ALEXANDER MACLEAY

from Scotland to Sydney

DERELIE CHERRY

ABBREVIATIONS

A.O.N.S.W.	Archives Office of New South Wales, Sydney
C.O.	Colonial Office Papers, Public Record Office, London
H.R.A.	Historical Records of Australia, Sydney
J.R.A.H.S.	Journal of the Royal Australian Historical Society, Sydney
P.R.O.	Public Record Office, London
R.A.S.	Royal Agricultural Society of New South Wales, Sydney

Published in 2012 by Paradise Publishers.
147 Cherry Lane
Kulnura, NSW 2250
Australia
phone +61 02 43761403
www.alexandermacleay.com

National Library of Australia
Cataloguing-in-Publication entry

Author: Cherry, Derelie Ann
Title: Alexander Macleay: from Scotland to Sydney/Derelie Cherry.
ISBN 9780646557526 (hbk.)
Notes: Includes bibliographical references and index.
Subjects: Macleay, Alexander, 1767–1848.
            Politicians—New South Wales—Biography
            New South Wales—Politics and government—1788–1900.
            New South Wales—Social life and customs—1788–1900.
Dewey Number: 994.402092

Design Diane Quick
Front cover Old Keiss Castle, Caithness, between John O´Groats and Wick, Scotland
  Photo Guy Edwardes
Back cover Portrait of Alexander Macleay aged about 58. *Reproduced with permission from Joan Downes, Brownlow Hill.*
Back flap Derelie Cherry at home with her two dogs. *Photo Peter Clarke*
Editor Peter Moore
Printer Everbest Printing, China

Contents

Alexander Macleay

1767, 24 June – Born near Ross-shire, Scotland, possibly in the village of Kilmuir Easter north of Invergordon

1786 – Aged 19, living in London, started work in the wine industry with William Sharp as business partner

1791, 15 October – Married Elizabeth Barclay (22 years old)

1792, 30 July – First child, William Sharp, was born – over the next 22 years another 16 children born

1793 – Napoleonic Wars began between France and other European nations

1794 – Elected Fellow of the Linnean Society in London

1795 – Commenced work as chief clerk in Prisoners-of-War Office in London

1797 – Prisoners-of-War Office transferred to the Transport Board and Alexander appointed head clerk of the Department of Correspondence

1798 – Appointed Secretary of Linnean Society – held this position until 1825

1802 – Alexander's first visit home to Wick, north Scotland

1806 – Promoted to Secretary of the Transport Board

1815, 18 June – Emperor Napoleon defeated at the Battle of Waterloo

1817 – Transport Board abolished and Alexander out of work

1817–1824 – Unemployed and looking for work

1824, December – Offered position of Colonial Secretary in New South Wales, by Lord Bathurst, Secretary of State for the Colonies

1825, 24 August – Sailed from Portsmouth bound for Sydney

1826, 3 January – Arrived in Sydney with wife and six daughters (aged between 11 and 32) to take up position of Colonial Secretary under Governor Ralph Darling

July 1826 – Elected President of the Benevolent Society charity

July 1826 – Elected Vice-Patron of the Sydney Auxiliary Bible Society

1826 – Elected Vice-Patron of the Agricultural and Horticultural Society of NSW

1826, 25 September – Appointed President of the Sydney Dispensary

Timeline

1828, April – Appointed Vice-Patron of the Australian Racing and Jockey Club

1829 – Sydney Museum established – Alexander key advocate of this

1829 – Appointed President of the first Subscription Library

1831 – Continued as Colonial Secretary under Governor Bourke, after Governor Darling was recalled

1835 – First stone laid for Elizabeth Bay House, Elizabeth Bay, Sydney

1836 – Committee of Superintendence for the Colonial Museum and Botanic Garden formed – Alexander elected to this Committee and appointed President of the Committee and Chair of the sub-committee

1837, 1 January – Removed from position as Colonial Secretary

1838, 29 May – Appointed President of Australian Club

1839, c. September – Moved into Elizabeth Bay House

1843, June – Won seat in local elections representing counties of Gloucester, Stanley and Macquarie – (from Port Macquarie to Moreton Bay) – he was nearly 76 years old

1843, 2 August – Appointed Speaker of the first partially representative Legislative Council

1844, 26 October – Asked to leave Elizabeth Bay House by son William to avoid bankruptcy

1845, 23 April – Alexander's library of 4,000 books offered for auction

1846, 14 May – Resigned as Speaker (Charles Nicholson replaced him)

1846, August – Suffered severe carriage accident outside Government House, Sydney

1848, June – Resigned seat in Legislative Council

1848, 18 July – Died aged 81, funeral at St James's Church, Sydney

1889 – Macleay collection bequeathed by Alexander's nephew, William John, to the University of Sydney (originally offered to them in 1874), now the Macleay Museum

This book is dedicated to my parents
Lynley Muriel Evely
and
John Lindsay Evely
who both gave me so much love

Acknowledgements

SINCE 1994 many people have helped this book come to fruition.

In particular I would like to acknowledge the enthusiasm and encouragement given to me by Hazel King, Noel Lothian, Howard Nicholson and Rodney Parker. They have all passed away now and it is sad that I cannot share the end result with them.

Others who have generously given me advice include Peter Stanbury and especially Scott Carlin, from the Historic Houses Trust. Scott was previously curator at Elizabeth Bay House and it has been wonderful to share an interest in the Macleay family with him, as it has been with James Broadbent and David Mabberley.

Macleay family relatives have also helped me, including June Underwood in London who guided me around the various sources of information such as the Public Record Office (now the National Archives) at Kew and the British Library. James Mitchell in Sydney was always delighted, from the very beginning, that I was writing the story of his ancestor.

Near Wick in North Scotland, Ian Stewart from Bilbster showed me historical records for the house, where my husband Bob and I stayed for several nights. Joan Downes from Brownlow Hill guided me around the house and garden, kindly sharing extraordinary knowledge of the years gone by. And Mitch McKay's marvellous Walking Tour brought old Port Macquarie back to life for me!

Numerous institutions have assisted me over the years and I thank the staff at the Mitchell Library and State Library of New South Wales, the National Library in Canberra, the Macleay Museum, the Archives of New South Wales, the Australian Museum Archives and the Botanic Garden Library in Sydney. Thanks also to the helpful staff on my visit to the State Library of Tasmania in Hobart, the Newcastle Region Public Library in Newcastle and the North Highland Archives in Wick. The staff at the fascinating Port Macquarie Historical Museum including Leonie Laws, Lyn Delaney, Lil Andrews and Des Grissell were most helpful and I thank them all. Also thanks to Gina Douglas of the Linnean Society in London, who even took me downstairs to see some of the original Linnaeus collection.

Experts in their different fields have read and advised on selected chapters. I thank Richard Clough for his input into chapter 7 on plants and Woody Horning and Jeremy Holloway for their input, especially in relation to technical details, in chapter 6 on natural history. And thanks to John Gascoigne from the University of New South Wales for his encouragement of my work about Alexander Macleay. My sincere gratitude goes to Stephen Garton for his magnificent foreword – which would make Alexander himself proud, let alone this author!

There is one person who I must single out, for since we met in 1994, Brian Fletcher has given me the greatest support in unravelling the life of Alexander Macleay. I thank him for his enduring interest in my research and also for his expert historical advice which forms such an integral part of this book.

Once again my designer, Diane Quick, has produced a book of lavish proportions and stunning elegance. I always wanted you to design the cover and how thrilled I am that you took on the whole book. Thank you Di! Sincere thanks to my excellent editor, Peter Moore, whose experienced editorial input, particularly in the areas of Australian history and biography, was just what my manuscript needed. Thanks also to Julia Cain for her meticulous attention to detail in reading the manuscript.

Finally I thank my long suffering husband, Bob Cherry, and mother, Lynley Evely, for their patience as I researched and wrote this biography that plays such an important role in the history of Australia.

Foreword

ALEXANDER MACLEAY was a controversial and important figure in early colonial New South Wales. The breadth and depth of his activities were extraordinary and his impact very evident in the numerous streets, lakes, rivers and islands that bear the Macleay name. His stately colonial mansion Elizabeth Bay House is now a vital part of Sydney's modern heritage industry and his name borne by a major natural history museum at the University of Sydney.

Until now, however, there has been no comprehensive account of the life and work of Alexander Macleay. This is partly because Macleay fits centrally into a history of colonial conservatism, a tradition that has tended to be overlooked by the majority of Australian historians. Another factor in this neglect is the difficulty of reconstructing Macleay's life from the diverse and scattered sources. This book is a path-breaking piece of forensic research, piecing together a large picture from many parts.

It represents the first substantial effort to document the life of this complex man, providing a total picture of Macleay's social, cultural, scientific and political interests. We see the man in action, his conflicts with other colonists, his trials and tribulations, setbacks and achievements. Previous accounts of his life are corrected and new insights into a range of important political and social issues in early colonial history are detailed. Alexander Macleay emerges as far more significant and less tyrannical than previous historians have claimed and our knowledge of early colonial New South Wales is much enhanced through this story of his life.

Professor Stephen Garton
Professor History and Provost and Deputy Vice-Chancellor
University of Sydney

Introduction

ALEXANDER MACLEAY was born in Scotland in 1767. From 1786 to 1825 he lived in London and his last years, from 1826 to 1848, were spent in New South Wales. Although he achieved prominence in public life in England through his association with the Linnean Society, it was in Australia where he took up the position of Colonial Secretary from 1826 to 1836, that he was catapulted into fame. Amidst rising political agitation in New South Wales, in the transition from penal colony to free settlement, Macleay triumphed when he was appointed Speaker in the first partially representative Legislative Council in 1843.

But it is not only through his prominent official positions that Alexander Macleay's name is remembered today. He was important also in the wider context as an outstanding example of the influence of the Scottish Enlightenment. Intrinsically linked to the development of trade[1] in his home town of Wick, where the herring industry flourished at the end of the 18th century, he was astonishingly versatile in his interests and capabilities. In the history

1

of New South Wales he is unique, for not only was he an administrator but also a political figure, a pastoralist with scientific interests, and an individual who became involved in the intellectual life of the colony. It is this unusual combination of talents that identifies Macleay as an outstanding contributor to so many different aspects of the development of colonial New South Wales.

Despite his obvious importance, it is surprising that no biography has been written about Alexander Macleay, although several books have been published which cover different aspects of his life. The most important of these publications was the release in 1993 of *Fanny to William: The Letters of Frances Leonora Macleay 1812–1836*.[2] The introduction regrets that 'there is no definitive biography of Alexander Macleay'[3] and now these letters, from eldest daughter Fanny to her brother William, discovered in 1950, have been used extensively for the first time to help tell the story of Alexander Macleay. Four further publications covered specific aspects of Macleay's life but not the wider picture. *Mr Macleay's Cabinet* was published in 1988, as was *Taste and Science the Macleay Women*. *Mr McLeay's Garden* and *Elizabeth Bay House: A History and Guide* were both released in 2000. David Macmillan's 1957 publication about Alexander's nephew, William John, entitled *A Squatter Went to Sea*, covered his expedition to New Guinea in 1875 and his life in Sydney but not his earlier years there before his uncle died.

In the late 20th century, the person most passionate about the subject of the Macleays was Annabel Swainston but, sadly, she died in 1988 before she could complete her work. She hoped to write two books from her research over nearly 30 years in England, Scotland and Australia and, after she passed away, some of her notes about Fanny's original letters were used in the publication of *Fanny to William*. The other book Annabel hoped to write was about the Macleay family to whom she was related,[4] and her extensive notes and writings are now in the Macleay Museum. Swainston herself realised that the Australian details were insufficient and she had hoped to return to Australia to carry out further research. Nevertheless she published two articles: one about William, Macleay's eldest son, in the Linnean Society newsletter in 1985,[5] and the other in 1975 about Alexander's involvement with his family's Scottish bank.[6]

Many details in these two articles had not been published before, including her fascinating conclusions about the bank that the family set up in Wick, and they are now part of the Macleay story.

Although Alexander's name frequently appears in general Australian histories and other biographies, as well as articles about natural history or colonial politics in New South Wales, few of these writings concentrate on him alone. Hazel King's article 'Man in a Trap: Alexander Macleay, Colonial Secretary of New South Wales', published in 1982, shows how his colonial life was affected by the fact that he was 'trapped by his debts'.[7] Another article, by Stephen Foster, published in 1975, entitled 'A Piece of Sharp Practice? Governor Bourke and the Office of Colonial Secretary', describes the dubious circumstances under which Alexander was removed from his official position.[8]

Articles connected with Alexander's interest in natural history cover only his years in Australia. Dymphna Clark, in 1989, wrote about 'Baron Charles von Hügel and the Macleays', basing her article on von Hügel's journal of 1834 when he visited Australia.[9] Michael Van Leeuwen's article entitled 'The Plan of a Museum — Alexander Macleay's proposal for the Australian Museum' was published in 1992 and the author, providing evidence through a letter he had only just discovered, acknowledged Macleay's important role in the development of that institution.[10] In 1989 Ronald Strahan wrote the article 'The Dog that did not bark: Alexander Macleay and the Australian Museum',[11] but Van Leeuwen's later conclusive research contradicted Strahan's ideas. Earlier, in the 1920s, Joseph Fletcher prepared various notes and speeches on the role of the Macleay family in relation to the Linnean Society of Australia.[12] Other articles have appeared sporadically, often in association with Historic Houses Trust exhibitions at Elizabeth Bay House, and Lionel Gilbert's unpublished thesis of 1989 covers the garden at Elizabeth Bay as well as Sydney's botanical community from 1825 to 1865.[13]

This book amalgamates, for the first time, the many different components of Alexander Macleay's life. Contemporary and later descriptions and references to him are extraordinarily contradictory. Why did Manning Clark make the following unsubstantiated claim:

Elizabeth Bay House, completed in 1839, is today engulfed by surrounding buildings. Photo: Derelie Cherry

It was typical of the pompous Alexander Macleay, whose eyes were specially moistened on public occasions by the waters of loving kindness, to take the chair at the temperance meeting: because everyone in Sydney knew that if McLeay had a chance to revise the Lord's Prayer he would add the words "Give us this day our daily clap".[14]

And why should Stephen Roberts in his 1935 book, *The Squatting Age in Australia 1835–1847*, dismiss Alexander at the time of his conflict with Bourke as 'a tenacious Scotsman of over sixty-five years of age' who had been a 'local tyrant'.[15] Such aspersions on Alexander's character have been previously challenged, but only in private correspondence. When Douglas Pike, editor of the *Australian Dictionary of Biography*, was preparing for publication the entry about Alexander Macleay in 1965, he corresponded with Annabel Swainston. In the files in Canberra there is a letter to Pike from a person identified only as J. Iltis. He had obviously been in contact with Annabel and wanted to tell Pike about Annabel's opinion regarding Alexander's character. He wrote that:

> statements that he was testy, autocratic and unpleasant — emanating from Australian sources only, she assures me, as to everyone else he was all sweet and light — are pernicious rumours started by Lord Glenelg and perpetuated by Stephen Roberts (Sir) in *The Squatting Age*.[16]

Another letter from Swainston to Pike continued:

> I have been reading *The Squatting Age in Australia* — with certain references to Macleay which are so unlike the man [as] I've learned to know him in firsthand letters to, from and about him over the 1790-1826 period when he was loved, honoured and revered by people as widely dissimilar as Lord Castlereagh — and his own gardener — a simple country clergyman and learned international scientists — a man whom Banks referred to …[17]

In this same letter Swainston wrote that she had quoted extracts describing Macleay's character in *The Squatting Age*, to a visiting American university lecturer who had been researching the story of Sir James Smith and the Linnean Society for two years. Swainston recorded that 'he was as dumb-founded as I was — this was a stranger to both of us'.[18]

Pike replied to Swainston in 1965:

> I do not mean to suggest that Macleay and many others deserve their current reputation, but at the same time I do not think that Robert's *Squatting Age* has moulded opinion. A scholarly book or even an objective Dictionary entry might help to change the picture. This is the kind of thing we are trying to do, although time and space some-what limit our capacity for a thoroughly argued case.[19]

But only the *Australian Dictionary of Biography* entry about Alexander eventu-ated from this exchange of ideas.

This comprehensive story of the life of Alexander Macleay is structured chronologically as far as possible although, unfortunately, information about his early years in Scotland is scanty. More extensive details about his working days in London at the Transport Board and his involvement with the Linnean Society provide substantial background for this enigmatic Scottish gentleman who was about to become the New South Wales Colonial Secretary. With the experience of the Napoleonic Wars and their aftermath behind him, Macleay found himself involved in New South Wales during a particularly tumultu-ous era. His work as Colonial Secretary, from 1826 to 1836, was his most significant contribution to the colony. And, too, his large circle of family and friends, his enthusiasm for gardening, natural history and pastoral concerns are all included. During his last years Macleay was still actively involved in the development of the colony, amidst a turmoil of personal circumstances.

Elizabeth Bay House, undeniably the finest house in colonial Sydney, still proudly stands as a lasting testimony to the foresight, taste, and signifi-cance of Alexander Macleay. The interior of this mansion, with its beautiful spiral staircase and impressive dome, continues to impress the public. On the eve of his departure from London to Sydney in 1825, Alexander's brother-in-law, the Reverend Robert Phin, prophesied: 'I have no doubt that your name will be transmitted to future generations among the benefactors of the human race.'[20] Hopefully, this first biography will help fulfil that prophecy.

one

FROM WICK TO LONDON

1767–1825

STARTING IN SCOTLAND

Alexander Macleay was born on 24 June 1767 in the Scottish Highlands county of Ross. The exact village is not known but it was possibly Kilmuir Easter,[1] which is situated several miles north-east along the coast from Invergordon, for it was there that Alexander's grandmother, Catherine, was buried in 1783.[2] Around 1773[3] the family moved north to Wick in the county of Caithness where Alexander grew up. In 1786, when he was nineteen, he began work in London where he lived for the next 37 years until departing for Sydney in 1825 to take up the position of Colonial Secretary. He remained in New South Wales until his death in 1848.

THE MACLEAY CLAN

The clan of Macleay in Scotland, from the region of Ross-shire, dates back to the 15th century and is associated with the Stewart clan from Appin.[4] The first Stewart king in Scotland was recorded in 1371 and the Appin branch of this clan appeared in 1469.[5] However, the Macleay name has been traced back even further to ancient kings and saints from Ulster in Ireland who came to Scotland in 560 AD.[6] Other names associated with the Macleay clan are Maclae, Maclay, Maclea and Maclew,[7] and the name itself means 'son of the physician'.[8] Alexander's ancestors, on his paternal grandmother's side of the family, also came from the well-known Munro lineage. In the 17th century this clan was one of the three largest, along with the Mackenzies and the Rosses, in Ross-shire.[9] Tradition has also given the name of Munro an Irish origin, dating back about eight centuries.[10]

By the mid-16th century the Macleay family 'had substantial landholdings in Scotland' but they 'suffered severe losses' from the wars instigated by Prince Charles Edward Stuart which culminated in the battle of Culloden on 16 April 1746.[11] The Jacobites, most of whom were Highlanders, had fought for the restoration of the Stewarts who they believed were the rightful heirs to the British monarchy, but they were badly defeated and the country suffered terribly as a result. Vast land holdings and estates were taken from their owners and the Highlanders' native language, Gaelic, as well as the wearing of tartan, were both banned. The young and daring 25-year-old Bonnie Prince Charles fled to Europe, never to return.

Alexander's father, William, grew up in those troubled times. He was born in 1740 to Kenneth Macleay and Catherine Munro. Described as 'a native of Invergordon',[12] he had two sisters, Catherine and Martha, and a brother named Andrew. William commenced work in Invergordon as a ferryman on the Cromarty Firth amidst the great changes that were taking place in the north of Scotland. A decision was made to assist the dispossessed highlanders 'by introducing Agriculture, Fisherys [sic], and Manufactures'[13] and a Highlands Society was formed to promote the interests of these

Provost William Macleay (1740–1820), father of Alexander Macleay.
Artist Sir Henry Raeburn (1756–1823). Wick Town Hall. Reproduced
with permission from the Highland Council

Barbara Rose Macleay (1740–1842), mother of Alexander Macleay.
Artist unknown. Reproduced with permission from the Stanham Macarthur family,
Camden, New South Wales

backward people, amidst that generally 'enlightened age'. If they worked hard and proved to be astute there were now opportunities to become wealthy if they so aspired. William was such an individual and, after marrying Barbara Rose around 1760, he decided to seek out his fortune. Donald Sage recorded in his 1840 *Memorabilia Domestica, or Parish Life in the North of Scotland*, that since leaving home, William had risen 'rapidly to wealth' from his 'humble sphere after having emigrated to Caithness',[14] and this was undoubtedly true. Migrating to Wick with his wife and growing family, which eventually consisted of four sons and three daughters,[15] he established a business as a merchant just when the herring fishing industry was beginning to flourish. After the British Fisheries Society was established in 1786, William became Inspector of Fisheries for Caithness and, through his active participation in community affairs as a Burgh Councillor, he became a prominent local citizen.

According to the editors of the published version of his daughter Fanny's letters, Alexander's mother, Barbara Rose, was 'a member of the Rose family of Kilravock'[16] from Nairnshire who originally came from Normandy and settled in Scotland around the 12th century.[17] A note, discovered behind a portrait of an elderly Barbara wearing a red shawl, referred to her as 'kin to the Rose-Rosses of Cromarty House'.[18] It is recorded that a Barbara was born to William Ross in the village of Fodderty in Ross-shire in 1739.[19] More than likely it was this woman who became William's wife, for by the time they married she would have been in her early 20s and when she died in May 1842 she was 103. In the 17th century the Ross family (from the Norman family de Ros) purchased land from 'the Clan Ross chiefs', and consequently many Rosses 'are really of the same ancestry as Clan Rose, pronounced also Ross',[20] which gives credence to the note found with Barbara's portrait. William's brother-in-law, John Rose, who became Sheriff Clerk in Caithness, appears to have moved to Wick at the same time as Alexander's family.[21]

After Barbara died her obituary in the local paper recorded that she was 'a native of Ross-shire' and that she:

> retained in her memory through life impressions of several important
> events which took place in that locality. In her early days, relative to

the contests of the loyalists with the partisans of Charles the Pretender. — When some of the rebels were one day passing her father's dwelling, one of them threatened to fire a musket at her, because she was the child of a loyalist; and she had a distinct recollection of the day, 1746, when one of the rebel chiefs (the Earl of Cromarty) was taken as a prisoner aboard a ship-of-war lying in Cromarty Firth. She heard the firing, and frequently mentioned it, as the event took place on the birth-day of her respected brother, the late John Rose, Esq., Sheriff Substitute of this county, and Collector of Customs.[22]

Exactly where the family first lived in Wick is unknown but in March 1790 they rented a tenement from Benjamin Dunbar of Hempriggs and Alexander Miller, a merchant from Staxigo.[23] By November 1809 it was recorded that William, Barbara and their eldest son, John Macleay, were living in 'tenements of land & Houses on the south side of the High Street' which they rented from Sir John Sinclair of Ulbster.[24] Both Dunbar and Sinclair were the two main 'local improvers' of Wick at this period and they were actively involved in agricultural and political reform, with Dunbar described as 'a decided Liberal'.[25]

Barbara's relative, George Rose, who was 'Pitt's influential Secretary to the Treasury',[26] possibly helped William set up his new life in Wick, but another family relative, Sir John Ross, was more likely to have been involved. As a great landowner from Ross-shire, and a Member of Parliament representing the Northern Burghs, Ross would have had many political and economic connections and he may have been responsible for William's appointment as Inspector of Fisheries.[27] However, the name most frequently associated with the Macleays over the years from 1770 until his death in 1835, was the influential Sir John Sinclair. The Sinclair or St Clair family first came to England from St Clare in Normandy 'with William the Conqueror' in 1066 and settled in Scotland in the 12th century. In 1379 a member of the family married the heiress to 'the earldom of Caithness' and the northern Sinclair clan arose.[28] In 1718 the family bought the title for Wick and its surrounding lands which had belonged to the Earldom of Caithness since 1589 when the village was made a Royal Burgh.[29]

BAILIE MACLEAY
OF WICK

Only a few years after his arrival in Wick, William's substantial contribution to the improvement of the local community was noted. In July 1780 it was decided to carry out a survey in the counties of Scotland to research the best methods of husbandry. Andrew Wight was commissioned and his research in 1781 included references to William Macleay's farming activities. Wight reported:

> The good people in Wick are wonderfully thankful to their bailie for cleaning the streets and carrying off the dung, judging that it is all done for their sake. The improved state of his farm shows the great efficiency of royal-borough dirt.[30]

Although this quotation implies that William was taking advantage of his situation as bailie (a council officer) to obtain free manure, he was nevertheless responsible for introducing innovative reforms in agriculture. One of his ideas, which was adopted by the community, was to plough the fields several times a year in order to improve the soil. He also raised a number of new crops including the potato and Wight observed:

> Were they known, then the people eat them greedily; and, to raise the greatest crop, they planted them in their very best land. Bailie Macleay taught them to raise potatoes at less expense on worse ground, and better too for food. He broke up an ill swarded ley in his outfield, ploughed it in November, and again in February, when dry, harrowed it to perfection, gave it abundance of dung, and ploughed it again in March. If any rough clods remained they were cut with spades, and carried off. The potatoes were planted in rows, with intervals of eighteen inches. Horse-hoing was unnecessary, because very few weeds appeared; and these were taken up with the hand. Harrows with iron teeth were used; a rare thing in that country. This great labour was necessary in the ground chosen for his experiment; but very improper

for the country-people to copy after. Avoiding this stiff kind of soil, he might have got land of a middling kind that would have cost much less labour.

Wight described William's experiments in some detail and he obviously considered his methods of farming to be useful. He also included information about William's attempts to change the community's outlook on growing oats:

> To remove the prejudice imbibed by the people against white oats, as improper for their land, white oats were sowed in the middle of a field, and black oats on both sides. The white oats yielded two balls per acre more than the black kind; not to mention the very great difference between them in meal. But the people were not thoroughly convinced; for, say they, the white impoverishes more than the black. To convince them of the contrary, he made the following experiment. A field cropped with white oats last year, was sowed this year with black oats, except a few ridges in the middle on which white oats were sowed. Change of seed was so far favourable to the black kind; and yet the white crop promised to be much better. We admire the zeal of the Bailie in giving this instruction; and, that it might be general, he made these experiments on the side of a public road, visible to all.[31]

In 1784 Wight, again with a wry reference to the 'public' manure, noted that:

> Bailie Macleay of Wick, inspector of herring, brought the knowledge of husbandry with him from Ross. Pease and beans are as much the aversion of Caithness, as nettles are of other parts in Scotland, and a much rarer sight. The pease that Mr. Macleay propagates in his farm, are as luxuriant as any I ever saw … He also saved the parish expense by collecting manure from the streets to use on his land.[32]

A supply of potatoes and peas provided welcome relief from the local diet which was heavily reliant on staples such as oats, barley and corn. William's claim to fame in 1784 even extended to an inn that he had established in Wick which Wight also referred to:

> Before taking leave of Bailie Macleay, I must mention that his public spirit has led him to open an Inn at Wick where a traveller gets good provision of fish, flesh, and fowl, well dressed, ready service, good clean beds, all at a moderate rate; and excellent claret for half a crown the bottle.[33]

In all probability Wight would have resided at this inn during the course of his travels and no doubt there would have been some agreement with William to cover his accommodation expenses in exchange for 'advertising' the inn.

On 29 September 1778 William was appointed as a Burgess (magistrate) in Wick.[34] At the time, Sir John Sinclair was Provost (Mayor) and William, as one of the two magistrates, chaired council meetings and signed the minutes during Sinclair's frequent absences on other business, effectively acting as deputy Mayor.[35] Over the next 40 years he continued to actively participate in council affairs and not only was he appointed Deputy Lieutenant of Caithness, but from 1814 until 29 September 1818, he was their Provost. His portrait by Sir Henry Raeburn still gazes down upon proceedings in the grand upstairs room of the 1825 Wick Town Hall. Raeburn, who also painted a portrait of Sir John Sinclair which is now in the National Portrait Gallery in London, was based in Edinburgh and was considered to be the leading Scottish portrait artist at that time. On the landing of the impressive wooden staircase in the Wick Town Hall there is also a magnificent, enormous portrait of Sir John Sinclair, Baronet and Laird of Ulbster, which was painted by the American artist, Benjamin West. Sinclair is dressed in splendid military attire and is holding a letter from George Washington which, it is believed, he was so thrilled to receive that he wanted it included in the portrait.[36] In 1882 this portrait was in the same upstairs room as that of William Macleay and 'other local celebrities'[37] whose importance in the history of Wick was publicly displayed.

EDUCATION AND WORK
PROSPECTS

Alexander was to follow the examples set by his father. Although there is little evidence to show how he, or Sandy as the family often called him,[38] spent the first nineteen years of his life, it is most likely that he helped his father in Scotland. As a measure of economy it was common practice to employ family members, rather than 'hired servants' or 'day labour'.[39] With a father so prominent in the local community and interested in the welfare of others and his country, Alexander's family upbringing was a fertile ground for his future broad interests and working life. Like his father he retained an interest in horticulture and agriculture and became a prominent figure after moving to New South Wales, where his position as Colonial Secretary also enabled him to influence the development of public policy.

Although Greek and Latin were universally taught throughout Scotland in Alexander's youth, his broad general knowledge implies a good education, but whether this extended beyond local school to university is not known. The fact that he also spoke Gaelic is unusual, as during the second half of the 18th century it was reported that 'little or no Gaelic' was spoken in the district around Wick.[40] He probably learnt this from his parents for Gaelic was commonly spoken in their native Ross-shire. None of Scotland's four oldest universities, namely St Andrews, Aberdeen, Glasgow and Edinburgh, have a record of Alexander attending any classes. However, at the University of Glasgow, prior to 1853, students could attend without having matriculated though class lists did not begin until 1794 and by that time Alexander was living in London. Although there is a Macleay Hall, named after a Lord Macleay, at the University of Glasgow today,[41] it is more likely, if Alexander attended any university classes at all, that they would have been at Aberdeen which was closest to home. Conversely, Sir John Sinclair, who was born in Thurso in 1754, and was a Member of Parliament for Caithness for many years after 1780, attended high school in Edinburgh followed by university at Glasgow and Oxford.[42]

The prospects of work for Alexander in Wick were very limited. Fewer than 1,000[43] people lived in the town and employment was mostly in fishing and husbandry. One contemporary observer reflected that the:

> want of manufactures and other means of employment, make young
> men who are averse to labour in husbandry, and have no good way of
> livelihood, readily betake themselves to the army and navy.[44]

Worse still for Wick, when the oats crop failed in 1782 and 1783, near-famine conditions were experienced and it was only through Sir John Sinclair's intervention that government assistance of £15,000 was granted and the people were saved from starvation.[45] In 1787 Donald Williamson from Spittle in Caithness wrote to James Horne in Edinburgh describing the conditions and prospects. He referred to the 'most dreadful weather' and that the hills were 'all white with snow' and was concerned that 'victual will be very scarce and dear in this country. My young folks are in distress'.[46] With such bleak prospects at home, Alexander decided that his future lay elsewhere. The great southern city of London, with a population of around 1,000,000, would have offered opportunities unheard of at home and by 1786 he had moved to this great metropolis.

A NEW LIFE IN LONDON

Thames Street was Alexander's first known address in London. There he commenced work in the wine industry, becoming a partner in a business with William Sharp that moved to 6 Little Bush Lane off Thames Street in 1789.[47] Possibly, suggests Annabel Swainston, Alexander acquired this job through the family connection of 'Archibald McLeay who lived in Bute [and] had married an Isobel Sharp in the first half of the century'.[48] Until the mid-19th century, the prefix of Mac was 'commonly abbreviated in written records to

Mc or even M'[49] and so Archibald may have been related. Because of his youth, it is unlikely that Alexander would have relocated to London without a definite job prospect. His experience, working with wines in his father's inn at Wick, would have helped secure the position. Several years later Alexander incorporated his business partner's name into that of his first-born son, William Sharp, who in the Scottish tradition, was usually named after his paternal grandfather. Alexander remained working in the wine industry for the next seven years.

On 15 October 1791, aged 24, he married 22-year-old Elizabeth Barclay in the Church of St Dunstan in the West near the centre of London.[50] Elizabeth was born on 13 March 1769 and baptised on 29 March 1769 at St Ann's, Blackfriars in London. Her father, James Barclay, and her mother Frances, who came from the Le Fevre family in Guernsey, lived in Fleet Street, London. James was thought to be a brewer and may have been one of the Barclay family of Urie who were Quakers. This branch of the Barclay family was related to the founders of the famous Barclays Bank who came to London from near Stonehaven south of Aberdeen in the 1750s.[51] So Elizabeth may have been one of their descendants. Perhaps Alexander met his future wife through his work in the wine industry or perhaps it was through the acquaintance of Robert Barclay at the Scots Corporation where 'fellow countrymen' met regularly for dinner.[52]

Within a year, on 30 July 1792, their eldest child, William, was born. Over the next 22 years a further 16 children arrived, including two sets of twins. Elizabeth, known as Eliza, gave birth to her last child, Barbara Isabella, at age 47 in 1814. Infant mortality was high and with widespread health problems only ten of the Macleay children survived to adulthood.[53]

In the 1790s, faced with a rapidly expanding family Alexander needed to find appropriate accommodation and in the early years of his marriage he moved several times. In 1794 the family of four lived in rented premises at 2 Montpellier Row on Stockwell Common for £16 a year and in 1796 at Clapham Road Place near Kensington. By 1797 they had moved to 3 Prince's Court by the Storey Gate in St James's Park near Westminster[54] where they remained until 1805.[55] In 1806 Alexander bought the lease for a house at 32 Queen

Anne's Gate, now 12 Queen's Square,[56] which was conveniently located near his work in the Transport Board at 44 Parliament Street, Westminster.[57] This house was built in 1706 and it was here, where the family resided until 1825, that Alexander housed his vast entomological collection. In 1803 he also purchased a country estate called Tilbuster[58], which was located south of Godstone village in the scenic countryside of Surrey. The family commuted between this house and their London residence especially during the summer months when it would have been so pleasant to exchange the heat and dust of the city with fresh country air and a garden. Christmas was always spent at Tilbuster.

APPOINTMENT IN THE
PUBLIC SERVICE

Not only was more money needed to support his growing family, but French wine became more difficult to obtain due to the French wars which began in 1793. Alexander became anxious to secure a more reliable job with better prospects for the future and in 1795 he took up his first appointment in the public service as chief clerk in the Prisoners-of-War Office. After he became a Fellow of the Linnean Society in 1794, Alexander was well-placed to make many useful contacts for himself. Sir Joseph Banks was one of numerous influential friends who possibly helped him find new employment. Or perhaps his relative in Ross-shire, Sir John Ross, was instrumental in obtaining another position for Alexander, as his wife's nephew was Henry Dundas, whom Sir John Sinclair described in 1793 as 'Scotland's pre-eminent politician'.[59] Considering that Dundas (later Lord Melville) was Treasurer of the Navy from 1783 to 1800, Home Secretary from 1791 to 1794 and Secretary for War from 1794 to 1801 when William Pitt was the Prime Minister, such a connection seems feasible. His relation George Rose, through his official capacity in the government, may have also helped Alexander at this time.

Original 18th century wooden panelling inside a house adjoining 12 Queen's Square. Photo: Derelie Cherry

Alexander's London residence at 12 Queen's Square, Westminster from 1806–1825.
Photo: Derelie Cherry

PROMOTION IN THE TRANSPORT BOARD

Alexander's work now involved him in all issues concerning prisoners-of-war, including French and Spanish prisoners in England, and British prisoners in France. Duties included responsibility for the prisoners' provisions and living conditions as well as their date of release and Alexander devised 'new forms to monitor prisoners' food'.[60] Administrative reorganisation in 1797 resulted in the separation of records for prisoners from records relating to the transport service, as initially there had been some confusion.[61] The outcome of this was that the Prisoners-of-War Office was transferred to the Transport Board which had been established in 1793 to handle the extra demands of war-time and Alexander was appointed head clerk of the Department of Correspondence. In 1806 he was promoted to Secretary of the Transport Board 'as a result of administrative efficiency' with a salary of £1,000, which was substantially more than he had previously received as a clerk.[62]

In 1806 the Transport Board also took over the Sick and Hurt Board. Under these new arrangements the Transport Board was composed of 'three sea officers, one of whom was the Chairman, two civil commissioners and a senior physician' and they worked six days a week during the war years.[63] They were busy times and in 1805 Alexander informed the President of the Linnean Society, James Smith, that 'for the last six weeks I have been constantly engaged with public Business from 8 in the morning till 2 and sometimes three in the morning'.[64]

There were three main areas of concern for the Transport Board: shipping (including the movements of troops and convicts), prisoners-of-war, and looking after sick and wounded seamen.[65] Because it was the official body through which decisions of the Secretary of State regarding the movement of troops were conveyed to the Admiralty for implementation, the Transport Board held a position of considerable authority and importance.[66] Also, this period experienced an enormous growth in the number of soldiers and seamen. In 1794, there were 60,000 in the army and 72,885 in the navy, but by 1814 these numbers had increased to 190,800 and 140,000 respectively.[67]

Alexander's duties, as Secretary, were very similar to those that he took on as Colonial Secretary twenty years later, though little did he realise, in 1795, where his future lay. He was:

> The Board's instrument for the performance of whatever relates to the Correspondence of the three branches, and he accordingly arranges and prepares it for the Board's approval and signature. He reads all Letters and Addresses made to the Board upon every part of the business; takes Minutes of the answer or determination of the Board thereon, or makes the necessary References for further information: He observes that all Minutes of Transactions of the Board are properly kept, that all Letters are duly entered in the several books of correspondence, and that all Letters are properly arranged and preserved: He superintends the general running of the Office.[68]

Twenty clerks assisted Alexander with the 'correspondence and with the voluminous minutes which, during the war years, averaged some ten pages of foolscap a day'.[69] Historian Hazel King claimed that the minutes of the Board meetings indicated no active participation in decision-making by Macleay, albeit he 'may have contributed verbally', but such behaviour was not decreed in his job specification.[70]

Sorting out shipping transport for soldiers, prisoners-of-war and convicts, as well as their supplies, would have been no easy task. Despite British naval supremacy, as evidenced by Lord Nelson's victories at Aboukir Bay in 1798 and the Battle of Trafalgar in 1805, there were still major shipping problems due to a shortage of vessels and it was up to the Transport Board to deal with this situation as best it could.[71] Still there was time for personal favours such as the request from Alexander's friend in the Linnean Society, William Kirby, for 'a good head of the late Lord Nelson — any that is judged to be a good likeness will do'.[72]

As he was the officer in the Transport Board who handled general correspondence, Alexander was often directly ordered to track down missing relatives to send them monies or even to determine if they were still alive. This was well before the Red Cross was established and Alexander's responses from the Prisoners-of-War office reveal that he was 'kindly and conscientious'.[73] Yet this important office, upon which such heavy responsibilities were placed, was by no means free from public criticism and satire. In 1812 the Transport Board received a letter which referred to an article that had been published in a Sunday newspaper about British prisoners in France. The author of the article claimed, with regard to those employed at the Transport Board, that:

> the redemption of our countrymen would remove from these honest and disinterested Gentlemen their valued and profitable flock of French prisoners which affords them and their friends an immense and inconceivable mine of riches.[74]

The man behind this article, identified only as Leavell, was described in the covering letter as a 'hardened libeller' who attacked everyone. Such experiences and confrontations could have been later recalled by Alexander in New South Wales where he experienced continual personal attacks from the local newspapers. Yet Alexander was confident that his country had the power and ability to forestall Napoleon. In one of his letters to James Smith in 1803 he wrote:

> There is no doubt of his determination to invade us, and certainly the sooner he comes the better ... I am sure we need not be at all apprehensive about the issue of any Attack which the Corsican and his miserable Slaves can make upon us, although the very landing of a French Force will, in the first instance, occasion much bustle and confusion especially in the metropolis.[75]

Fortunately, the very real threat of an imminent invasion was averted as Britain signed yet another coalition with Austria and Russia which forced Napoleon to change his plans.

HERRING INDUSTRY
DEVELOPS IN WICK

Meanwhile, back in Wick, exciting developments were taking place in the fishing industry and Alexander was actively involved in them. It was well known that the Dutch had been successfully fishing herring in the North Sea for several centuries and in 1800 Provost Sir John Sinclair received a letter from Alexander Macleay of the Transport Office advising him that he had learnt:

> that nine Dutch Fishermen who were in the Prisons of the country [almost certainly interned], were willing to be sent to Caithness to prosecute the Fisheries if met with encouragement.[76]

Over the next decade the fishing industry was further encouraged. In 1803 an Act was passed that gave £20,000 'towards making roads and bridges in the North of Scotland'. The other half of the costs involved was to 'be paid by the county or district'.[77] The most important news for Wick was that the British Fisheries Society had proposed building a harbour there and Thomas Telford was to be responsible for its implementation. An entirely new town, to be called Pulteneytown, was planned to be built on the south bank of Wick where the new harbour was to be located and the old town would be connected to it by a bridge upstream. Built between 1803 and 1807, the new harbour provided great impetus for the expansion of the herring fishing industry and the increase in the number of boats alone, from 214 in 1808 to 822 in 1814, confirms this.[78]

When Alexander returned home to Wick for four months in 1802[79] he would have watched plans develop for the new harbour with great interest. He wrote an account of his stay to the Reverend William Kirby, describing how he had been 'prevented from looking after insects by continued rains, snow, and high winds, during the whole of my stay in the county'. Although he was unable to collect natural history specimens because of the weather, Alexander did observe improvements in agricultural practices that had taken place since his departure in 1786. He reported:

Indeed, so bad a season was never known; and a more serious consequence than my entomological disappointment is that the crop of oats
in Caithness has almost entirely failed. Notwithstanding the unfavourable state of the weather, however, I was much gratified by my visit to
the north. I had reason to believe that very considerable improvement
had been made in my native county during the sixteen years I had been
absent; but, I assure you, I found the county improved far beyond my
most sanguine expectations.[80]

He also noted the assistance given by Sir John Sinclair: 'What has been done
within the last few years is truly astonishing … Sir John Sinclair has this year
ploughed up about 600 acres of waste Land, which was in fact before good for
nothing.'[81]

Alexander was made a director of the British Fisheries Society in 1812 and
his brother Kenneth became their agent in 1825.[82] So when the new town was
completed by about 1827 and the streets were named after directors and other
officials of the British Fisheries Society, naturally a Macleay Street was designated.[83] This short street, in Upper Pulteneytown, has a grim appearance today
with severe looking houses facing the street and not a garden in sight. On 22
June 1812, 2½ acres of the Barony of Hempriggs known by the name of 'Samuel's
Croft, Bankhead of Wick' was granted on a leu or perpetual lease at fixed rent,
to Alexander's brother, John Macleay, by the 'British Society for extending the
Fisheries and improving the Sea Coasts of Scotland'.[84] Sir Benjamin Dunbar
owned all the land in this area and John built a 'very elegant house' on his portion which Kenneth renamed 'Rosebank' in 1824.[85] Local legend says that it was
named after the wild white rose, the traditional flower of Scotland, which grew
there on the bank.[86] It is regrettable that this house was demolished but a lovely
fireplace, with tiles depicting nursery rhymes, was removed to the Wick Heritage Centre in a last salvage attempt just before the walls came tumbling down
to make way for the new Caithness General Hospital in 1975.[87] Also in 1824,
Alexander's parents moved to 'a Tenement compound the ground whereon the
late Manse and houses of Wick stand, with the Garden, Corn Yard, and Stackhill, Mansion house and Office houses' which belonged to Sir John Sinclair.[88]

FAMILY AFFAIRS

Ties with the family in Scotland were regularly maintained and in 1797 Alexander's brother William escorted young William and James to Wick,[89] where they lived with their grandparents for several years. How different and exciting this remote place must have seemed to such young children. And what a help it must have been for their mother, that these elder boys were away, for each year, from 1796 to 1798, Elizabeth gave birth to yet another child.

By 1801 there were nine children in the family, and it seems that Elizabeth's only sister, Frances, was also living with them at that time. The extra support to look after the nine Macleay babies, who were then all under the age of ten, would have been much appreciated. But it was Fanny, as the eldest daughter, who inevitably had to assist her mother with the ever-growing number of young children and babies. Aged seventeen by 1810, she shared the responsibility for looking after eleven children, six of whom were under ten

'Rosebank' at Wick, home of Alexander's brother John Macleay.
The Johnston Collection. © The Wick Society

years old. In her letters to her brother William, Fanny made constant reference to illnesses. For example, in May 1813 she told him that Johanna had a knee problem and would need a high shoe if she lived, otherwise she would become 'as lame as our poor James was'.[90] In the same letter Fanny informed William that 'Eliza's cheek looks no better, indeed I greatly fear it will break in another place. It is a great pity and I doubt whether it has been properly treated'.[91] By 8 February 1814 Fanny wrote to William that 'It is supposed now, that Eliza has the liver complaint'.[92]

James had fallen and injured his leg when he was seven years old. He never recovered from this accident and in 1810 Kirby wrote: 'I am much concerned to learn your second son is so hopeless an invalid'.[93] James died later that month when he was only sixteen though Johanna survived another ten years. Kirby again referred sympathetically to the loss of Barbara in 1812, and he also mentioned another sick daughter,[94] presumably Catherine, who died the following year. On 7 October 1814 he wrote once more about the 'heavy loss' that the family sustained when Elizabeth died, aged fourteen.[95] It is sad to reflect that five of the Macleay children died in their teens and another died aged just two.

Fanny provided a very clear picture of her domestic duties in 1814 when she wrote to William:

> I have been alternately nurse, cook and housemaid, to crown all, we
> had until last night, but two servants, while we had all sick from Susan
> downwards. Oh I am sick, very very sick of Children! You can have no
> idea what numberless miseries I have been obliged to bear patiently.[96]

The Macleay London residence would have felt like a prison to Fanny. Spanning five floors with several rooms on each landing, quarters would have been very confined, especially in bad weather. And although the tiny backyard was just across the street from St James's Park, the house must have constantly resounded with the noise of children. Alexander's library, on the ground floor, was fortunately located some distance away from the bedrooms upstairs.

Good servants were also difficult to obtain and anyone who proved worthy was likely to move on as was the case with their cook, Elizabeth, who in 1815 was 'genteelly enticed away' by Lady H.[97] Kirby tried to help wherever he

This marble cherub rests above the fireplace in the library of the house at Queen's Square, London. It is a poignant reminder of when the large Macleay family lived there in the early 19th century. Photo: Derelie Cherry

could and in 1813 he procured a servant for the family, the young William Hiliyard, who was also keen to improve his written English whilst he worked for the Macleays.[98] Fanny mused in 1816 that she might one day keep house for William based on a promise he made to her. What a tempting and respectable alternative life he suggested, especially with the added bonus of no children.[99] It was fortunate for their father that he could escape to an office each day but, for Fanny, there was no such escape.

Alexander was back in Wick again in 1811 recovering from a serious bowel illness.[100] Kirby wrote on 11 November 1811 saying how grieved he was to learn that Alexander's 'health had been so indifferent as to render it advisable' to try his 'native air'. His words of encouragement were profound:

My good & valuable friend, yours is a life of great consequence both to your family & the publick, & therefore you are bound by every tie to spare yourself for the good of others; & as the case now stands with your health you have the strongest plea to urge, to be permitted to relax the too great intenseness of your application to publick business.[101]

Over the next two years, Alexander seems to have been constantly unwell. During that time, from 1809 to 1811, he was absent from all Linnean Society meetings. Smith, the president of the Society, was familiar with his health problems, Alexander having advised him in December 1811: 'I know that you have heard of my long absence from London and the cause of it. — I am, thank God, very much better than I was, but I am told that my perfect recovery will require much time.?'[102]

Alexander's brothers and sisters also came to stay with him in London. Margaret and Barbara were there for Christmas in December 1808, as were John and Kenneth, and John had also stayed there in 1801.[103] In 1798 brother John had even worked as an extra clerk in the Transport Board with Alexander.[104] His three brothers had joined the navy by the early 1800s but unfortunately William, who was Commander of the ship *Diana*, died in Tobago of yellow fever in 1802 when he was only 32. Kenneth and John also worked commercially in the West Indies before returning to Wick.

FANNY'S FIRST
VISIT NORTH

Family ties were strengthened when Fanny visited the north for the first time in the summer of 1817, accompanied by three of her sisters: Christiana, Margaret and either Kennethina or Johanna.[105] She informed William that: 'I have much pleasure in remembering all the stories you have told me of your several feats performed here & in listening to others related by your Aunts. You are a favorite [sic] wherever you go'.[106]

In her graphic descriptive style Fanny wrote in detail about her first encounter with Wick. The reception that the Macleay sisters received upon their arrival makes amusing reading through Fanny's eyes:

> I was happy enough to get on shore amongst Herrings & dirt on the 22d of last month for we were all quite overwhelmed with sickness & any thing was better than the close cabin of the Broughty Castle. You must know I was far from having sanguine expectations of the beauty of the place. On landing I found I could not walk at least it appeared to me that I stepped in air & that I was tossed up & down most unmercifully by that element … dark colored Houses, the queer dresses of the Women & Men I could scarcely make myself believe I had not quitted the Kingdom of Gt.Britn besides I could not hear them speak, but I was vexed to find I comprehended it not (tis not the case now but in few instances where gaelic is spoken) they seemed to speak very fast & indistinctly of course. We appeared to be a greater wonder to the good people here, than they to us for though it was but six o'Clock, both piers were covered & all eyes fixed upon your seemingly tipsy sisters.[107]

One of the pastimes that Fanny and her sisters enjoyed whilst in Scotland was riding around the countryside.[108] She complained about the 'flat bare ugly country' but was delighted that 'Uncle Kenneth took Chris & I to see the old Castles with which I was very much pleased. I intend to try my pencil …'.[109] The original Girnigoe Castle, built in the 15th century, was added to in the 17th century and is now Castle Sinclair Girnigoe. Like her contemporaries, Fanny thought there were actually two castles. Built of local slate on a 'rocky promontory', which makes a wildly romantic and dramatic setting, these ruins have attracted visitors over the centuries.[110] They are extraordinary feats of architectural ingenuity. Bishop Forbes, in the 1760s, recorded that they were 'the grandest I ever looked upon'.[111] Another fun venture was to ride six miles along the coast north of Wick, to visit the 18th century Keiss Castle, next to the earlier 16th century Keiss Castle, both of which her Uncle John had acquired on disposition from Sir John Sinclair in 1813.[112] Fanny was pleased when her brother Alexander Rose presented her with a 'beautiful pony' in 1820 for such excursions.[113]

Alexander subsequently returned home to Wick on a number of occasions. When Fanny and her father were there in September 1820, only three months after Alexander's father died in June, she referred to Alexander's 'three last journeys to the North'[114] and also mentioned that he had been elected councillor and her Uncle John, head bailie, both for the Burgh of Wick, following the family tradition that had been instituted by her grandfather.[115] In 1825 Kenneth was also made a bailie in the local council.[116]

MONEY MATTERS

In 1823 Alexander was back in Wick again and the following year he wrote to James Smith saying: 'You probably heard of my having been upwards of 5 months about in Scotland last year, and of the cause'.[117] Alexander's mention of his extended stay in Scotland in 1823 was a reference to financial problems, in particular, those experienced by the family bank, the Caithness Banking Company. This bank had been formed in 1812 by a partnership between Alexander, John, Kenneth and their father William. With the new harbour at Pulteneytown completed by this time, it was timely for the British Fisheries Society that a local bank was setting up in the area. In the ensuing years this Society worked closely with the Macleay bank and in 1815, when their Secretary came to inspect the scene, he stayed with Provost William Macleay for two months. During this time not only did he attend Margaret's wedding, but he also met with Joseph Rhind, the bank's accountant.[118]

By 1812 Alexander's father, William, had amassed considerable monies through his mercantile ventures in Wick. John and Kenneth, back in England by 1807, were also in a position to invest through profits they had made in the West Indies. Kenneth had originally worked as deputy paymaster in Martinique and John had worked in 'the Exchequer Bills Office for Grenada & St.

Vincent'.[119] During this time, Kenneth had also taken on the extra lucrative enterprise of selling his father's herrings which were exported from Wick. The money he used to finance these ventures was borrowed from official funds and spent with the navy's consent on the proviso that he continued to pay for provisions and salaries.[120] Perhaps these brothers conceived the idea of a bank when they stayed with Alexander in December 1808. It would have seemed a sensible venture, bearing in mind the recent expansions in the vicinity of Wick primarily related to the herring industry.

Alexander also appears to have accumulated enough money to invest in the family bank as a partner. Of particular interest are reports in the Sasines (records of transfers of land titles, held by The National Archives of Scotland) that he acquired the titles to many parcels of land throughout Caithness in 1804 'in security of' £1,800 from William Wemyss and his wife, Henrietta Sinclair.[121] Whether Alexander actually bought these lands outright or borrowed money to buy them, or even whose land it originally was, is not clear. He further acquired a third part of a mill at Brabsterdorran, and several other mills and mill land in other areas, which would all have brought in extra money. Another reliable source of income for Alexander over some years, in addition to his salary at the Transport Board, was indirectly referred to by Fanny in 1814, when she informed William that Mr Miles was dead and that 'Mama says his death is a great loss to Papa, he having every year given Papa a share in the Loan'.[122] What this loan was for is not known but it must have been lucrative and sorely missed when it ceased.

EDUCATION FOR THE CHILDREN

A good education was considered important to Alexander and he endeavoured to provide his family with the best education he could afford. In 1817 Fanny acknowledged his generosity:

What a kind Father we have … I can never be sufficiently grateful for his goodness to me. He has been so good as to give me a Drawing Master, Singing & Harp Master, so that really I am much engaged in practising for each, for they are very expensive (each charging 15/- a lesson) & consequently I have two reasons for getting on as fast as possible.[123]

These lessons were not restricted to Fanny for she reported to William in 1817 that 'Chris … has been making a most dreadful noise all time with the Harp'.[124] According to the common prevailing practice of the time, the Macleay daughters studied at home under a governess, although Christiana attended a private school in Kensington for a brief period. However, Fanny wrote to William in August 1816 that she thought Christiana would not be returning to this school:

> for my Father finds great fault with Mrs. S's [Slaveley] charges: Indeed they are very high considering the short time she was at school, which you will allow, when I tell you for about 4 months, Mrs. S demands £100… [125]

It was just as difficult to find suitable governesses as it was to find good servants. 'Poor Miss Hughes' in 1812 was succeeded by yet another inadequate governess whose manners were described by Fanny as 'far from genteel … although she certainly is every way superior' to her predecessor.[126] Fanny wrote to William that the new governess, Miss Beck, who was with them in 1814, 'knows no more of drawing than the cat', although she did play music very well.[127] Sometimes Fanny was asked to play a part in the education of her younger siblings. In 1814 Alexander specifically requested that she observe Miss Beck's methods of teaching but Fanny's response was that this was to be 'exceedingly awkward for me as I already perceive, she does not act as Papa & Mama wish her'.[128] Fanny came to the conclusion that Miss Beck was just too lazy to teach so many and she also thought her general reading was lacking. But she was pleased to advise William that their father had 'subscribed to Cawthorns Library, and I have proposed that we should get some good historical works from it, which are to be read out every evening'.[129]

In 1796 Alexander had been Librarian at Clapham Road Place in Surrey and in 1798 he was Secretary and Librarian for the Westminster Library Society at Prince's Court,[130] which possessed 'one of the finest collections of books in London'.[131] Fanny's parents were fortunate that their eldest daughter was capable of supervising her brothers and sisters and also innovative and patient enough to encourage further reading and the learning of history each night.

But there was possibly another motive behind Alexander's request for Fanny to sit in on classes. Perhaps one day she would need to earn her own money and such experience would help.[132] Only twelve years later, in New South Wales, both Fanny and Kennethina did teach in the School of Industry using the pupil monitor system, although their efforts were unpaid. Sister Margaret also helped educate her own children, with the aid of a governess, in the years to come when she lived near Port Macquarie in northern New South Wales.[133]

As the eldest son, William was the most privileged child. He was given the maximum opportunities and encouragement as it was understood that, if Alexander died, it would be his duty to look after the family. When the Reverend Samuel Goodenough, who was then Dean of Rochester and later became Bishop of Carlisle from 1808 to 1827, recommended in 1805 that William should attend Westminster School,[134] Alexander took up his suggestion to call on the headmaster Mr Carey. Once again Alexander's friends in the Linnean Society were useful, for in 1805 Goodenough was Vice-President of the Linnean Society.

William entered Cambridge University in 1810, graduating as a B.A. with honours in 1814, and an M.A. in 1818.[135] He was the only member of the family to acquire university qualifications and how proud his father would have been of his eldest son's achievements. Alexander's Linnean Society connections again helped William during his tertiary studies. The Reverend William Kirby, who lived at Barham near Cambridge, encouraged William's interest in entomology and enthusiastically followed his budding career for many years afterwards. On numerous occasions William visited the Kirby household and often stayed with them on holidays such as Easter. Kirby had many personal contacts including the Master of Sidney College at Cambridge, Mr Davie, who was also a friend of Alexander's.[136] He did not hesitate to use his own acquaintances to assist William and in December 1811 he wrote to Alexander to inform him that William and Mr Davie had recently dined together,[137] a social occasion that no doubt fostered William's academic studies.

In September 1815,[138] only three months after Napoleon was finally defeated at the Battle of Waterloo in mid-June, William moved to Paris to take up an appointment initially as Attaché to the British Embassy. By the end of the year he held the position of 'Secretary to the Board for liquidating British claims in France'.[139] He had his father to thank for this opportunity as Alexander had written to Sir Henry Bunbury, head of the War Department, seeking a diplomatic posting for William. Further help came from Viscount Castlereagh, the Secretary of State for Foreign Affairs, who approved the idea.[140] Previously, in 1812, Alexander had approached the Prime Minister, Lord Liverpool, through the Chairman of the Transport Board, Rupert George,[141] to see if he could secure a position for William with him at the Transport Board but this application had been rejected.[142] However, Alexander's third eldest son, Alexander Rose, did work at the Transport Board from around 1813 to 1816. But it must have been under a special arrangement with his father because Fanny informed William that Alexander Rose was most unhappy with the gratuity of £75 that he finally received for his services.[143]

Whilst William was keen to have his father visit him in Paris, it appears that he did not relish the thought of his sisters staying with him. Alexander never did make the trip and Fanny, who would have dearly loved to have visited her brother, admonished him sternly in 1817 by writing:

> You know I hinted my wish to pay you a visit but you did not choose
> to see me Unfraternal Wretch … My Father asked me the other day
> which I would rather do — take a trip to see you or go to Scotland
> this Summer — I am more than half inclined to plague you & tell you
> that it was determined you should be tortured with a visit from us. But
> I am too good for that, so you may take breath — for I am afraid my
> choice will not be my Father's.[144]

Previously, in 1815, Fanny had suggested that a visit by herself and sister Christiana might not have been 'so very troublesome as you seem to express'.[145] Clearly William wished to be left alone to discover French society and natural history, no matter how fond he claimed to be of his favourite sister!

Not all Alexander's sons were as clever as William. George and James also attended Westminster School which would have been expensive but considered worth the cost at the time. Alexander would have fostered eight-year-old George's 'love of Natural history',[146] although some years later in Australia he was so upset upon hearing that George had been expelled, that he had to be bled.[147] James also never completed his schooling at Westminster,[148] perhaps being adversely influenced by his older brother.

THE IMPORTANCE OF RELIGION

Like education, major emphasis was placed on religion by the Macleay family. Alexander was a member of the Church of England and in the 1790s attended St Mary's Church at Lambeth in South London.[149] When he was at his country estate near Godstone in Surrey, he worshipped at the 13th century Church of St Nicholas, where Charles de Coetlogon was the Rector from 1794 to 1820 and Charles Hoare from 1820 to 1865.[150] This picturesque church, situated only half a mile from Godstone and not far down the hill from Tilbuster, was where the family regularly attended service each Sunday when they were in residence. Five of Alexander's daughters[151] and other Macleays are buried in a family tomb in the graveyard adjoining this beautiful old church. Inside the building is the Macleay Chapel which was founded by son George Macleay, of Bletchingley and Elizabeth Bay. Within this small chapel, which is on the right of the main section of the church, several Macleay memorial plaques are displayed and there is also a marble effigy of Barbara St Clair Innes who was George's first wife.

St Nicholas's Church at Godstone, Surrey, where the Macleays worshipped when they stayed at Tilbuster. Drawing by John Hassell in 1821. Reproduced from *Bygone Godstone* by Juliette Jacques in 1992

Evidence of the importance of religion in the lives of Alexander's parents also is in Wick. Their grave lies behind a high wall next to the road in the terraced cemetery of the old parish church which was built in the 1820s on the site of an earlier church.[152] The popular Reverend Phin and his wife, Margaret (Alexander's sister), are also buried there with their daughter, Barbara Rose, who died aged only five in 1820. Robert Phin, who was minister of this church from March 1813 until his death in 1840, married Margaret in 1815 but, sadly, she died in September 1822.

Alexander was a great believer in upholding Christian principles in his daily life and found it difficult to accept shortcomings in others. Kirby thought that he was too sanctimonious. He wrote to Alexander in 1817 about their Linnean Society friend, Sheppard, who had had a 'sad lapse' with a married woman,[153] and specifically stressed that the letter was secret and that it should be burnt or at least the part containing the reference to Sheppard destroyed. Concerned with the wording of an acknowledgement to Sheppard in one of his writings

*Today St Nicholas's Church is much the same as it was nearly 200 years ago. Buried
in the Macleay grave in the foreground are James, son of Alexander, his wife Amelia
and one of their children also named Amelia.* Photo: Derelie Cherry

about to be published, Kirby explained that he had only raised the matter as he
thought that it should probably now be changed because of public opinion. A
few days later he wrote to Alexander on the subject again:

> Excuse me for saying I think you are rather too bitter with respect to
> S —. I by no means wish to extenuate a crime of so deep a die, but
> we should always separate the sin from the sinner, & while we hate &
> abhor the one, not extend those feelings to the other.[154]

One is left to contemplate why Alexander did not destroy these details as
Kirby had instructed. He must have felt very strongly about the situation to
not do so.

The Macleay family motto 'Spes anchora vitae' *translates as* 'Hope is the anchor of life', *a creed that the family firmly believed in.* Photo: Derelie Cherry

Scottish granite used for this family grave signifies the Macleay heritage. Photo: Derelie Cherry

This communal monument in the grounds of St Nicholas's Church is the resting place for five Macleay sisters. Photo: Derelie Cherry

BARBARA MACLEAY,
DIED AUG.ᵗ 31ˢᵗ 1812. AGED 15 YEARS.
CATHERINE MACLEAY,
DIED SEPᵗ 10ᵗʰ 1813 AGED 14 YEARS.
ELIZABETH MACLEAY,
DIED JULY 18ᵗʰ 1814. AGED 13 YEARS.
JOHANNA MACLEAY,
DIED JANᵃ 27ᵗʰ 1820. AGED 16 YEARS.
KENNETHINA MACLEAY,
DIED AUG.ᵗ 29ᵗʰ 1864. AGED 58 YEARS.

The inscription evokes sad memories of that era in Alexander Macleay's life.
Photo: Derelie Cherry

CONCERNS FOR THE
FUTURE

After he arrived in Australia in January 1826, Alexander worked extremely long hours in his official capacity as Colonial Secretary but still found time to devote to numerous local charities and societies. It was the same in England, where apart from his work at the Transport Board and the Linnean Society, he became a member of 'many learned societies including the Royal Society, the Antiquarian Society, the Horticultural Society and the Zoological Society'.[155] How difficult it must have been for him to adjust to his new status after the Transport Board was abolished in 1817 and its affairs were transferred to the Navy Board.[156] With no firm offers of employment, and his pension not immediately forthcoming, Alexander was very concerned about his future. Fanny wrote to her brother William in 1818 that:

> Papa … is very anxious to know what situation they will give him —
> I know not whether he had told you, but he has some hopes of getting
> the situation of Chairman of the Custom House … It would be an
> excellent thing for him if he should get it but somehow or other I fear
> such luck is not for us.[157]

Her predictions proved correct. Chances of employment for her father were very slim amidst the social and economic turmoil that Britain was experiencing. Unemployment was widespread and there was talk throughout the country of general discontent and possible riots against increased taxes and the distribution of wealth. Fanny referred to this situation in 1817 when she wrote to William about a planned uprising by the people and that they had already begun 'to calculate the share each man is to get on the general distribution of Land'.[158]

Things became so dire that Alexander even contemplated permanently returning home to Wick. Kirby wrote to him on 10 May 1819: 'A rumour has reached me from town which affirms that you are about to quit London & its vicinity & retire to your native land. A lamentable thing this would be for science & your friends'.[159]

THE OPPORTUNITY
TO BECOME
COLONIAL SECRETARY

In addition, William had returned from Paris to London in 1818 and he too had found no work which must have created another worry for Alexander. Little wonder then, when the offer of Colonial Secretary with a salary package of £2,750 was made in 1824, that Alexander took only a couple of weeks to make up his mind.[160] In his letter of acceptance to Lord Bathurst, the Secretary of State for the Colonies from 1812 to 1827, Alexander wrote of his concerns in taking his large family with him to the other side of the world. What would happen to them if he died? Could not a position be given to his eldest son who would need to take over responsibility for the family if this situation ever arose?[161] His request was again rejected and a year later William accepted an appointment in Havana in the West Indies, which he had obtained through the patronage of the Marchioness of Stafford. Fanny reminded him in due course to send a present to Lady Stafford so that she and her son, Lord Granville, would not forget him.[162] Patrons were of the utmost importance and were to be treated as such, a fact which Fanny fully appreciated. William's new position was 'British Commissioner of Arbitration to the Mixed British and Spanish Court for the Abolition of the Slave Trade'[163] and in 1830 he became a Judge there in the Mixed Tribunal of Justice. Commencing on a salary of £1,850,[164] and even though he was far removed from his family, he had excellent prospects for the future.

POSSIBLE PATRON
SIR JOHN SINCLAIR

Undoubtedly there was a patron who influenced Bathurst's decision to appoint Alexander as Colonial Secretary. Although this person remains unknown, there are many indications which lead to the conclusion that it was Sir John Sinclair. Apart from his agricultural reforms and political activities, Sinclair's enduring contribution to fame was his 27-volume *Statistical Account of Scotland*, the first volume of which appeared in 1797. In 1826, less than two months after Alexander arrived in Sydney, a biography of Sinclair printed in the *Sydney Gazette* informed the public that 'he may justly lie [sic] characterised as one of the most useful, active and zealous patriots of his age'.[165] Perhaps Alexander was responsible for the publication of this article.

With the best political connections and vast personal wealth, Sinclair was well placed to influence those in authority. The following quotation from his correspondence in 1834 with the Prime Minister, Sir Robert Peel, revealed the extent of his power, especially in terms of the incredible amount of money that he hoped to raise in order to win the forthcoming election. This passage also reveals his strong political allegiance:

> It is the duty of every real friend to the prosperity and happiness of his country, to give you every possible assistance in carrying through the important task you have undertaken, and if you wish for it, I shall, from time to time, send you such hints, as my great experience in political matters can furnish.
>
> As it will be necessary to provide large funds for the expenses of the Election, I have mentioned to Mr. Alex Baring, a channel by which I am in hopes, that £200,000 for election purposes may be obtained. As this is the last chance we have for establishing a Constitutional Government on Conservative principles, no expense necessary for so great an object should be spared.[166]

This was written only a year before he died in 1835 and even then Sinclair's reputation was still remarkable, as he himself commented in another letter to Peel which expressed his determination to remove the protectionist malt tax:

> It has just occurred to me, that my going to London, to bring forward the plan for extinguishing 'The Malt Tax' in person, might be of essential consequence to the country at the present crisis. For that purpose, it would be necessary, to give importance to the measure, that you

sent a King's Messenger to Edinburgh, requesting my attendance, as a Member of the Privy Council, and the circumstances should be mentioned in a paragraph inserted in the London Newspapers. The idea of an old Senator, who had completed his 80th year of his age, coming forward at such a crisis, would make a great impression on the public mind.

You can hardly conceive the mental resources of a Man of Eighty, who has made Politicks and Finance, the peculiar objects of his study.[167]

As a friend of the Macleays in Wick for at least 50 years, Sinclair would have been pleased to help one of old William's sons, especially now that their father had passed away and the family bank was in serious trouble. It was Sinclair who had first suggested to the British Fisheries Society that Wick would be suitable for development and his 'zeal in promoting' Pulteneytown 'which has so greatly tended to the prosperity of the Town of Wick and its vicinity' was publicly acknowledged in 1821.[168] He must have been considerably upset when the first bank in the area failed, apart from taking into account all the business transactions that he had with the Macleays since its establishment. Evidence of such sentiments is portrayed in a letter he wrote to Alexander on 30 January 1825. Full of practical advice, he spoke in most encouraging terms of the opportunities ahead for his friend and also how pleased he was that he would be leaving Caithness far behind. He wrote:

I was very glad to hear of your Appointment in New South Wales
1. Because it may do good to your family
2. Because it may do good to yourself, being so healthy a climate that you may live there ten or twenty years longer than you would do in Europe, more especially if you study 'The Code of Health and Longevity' and
3. Because it will do much good, both to that rising settlement and ultimately to the Mother Country. I am glad also that it puts an end to your political connexion with Caithness.[169]

Sinclair concluded that he should 'probably be in London before you leave it and we may then discuss together what additional improvements can be introduced in to the Colony'. When Sinclair's son, George, wrote to Alexander in June 1825 from Thurso Castle on his wife's prompting, to see if he could obtain an appointment for his brother-in-law in New South Wales, he wrote:

> She has imagined I know not why, or heard, I know not where, that you are likely to have considerable patronage — and wishes, that, if this is the case, you will after having provided for your own relatives and friends, endeavour to procure an appointment ...[170]

Later in this same letter George noted: 'I suppose you often see my father', with the associated implication that he, in turn, could ask a favour because of this connection. Although no evidence has yet surfaced to officially confirm that Sir John Sinclair was Alexander's patron at this time, his background, personal response and continual advice strongly suggest this was so.

In his letter of acceptance to Bathurst, Alexander requested delaying his departure date to April or May 1825. There were other matters that he needed to settle, not the least of which were those of the family bank in Wick, which ultimately were so complicated that they prevented him from leaving England until August 1825.

A LOOMING FINANCIAL CRISIS IN WICK

Since their father's death in 1820 and John's death in 1821, the remaining partners in the bank, Alexander and Kenneth, were left facing a looming financial crisis. For some years the Macleays, especially John, had been buying up land and property in Caithness and a number of these purchases appear to have been on behalf of the bank. In 1813, the year after the bank opened, John purchased 'several tenements & pieces of land in & around Thurso' which he rented out 'in security and relief to the said Bank for the intromissions of the said William Wilson, as their Agent in Thurso'.[171] By November John had purchased further 'land with houses, shops, yard & Stackhill' for £300 in High Street, Thurso, so business was booming in those early years. In fact the Commercial Bank of Scotland was so concerned about the new competition that they set up an agent in Thurso that very same year.

In 1816 John acquired land with houses and garden on the 'north side of High Street' in Wick from his father-in-law, Benjamin Williamson,[172] and in 1818 a further three lots of land, including two with houses and buildings thereon in Pulteneytown for £500.[173] But in February 1815 he actually disposed by title deed of some land in 'south and north Keiss' to Sir John Sinclair 'in security of his purchase'.[174] Later that year, in September, Sinclair sold parts of land in the north area of Keiss to William Macleay,[175] whilst it appears that John mortgaged parts of the south of Keiss.[176] In September 1815 John and William acquired 'in liferent and fee respectively' land at Myrelandorn from Sir John Sinclair, at the same time that Sinclair acquired land at Keiss from William.[177] And in 1817 John acquired further lands in the area of Myrelandorn 'in security of' £810 from William Wemyss and his wife, Henrietta Sinclair'.[178] Family connections were strong. William's wife, Henrietta, was the sister of John Macleay's wife, Janet Williamson. Furthermore, William Wemyss was a relative of the Marchioness of Stafford,[179] who some years later helped Alexander's son, William, secure a position in the West Indies.

By July 1820, the Caithness Banking Company had started to sell off some of John's properties including those in the High Street in Thurso[180] and the lands at Myrelandorn and Brabsterdorran.[181] In that same year Alexander sold lands in the area that he had acquired in 1804 which included 'part of the town & lands of Myrelandorn' and 'town & lands of Brabsterdorran..., with the Mill & Mill lands thereof' back to William Wemyss's widow, Henrietta.[182] Obviously these arrangements were made so that the lands involved would stay within the extended family. John had married Janet Williamson in 1815 and in the years to come she acquired considerable land through inheritances received from both her parents.[183] On 24 March 1820 the Caithness Bank took over the deeds of an inheritance for lands that Janet received from her mother, Janet Sinclair, in 1819.[184] The Bank received £2,500 for this transaction[185] and, as John had only died in February, it was obviously arranged at that time to help ease the financial stress. Kenneth also took over the security in December 1820 for the lands that Alexander had sold back to Henrietta in October for £1,800[186] and he took over further lands as security from Henrietta Sinclair for around £4,184.[187]

Such a situation would have been difficult enough for Kenneth, who by 1824 was in a poor state of health, but it was even worse for Alexander in London who had been unemployed for seven years and had to rely on second-hand information. Furthermore, Alexander was already in debt to his own son, William, who had lent him £550 at 5% interest in 1824, and many more loans were to come from him in the following years.[188]

Amidst these trying circumstances Alexander must have wondered who he could trust and turn to for help in Wick. He chose as his confidante his brother-in-law, the Reverend Robert Phin, and some of their correspondence from this period is still in the Linnean Society in London. On 12 April 1825 Phin wrote to Alexander suggesting that Kenneth 'should surely be advised to curtail his business if not to settle it entirely. The advice can come from no one with such propriety or effect as yourself. I know it is his own opinion. But he puts off & puts off'.[189]

Interference in the family's affairs was not taken lightly by Phin, who in the same letter expressed to Alexander his concern about not upsetting relationships with his relatives. Living amongst Alexander's mother and his brother and sisters in Wick, Phin would have been placed in an awkward position, especially as he was not able to discuss Alexander's plans with them.

Later that month Phin wrote again to Alexander from Wick stressing that the 'very confidential' communication about his brother should be 'committed to writing' and that he should do so before he departed from Britain. Phin assured him that if he was given these details, he would ensure 'by everything that is solemn and binding among men, that they shall be observed with a punctuality and fidelity that cannot be exceeded'.[190]

Two months later, on 24 June 1825, the Caithness Banking Company was sold to the Commercial Bank of Scotland. From this sequence of events it appears that Alexander alone initiated this ultimatum as the only line of action he could take to solve the crisis before his departure for New South Wales. The very next day Phin wrote to Alexander advising him that he had left a letter with Mr Donald Horne who was related to Kenneth's wife Isabella Horne and was a Trustee for Kenneth's estate after his death. In this revealing letter he declared that he was preparing 'to exert himself in concurrence with you, in getting Mr. Macleay relieved from the concerns of the Bank'.[191] Phin also mentioned that Kenneth, who had been suffering 'severe attacks' from his illness, was a little better and hoped that such news would relieve Alexander's 'mind from the anxiety so natural to your kind and affectionate heart'.[192]

Affairs must have become so complicated that Phin even travelled to London to see Alexander[193] and Alexander himself returned to Wick in July just a month before his departure for Sydney. Because this poignant personal correspondence between Phin and Macleay is still on public record it seems likely that Alexander wanted his own perspective on the situation recorded for posterity to judge. Another letter referring to his 'trying crisis' at this time is also held in the Linnean Society. Kirby obliquely referred to the bank's financial crisis in January 1825 when he wrote about this 'event so unexpected' and declared, in relation to Alexander's new appointment, that 'the only thing that affords an alleviation to the loss is the prospect it holds forth of making a provision for your large family'.[194] A month later he wrote again to Alexander saying 'what a variety of affairs you have to settle & arrangements to make'.[195] In retrospect it was fortunate that Alexander took such action when he did as in August the following year Kenneth died in Edinburgh.

TRUSTEES AND ESTATES

Curiously enough, Alexander did not part with all his possessions before he left England. In fact Kenneth lent him the substantial sum of £6,000 'as Factor and Commissioner' on 12 September 1825 'in favour of said Bond and Disposition in Security of Alexander Macartney then Manager of the Commercial Banking Company of Scotland'.[196] On 24 and 25 May 1824 the trustees of James Sinclair's estate had specified the disposition of Bilbster, whose records dated back to 1642, to Alexander Macleay of Queen's Square.[197] The acquisition of this grand estate, which originally extended to 5,000 acres, and had been owned by James since 1785, firmly placed Alexander and his extended family among the gentry. Indeed, by 1825 Mrs John Macleay and Mrs Provost Macleay who were living in High Street were listed amongst the 'nobility and gentry' of Wick.[198]

Kenneth, as factor and 'mercantile agent' for Alexander, was 'a party entrusted with the possession of goods or documents of titles to goods, the latter being a mere intermediary without possession'.[199] Only five days before the Caithness Bank closed, on 19 June 1825 the Commercial Banking Company took over the mortgage that Kenneth had on Bilbster on behalf of Alexander for 'the Town and lands of Over and Nether Bilbster, with the Mill of the same, and Manor Place of Bilbster, and Pendicles of said lands commonly called Old Crooke, and Quoy Jacks'.[200] These same lands were given to Alexander on 28 September 1829, on disposition, after Kenneth's death.[201]

Not only did Kenneth come to Alexander's aid at this time but he also disposed of lands in the estate of Keiss and at Auckhorn, including the 'Miln and Miln lands thereof, Salmon Fishings & Teinds'[202] to Alexander Rose who had taken over the position of Collector of Customs at Thurso from his Great Uncle John Rose who had died on 9 January 1818. This transaction was in May 1824, thirteen months before the Bank was taken over, and it seems a very generous gesture towards his nephew. However, on the same date in May, Alexander dispensed with lands in the same area to Kenneth so there were obviously internal land transfers taking place.[203] Barbara Rose was also provided for in July 1825 as she arranged for the transfer of lands to Kenneth 'in security of a restrictable liferent annuity' of £200.[204] This was scarcely two weeks after the Caithness Bank had been sold so it is evident that the family were making future provisions for all members wherever possible.

FRIENDS' ADVICE FOR
THE FUTURE

William Kirby, at 65 years, was almost envious of his friend's new appointment and wrote that if he was '15 years younger I should request you to use
your interest to procure me some appointment that I might accompany you,
& unite my labours to yours as a naturalist, & do what good as divine circumstances might enable me'.[205] He added:

> I am sure [the] Government could not have fixed upon a person better
> qualified both by temper & talents to allay the heats & bitterness pro-
> duced by dissentions in the Colony & to place things upon a better foot-
> ing, than yourself, & as so intimate a friend of your brothers is to go as
> Governor — there seems every probability of discord giving way to peace.[206]

Kirby probably referred to Kenneth in this letter as by then he was Alexander's only surviving brother. It is assumed that Kenneth knew the new Governor, Ralph Darling, in the West Indies where Darling had been military
secretary and Lieutenant-Colonel from 1785 to 1802. Nevertheless, Kirby was
deeply grieved by Alexander's impending departure and told him that 'to your
friends here & science the loss will be irreparable'.[207] He managed to console
himself with the thought that all was not entirely lost as he thought that bright
young William was to stay on in England. How upset then he must have
been when William departed for Cuba a month after his father sailed for New
South Wales. A couple of years later, Fanny wrote to William saying that she
had received a letter from Mrs Kirby expressing 'her husband's great disappointment at not hearing from you once since you quitted England!'[208]

Robert Phin was particularly keen to promote the spiritual welfare of the
colony although he did admit that 'It would be presumptuous in me to suggest
what objects I thought best entitled to your patronage'. He reminded Alexander of how important 'religion and morals' were to men in power, especially
in relation to his brother-in-law who was such a 'zealous friend to the Gospel
of Christ'. He was confident that Alexander would 'employ every Talent and

embrace every opportunity for its advancement' more than anyone who had ever left England to work in the 'Government of any of her Colonies'. Still mindful of the strained circumstances under which his brother-in-law was departing, Phin declared that the idea of helping others in the colony on religious grounds was the only way in which he could 'reconcile' Alexander's 'aged and venerable Mother to the thoughts of your Departure', bearing in mind that they would probably never see each other again 'in this world'. Barbara Rose, he considered, was 'the most wonderful person of her age that I ever saw. Your Departure and your Brother's ill health are weighing her down', but her religion was giving her extra strength to face the future. He hoped to live long enough:

> to know that you are at the heart of many Christian & Benevolent
> Institutions in the country ... and are the means of giving ...
> education to the young & the unspeakable benefits of access to
> Religious Ordinances in every part of that immense country.[209]

Apart from Kirby's sadness and Phin's words of spiritual advice, after his new appointment was announced, Alexander also received many congratulations which bore testimony to his capabilities. Mr Duncan McArthur, of Walmer Deal, wrote to him on 7 January 1825 offering support and advice for his future career. He believed that Alexander's 'conciliatory manners will bring back those, whom the misconduct of your Predecessor alienated from the Government'.[210] James Loch, who at the time was staying at the palatial Castle Howard in England, wrote:

> the colony is in vast luck to obtain the benefit of your active services
> and you will I have no doubt much satisfaction in the exercise of your
> benevolence, by promoting the improvements of that infant Empire
> ... do not attempt too much and don't expose yourself too much to the
> climate, tho' it is a fine one or take too much exercise.[211]

Alexander must have been very gratified to receive this letter. Loch, as an agent for the Marquis and Marchioness of Stafford during the years 1810 to 1830, helped clear their land of tenants and replace them with sheep,[212] though this did not affect his popularity and from 1830 to 1850 he was 'repeatedly re-elected Liberal MP of the Northern Burghs'.[213] Alexander supported such action in the spirit of progress and Fanny reported to William that Loch was present at a grand dinner held at the Stafford's wonderful old Dunrobin Castle in September 1820. Kenneth and Alexander were greatly excited that they had been invited to stay at the Castle for two nights on this occasion. On her father's return to Wick, Fanny wrote to William that he 'almost covets his [Loch's] place & seems inclined to look out for some thing similar — You know he is fond of improving'.[214] Moreover, at that time Alexander was badly in need of a position.

TO THE VERY
ANTIPODES

Alexander's own thoughts on his new appointment were succinctly expressed in a letter that he wrote to James Smith in January 1825:

> My Friends generally congratulate me on this appointment, but I cannot think it any subject of Congratulations to be sent at my time of life with a large family to the very antipodes of all my Friends and Connections. — The truth is that the Situation was offered to me in a very handsome and flattering manner, and the temptation was so great that after taking a fortnight to consider of it, I felt that in duty to my Family I was bound to accept of it.[215]

But what alternative did he have? Because of the bank's problems and the fact that he had not been able to find work since 1817 there seemed to be no other solution, and so, accompanied by his wife, six single daughters and several servants, Alexander embarked for Sydney from Portsmouth on 24 August 1825. In May 1825 he had originally requested passage out with the Navy for his family including his wife, one son, six daughters, a governess and six servants.[216] Even though in January Lord Bathurst had made it clear that he could not provide employment for William in the colony, Alexander must have still held hopes that his eldest son would accompany them.[217]

Looking back as he left England forever Alexander must have felt emotionally exhausted, especially as he was not really looking forward to moving to the 'very antipodes' on the other side of the world. Yet the role that his father William had played in his upbringing and his administrative experiences in his work at the Transport Board and the Linnean Society were to all stand him in good stead for the future. From his earliest days of helping his father with farming ventures and becoming familiar with local politics through William's participation in the Wick Burgh Council, Alexander had been well trained to handle most situations. His father would have been proud that this son was embarking on such a courageous venture.

Contentious issues resulting from the demise of the family bank were still being mentioned to William by Fanny over the next two years and they continued to be a source of grievance for Alexander. In September 1826 Alexander received a letter of complaint from Isabella, Kenneth's widow. Fanny reported: 'My poor Father had been rendered very unhappy by Mrs. McLeay's letter — as for me I had expected worse accounts therefore cannot quite enter his feelings'.[218] In August 1827 there was another 'annoying' letter to Alexander from Isabella stating that she hoped:

> he will not allow his Brothers Children to be losers by him as she finds
> he (Papa) is greatly in his Brothers debt — Poor dear Papa — he must
> have been greatly involved ere we came here for all his Salary is sent
> Home to pay off debts — He never seemed so poor before …[219]

Isabella was right as Alexander had his brother to thank for Bilbster, apart from numerous other arrangements which were put in place before the Bank closed. Alexander retained Bilbster until April 1833 when it was transferred by conveyance to the trustees of Kenneth's Estate.[220] In 1849 James Henderson, who was by then living at Rosebank, having married Kenneth's daughter, Elizabeth, on 4 June 1845, acquired the property by disposition from Kenneth's trustees.[221] Bilbster and Rosebank remained within the Macleay family until 1927. Bilbster was then sold and James's last

Alexander Macleay (1767–1848). This portrait was later copied by Margaret Carpenter, whose paintings are on display at the Australian Museum and Australian Club in Sydney. Artist Sir Thomas Lawrence (1769–1830), 1825. By permission of the Linnean Society of London

> *Elizabeth Macleay, wife of*
Alexander Macleay(1769–1847).
Copy of a portrait by artist John
Hoppner (1758–1810), c. 1800.
Mitchell Library, State Library of
New South Wales

< *Remains of an icehouse*
from the heyday of the herring
industry in the early 19th
century that still exists at
Keiss harbour north of Wick.
Photo: Robert Cherry

< *Spectacular wild gorse, which*
the Macleays would have enjoyed
on their visits home to Wick, is the
plant badge for the Sinclair clan.
Photo: Derelie Cherry

> *Sir John Sinclair, Baronet*
and laird of Ulbster (1754–1835).
Artist Benjamin West (1738–1820).
Wick Town Hall. Reproduced
with permission from the Highland
Council

Castle Sinclair Girnigoe solemnly guards the sea from its spectacular cliff face. Photo: Derelie Cherry

Bilbster House near Wick was once owned by Alexander Macleay although he never lived there.
Photo: Derelie Cherry

< *Fantastic ruins of Castle Sinclair Girnigoe , north of Wick, a place that Fanny loved to visit.*
Photo: Derelie Cherry

18th century Keiss Castle north of Wick, which was once owned by Alexander's brother, John Macleay. Photo: Derelie Cherry

> *Ruins of the original 16th century Keiss Castle on its rocky perch.* Photo: Derelie Cherry

Two centuries later, Barham Church still exudes rustic charm. Photo: Derelie Cherry

Barham Parsonage, the elegant home of Reverend William Kirby, one of Alexander's closest friends in the Linnean Society. Reproduced with permission from the Linnean Society of London

PRISON-SHIP IN PORTSMOUTH HARBOUR.
CONVICTs going on board.

Drawn & Etched by Cap.t W.m Cooke 1828.

Prison ship in Portsmouth Harbour, with convicts going aboard. This hulk, the HMS York, housed around 500 convicts and the Macleays would have seen it as they left England. Artist Edward William Cooke (1811–1880), 1828. The National Library of Australia

surviving daughter, Adelaine Florence, left Rosebank as a legacy to establish the Pulteneytown District Nursing Association which in 1931 became the Henderson Memorial Nursing Home. With an estate valued at £81,851 on her death,[222] Adelaine was one of the wealthiest women in the district.

It is somewhat ironic that both Alexander's brothers' widows remarried within six years, although Janet had only been married to John for six years before he died whilst Isabella's marriage to Kenneth spanned fifteen years. But outspoken Fanny was not impressed by this news from home in 1831. She informed William that Uncle John's widow had married 'old Mr. Henderson of Stempster … so that she is now Mother to her [own] elder Sister!' Fanny was mistaken: Janet had actually become mother-in-law to her sister Marjory Williamson, the wife of Captain David Henderson. Also, Fanny wrote, Isabella Rose was to marry Peter Brodie Henderson, who she described as a '*poor Mad* surgeon, whom we have seen here' in New South Wales.[223]

With so many miles separating Alexander from his homeland for the remainder of his life, the extensive network of contacts he had established were to provide a link with the past in the years to come. Taking up the gauntlet he moved on to another era, far removed from the small village of Wick where he had spent his youth and the hectic daily routine he had experienced in London for 40 years.

two

COLONIAL
SECRETARY

1826–1831

BOUND FOR
SYDNEY TOWN

Alexander Macleay held the position of Colonial Secretary in New South Wales from 1826 to 1831 under Governor Ralph Darling and from 1831 to 1836, under Governor Richard Bourke. Because of the recall of his predecessor, Frederick Goulburn, who was the first official Colonial Secretary in the colony, Macleay's performance would be under stringent examination from both the Colonial Office in England and the rising political factions in New South Wales. Dramatic developments during this turbulent period included a new constitution in 1828 and much public discussion about issues such as trial by jury and the rights of ex-convicts and free immigrants. In addition, there was continual conflict with the expanding press, and the colony's geographical boundaries, opened up by explorers, began to expand because of the surge of interest in pastoral activities.

The Macleay family set sail for Sydney from Portsmouth on 24 August 1825 aboard the *Marquis of Hastings* and in September William left England on the *Bustard* to take up his new appointment in Havana, Cuba. The four-month journey out to New South Wales was far from pleasant. The soldiers in charge of the 152 male convicts on board[1] were mostly Irish and, according to Fanny, were no models of good behaviour. During the stopover at Rio de Janeiro for a couple of weeks some of them became so drunk that they had to be put in irons and two of the Macleay servants also disgraced themselves by getting drunk on the same occasion.[2] The soldiers, too, were a rowdy lot, seasickness was rife and the horrible smells, many of which came from bouts of diarrhoea amongst the convicts, were all-pervasive.[3] In addition scurvy had broken out but the ship's doctor, Dr Rutherford, managed to control this by insisting that the boat stop at Rio de Janeiro for fresh supplies.[4]

Nevertheless there were opportunities for sightseeing in the new and exotic places en route and Fanny's letters to William recorded some of her observations. The family attended church at Rio de Janeiro and Fanny very much liked the 'splendid' shops in that port, where merchants from France, England, Germany and other countries occupied streets that were devoted solely to one industry such as shoemaking or goldsmithing.[5]

How relieved everyone would have been to finally arrive in Sydney on the midsummer's afternoon of 3 January 1826. With a population of nearly 12,000 and only 1,000 houses, the township appeared tiny situated on the vast harbour amidst wooded surroundings.[6] The remarkable physical features of this new country, so different to those of England, must have amazed the Macleays. Just ten months before, the new Chief Justice Francis Forbes and his wife had sailed up that same magnificent harbour. The views they admired, as recorded by Lady Forbes, would have been similar to those that the Macleays saw during the four-hour sail in from the Heads:

> The numerous bays, the white sandy beaches, and the green-capped islands which rose from the limpid plane of blue water, seemed to me rather like some glimpse of a fairy dream-land than actual reality — And this Paradise was to be our future home![7]

Paradise it may have appeared on the surface, but Alexander must have felt some trepidation as he reached his destination knowing he was to start work only five days later on 8 January. Although he had never visited New South Wales, he was familiar with the nature of the colony from his days at the Transport Board. But the position of Colonial Secretary and Registrar of Records, as it was described, was such a relatively new one in the colony that there were bound to be problems. Inherent in these potential problems was the evolution of the position itself. The duties of this office, prior to 1820, had been carried out by the Governor's personal secretary,[8] although in 1808 John Macarthur had unofficially declared himself Colonial Secretary for a brief period following the military overthrow of Governor Bligh.[9] In 1817 Governor Macquarie had recommended that his secretary, John Campbell, be given the title of Colonial Secretary,[10] but it was only after Campbell was also made Provost Marshall by the Governor in 1819 that the Colonial Office sanctioned the position. Major Frederick Goulburn was subsequently appointed, commencing work on 31 December 1820.[11]

The recall of both Goulburn and Governor Brisbane in 1824, partly because they had clashed with each other, would have made Alexander realise the need to exercise extreme caution and tact in his forthcoming role. Yet he would have been buoyed up by the fact that he had been appointed, not by the Governor of New South Wales, but by the Crown, which would have attached additional prestige to his office. It was fortuitous also that he and the new Governor Darling, who had arrived only two weeks before him, were acquainted in England and that they both held similar conservative political views.[12]

Goulburn, who was aged 35 at the time of his appointment, initially worked under Macquarie from 1 January 1821 until 7 November 1821 when Brisbane arrived. Four days after Macleay's arrival, his predecessor left the colony but before he departed Goulburn met Macleay to discuss matters which most certainly would have revolved around recent events.

IMPENDING CHANGES IN
THE COLONY

Alexander had arrived in a colony that was in a state of transition. Although some changes had already been implemented, many more were recommended following three reports emanating from the Bigge commissions of enquiry which were released in London in 1822 and 1823. Several years earlier the Secretary of State, Lord Bathurst, had received complaints from New South Wales about how the colony was run and he was anxious to gain first hand knowledge of the situation so that he could decide upon appropriate policies. In 1818 he commissioned John Thomas Bigge to undertake an inquiry to determine whether the settlement was suited to convict purposes. From 1819 to 1821 Bigge investigated specific aspects of New South Wales and interviewed many of the colonists. His brief was to cover three main areas: the state of the colony, the judicial system, and the state of agriculture and trade.[13] Bigge had been Chief Justice in Trinidad from 1813 to 1818 and he carried out his new commission enthusiastically.

Emerging from his report were specific recommendations regarding convict punishment in the colony. The Colonial Office was worried by the fact that more convicts than ever had been sent to New South Wales after 1815 and the cost of supporting them had grown. Britain was still experiencing severe economic retrenchment following the Napoleonic Wars, as evidenced by Macleay's own job loss following the closure of the Transport Board in 1817. The government believed that Macquarie had treated the convicts too leniently and, in order to increase the punitive aspects of transportation, Bigge recommended that they be sent into the interior where they would be isolated and removed from temptation. Closely related to this idea was Bigge's emphasis on developing the wool industry which would not only provide England with much needed fine quality merino wool, but also usefully employ convicts on the farms. To encourage this, Bigge suggested that large land grants be given to settlers with capital and he was especially supported in this idea by John Macarthur who was keen to establish the wool industry and a colonial landed gentry. Following Bigge's recommendations, the colony began physically to expand in 1822 to the north, west and south of the Cumberland Plain to accommodate the increased need for pasture.[14] Exploration was encouraged for this purpose and, as Bigge had recommended that the colony be surveyed for colonisation, the number of staff in the Surveyor-General's office was also increased.[15] As far as the Colonial Office was concerned, the colony was to serve a dual purpose. It would continue to operate primarily as a gaol, but provision was also made for the expansion of pastoral enterprises which could assist the economy and offer financial return to England.[16]

STILL A CONVICT COLONY

When Macleay arrived in Sydney the total population of the colony was nearly 37,000. Two-thirds of this total were either convicts or of convict origin, women made up 25%[17] and emancipists 45% of the population.[18] Alexander would have recalled also that it was only eighteen months since Macquarie had died amidst continued opposition about the way in which he had governed the colony. To ensure that the activities of the governor in future rested on a secure legal basis, the decision was made to provide him with proper legal advice. In July 1823 Bathurst appointed, as the colony's first Chief Justice, Francis Forbes, who had returned to England the year before from Newfoundland where he had been Chief Justice. James Stephen, legal advisor to the Colonial Office, was instructed to draw up an Act 'for the better administration of Justice in New South Wales'.[19] Under the terms of this Act the Governor, before introducing legislation, was obliged to consult with the Chief Justice to ensure that it was correct according to British law.[20] Other administrative changes were also made, amongst them the appointment of Saxe Bannister as Attorney General in October 1823. As far as the position of Colonial Secretary was concerned, under the Act of 1823, both the Chief Justice and the Colonial Treasurer were to report to the Governor through the Colonial Secretary thereby changing his role significantly. The fact that Bathurst did not specify how these officials should relate to each other proved to be a constant source of friction in the ensuing years.[21] James Stephen, too, had commented in 1823 that the position of Colonial Secretary was not one 'known to the Law of England', and in other colonies it had been left to the local legislative assemblies to clarify the matter.[22]

FIRST LEGISLATIVE COUNCIL

The burdens imposed on the Governor had grown as a result of the increase in the number of convicts and of the free population, and the British government was prompted, in 1823, to establish a Legislative Council to help run the colony. All members of this Council were nominated and their powers were advisory only, with the Governor retaining the final authority. The government officials who formed this first Council included Chief Justice Forbes, Colonial Secretary Frederick Goulburn, Lieutenant Governor of New South Wales William Stewart, Surveyor-General John Oxley and Principal Colonial Surgeon James Bowman.[23] In December 1825 three non-official members replaced Bowman and Oxley with the intention of widening the representation to incorporate merchants and pastoralists. They were John Macarthur, Charles Throsby and Robert Campbell, and Archdeacon Thomas Hobbes Scott, who was head of the Church and School Corporation, was also appointed as an ex-officio member.[24] Scott had accompanied Bigge to the colony as his secretary when he carried out his important commission and had since returned to New South Wales in May 1825 to take up the position of Archdeacon on a salary of £2,000 per annum plus allowances.[25] The Act of 1823 also introduced trial by a jury of twelve colonists for civil cases where both parties agreed to their use, but criminal cases continued under military juries. This change alone was an admission by the British Government that the colony was changing from a

Frederick Goulburn (1778–1837), the first official Colonial Secretary of New South Wales 1820–1825. This portrait of Goulburn hangs in Parliament House, Sydney.
Artist unknown. Mitchell Library, State Library of New South Wales

penal colony, as previously it was considered that there were simply not enough free men to make up such a jury. Ex-convicts, however, were still excluded from acting as jurors in civil cases.

CONFLICT BETWEEN BRISBANE AND GOULBURN

Goulburn had been an unpopular choice as Colonial Secretary. Not only had he been a soldier with no experience in civil administration, but it was also rumoured that he was a 'political appointee'[26] because his eldest brother, Henry, was Under-Secretary of State for War and the Colonies from 1812 to 1821.[27] Appointed on a salary of £365 per year plus fees, Frederick's salary was later increased to £1,200 per annum.[28] At the time he accepted the position Brisbane, who came from a distinguished Scottish family, had behind him a successful military career, for which he was made Knight Commander of the Bath in 1814. He had been soliciting the position of Governor in New South Wales since 1815, albeit one of the reasons for his keen interest was to enhance his astronomical knowledge.[29]

After his arrival in Sydney, Governor Brisbane arranged for an observatory to be built at Government House, Parramatta, a decision that caused many of his future problems as he decided to live there with his family. Because he came to Sydney on only the 'first and third Tuesdays in each month',[30] much of the daily administration was left to Goulburn. With little administrative experience himself, Brisbane instituted this arrangement which, if he had lived in Sydney, would probably have worked reasonably well. But his removal from the hub of activity isolated the Governor from what was actually going on and it was perceived that Goulburn was assuming too much authority. On occasions Brisbane was known to interview people at Parramatta and issue instructions which were contradictory to those that Goulburn, unaware of the Governor's behaviour, had issued simultaneously in Sydney.[31] His absence from Sydney was noted by the Colonial Office and James Stephen wrote to

Portrait of Sir Thomas Brisbane (1773–1860) proudly displaying medals awarded for his distinguished career in the army. He was appointed Governor of New South Wales when he was 48 years old. Artist Frederick Schenck (1811–1885). The National Library of Australia

Governor George Arthur in Van Diemen's Land suggesting that Brisbane was:

> more addicted to stargazing than is quite compatible either with his
> own comfort or with the well being of those who live under his control
> … I take the case to be that Major Goulburn is Viceroy over him, and
> I do not think the Major excels in discretion.[32]

Brisbane later complained to Bathurst that the Colonial Office would have
gained the impression that the Colonial Secretary 'entertains that He is Secretary of State for the Colony, and embracing His powers, without, I am fully
aware, shareing [sic] in the smallest degree His responsibility'.[33] When he
finally realised the extent to which Goulburn had taken over his own duties,
the Governor appointed Major John Ovens as his personal secretary in May
1824, in order to separate some functions away from the Colonial Secretary.
Ovens had served as his aide-de-camp in Spain[34] and would therefore have
been a person whom Brisbane could trust. Differences in personality also
exacerbated the conflict between the Governor and Colonial Secretary. When
Forbes arrived in the colony in August 1824, he informed the Colonial Office
in London that he 'found the whole affairs of the colony in the hands of the
Colonial Secretary'.[35] Forbes further advised that Brisbane had informed him
that he and the Colonial Secretary had:

> so serious a misunderstanding … as to suspend all private intercourse
> between them. The Governor told me that Major Goulburn's language
> and manner had been so loud and offensive, that he had abruptly quit-
> ted his office, and felt himself insulted.[36]

Conversely, Goulburn thought that Brisbane had affronted him.[37] The relationship reached a crisis in April 1824 when Goulburn and Brisbane clashed
over orders that the Governor had issued directly to the Surveyor-General
without first consulting the Colonial Secretary. Both parties differed about
the way in which grants of land should be formalised and Goulburn requested
that the matter be resolved by the Secretary of State in England. Under such
circumstances, the Colonial Office was not prepared to endure the problematic
situation any longer and both officers were recalled.

A NEW GOVERNOR AND A NEW COLONIAL SECRETARY

Because of these preceding events and recent discussions about the relative duties of the Colonial Secretary and the Governor, Bathurst issued specific instructions to Darling, two weeks before his departure for the colony, about the role of the Colonial Secretary. He decreed that 'the Colonial Secretary will have no pretension to controul [sic] your Judgement or to direct your decisions in any particular case', and confirmed that the Governor would maintain exclusive responsibility for each law passed. Bathurst clearly spelt out that the Colonial Secretary was:

> to conduct, under your direction, all Official Correspondence in the Colony, and is to act on all occasions as the general medium of Communication, through which your orders are to be signified either to the community at large, or to private persons. He is also to render you his Assistance in the various details of your Administration on every occasion, on which you may require such assistance, and in the manner which you may think fit to prescribe.[38]

Darling, who was 50 when he left England with his family on 29 July 1825, arrived in New South Wales on 17 December. Having worked as military commander and Acting Governor in Mauritius for several years, he was well experienced for the difficult tasks that lay ahead in the colony. Upon his arrival Darling was reunited with his brother-in-law, Henry Dumaresq, who had worked with him as military secretary in Mauritius where he had also been appointed as the Governor's private secretary in 1823. Dumaresq had arrived in New South Wales two months earlier and Darling soon nominated him to be his Private Secretary and Clerk of the Executive Council. Henry's father, who died in 1804 leaving his mother to raise a family of five children, had even worked for Alexander at the Transport Board on 'secret service work' from his home in Jersey[39]. Furthermore, Darling had actually recommended Henry for the position of Colonial Secretary before he left

England but by that time Alexander had already been nominated for the position.[40]

In addition to his regimental service, the new Governor had served as military secretary in the West Indies from 1796 to 1802[41] and constantly liaised with the War Office in London.[42] Alexander's years of administration at the Transport Board and the Linnean Society in London were also highly regarded and considered appropriate background for his new position. The *Sydney Gazette* announced in February 1826 that the appointments of both the Governor and the Colonial Secretary owed 'their nominations to merit and talent alone' and that Alexander had 'performed the most arduous duties' at the Transport Board 'during the whole of the late war with great zeal and unremitting labour'.[43] Whilst Darling's patron was assumed to be the Duke of York,[44] Macleay's patron was not acknowledged. The article further declared:

> In such hands as these we may confidently look forward to the increased prosperity of the colony, which has already become an important acquisition to the Mother Country, and cannot fail in a few years, from the fertility of its climate, and the enterprise of its inhabitants, to stand amongst the very first of British possessions.[45]

Naturally, residents in New South Wales wanted to know what sort of a person their new Colonial Secretary was. They would have been interested to read the following comments that John Macarthur's son, also named John, wrote home from London to his father in 1824:

> Lord Bathurst has determined to have a Civilian ... Mr. McLeay ... is a most agreeable man, of considerable talents, having great knowledge of official duties, and generally respected here. He is one of the Council of the Royal Society and is thought to profess an enlarged mind on all subjects of commerce and agriculture. I have known him several years, and he has always lived on terms of great intimacy with Barnard ... Mr. McLeay[,] Barnard[,] Scott[,] and myself dined together yesterday ... If his age be not a great disadvantage as diminishing his activity of

mind and body, I think it would be difficult to select a further person, as certainly a man more generally esteemed could not be found.[46]

As Edward Barnard worked in the Colonial Office, he would have heard all the gossip about the new appointments. And certainly Macleay would have perused the Bigge Reports, as had Darling, and there would have been numerous opportunities to discuss their content and implications with the author. With the recent changes to the judiciary in New South Wales, Alexander may have even studied the application of English law in a penal colony.

Six months after this first encounter, young John Macarthur changed his opinion as he now wrote that Alexander was 'too old and inactive for the Situation of Colonial Secretary' and he also implied that Alexander's private pursuits could interfere with his official duties. But he thought that with Darling at the helm this would not present a major problem.[47] What caused him to alter his opinion within such a short time frame can only be speculated upon. He also changed his initial favourable impression of Darling. Brian Fletcher, in his biography of Ralph Darling, suggests that this may have been because the new Governor had made it clear that he would be unwilling to identify or align with any particular section of New South Wales society, including the Macarthurs.[48]

CONFUSION AND DISORDER IN THE PUBLIC SERVICE

When Darling arrived in New South Wales almost 700 people, including unpaid convicts, were employed in the public service.[49] Not only was the daily routine business carried out by untrained and inept convicts, but the colony's finances were quite uncontrolled. The new Governor claimed that 'the confusion and disorder of the Government, when I took charge of it, was unparalleled and inconceivable'.[50] This situation was made worse because each department had been allowed to function separately without any coordination by Brisbane. It was time to take effective control. A further challenge was the fact that the Colonial Office had issued a directive to Darling to increase local revenue which it envisaged could be achieved by fostering emigration and economic growth. Whilst all matters connected with convicts were still to be financed from Britain, the intention was that the colony would gradually take more responsibility for other areas of its administration. Such orders to his superior must have appeared daunting to Macleay. Darling claimed that:

> every Department appeared to act for itself, without check or control, and indeed without any apparent responsibility. Money was drawn without any specific authority, and issued without any Regulation, or even a Voucher of any validity for its expenditure. Contracts were agreed upon without any written Document to render them binding; and purchases were made and supplies furnished without any representation of the necessity or Authority for the Expence.[51]

NEW ADMINISTRATIVE STRATEGIES IMPLEMENTED

Only one week after his arrival, Darling implemented his first major administrative strategy by appointing a Board to investigate and advise on ways to improve the public departments through reorganisation.[52] Two months later, in February 1826, he appointed a Board of General Purposes to compile a report on each department. Four government officials were appointed to this Board: William Stewart (Lieutenant Governor), Henry Dumaresq (Private Secretary), William Wemyss (head of the Commissariat), and Alexander Macleay.

Of the twelve departments in existence, the office of the Colonial Secretary was considered, by Darling, to be the most important and it was the first department to be affected by the ideas of the new Governor. Only two days after Macleay's arrival an official order on 5 January 1826 directed that all 'Heads of departments and commandants of out-stations'[53] must address their applications and reports to the Colonial Secretary. Previously, Brisbane had been unsuccessful in implementing this order and Darling now gave it priority. This order also confirmed the Colonial Secretary's role as the 'custodian of all official papers and records, except those of the Courts'.[54]

BOARDS AND COMMITTEES OF INQUIRY APPOINTED

In March 1826 a Land Board was established composed of William Stewart, William Lithgow who had been appointed head of the new accounts branch, and John Campbell. It was set up to take over from the Colonial Secretary's office the time-consuming tasks of land grant applications and the processing of assigned convicts.[55] Darling hoped that such changes would alleviate some of the extra workload imposed on the Colonial Secretary as a result of his directive that Macleay's department become the central link with all others. Nevertheless, the volume of mail received at the Colonial Secretary's office increased substantially because of this measure: from 8,849 letters in 1826 to 12,005 in 1827, and by 1835 the average was about 9,500 per year.[56] Furthermore, Macleay seemed to be involved in most aspects of Darling's changes.

Additional committees, such as the one formed in March 1827 to investigate salaries, were appointed under the Board of General Purposes to examine specific issues. As Darling wanted to replace convicts in the public service with free employees, it was essential that salary levels were sufficiently attractive and this committee subsequently recommended a graded salary structure and incentive scheme both of which were introduced in June 1827. Macleay, Stewart and Lithgow sat on this committee[57] and Alexander, William Dumaresq and six other colonists also sat on a committee which was appointed in August 1826 to propose improvements for the Female Factory at Parramatta, which housed all unassigned female convicts and children.[58]

The Governor was especially pleased to be able to draw on Macleay's banking expertise in May 1826 when he appointed a Board of Inquiry into the troubled financial affairs of the Bank of New South Wales. Alexander was appointed as one of the three Board members and, as a result of their investigations, the government provided funding to the Bank. Darling's report to Bathurst concluded: 'I beg to add that Mr. McLeay's Services have been also important in these arrangements, and that he has on all occasions afforded me the most zealous assistance, and has proved himself a most useful and able servant of the Government'.[59] In 1828 Alexander sat on yet another committee, this one to examine the postal system.[60] Under its recommendations, the government assumed charge of postmasters in major country towns and postal revenue was to be paid into colonial funds.[61] This directive proved financially beneficial to the colony as considerable sums were raised through the increased number of letters from 15,595 in 1829 to 168,551 in 1838.[62]

STAFF CHANGES IN THE COLONIAL SECRETARY'S DEPARTMENT

In July 1826 the Colonial Secretary's department employed nineteen staff with the following duties:

Clerks:	first class:	R. Crawford £360
	second class:	[no appointment]
	third class:	Wm. Elyard and Jno. Layton £150 each, C. Nye, Thos. Ryan, C. Greville, G. White and P. Brodie all £100 each
Extra third class clerks:		J. Vaux £95, M. Gregson £75, J. Watt £52, F. Stannard £52
Office keeper:		Mrs Watson on 2/6 a day, two messengers on 1/3 per Diem
Four temporary clerks:		R. Martin, J. Erskine and D. Mills on £100 per annum and W. Howarth on £52[63]

By November 1826, Robert Crawford had resigned. He was the son of Brisbane's agent in Scotland and had come out to the colony with the

Governor and taken up his appointment in November 1821. Darling considered that he had 'little pretension as a man of business' and was not much help to the Colonial Secretary.[64] Furthermore, he was living with Mary Campbell who had left her husband, Lewis Campbell, a 'former sergeant of the 48th Regiment'.[65] Such behaviour was deemed inappropriate by the new Governor who was keen to set the highest moral example in the public service. Darling's acceptance of Crawford's resignation was condoned in England, Under-Secretary Hay advising him: 'you did right in accepting his Resignation, as he does not appear to be a person, whom it was desirable to retain in the public Service'.[66] Crawford had been unhappy with the new regime as under the new salary arrangements of 14 June 1826 he actually lost £180 per annum and no longer received the benefit of fees.[67] However, by that time he had managed to obtain a grant of 2,000 acres on which he employed 40 convicts and also possessed 800 cattle, 600 sheep and 18 horses.[68]

THE APPOINTMENT OF
THOMAS HARINGTON

Immediately after Crawford's departure a new appointment was made in the Colonial Secretary's office which was to have a major and lasting impact upon Alexander. Thomas Cudbert Harington became Alexander's unofficial Assistant Colonial Secretary on 1 November 1826. Born in India in 1798, in 1819 he had moved to England and embarked from there for New South Wales where he arrived in June 1820. Hoping to become a prosperous landowner, he settled at Elderslie in the Camden district. By 1822 it seems life on the land was not all he had envisaged and he entered the public service as a clerk in the Commissariat. McMartin suggests that this change was stimulated by the fact that his father, who worked as a senior official in the East India Company, was 'a devoted administrator',[69] but as events turned out it seems more likely that personal ambition was his motive. In 1823 Harington decided to sell property he owned in India and use the substantial sum that he received to resign from the

Commissariat and return to his rural property. It was reported that he brought £6,600 into the colony which, at the time, was 'the largest money capital' that had ever been introduced by one person.[70] Based on this amount, he requested a grant of 6,600 acres from Brisbane.

From November 1824 to April 1826, Harington worked as secretary for the newly established Australian Agricultural Company, on a salary of £500 per annum. He ultimately resigned from this position in 1826 because of a disagreement with John Macarthur. Fortunately for Harington, Brisbane had noted his 'charm and intelligence' and in 1825 appointed him a Justice of the Peace,[71] and Darling also recognised his capabilities. Although the Colonial Office refused to acknowledge the title of Assistant Colonial Secretary because of the higher salary it would entail, Darling kept this fact hidden from Harington. The new Colonial Secretary of State Viscount Goderich later defended his refusal by stating that he had been directed to reduce expenditure in other colonies and was therefore unable to make an exception in the case of New South Wales.[72] That Harington was adamant about the title reinforces his underlying reason for rejoining the public service. As Macleay was approaching the age of 60, he probably thought it would not be too long before the position became vacant and he could then succeed him. Later events confirm this for when Alexander did finally leave office in 1836, Harington applied to become Colonial Secretary.

Harington's salary was £450 per year. It must have eased Macleay's workload considerably to have the assistance of such a capable young man. They were to have a harmonious working relationship for the next ten years, culminating in the marriage of Harington to Alexander's eldest daughter Fanny in 1836. Fanny had drawn attention to Harington's talents not long after arriving in the colony, having advised William in May 1826 that he was 'a person of great abilities and excellent principle'.[73] Although his British father was also a 'distinguished linguist, and for some years honorary professor of law and regulations of the British government in India at the college of Fort William',[74] the fact that Harington's mother was Indian was used by the colonists to criticise him from time to time. But Macleay had no such prejudice against him and Harington exerted himself and worked extraordinarily hard.

On the eve of his wedding he wrote to Alexander requesting him to obtain the Governor's permission 'to be absent for three weeks upon important Private Affairs. During nine years, I believe I have only asked leave three times'.[75]

An examination of the correspondence and memos in the Archives Office of New South Wales reveals the influence that Harington held in the Colonial Secretary's office. He kept the Colonial Secretary well informed as to how his department was performing, and unlike Alexander's mostly illegible scrawl, his handwriting was precise and neat, his instructions meticulous, and the tone of his memos consistently polite and intelligent. But when Alexander left office for a week in 1829 to inspect his rural properties, the inflammatory *Australian* could not refrain from having a sly dig at both men:

> The absence of this Hon. and well paid functionary did not put a stop
> to business, for things went on tolerably well in the usual ding dong
> method, though we hear the principal parts were but 'half-caste'.[76]

REORGANISATION IN THE COLONIAL SECRETARY'S DEPARTMENT

It was the turn of the Colonial Secretary's office to be examined by the Board of General Purposes in September 1827. The results of this investigation were submitted to Darling in the 'remarkably short time of four days', no doubt because of prior recommendations by Harington who, by then, had been working in the department for nearly a year.[77] It was understood that the inquiry was to concentrate on four issues, namely: its establishment, the effective organisation of its activities into separate branches headed by a competent clerk, the role of the assistant secretary, and salaries.[78]

In a memorandum to Macleay the previous February, Harington had already addressed many of the issues that the Board of General Purposes later examined. Noted on his memo are the words 'for approval', indicating that Alexander should give his consent to the way in which the office was structured under the Assistant Colonial Secretary. Harington suggested that office correspondence should continue to be handled by Elyard, Prout, Polleck and Brodie; the first two writing the original letters whilst Polleck and Brodie made copies for despatch and the public records. Nye was to register incoming mail and was also responsible for musters on the convict ships. Elyard was to collect and record fees twice each month and was general superintendent above stairs. Downstairs duties were to be handled by Ryan, Newcombe, MacDonald and Stanmod. With Newcombe as superintendent, their tasks involved the preparation of certificates of freedom, tickets of leave, licences and registers of vessels, bonds, grants and leases of land. Gregson was responsible for the Stationery Office. Normal office hours were from 9 to 6 'but the whole of the Clerks down stairs will remain by turns, two each day in regular rotation, until dark or the actual closing of the office'.[79] Before presenting his ideas to Macleay, Harington circulated them to his staff eliciting a written response from Ryan referring to the 'new Code of Regulations for the guidance of clerks'.[80] The fact that Macleay accepted Harington's proposals conveys the degree of confidence he placed in his opinions.

The vast amount of paperwork emanating from this office often involved triplicate copies of documents and correspondence which had to be laboriously copied out. By the time the department was officially investigated, Harington had already made substantial improvements to the way in which correspondence was handled and filed. Internal letters from other government departments were filed in separate pigeonholes in a newly constructed press specifically designed for that purpose, whilst external and private letters were registered by number upon receipt and filed alphabetically in another compartment. Outgoing correspondence was filed in the same manner and copies were kept in 26 registers under a system 'so methodical and complete, as scarcely to admit of improvement'.[81]

The Board passed its recommendations on to Darling, who by this time had clearly defined in his own mind the role of the Colonial Secretary. He spelt out his ideas to Alexander on 10 October 1827, insisting that:

It is not enough that Orders are issued, or regulations made; There must be an immediate controlling power somewhere; and, under the

The Colonial Secretary's Office (second from left) and Residence (adjoining) in Bridge Street, Sydney. Such close proximity suited Macleay well. This image, though dated 1904, depicts a much earlier era, probably around 1835. Government Printing Office, Mitchell Library, State Library of New South Wales

Governor, it is the special and indispensable duty of the Colonial Secretary, to see that all orders and regulations are properly followed up, and carried into effect — and that they are not, by the supineness of others, allowed to become a dead letter.[82]

In the Governor's opinion, the role of the Colonial Secretary's office was to help 'in considering framing and perfecting which Measures as might be requested for the better Government of the Colony'.[83] On 27 October 1827 Darling despatched his report to the Colonial Office which, in due course, accepted all the proposals put forward. The office was duly restructured, according to the recommendations laid out, into six branches of responsibility namely: finance, the Commissariat, the Medical Department, the out-settlements, land matters including agricultural and stock establishments, and the Military Department. Each branch had a principal clerk who reported direct to Harington and two junior clerks also worked in each section.[84] According to historian Arthur McMartin, one result of this reorganisation

was that clerks in the Colonial Secretary's Department came 'to be looked upon as the elite of the public service, a reputation that was not wholly due to the fact that they were the best paid clerks in the service'.[85] To further the Colonial Office directive of separating colonial, civil and penal expenses, thereby reducing the burden for Macleay and Harington, Darling instructed that all correspondence concerning supplies for the penal settlement be transferred to the commissariat. In addition, other time-consuming matters such as the preparation of tickets of leave and certificates of freedom, as well as the supervision of returns and musters of those to whom the tickets were issued, and the processing of marriage applications, were all transferred to Frederick Hely, the Principal Superintendent of Convicts.[86]

THE BLUE BOOK

Another time-saving recommendation by Darling was in relation to the compilation of the Blue Book which had been prepared in the Colonial Secretary's Department since 1822 at the direction of Lord Bathurst. This book of colonial statistics was prepared annually and sent back to England. Prior to 1827 this arduous task had been completed by one person and, inevitably, if that person (as in the case of Matthew Gregson) became ill, delays occurred. Therefore Darling instructed that, in future, the data would be submitted from all other relevant government departments and that the Colonial Secretary's Department would only be responsible for compiling it.[87]

The preparation of this annual report was made increasingly difficult in 1828 when the Secretary of State, Viscount Goderich, specified that an additional book be prepared in tabular form, set out in debtor and creditor accounts, to furnish details of all revenue and expenditure in the colony for the previous three years.[88] By July 1829, 30 copies of the Blue Book for 1828 were despatched to England 'as far as the printing has been completed', and one copy was included with the few unfinished sheets enclosed in manuscript until the printed versions could be sent.[89] Whilst printed forms had been sent out for the compilation of all other statistics in the colony, nothing had been provided to meet the new requirement of financial estimates and revenue. Alexander documented his excuse to Darling for the imperfect state of the presentation: 'Your Excellency is aware of the difficulty, which I experienced in procuring satisfactory materials and information to enable me to make up the financial Statements'.[90]

He explained that as his office was not one 'of Account' he did not consider himself responsible for the correctness of the accounts as some of them were estimates only. Several receipt and expenditure items were wrongly classified and another problem was the difficulty in obtaining 'any printing containing what is called *Ruled-work* — or anything out of the common way done in this country'.[91] With the only printer that could handle such work already being used for corrections and remodelling, which 'occasioned much labour and delay', Alexander must have become increasingly frustrated. When Darling wrote to Hay in 1831 over the delay in the preparation of the Blue Book for 1829, he enclosed a memo from Alexander which stated that the delay this time had actually been caused by the late arrival in the colony of the printed data collection books from England. Added to the overall problem was the shortage of capable clerks, a situation that Darling and Macleay had complained about ever since they had arrived in New South Wales. In Macleay's defence the Governor wrote:

I am bound in justice to him to state that it is quite impossible for him to get through the Business he has to transact, which is not only very extensive but multifarious, without additional means. I state from my own observation and knowledge that no Man can be more zealous or indefatigable; Besides which, there are few so competent as Mr. McLeay, his official experience enabling him to get through business with greater facility than almost any person I ever met with. I have observed, with much concern, that his health has lately given way, and I am quite satisfied the failure is to be attributed to his close application to the duties of his office.[92]

Darling added that much of Macleay's time had been taken up with the 'legal Affairs of the Government' as the Attorney General, Alexander Baxter, and John Sampson, who was the Solicitor General, had both proved so incompetent that they were about to be replaced.

STAFF DUTIES IN THE COLONIAL SECRETARY'S DEPARTMENT

Emanating from the Board's report in 1827, staff duties in the Colonial Secretary's Department were clearly designated as follows:

Charles Nye, extra clerk:
Numbered, dated and arranged all letters received — entered abstracts of these in register — entered all warrants for disbursements — prepared muster rolls of prisoners on arrival of transports

Matthew Gregson, extra clerk:
Almost entirely occupied with preparation of Blue Book — also had charge of public records

William Elyard, 2nd class clerk:
Framed and wrote original letters connected with receipt and expenditure of revenue; public works, commissariat, except requisitions

Thomas Ryan, extra clerk:
Received, prepared and transmitted certificates of freedom — examined prisoners' applications for mercy and reported on numerous applications from prisoners

Alexander Manson, extra clerk:
Entered indents and muster rolls — copied returns of trials in the courts — additional sentences to chain gangs — folded, endorsed, and sealed dispatches and letters sent out — entered commissions and miscellaneous papers — assisted in making copies

Patrick Brodie, 3rd class clerk; Cornelius Prout, 3rd class clerk: William Vallack, 3rd class clerk:
Entered all letters dispatched and copies of enclosures — framed indexes for letter books

William Newcombe, 2nd class clerk:
Entered tenders and related letters — entered deeds and grants — wrote commissions and documents in an abstract or tabular form

Charles Greville, 3rd class clerk:
Entered and transmitted all requisitions and related tenders — arranged and endorsed all returns

William Shairp, 3rd class clerk:
In charge of all ticket-of-leave business

Alexander Still, 2nd class clerk:
Exclusively employed in the muster office

James Raymond, Jr extra clerk:
Made copies and carried out such duties as he was qualified for[93]

PROBLEMS CAUSING
INEFFICIENCY

Yet the work continued to mount up and in 1830 the critical *Sydney Monitor* referred to the enormous number of letters that Macleay had to deal with and complained about the length of time it seemed to take in getting a reply. The editor suggested facetiously that the Colonial Secretary should 'reflect upon the numbers of letters that are not answered by him for months, till the subject matter dies a natural death'.[94] However, the type of correspondence that had to be dealt with often involved extensive background research before it could be answered, while many of the incoming letters, although trivial in content, still required a response. By 1831 there was so much public complaint about the delay in issuing tickets of leave that Alexander decided individuals could apply three months earlier than before. He claimed that much of the delay had been caused 'by the non communication of the replies transmitted to the Mag-istrates, and partly by the recommendation of Prisoners who had been recently punished, or were otherwise disqualified'.[95]

The Colonial Secretary's office was initially poorly equipped and work-ing conditions were cramped. In 1829 Greville complained that the table he worked on was so small that he could barely write on it.[96] By 1829 the layout of the office, which was conveniently located next to Alexander's residence in Bridge Street, consisted of: Room 3 Land, Room 4 Revenue, Room 5 Con-victs, Room 6 Musters, Room 7 Harington, Room 8 Ante-Room, Room 9 Records. One assumes that rooms 1 and 2 were for the Colonial Secretary himself. The furniture for the whole office in that year consisted of '12 tables of various sizes and 4 upright desks', excluding seating and bookcases. Various items such as 'tables, stools for tables, pigeonholes for tables, sloping desks for tables', and 'office chairs' were all listed as items needed.[97]

ALEXANDER'S APPLICATION
TO HIS WORK

Darling was greatly satisfied with Macleay's performance as Colonial Secretary right from the start. In November 1826 he reported to Bathurst that whilst the office hours of the Colonial Secretary's Department were from nine to six for six days of the week, he was aware that Alexander's official day usually started at six in the morning when he presided over Public Board meetings and extended long beyond the closing time of his department.[98] Fanny had written to William seven months earlier that: 'My Father is still greatly occupied — many nights he spends but four hours in bed, notwithstanding this he looks well and seems to like the place'.[99]

And Henry Dumaresq informed Under-Secretary Wilmot Horton in a letter dated 10 January 1828 that: 'The Colonial Secretary is usually employed from 6 a.m.; or soon after daylight until 6 in the evening, and has occasionally been obliged to continue his labours until 12 o-clock at night'.[100] Even though Alexander was so busy, he still maintained his health and demeanour. However, to better manage his time, he issued an instruction in October 1826 for the public to call on him only between 11 and 1 to avoid constant interruption.[101] Three years later, daily meetings from 11 a.m. to noon were held exclusively between the Colonial Secretary and the Governor.[102]

NEW EXECUTIVE
COUNCIL

Just prior to Darling's arrival in the colony, the newly formed Executive Council had met for the first time. Composed of the Chief Justice, the Colonial
Secretary, the Lieutenant Governor, Archdeacon Scott and the Governor,
this Council was specifically set up to assist the Governor to formulate and
advise on policy. All members were also members of the Legislative Council, a factor which contributed to future conflict as the Governor expected
participants to support his measures rather than advocating their own views.
Macleay was obliged to attend 26 meetings of the Executive Council in his
first eight months; sessions were held over approximately three days each
month. The regularity of these meetings waned to 5 in the last part of 1826,
then 19 in 1827, 18 in 1828, 44 in 1829, 37 in 1830 and from January to
October 1831, 48 times.[103] Macleay also had to attend Legislative Council
meetings which took place on thirteen days each year from 1825 to 1831
and agreed to 45 acts during that period.[104] All these meetings were time-
consuming and had to be fitted in around his routine work as Colonial
Secretary.

Meetings for both Councils were held, during the first few years, at
either Government House or the nearby residences of the Colonial Secretary or Chief Justice until rooms were made available in 1829.[105] In its first
year the Executive Council dealt with numerous important issues, including the introduction of a new currency and reform proposals for the Female
Factory. In addition it helped avert the collapse of the Bank of New South
Wales, discussed libel laws and trial by jury, and investigated land regulations and the problem of grain shortage in the colony.[106] Alexander Macleay
played an integral part in all these proceedings, and in the case of the Bank
of New South Wales, his role was especially significant. Considering these
public responsibilities, he would scarcely have had the time to discharge
his duties as magistrate, a position to which he was appointed in March
1826.[107]

INITIAL FAVOURABLE
IMPRESSIONS

For their first twelve months in office everything seemed to progress satisfactorily for both Darling and Macleay. Chief Justice Forbes was initially impressed with their abilities, although he professed a personal dislike for Macleay,[108] and in March 1826 he wrote to Under-Secretary Horton that:

> The Governor has proved himself to be a cautious, reflecting man, and is in possession of many of my views. The new secretary is a man of business, practised in office, and not likely to be taken by surprize. [sic] I like his Excellency much — and I much approve of the secretary. I believe I am well with both, and I anticipate that we shall work marvellously well together.[109]

A couple of months later, Forbes was still pleased with the situation and wrote:

> We are now fairly entered upon the annals of a new dynasty — the Governor does me the honor to advise in the most unreserved manner with me upon most subjects of importance, whether they relate to the courts or to the ordinary business of the colony.[110]

For the first few months of 1826 Forbes was actually ill and, being absent from Sydney, was unable to attend Council meetings. A year later his opinions, as well as those of the public about the Governor and the Colonial Secretary, changed and the opposition newspapers perpetuated the situation by capitalising on a series of unprecedented events that unfolded in the colony.

Stephen Foster claims that Macleay 'as an administrator' was undoubtedly 'industrious and conscientious during Darling's period of office. Yet there is little evidence in the archives of his department that his activities involved or required much initiative'.[111] Foster further suggests that Darling issued clear instructions and Macleay's role was routine, not that of a decision maker. But Macleay's influence with the Governor extended beyond the records in the

Colonial Secretary's archives and it is hard to imagine that such an astute and experienced man, who was also a personal friend of the Governor, would not have been allowed considerable latitude in advising on policy outside of his role as a councillor. The *Australian* harshly designated Macleay as 'Colonial Secretary, Legislator and Executor of the Laws etc. etc.' in May 1827 in specific relation to the proposed Stamp Duty on newspapers of four pence.[112] Such a tax, purportedly on knowledge, was considered anathema by the editors of the *Australian* even though stamp duty had been paid in England since the 1790s. Another indication of how important Macleay's position was considered to be by the Colonial Office was when Sir George Murray, Secretary for War and the Colonies, suggested to Darling on 10 November 1830 that he undertake a:

> commission of enquiry consisting of the Chief Justice, the Colonial Secretary, the Treasurer and any other persons most conversant with the course of public business in the financial and judicial departments who might report to you on the extraordinary amount of litigation and on the most convenient mode of applying a remedy.[113]

Gordon Richardson, in his Sydney University 1951 M.A. thesis on the history of the Colonial Secretary's Department, declared that 'it was Darling and Macleay who really established the working basis for the Colonial Secretary that lasted until 1856, and Goulburn's term was essentially one of transition'.[114] Whilst this statement is essentially correct, it was unfortunate that Richardson did not have access to Fanny's letters for if he had read them he might not have written the following about Alexander:

> But Macleay's very efficiency and ability in the company of mediocrity that graced most of the public offices had made him not only nominally but in fact by far the most influential officer of the crown in New South Wales; with a capacity as well as a taste for engaging in multifarious activities he was not slow to follow his inclinations and seize the opportunity of building himself up as a powerful permanent head of the government and something of a local tyrant.[115]

In direct contrast to Richardson's opinion, Fanny's letters constantly convey how despondent her father was in the face of the relentless criticism he was forced to endure whilst in public office in New South Wales. Naturally, he accepted the benefits and privileges that came with his position but he was not manoeuvering to usurp the Governor's position of authority. As to the idea of him being a local tyrant, it was inevitable that the authority associated with his position as Colonial Secretary would upset those in opposition to his policies and ideas.

By the time Darling departed, as McMartin points out, 'the primacy of the Colonial Secretary's Department among the other departments had been finally established'.[116] Macleay had successfully carried out his brief to convey and implement the Governor's regulations to the satisfaction of the Colonial Office. But there were other factors that contributed towards Alexander's behaviour, including the major influence the local newspapers held on public opinion which were to make life increasingly difficult for him.

three

IN THE
PUBLIC
EYE

EMANCIPISTS AND
EXCLUSIVES

Whilst Darling's initial thoughts on arrival in New South Wales in 1825 were to calm and control the situation of developing tension between the various political factions, events partly beyond his control initiated a dramatic period of turbulence over the next six years. In the lead-up to the constitutional changes due in 1828, colonists pressed for their demands and, as one of the leading government officials in New South Wales, Macleay was inextricably involved. Through his association with the Governor's increasingly unpopular measures some of the animosity against Darling during this period also turned against the Colonial Secretary.

By 1826 two distinct political groups had emerged, commonly known as the emancipists and the exclusives. The word 'emancipist' had been used by

Edward Eagar when he returned to England in 1821 to advocate the rights of ex-convicts.[1] Eagar had arrived in the colony from Ireland in 1811 with a life sentence but was pardoned in 1818.[2] He had then returned to his profession as a lawyer and also became involved in commercial undertakings.[3] By 1825 other emancipists, together with liberal free settlers such as Sir John Jamison, and some of the prominent local born, including William Charles Wentworth, had also identified with this cause, and established a distinct political group which was occasionally known as the 'Botany Bay Whigs'. Drawing support from newly-founded newspapers such as the *Australian* and the *Monitor*, they advocated representative government and also sought to remove the restrictions placed on the use of juries in the civil and criminal courts.

The term 'exclusive' was first used by William Charles Wentworth in 1825.[4] Eagar referred to them as 'the Judges with a few of the old Emigrant settlers'.[5] Headed by John Macarthur, they emanated from a group of wealthy free settlers and were sometimes known as the 'Botany Bay Tories'. Conservative in outlook, they opposed the idea of representative government which they saw as a threat to their own position and authority, and out of place in a penal colony. They also opposed the idea of juries being used in the civil and criminal courts, and again argued that the system would not work in a penal colony.

WILLIAM CHARLES
WENTWORTH

Even before Alexander arrived in the colony there were changes taking place in the press. The first independent newspaper, the *Australian*, was published on 14 October 1824 by William Charles Wentworth, who later became Alexander's most outspoken opponent, and Robert Wardell. Both men had met at Cambridge when studying law and Wardell, whom Wentworth persuaded to come to New South Wales, had worked as an editor with the London evening newspaper, the *Statesman* as well as the radical *Constitution*.[6] They transported a press and plant out from England and set up the *Australian* for the express purpose of disseminating their political opinions. With a legal background that was to prove very useful in the years to come, as both were barristers, they were also admitted to the Supreme Court in September 1824. By the time Darling arrived a few months later, Wentworth had left the paper in Wardell's hands. Initially, the *Australian's* moderate independent approach to political matters, 'unmoved by favours and by fear', was probably influenced by Wardell's hope of becoming Attorney General.[7] Wentworth had bigger things on his mind. He was very soon to acquire considerable wealth and property, for after his father, D'Arcy, died in July 1827, it was the eldest son who gained the most. It was reported that there were 34,145 acres in D'Arcy's estate, acquired through grants and purchase,[8] and the month before his father's death, William had bought his own estate at Vaucluse in Sydney.

His family background would have inevitably influenced William's very public and aggressive agitation for political reform. D'Arcy, who had originally come from Ireland, had committed highway robbery on a number of occasions in England when he was a young and debonair, though poverty-stricken 25-year-old. With the assistance of a number of influential friends, not the least of whom was the family relative, Earl Fitzwilliam, he was discharged and sailed to New South Wales with the Second Fleet in June 1790. William was born on Norfolk Island in August 1790 where his father had been appointed as Assistant Surgeon. His mother, Catherine Crowley, was a convict who D'Arcy had met on the voyage out to Sydney. She died only ten years later at age 27.

When he was twelve William was sent to England for his education, and after returning to Sydney in 1810, he achieved early fame by accompanying Blaxland and Lawson in their journey of discovery across the Blue Mountains in 1813. In 1816 he was in England again to study law and he returned to the colony in July 1824, accompanied by Wardell, their newspaper press and zealous ambitions. During his second stay in England William was pained to learn, for the first time, that his father had narrowly escaped conviction as a criminal on charges that usually carried the death penalty.[9] D'Arcy had never talked about his past with his children and this information, received from secondary sources, shocked his eldest son. Combined with the fact that he was the illegitimate child of a convict, William had been rejected as a suitor for John Macarthur's daughter, Elizabeth. Well aware that his father was not made welcome amongst the self-styled 'gentry' in the colony, he adopted a stance opposed to them. In his opinion, the background of families such as the Macarthurs had no comparison with that of the Wentworths whose lineage was aristocratic. Their family claim to fame, Earl Fitzwilliam, along with his agent, Charles Cookney, became patrons for D'Arcy and his siblings and a useful source of financial assistance until the Earl's death in 1833.

William wrote extensively, and in England he devoted many hours to the preparation of a two-volume work, the third edition of which was published in 1824 under the title, a *Historical Statistical Account of the British Settlement in Australasia.* This work provided a platform in print for presenting his political opinions, especially after he met Edward Eagar in London where they shared their opinions on the future of New South Wales. William compared the situation in the colony with the American experience where constitutional reform had provided all individuals with the rights that they were entitled to through 'representative government, free press and complete trial by jury'.[10] It was not long after his return to New South Wales in 1824 that he publicly identified with the emancipist movement. Here was a cause through which he could attack the exclusives who were keen to establish themselves as the ruling landed class, and, at the same time, further his own political career. Espousing constitutional rights such as unlimited trial by jury and an elected Legislative Assembly with eligibility based on property ownership, along with the removal of trade restrictions and an increase in immigration, Wentworth looked forward to the time when there would no longer be convicts in the colony.[11] Founding a newspaper gave him the opportunity to influence public opinion along these lines. Over the ensuing ten years the *Australian* was at the forefront of the opposition against Macleay.

*William Charles Wentworth (1790–1872), acclaimed explorer, barrister,
newspaper publisher and politician in colonial Sydney.*
Artist unknown. Mitchell Library, State Library of New South Wales

Wentworth's opinions inevitably caused bias in the newspaper and the fact that he was independent from the Crown, would have aggravated the exclusives even more.

THE RISE OF
THE PRESS

Echoing the politically partisan press in England at that time, the next independent newspaper in New South Wales was the *Monitor*. It was first published eighteen months after the *Australian*, in May 1826, not long after Macleay began his new job. The editor and joint owner, Edward Smith Hall, had arrived in the colony as a missionary in 1811 and, after a failed venture as a pastoralist, had worked with the Bank of New South Wales and the trading company, Jones and Riley.[12] As 'an evangelical Anglican and philanthropist',[13] Hall's views had been significantly influenced before he came to New South Wales by the leading English radical William Cobbett[14] who advocated civil rights, including the franchise for all male adults, through his newspaper *Cobbett's Weekly Political Register*.[15] Hall wrote well and, according to some, was the only good journalist in the colony. The visiting horticulturist from Austria, Baron von Hügel, mentioned him in his diaries in 1834, commenting that 'the only talented writer among them is Hall ... but he imagines himself un [sic] untutored genius, and his manner of demonstrating it is to heap abuse upon everybody'.[16]

Von Hügel's observations were incisive for it was Hall's paper which proved to be the most offensive to the exclusives and which caused Alexander the greatest amount of trouble. By 1827, Henry Dumaresq claimed that it was impossible to prevent assigned servants from travelling sometimes four to five miles on the evenings the *Monitor* arrived, to peruse 'its intemperate Columns'.[17]

Meanwhile the government found support in the *Sydney Gazette*. Established in 1803, mainly to print government orders and regulations, it was the longest-running newspaper in the colony in 1825. By then, Robert Howe had taken over the position of editor from George, his emancipist father who had died in 1821. Each edition contained official information for which the paper received an annual subsidy of £150 and in turn the government received 25 free copies which included copies to be despatched to England.[18] Initially, this newspaper claimed that 'Information is our only purpose'[19] but after the *Australian* was established in 1824 and allowed to print what it liked, Howe, with the permission of the Governor, adopted the same policy. With the new motto of 'Advance Australia', and because he was an 'ardent Methodist' more concerned with reforming morals than politics, his writings reflected an anti-exclusive attitude.[20]

For some time Alexander was favourably looked upon by this government newspaper though later it turned against the exclusives. Although Robert Howe was only four in 1799 when his father was transported to New South Wales for shoplifting,[21] he held Alexander in 'personal regard'.[22] This attitude was influenced by the fact that Alexander had 'befriended his father and grand-mother' back in England.[23] Before his untimely death on 3 February 1829, it was therefore not surprising that Howe's editorial features often provided entertaining details of the Macleay family's daily activities. Instead of stirring up criticism against Alexander, he was ready to defend his behaviour. When Macleay sailed with Henry Dumaresq and John Oxley to Bateman's Bay in 1827, with the explicit intent of establishing a settlement there with the help of voluntary mechanics, Howe categorically pointed out that 'None of the Gentlemen of the expedition went in quest of land for themselves!!!'[24] His remark presumably was to dispel the growing controversy over land grants, particularly those recently given to Alexander, including his grant at Elizabeth Bay.

This influential channel of public support for Alexander was removed after Howe's gruesome death in a boating accident on Sydney Harbour. The *Australian* felt a duty to inform the public that Alexander's own boat, manned by Howe's servants, had been sent out in the rescue party.[25] Yet only a few weeks before this incident, its editors had furnished evidence that, in their opinion, the Colonial Secretary had given Howe advice on what to print in his paper. They quoted a specific example of an instruction in a letter from Alexander to Howe, dated 7 January 1829.[26] By then, the Methodist Minister and missionary, Ralph Mansfield, had joined the paper as co-editor and he succeeded Howe and assumed sole responsibility until 1832 and from 1840 to 1854 worked for the *Sydney Herald*. However, Mansfield, too, was accused by the *Australian* of bias in the *Sydney Gazette* in favour of Macleay. It was claimed by the *Australian* that Macleay and Mansfield had been seen 'striving to correct proofs' prior to its publication and brazenly asserted that 'Mr. M'Leay *does* dictate, *does* furnish matter, *does* give directions to his Reverend *protégé*'.[27]

Another paper, the *Gleaner*, was first published on 5 April 1827 by an Anglican clergyman, Dr Laurence Halloran. After being transported to New South Wales in 1819 for 'stealing a tenpenny frank',[28] Halloran had been employed as a schoolmaster and his editorial approach supported the government. But Halloran was no businessman and his weekly paper lasted less than six months.

With the *Australian* and the *Monitor* striving to arouse public opinion, and the emancipists organising political meetings, the government became increasingly concerned about retaining its position of authority. The atrocities of the French Revolution were still remembered and the colony also had its share of upheavals, commencing with the Castle Hill uprising in 1804 when around 300 convicts, most of whom had an Irish background, rebelled. Darling would also have recalled the ousting of Governor Bligh in 1808 by the New South Wales Corps in retribution for his autocratic manner and he was particularly anxious to ensure that discipline was maintained within the penal colony. For John Macarthur, the situation was quite clear cut. His attitude was that:

> Four newspapers are published, all in the convict interest, and the editors are all desperate radicals, alike shameless and unprincipled. Our Chief Justice is their idol, and on him they rely for protection, whether their libels are aimed at individuals or against the Government — the most intimate companions of Forbes are Wardell, Wentworth and Dr. Douglas ...[29]

PRESS CRITICISM OF THE
COLONIAL SECRETARY

The opposition newspapers availed themselves of every opportunity to demean the government and, inevitably, Alexander's close association with the Governor made him one of their targets. Because of the unique circumstances surrounding his appointment as Colonial Secretary, Alexander seemed to suffer more grudges than his colleagues, with the exception of the Governor himself. One of the issues that was continually raised was payment of the pension for his work at the Transport Board which had been agreed upon by Lord Bathurst before Macleay left England. His salary was £2,000 and the fact that he received an additional £750 from colonial sources, 'in lieu of the pension that he had been receiving since he retired from the English public service in 1817',[30] was considered entirely unwarranted. Further resentment arose over the question of where the funds for the pension were to come from. Originally they were to be paid from public accounts in the colony after fees had been abolished, but in August 1825 Bathurst instructed Darling to make up possible shortfalls 'from any fund at your disposal'.[31]

The *Sydney Monitor* was adamant that Alexander's salary of £2,000, which was nearly a 50% increase on his predecessor's salary of £1,200,[32] was unnecessary, conveniently choosing to omit the fact that Goulburn's salary had increased to £2,000 in 1824.[33] In addition there were claims that costs in the Colonial Secretary's office had increased dramatically without justification. Between 1825 and 1831 expenditure on salaries virtually doubled from £2,649 to £5,715 in 1831,[34] an increase that would have been expected considering the changes that were being implemented. The rapid escalation in expenditure over the 1825 to 1826 period was a direct result of the Governor abolishing the system of fees and replacing it with higher salaries to attract better staff. The press, however, drew no attention to the salary of the Governor which had risen substantially from £2,500 for Brisbane to £4,200 for Darling.[35] This was a conservative figure in Chief Justice Forbes's mind, for, according to him, in 1827, the cost to the Crown of maintaining the Governor's services in the colony was 'not less than ten thousand a year'.[36]

Another complaint raised against Macleay was in connection with the house that he occupied, rent free, in Bridge Street. This house was comparatively new, having been built for Judge Ellis Bent during Macquarie's time, but when the Macleay family arrived it was far too small and Fanny informed William:

> Here we have but one bedroom at present, the remaining holes are
> unfit for a cat to sleep in they are so small & close. The Veranda is
> quite necessary, for already our furniture has suffered from the Sun.[37]

She added in December 1826 that 'you must remember that I mention'd our House as being one of the worst & ugliest in Sydney'.[38] Extensions were soon made and by 1827 four additional bedrooms, a verandah and french windows had been added. The house had also been cleaned and painted, and minor repairs undertaken at a total public cost of £395,[39] yet the fact that it continued to be rent free irked those who opposed Macleay.

54 ACRE LAND GRANT AT ELIZABETH BAY

But the issue that caused the most discontent was the land grant of 54 acres at Elizabeth Bay which was promised to Alexander by Governor Darling in 1826. Resentment increased even more as Macleay developed the site and, with the aid of convict labour, laid out a magnificent garden and made plans to build a splendid house facing the water. In 1827 Hall claimed that this land, situated a mile from the capital, was in one of the most valuable positions on the harbour and that it was worth £100 an acre and increasing daily in value.[40] By the time Elizabeth Bay House was nearing completion in 1837 the site was given an estimated value of £50,000 based on the sale of the nearby residence of Craigend.[41]

The *Sydney Gazette*, under Howe, attempted to combat such criticism in February 1827 and responded:

> The *Monitor* of Saturday — says that the Honorable the Colonial Sec-
> retary has obtained a swinging grant of land; and the *Australian* also
> ... we admit that the Honorable Gentleman has been indulged by HIS
> EXCELLENCY with 5 ... acres of rock and sand at Elizabeth Bay in
> which, however, the rocks on the sea shore happen to be included.[42]

Because of the opposition to this grant Darling was forced to justify his action. He declared that the Colonial Secretary was the best person to develop the land there and the *Sydney Gazette* supported him by announcing that the grant ought to be 'the topic of Editorial praise; since that Gentleman is converting a very small fragment of the most sterile part of the creation into an epitome of the far-famed Eden'.[43] It is ironic that Forbes had been offered the same site by Governor Brisbane but had declined, presumably because of the difficulties and expense involved in developing the terrain.[44]

Controversy over the grant continued to rage, and in 1830 Darling officially justified his actions in a despatch to Sir George Murray in England stating that:

> As to the Land which he has obtained, he [Macleay] has received it on
> precisely the same terms that Land has been granted and sold to other
> Public Officers and private Individuals, and not under any peculiar or
> more favourable conditions ... He is indefatigable in the performance
> of his duties, which are very extensive and laborious, and has acquitted
> himself with a degree of Ability highly creditable to him.[45]

Whilst Darling sincerely believed that he was astutely adhering to the law, the disparity between the size of Macleay's grant and that of between eight to ten acres for other individuals in the same area including Clerk of Council Dr Douglas, Treasurer William Balcombe, Attorney General Alexander Baxter, Mineral Surveyor John Busby, Judge John Stephen and merchant Alexander Spark, only magnified the problems.[46] Further opposition to this situation was

voiced by the Chief Justice who privately wrote to Horton at the Colonial
Office on 7 March 1828 that:

> The governor and his family are becoming proprietors of land and
> stock, and consequently anxious to enrich themselves by all lawful
> ways and means. My example of refusing everything but what is open
> to every colonist, and determined hostility to abuse in office, make me
> an unpleasant spectator.[47]

However, Forbes was not entirely innocent himself as in March 1826 he had
requested a favour from Horton for land grants so that his family would be provided for in the colony in the event of his death. One of the grants he requested
was in lieu of money for the eleven-month period from the date of his nomination to the date of his leaving England for his new position. This grant and
other purchases that he requested, 'at the valuation fixed by Sir Thomas Brisbane', came to the grand total of 10,000 acres![48] Yet the Governor himself and
Alexander were entitled to their grants, as indeed was the Chief Justice.

CONTINUING
CONTROVERSIES

In September 1829 the *Australian* mentioned Alexander as trustee of the
'Clergy and School Lands' which had been set aside for the Church of Eng-
land,[49] referring to the fact that he was one of the appointed trustees of the
Church and School Corporation which had been established in 1825 and
allocated one seventh of the land in each county in the colony. But, when in
December 1829 this newspaper hinted that Alexander used some of this land
to his own advantage, it was deliberately stirring up trouble. It described the
Colonial Secretary's visit to his:

> numerous dairy, grazing, and arable possessions all about the Territory
> — Shoalhaven, Bateman's Bay, Cowpasture, Argyle, and Bathurst to

say nothing of Elizabeth Bay [and suggested] … he will have to dis-gorge a few thousand acres, held by him from the Church-reserves …[50]

When Hall, in the *Sydney Monitor* in 1830, accused Henry Dumaresq and Alexander of renting Crown pastures, the charge was 'denied in insulting lan-guage by Mr. M'Leay'.[51] Numerous other incidents involving Macleay during this period were used against him by the opposition press. Even the report by the *Monitor* in 1827 that the Colonial Secretary had served up a 'fine turtle' at a grand dinner for the principal civil and military officers in April was face-tious.[52] In 1829 the *Australian* reported that a boat named *Alexander Macleay*, used for coastal shipping, was quarantined outside Sydney Heads because a prisoner on board had measles. Wardell observed: 'We suppose this craft will be looking for demurrage-money',[53] having previously enlightened readers that 'Her hull is adorned with a figure-head — being a well carved likeness … of the individual after whom the snug vessel has been christened'.[54] Although most ship's names were then evoked in their figureheads, Wardell's suggestion that Macleay could be pocketing more money through demurrage was obviously intended to damage the reputation of the Colonial Secretary. Considering his long working hours, Macleay must have felt particularly offended by Hall's vindictive attack in the *Sydney Monitor* in 1828 when he commented that:

> You, Sir, after a few hours labour in your office, can retire to your saloon, and recline at leisure on your sofa to spend the evening in pleasing rec-reation, study or in contemplation suitable to your declining years; while I must labour by night as well as by day to sustain my family.[55]

Hall's attitude would have been further aggravated by the sad loss of his wife through childbirth in August 1826, leaving him to raise seven daughters and one son. Although, publicly, Alexander appeared to ignore this constant carping from the press, he personally found it distressing, as Fanny reported to William. In 1830 she wrote:

> My Father however has too much on his mind, which you know is an anxious one. I had no idea that my Father was so sensitive as to what

People thought or said of him. He is greatly annoyed by the
Opposition papers, which, having been prevented from their daring
attacks on the Govr., now wreak their vengeance on my Father —
Their tissue of falsehoods would astonish you — long stories without
the slightest foundation — but which may be believed by the Supine
Chiefs at home — because, to enquire into the truth of each
statement might be troublesome and surely it is easier to commit
an act of injustice, particularly, if by so doing we have an oppory
[opportunity] of obliging a friend, than to punish false witnesses.[56]

Neither were Alexander's extended family precluded from public inspec-
tion and criticism. The opposition papers were up in arms in 1833 about a
50-foot wooden 'family bridge'[57] at Maitland which they claimed was to be
unfairly compensated for by the government because of the intervention of the
Colonial Secretary in the Legislative Council. In 1827 two local settlers had
approached the Dumaresq brothers, who had property in the area, to help pay
for the bridge's construction. Because the bridge was built on the King's Highway, the men were permitted by Macleay, according to the *Australian,* to exact
tolls for a period of seven years on the understanding that they also built an inn
and established a stockyard in the vicinity.[58] It was convenient to their cause at
the time that William Dumaresq, who married Christiana Macleay in 1830,
was Chief Engineer and Inspector of Roads and Bridges. But after Darling's
departure from the colony in late 1831, it was revealed that the tolls were both
exorbitant and illegal as no official Act of Council had been passed to authorise them. After Bourke's arrival the government decided to take over control of
the bridge but controversy broke out about the costs involved and the degree of
compensation to the Dumaresqs who by that time had sole ownership. When
Henry threatened to take the matter to the Secretary of State, the whole issue
was raised in the Legislative Council for resolution. Alexander, in his official
capacity, suggested compensation of £500 in lieu of lost tolls, and when only
three members of the Council objected, the *Australian* claimed it was a 'shame-
less application'[59] of revenue and 'a more barefaced piece of impertinence than
the claim itself'. The editor added that:

when we find the Father-in-law in his judicial capacity (a situation which ought to have prevented his taking any part in the proceedings) moving a vote, which had been procured by private influence, contrary to the declared opinion of the Head of the Government — we may venture to assert that had Mr. McLeay (himself so large a pensionary) proposed the vote, there would have been the same convenient majority to carry it.[60]

Adding to the injustice, the *Australian* claimed that the architect's estimate of the cost to replace this bridge, which finally collapsed in July 1833, was £223.[61] The new bridge, built later that year by the government, cost in fact less than £25 and lasted a further 19 years. In the end, the Dumaresqs received compensation of only £223.[62] The public controversy over this bridge was another example of Macleay's growing unpopularity even though it was the Dumaresqs who were really the culprits.

THE SUDDS AND THOMPSON AFFAIR

An incident that occurred in the colony in late 1826 was to have lasting repercussions for the Governor, his chief advisors and the freedom of the press. Inevitably the Colonial Secretary was caught up in the drama as well. On the evening of 20 September 1826, Joseph Sudds and Patrick Thompson were arrested for stealing twelve yards of calico from a shop in a deliberate attempt to be dismissed from the army. They considered that the life of a convict, which would entail an eventual pardon, was a viable alternative to that of a soldier until death. Such robberies were not uncommon among the military and cases of self-mutilation and suicide had even been reported with the same motive in mind. On this occasion both men were given a seven-year sentence in a penal settlement. However, two weeks later, Darling commuted this decision to work on the road chain gangs for seven years, after which they were to rejoin the army. In order to avoid similar occurances in the future, the Governor singled out these two soldiers for public humiliation in a ceremony at the Wynyard Barracks on 22 November 1826. Wearing heavy chains, iron collars and convict clothes, they were paraded in front of the soldiers, and whilst the band played 'The Rogue's March', they were marched back to gaol. It was most unfortunate that Darling was unaware that Sudds had been seriously ill for the preceding two weeks. He died five days later.

When Darling wrote to Hay in 1827 concerning this outcome he noted that the *Monitor:*

> has from the first been seditious and inflammatory in the highest
> degree. With respect to the 'Australian', it has, ever since the affair of
> Sudds and Thompson continued to publish the most perverted and
> distorted Statements of facts, and in many cases the most groundless
> and unfounded representations.[63]

RISING OPPOSITION FROM WENTWORTH

The *Monitor* accepted by 22 December 1826 that Darling was not to blame for Sudds's death, but that it was the fault of the medical staff who had attended him and not informed the Governor of the situation.[64] The *Australian* had initially challenged Darling's authority to alter the terms of punishment but it too moderated its opinion. Alexander's deposition on the episode, to the Executive Council, included results of an autopsy which revealed that Sudds had bronchitis.[65] He recalled that he and Darling had both stressed to the Assistant Prison Surgeon, James McIntyre, the importance of being 'particular in his statements', as it was a subject which the 'Rascally Newspapers' would take up.[66] Furthermore, the Council commented that McIntyre's statement had been 'confused and inconsistent', yet Council members excused him as he was relying on his memory and not upon a written record.[67] Wentworth, although he had written a letter of complaint to Bathurst on 15 December 1826, then let the matter rest but after the case was raised again in the House of Commons in 1828, he decided to request an impeachment for Darling in 1829.

Even after his first year in office, Darling had written to Horton about the potential threat of Wentworth, stating that he considered him a:

> vulgar, ill-bred fellow, utterly unconscious of the Common Civilities, due from one Gentleman to another. Besides, he aims at leading the Emancipists and appears to have taken his stand in opposition to the Government.[68]

True to Darling's predictions, on 26 January 1827 Wentworth called a meeting to convince the colonists of the need for a fully elected Legislative Assembly of 100 members based on property ownership to protect their rights. He also advocated that the right to serve on juries should be extended to include more of the population.[69] More importantly, the Constitutional Act of 1828 was still being prepared and Wentworth wanted to impress on the British government how the colony was changing and that it needed to adjust and revise laws to suit new circumstances. Darling, after consultation with Forbes and Macleay, rejected Wentworth's ideas and wrote to Under-Secretary Hay, explaining that because the colony was still 'in its infancy' the time was not yet right to introduce changes such as a Legislative Assembly.[70] He considered that the activities of the colony were still strongly oriented around convicts and pointed out that in England:

> The Members of Parliament are Men of Fortune, who are put to no inconvenience by residing in London for a period. Here the case is exactly the reverse — Where the Servants are all Convicts the immediate, the Constant Superintendence of the Master is indispensible [sic] to the preservation of his Property.[71]

Darling implied that there were simply not enough suitable men to form a Legislative Assembly and he spelt this out to Hay: 'I am satisfied that there are not three Settlers in the Colony, who would or could give up their time to the necessary attendance on a Legislative Assembly.'[72]

LIBELS AND LICENSING
FOR THE PRESS

Although Darling was concerned about the way in which the newspapers were expounding their own political views, he had not initially been prepared to take an open stand against them as he thought that any such action would lead to even more trouble. In July 1825 Bathurst had sent a despatch to the Governor specifically instructing him to propose a law to the Legislative Council to impose a licence fee on newspapers which would be 'forfeited upon the conviction of the Publisher, Printer, or Proprietor for any blasphemous or seditious libel'.[73] In addition, Bathurst proposed the introduction of a stamp duty licence 'to defray [the] charges of printing public Acts, Proclamations, and Orders' and directed that the Governor should decide on the amount of such a duty given the following directive: 'In fixing the amount of the Stamps, you will therefore so regulate the scale of the duty, that the produce of it may be adequate to provide for this charge'.[74]

By early 1827 Darling concluded that: 'The Press, formidable everywhere, is, from the peculiar composition of this community, extremely dangerous here'.[75] When public opinion began to move against the Governor after details of the Sudds and Thompson case reached England, Darling decided it was time to take action against the newspapers in order to protect the reputation of both himself and 'many of the legislative members',[76] as well as the safety of the colony. Acting according to Bathurst's original instructions, he attempted to introduce a Stamp Duty Act in 1827 to raise a duty of four pence on the sale of each paper with the publicised aim of subsidising the cost of printing government orders. In addition he attempted to introduce an act to license newspapers and thereby exercise some control over their content.

CONFLICT BETWEEN MACLEAY
AND FORBES

Referred to by the *Sydney Monitor* in 1830 as 'the gagging bill', both the proposed Stamp Duty Act and the Licensing Act were rescinded after Forbes refused to grant his authorisation, although he did approve a bill permitting prosecution for libel. Requirements under this new act were that 'printers and publishers had to lodge sureties with the government, register their place of abode and provide copies of printed material to the Colonial Secretary'.[77] The attempt to introduce the Stamp Duty Act was foiled by Chief Justice Forbes and brought him into direct conflict with Macleay. When the bill for this proposal was passed in the Legislative Council, Forbes was in the Supreme Court attending criminal sessions and 'Mr. Justice Stephen was confined to his bed with the gout'.[78] Forbes later claimed that Council was aware that he would be absent on that day and in order to obtain the necessary signatory approval from the Chief Justice before the meeting, Alexander called on him at home early one morning. He stated that Alexander spoke to him on that occasion:

> as he has since told me, upon the subject of the act generally with reference to a new clause, added at his suggestion by the Council — I cannot be held answerable for loose opinion given in this way — if I expressed my general assent to the Stamp duty of four-pence, as Mr. McLeay supposes I did, I can only say that it was so utterly unconscious on my part …[79]

It was not that Forbes was against the Act itself, rather it was the offending four pence duty which had been added. As to who suggested the introduction of a Stamp Duty Act in the first instance, Forbes later informed Horton: 'I cannot tell — I was not in the secret',[80] although such instruction had initially been issued by Bathurst to Darling. Forbes claimed that the space for specifying the amount of duty had been left blank when he saw the proposed bill, but when Darling later wrote to Bathurst he confirmed the blanks and also stated that the word 'fourpence' was written in pencil in the margin, and that Forbes had conveyed a message of approval to the Council.[81] However, Forbes, whilst confirming that there was a blank, denied any knowledge of an amount in the margin,[82] and accused the Colonial Secretary of taking him by surprise at the time.[83] Macleay asserted that Forbes had assented to the new bill that morning in line with his clarification in Council only the week before, 'that any alteration in any bill, rendered it necessary to be certified by me'.[84]

The Chief Justice further pointed out that during their discussion on the previous Sunday morning, Alexander had 'admitted that in consequence of the high rate of duty the sale of the newspapers would be so depressed, that it was calculated they would not realise a revenue of more than £500 per annum'.[85] As the explicit aim of this Act was to increase revenue, Macleay, by admitting that the increased revenue would amount to very little, implied the existence of other more politically oriented motives. And Forbes informed Horton on 27 March 1827 that 'the Colonial Secretary has admitted to me that such motive was, in short, to silence the opposition journals'.[86] Forbes was adamant Macleay had added the offending four pence duty without his approval, affirming: 'I vow to God that Mr. McLeay acted without authority from me'. He concluded it was probably Macleay's 'extreme anxiety to carry a measure, [that] might have led him to believe that [which] he had only imagined'.[87]

When Henry Dumaresq sailed for England in June 1827 to personally present the Governor's views about recent events to the Colonial Office, he prepared a paper on 'the Sydney Press'. He stressed that within the confines of the convict community it was vital to ensure that persons in authority had a high degree of protection because there was so much interaction and familiarity due to the nature and size of the colony. He succinctly pointed out:

> Now Government, like everything else to be preserved, must be
> beloved, and what can be expected from Soldiers, or others, who are
> thus in the habit of hearing and seeing the Government reviled, its
> Public Officers spoken of with insulting disrespect and alluded to with
> the utmost rudeness of Personal reflexion?[88]

Dumaresq stressed that the situation was made worse 'by the conviction that you [targets] are personally known and pointed at as the Person alluded to and as the subject of ridicule or perhaps of reproach'.[89] In addition he pointed out that both prisoners and emancipists had forfeited their rights by their past behaviour, and because the colony was still primarily a penal one, the freedom of the press should be restricted.[90] His views would have reflected those of the Colonial Secretary who had been the target of so much unwarranted criticism in the newspapers. Whilst the colony remained a penal settlement Macleay would also have agreed with Dumaresq's sentiments regarding the rights of convicts and emancipists and the need for the military to respect the governing body. Forbes disagreed with these arguments and claimed that if he had genuinely believed that the colony was under threat or insurrection, he would have acted immediately to suppress the press altogether.[91] As matters stood, however, he did not believe that the newspapers had 'succeeded in exciting a strong spirit of discontent amongst the prisoners'.[92] Conversely, however, Forbes approved of libel measures against slander and claimed that he had 'all along advised the government to resort to a vigorous course of prosecution in the Supreme Court'.[93]

Darling claimed that when Council meetings were held to discuss the Stamp Duty Act, Forbes was deliberately absent, excusing himself on the grounds of ill health, and that he 'reserved his objections to the last moment when the subject had come before the public' in order to gain popular support.[94] Even Fanny observed that the Chief Justice had attempted to ingratiate himself with the new Attorney General. She wrote to William that when Alexander Baxter arrived in the colony in August 1827 Forbes was obviously keen to make his acquaintance as soon as possible. However, Alexander upstaged him by boarding the ship not long after it had arrived and personally inviting Baxter and his wife to spend a day with his family:

> our Neighbour — the Judge is quite mad and I understand cannot say too much against both parties — The Governor, on the other hand complimented Papa on forstalling [sic] the Judge who it seems wished for his good purposes to have the first confab with the New Lawyer.[95]

The idea that Forbes was seeking popularity is refuted by Bennett in

Chief Justice Sir Francis Forbes (1784–1841). Artist Charles Rodius (1802–1860). Dixson Galleries, State Library of New South Wales

his introduction to the published volume of Forbes's papers. He claims that Forbes's existence in New South Wales was 'almost monastic' and that it was the Governor of Newfoundland, Sir Charles Hamilton, who had spread rumours about Forbes after both men clashed over the question of who held the ultimate legal authority in that colony.[96] How far Forbes's own political views influenced his behaviour is difficult to ascertain but they undoubtedly contributed towards his antagonism against Darling and Macleay as his sympathies generally lay with the emancipists.[97]

Darling's new libel laws failed to deter the vocal Hall. In 1829, was gaoled for just over three years for libels including a six month sentence for a libel retaliating against the Colonial Secretary who, the previous year, had called him 'a disturber of the public tranquillity'.[98] But even in prison Hall continued his radical behaviour. In 1830 he lodged another retaliatory complaint about the statement Macleay had issued, under the directive of the Governor, that 'the columns of the *Monitor* demoralised the community'.[99] Fanny described the situation adeptly in 1831 when she wrote to William that the editors of the opposition papers had:

> libelled the Govr, my Father, and all the respectable Members of Government … and owing to our Law Officers had escaped all punishment, either by evading the questions as to the real Editors or some other quirk equally honorable. Now the Libels were shameful falsehoods — You can perhaps have no conception of the vile stories & insinuations against my Father's character. In short the best Men here, were represented as the very worst of beings.[100]

FORBES OPPOSES GOVERNOR DARLING

By 1827 Forbes had formed definite ideas about where the power resided in the local government. According to him:

The Governor, his private secretary, and the Colonial Secretary, the real cabinet of the Colony, were not only new to the colony, but novitiates in the office of governing, that is, of governing according to the laws of England. The General was born in the army .... The Colonial Secretary is a very industrious officer, but knows little or nothing of the details of a subordinate board — and the private secretary is a young soldier of fortune.[101]

Furthermore, Forbes disapproved that Henry and William Dumaresq were related to the Governor in a colony, 'composed as it is, without anything like its fair proportion of the moral sense'.[102] But his views were unrealistic within such an isolated environment where it was only natural to discuss issues with relatives and friends. As a result of Forbes's reports to the Under-Secretary of State Robert Horton, the new Secretary of State, George Murray, directed Darling to consult the opinions of his Executive Council rather than outside opinion.[103] Murray believed that Darling had called the Executive Council to meet less frequently because Forbes was present, but this situation was to change under the 1828 Act. As far as the employment of relatives was concerned, Forbes claimed he had heard it mentioned by one of Alexander's friends that his own son William would succeed to the position of 'Collectorship of the Colony'. But the Chief Justice advised Horton 'that the Secretary has too much honor [sic] to contemplate such a reward for his visitatorial exertions in the Naval Office', and was convinced that the Colonial Office would never approve of such a measure.[104]

Bennett points out that Hamilton in Newfoundland had acted according to naval principles, and that Darling similarly applied military principles to his mode of governing. When constitutional measures were implemented to reduce the sole power of the governor, Darling was ill-prepared for such a change, and not having the legal background of Forbes, it was inevitable that they clashed.[105] Forbes advised Horton that the Governor's counsellors, 'with the single exception of the Colonial Secretary, partake of his feelings, and strengthen his principles — and the Secretary is no check'. He added that these men were:

very inferior to what was here before. They are very industrious, always at the desk, and ready to execute whatever they are commanded; but where is the spirit to command, to create, collect, animate, and to embody?[106]

Forbes's comment on Macleay in this letter contradicts his previous correspondence with Horton. He seems to imply that Macleay, unlike Darling's other close advisors, adhered to his own opinions even though he ultimately acquiesced with the views of the Governor. Forbes's assessment of Macleay's character proved correct in later years under Governor Bourke. The Chief Justice also felt that Darling was merely the 'medium' who communicated Bathurst's commands and was the 'local reporter of other men's opinion'.[107] He thought that because the Governor's legal knowledge was lacking and he was 'unacquainted with civil business', he took advice too readily from those who 'might happen to have his ear and his confidence'.[108] The following passage that Forbes wrote to Horton about the three 'cabinet' members expressed his confidential views on the subject:

> I have had occasion to see all these gentlemen, in situations which afforded me the best means of determining the measure of their abilities and the nature of their views. And they are not such as I am sure you would have selected, as the best fitted for directing the affairs of this Colony, of all others, under the British Crown, requiring at this moment the greatest share of talent, the nicest tact, and the widest reach of intellect to direct aright, and to prevent it becoming a future curse to its parent.[109]

Whilst the 'cabinet' was accused of collusion by Forbes, he too was accused of colluding with the emancipists. On 1 June 1827 he was forced to defend his own reputation in the colony. It was rumoured that he had leaked details, which were published in the *Australian,* to Wardell about how the Stamp Duty Act had been passed in the Legislative Council without his approval. As such information had not been officially released to the press the blame led to Forbes, but as to who initiated this idea, the Chief Justice could only state that it had 'been obscurely hinted at by a very low person, very high I am sorry to say in the councils of this place'.[110] There is reason to suggest that Henry Dumaresq, who had originally befriended Wardell soon after his arrival in the colony, was the person responsible in this instance.[111] Although Forbes criticised the Governor and his 'cabinet' for engaging in such activities, he too behaved in this way, although he apologised to Horton by stating that 'I would not have even so far lowered myself as to offer this abjuration if it had not reached me privately, from a quarter I cannot reveal …'.[112] Not even the Chief Justice was exempt from the politics of intrigue.

On the other hand, it may well have been Alexander who Forbes was referring to as 'a very low person' high within the council ranks, because of Macleay's involvement in the libel case of William Carter versus Wardell in February 1827. This case was brought against the *Australian* on 6 February 1827 for material it had published on 20 January 1827 about Carter who was chairman of the Court of Quarter Sessions and had been the magistrate who sentenced Sudds and Thompson. The grounds for this action were that Wardell had published an article in which he criticised Carter's acquittal of a woman who had been accused of stealing linen from Government House, 'a hasty and erroneous judgement based on mere intuition'.[113]

Although the trial was eventually ultimately dismissed on technical grounds on 26 June 1827,[114] the part Alexander played in the proceedings demonstrates the degree to which the Governor valued his decisions inasmuch as the case was allowed to proceed. It seems it was solely Alexander's idea for Forbes to handle this trial, as indicated by Darling's response to the Chief Justice on 9 March 1827, in reply to Forbes's letter that Alexander had requested him to try Carter:

> As to the merits of this particular question I have never thought of
> speaking to you respecting them, that I am aware of, and however
> anxious Mr. McLeay may have been that you should try the cause, you
> will recollect I did not second him very warmly.[115]

Forbes's reluctant attitude towards taking on this case, particularly as he had been requested to do so by the Colonial Secretary, was later used against him by Darling when the Governor attempted to justify to Hay why Alexander had approached Forbes with the request for a libel action before he had apparently consulted with the Governor. He pointed out that Alexander's aim was to:

> identify Mr. Forbes more immediately with the Government, and to show, if he could induce him to preside at the Trial, that Mr. Forbes was not disposed to shrink from his duty on account of his intimacy with Dr. Wardell. This appeal, on the part of Mr. McLeay, was perhaps not altogether judicious; and Mr. Forbes showed some dissatisfaction.[116]

Darling was caught in the middle of an awkward situation which required considerable skill to resolve. Not only had he to personally contend with Forbes and keep the Colonial Office in England informed, but on this occasion he disagreed with his closest ally, the Colonial Secretary. However, from his own 'judicious' wording to Hay, implying that Forbes was associated with the opposition press, Darling supported Macleay. Nevertheless, his suggestion that the Colonial Secretary acted improperly must have disappointed Macleay.

There is no doubt that Forbes had little time for the exclusives, who he described in September 1827 as the 'Parramatta party'[117] under their leader, John Macarthur. He considered that they assumed 'a prescriptive right to lands, convicts and influence', much to his annoyance.[118] But he also admitted to Horton in February 1827 that, in his opinion, 'a free press is not quite fitted to a servile population'.[119] Barron Field, when writing to the Reverend Samuel Marsden from England in 1827, expressed the same sentiment even more strongly. He exclaimed at 'The idea of freedom of the press in a vast penitentiary … One might as well permit a radical paper to be published in Newgate'.[120]

Forbes also implied to Horton that Darling was jealous of his authority and extensive legal knowledge and resented the fact that the Chief Justice was so popular with the public.[121] But Fanny had her own opinions on the matter and thought her father was 'too wise for' Forbes, especially in terms of his legal knowledge:

You would scarcely believe that my Father has been obliged to frame
& write all the Laws which have passed the Council, [sic] which
owing to the Villainy of some of our Law Gentry & the complete
Imbecility of others! ... My Father ... the other day ... differed in toto
from our Chief Justice, was found to be correct & good Law, consequently it was approved to the great disgust of his Honor, who recd a
severe reprimand!!![122]

THE ACT OF
1828

Meanwhile, within the community, knowledge that a new constitution
would be introduced in 1828 had sparked increased political agitation and
debate. The emancipists seized the opportunity to press for the introduction of representative government and to secure an extension of trial by jury
in the colonial courts. Public meetings were organised to secure these ends
and petitions were sent to the Colonial Office in London. These moves were
strongly resisted by the exclusives with whom Darling and his Colonial Secretary were allied. Against the emancipist demands for full rights as British
citizens, they adopted the view that, as a convict settlement, New South Wales
should be ruled in an authoritarian manner to preserve discipline and control.
Such views increased the unpopularity of Darling whose authoritarianism and
policy towards the press had generated considerable opposition. Adding to his
problems was the fact that the House of Commons had published much of
the correspondence and other details about the Governor's actions in relation
to Sudds and Thompson. This further increased hostility towards Darling and
was used by his critics to damage his reputation and the government that he
administered.

Although the British government was concerned by these developments
within the colony, it was determined not to change the system of government fundamentally whilst convicts were still arriving. This escalated Darling's

unpopularity even further amongst those who sought reform and added to the difficulties which he faced. Much of this opposition extended to Darling's associates, most prominent amongst whom, in the public eye, was Alexander Macleay.

Under the new Act of 1828, the powers of the Legislative Council were increased although the functions of the Executive Council remained virtually the same.[123] The size of the Legislative Council increased to fifteen members, including seven non-official members who were to be chosen from the 'more intelligent, wealthy, and respectable Members of the Commercial, Agricultural, and Professional Bodies of the colony'. Secretary of State, Sir George Murray, hoped that by representing all the 'varied interests of the Colonial Society',[124] the emancipists would conceivably be provided with more rights. However, as these extra members were still nominated by the Governor, the choices inevitably favoured the exclusives.[125] Provision was also made to alleviate the problems between the Governor and the judiciary by replacing the necessity of the Chief Justice approving new laws in the first instance, with the introduction of declaratory acts by the Legislative Council.

By 1829 rumours were rife in the colony that Darling and Macleay were under threat of removal. In April the *Sydney Gazette* announced 'from the best authority' that both men had been recalled and that 'their successors are actually on the way, and may be looked for by one of the first ships!'[126] In fact, in June of that year, Murray advised Bourke that there was no imminent vacancy in the office of Governor of New South Wales.[127] A couple of weeks later the *Sydney Gazette* described Alexander's celebrations for the King's birthday, reporting that his house was illuminated 'in front of the verandah' and that there was 'a handsome row of lamps, surmounted by a brilliant star, and the letters G.R. also in lamps'.[128] By publicly displaying his support for the Crown, Macleay was reinforcing his allegiance to the views of the Colonial Office. After all, he owed them his appointment in the first place.

GOVERNOR DARLING
DEPARTS

The rumours persisted. In January 1830, the *Sydney Monitor* emphatically advised that 'Governor Darling and Mr. M'Leay are both ordered home'.[129] In September the *Australian* dramatically announced: 'The Governor's Going! — Unless Mr. Sec. M'Leay goes too — General Darling may as well stay as of the two evils, to choose the lesser — we would even prefer a happy riddance of that high functionary first!'[130] By November the *Australian* claimed it knew the name of Alexander's likely successor but was unable to authenticate the information.[131] That same month Murray offered Bourke the position of Governor of New South Wales.

Soon after, the Whigs took over government in the United Kingdom and Viscount Goderich, who had become the new Secretary of State, wrote on 15 March 1831 to terminate Darling's appointment. The Governor received the news in July. In his official letter Goderich explained that Darling's recall was linked to the decision in 1828 to limit the terms of governors to six years and that it in no way cast a reflection upon his performance.[132] As Darling's understanding was that his term would end six years after his notification of the new ruling, he had anticipated remaining in New South Wales until 1834. When it is considered that Colonel Arthur in Van Diemen's Land stayed on beyond his six-year term, Goderich's explanation seems a subterfuge for the real reasons which he was not prepared to put in writing. By September 1831, the appointment of Governor Bourke to replace Darling was confirmed in the *Sydney Monitor* and it was hinted that Dudley Perceval, who was the son of the assassinated Prime Minister and son-in-law to Bourke, was likely 'to succeed Mr. Macleay'.[133]

Darling left the colony the next month, in October 1831, and inevitably Alexander expected his own recall at any time. This was scarcely surprising considering that Governor Brisbane believed that 'he had been sacrificed to cushion the fall of the Colonial Secretary'.[134] Perhaps it was the turn of the Colonial Secretary to be sacrificed this time. In anticipation of such an event,

Alexander lamented to his family that, after six years of the most arduous toil, he would be leaving the colony poorer than when he had arrived.[135] Considering his debts, this may very well have been the case. A few months earlier Fanny had mentioned to William that her father was upset with another rumour emanating from England that he was to lose £500 from his salary and that he had declared 'should these People break faith with him that he will resign his situation! & then what will become of us?'[136]

On the eve of Darling's departure animosity was running high against him and, as the Governor's public ally, Alexander bore much of this hatred as well. The *Sydney Monitor*, cynical to the last, decided that Darling's 'policy has been to seem to leave all to his Secretary, while we ourselves verily believe that all the Secretary did and does is *virtually* the General's'.[137] It announced that:

> The General, by means of maiden-portions, convict sawyers, and other
> oily substances, has moulded the Secretary, as a pastry cook moulds his
> paste. No man can handle a political rolling pin with more dexterity
> than General Darling.[138]

In addition it claimed that whilst Alexander was friendly by nature, he had behaved in a manner, over the last six years, that was inconsistent with his preceding life in England and that:

> while Mr. M'Leay has had to shoot the bullets prepared by the Gen-
> eral he has himself from disappointment and private pecuniary dif-
> ficulties, and the exposure and satire of the public Journals, engaged
> in scores of petty quarrels with the people on his own account; and
> thereby rendered himself obnoxious to hundreds of Colonists.[139]

The Colonial Office, however, did not concur with this idea and Macleay kept his office. Darling summarised the situation to Goderich when he learnt of his recall and his words echo Macleay's sentiments:

> If I have erred, surely, my Lord, some allowance might have been
> made, if only in consideration of the persons I have had to deal with.

These, I may say, habitual drunkards filling the most important offices, speculators, bankrupts, and Radicals, while I (and I only state the fact) have exerted myself strenuously to promote the views of His Majesty's Government and maintain His Majesty's Government and maintain His Majesty's authority. If it be your Lordship's will that I should be the sacrifice, I must submit.[140]

Prior to Darling's departure, Wentworth enthusiastically held a gigantic party at his Vaucluse home where he supplied free food and liquor to around 2,000 people. Alexander was so outraged by this event that he considered taking legal action on behalf of the Governor but was subsequently talked out of it.[141] The opposition newspapers also celebrated the Governor's departure with relish and on Darling's last night in the colony the *Australian* denigrated both the Governor and Macleay by recording that the:

Office of the *Australian* displayed a transparency painting the triumph of the press, with the fall of the oppressor — a dumpy Scotchman … while in the endeavour to waddle an escape, still catches at the loaves and fishes — the various reserves, grants, leases and promises of land which have escaped from his hat … a late great military figure appears in the attitude of falling …[142]

The fact that both Darling and Macleay were so intrinsically linked by the opposition papers, even though only the Governor had been recalled, indicates just how closely these two figures were aligned in the public mind. Whilst Alexander would have been most upset to see Darling depart, he would have been apprehensive about working with Bourke who was due to arrive in the colony in December. But hand in hand they undeniably were on the day of Darling's departure and Alexander was not ashamed to publicly display his support when the Governor took his arm. They walked together for the last time, on 22 October 1831, from the Domain to the barge which would take Darling out to his ship, the *Hooghley*, moored near Pinchgut Island.[143] As a final insult, on the Governor's embarkation, the 'bleeding head' of an ox that Wentworth had roasted 'was carried round the ship by some ruffians in a boat, to the great terror of Lady Darling' on board.[144] To make matters worse, Elizabeth was nearly eight months pregnant at the time. Nevertheless, the Governor managed a dignified farewell 'by waving his hat, and making a very low bow'.[145] The *Sydney Gazette* further observed on this occasion that:

> MACQUARIE was pursued with a rancour which we have every reason to believe hastened him to the grave; BRISBANE was dismissed with the hatred and the scorn of a very powerful party; nor has DARLING been permitted to descend from the unenviable post without sufficient to remind him that Botany Bay has not yet entirely lost the peculiarities of its character … When the hurricanes of faction shall have spent their fury, and the violence of personal animosity has given way to better feeling and sounder thinking, even his enemies … [may give] justice both to his private virtues and to his public measures.[146]

Four years later, after more attempts had been made to censure Darling, the Colonial Office finally acknowledged his ability and what he had achieved in New South Wales. He was acquitted of all charges and in September 1835 received the honour of Knight of the Guelphic Order by King William IV.

Currey, in his biography of Forbes, states that Alexander's 'exact relationship with Darling is difficult to determine. By virtue of his office, he was at his right hand and close to his ear, and he stuck to his desk with an application that only the Governor himself could rival'.[147]

Supreme Court Judge, Roger Therry expressed the same opinion as Currey on this point in a book published in 1863 about his own experiences in the colony. He wrote that in 1829 Alexander 'shared in the Colony for a time a portion of the unpopularity attached to some of the measures of Governor Darling'. But, Therry continued, as to 'What share he may have had in … [the] … initiation and progress' of the unpopular measures introduced by Governor Darling 'cannot now be easily determined'.[148] Why Therry even posed this question, as he later became a firm supporter of General Bourke, is interesting as it implies that Macleay played a more significant role than has previously been accorded.

Whilst Forbes put down on paper details of the Carter versus Wardell libel case, how many other unrecorded situations involved the direct participation and guidance of the Colonial Secretary? The *Australian* summed up its own attitude towards Macleay's involvement and bluntly asked him, in print, if he had:

> never given the public cause to infer that you have been a powerful
> wiremover behind the curtain, in the political puppet show which
> has so attracted and distracted this community for the past five
> years?!!!![149]

Although, in the public eye of the colony, Macleay was associated with Darling's unpopular measures and criticised for what were considered to be the unfair privileges associated with his position, he remained in office for the next five years. His clashes with the Chief Justice were unfortunate but they seemed to emanate from a personal dislike that Forbes took to Macleay on his first meeting. He later mentioned that Macleay was 'altogether … the sort of body that I took a dislike to, Such is the force of first impression. This impression I have never been able to get over …'.[150] But even Forbes acknowledged how wary he was of the colony not long after he arrived when he informed Horton: 'You have not placed me on a bed of Australian roses'.[151]

Between 1831 and 1836 Macleay continued to work as Colonial Secretary under Governor Bourke. Although Darling had taken measures to reduce the freedom of the press, he had been unable to suppress the growing demands of the emancipists. Reflecting political changes that were taking place in England, New South Wales experienced major developments over the next six years which would eventually lead to the abolition of transportation in 1840. It was during this time that Alexander's appointment as Colonial Secretary came to an abrupt end.

four

COLONIAL SECRETARY

1831–1836

GOVERNOR BOURKE ARRIVES

Born in Dublin in 1777, Governor Richard Bourke arrived in New South Wales on 3 December 1831 accompanied by his wife, Elizabeth, daughter Anne, and son Dick who was to become his father's private secretary. He left behind another two daughters in the United Kingdom, and a son who was blind and 'needed special care'.[1] Although he had extensive army experience during the Napoleonic Wars, Bourke came from quite a different background to Darling. His family were among the Irish landed gentry and he graduated with a B.A. from Oxford in 1798 and between 1826 and 1828 served as Acting Governor in the British colony at Cape Town, South Africa. In 1828 he returned to his family estate near Limerick in Ireland to resume the life of a gentleman farmer, but money shortages led him to seek the governorship of

New South Wales. He was said to be 'equal in zeal, energy, and common sense to Macquarie, and superior in the liberality, humanity, and statesmanlike far-sightedness of his views'.[2]

The new Governor had gained a reputation for acting in a liberal and humane manner during his years in Cape Town and he was greeted with an enthusiastic reception upon his arrival in New South Wales. However, Bourke entered a colony fraught with change as it developed its own identity. Large numbers of convicts continued to arrive and after 1831 the number of migrants and emancipists also increased. By 1831 the population had expanded significantly from 31,016 in 1825, to 51,115 and by 1838 there were 97,912 residents in the colony.[3] An average of 2,368 convicts arrived each year from 1826 to 1831, and by 1832 more than 40% of the total population were convicts.[4] The remainder were either emancipated convicts, free settlers, government officials or those born locally. Immigration was further encouraged after land sales replaced grants in 1831 and the monies raised were used to fund migrant passages from Britain. Immigrants with skills rather than capital began to settle in the colony and gave voice to a new middle class with its own agenda for political change, as had taken place in England following the Great Reform Act of 1832.

Amidst all these changes Alexander, and most members of the Legislative Council, emerged as a 'faction' in direct opposition to the policies proposed by Bourke. When this Governor arrived in the colony the Executive Council was largely composed of Tories, to the extent that he compared the situation with how Lord Grey, the new Whig Prime Minister of England, would have felt if he had found that 'all the Members of his Cabinet were Ultra Tories and he could neither turn them out nor leave them'.[5] Not surprisingly, Bourke became increasingly threatened by this state of affairs amongst the members of his chief advisory body. Tensions increased and by December 1833 Bourke complained to the Secretary of State, Stanley, about 'the evil of legislating for the whole community by means of a Council composed of one Party'.[6]

When the Governor raised the controversial issue of extended trial by jury and introduced an Act in 1832 to diminish the powers of individual magistrates to authorise severe sentences for convicts, there was strong resistance. According to the exclusives, who were mostly wealthy property owners of free origin and rich merchants who employed large numbers of convicts, the only way to successfully control the colony was through maintaining strict severity in dealing with the convicts. To ease the situation and meet the increasing political agitation of the emancipists, Bourke recommended, at the end of 1833, the introduction of a Legislative Council composed of 24 members, a third of whom were nominated by the Crown and the remaining majority elected.[7] But his ideas were rejected by the Colonial Office which considered that the colony was not yet ready for such a change.

Despite differences in political agendas amongst the colonists and the Tory bias in the Legislative Council, hopes were initially held that the new Governor would work amicably with his colleagues. But the *Australian* felt obliged to warn Bourke, even before he arrived in the colony, that:

> should Mr. M'Leay continue to hold his present office, however, we fear that his counsels may mar, or will protract the goodly work which we anticipate. We sincerely hope, therefore, that so venerable a bigot — so grasping, avaricious, and insatiable a pensionary, will not be allowed to burthen the civil list of the Colony, or to retain office of any kind under the new Governor.[8]

This editorial further advised that if Bourke retained the services of Macleay and 'valued his reputation, his peace of mind, the public esteem and benefit', he should 'utterly … disregard every crafty insinuation or sidewind remark, of the Official cormorant'.[9] But when Bourke failed to defend his predecessors, in response to a public welcoming speech two days after his arrival, his unorthodox behaviour was noted in England, and in due course he received a severe reprimand from the Secretary of State, now Lord Goderich, who considered that some parts of his speech had the effect of:

> a direct censure on your Predecessor's mode of conducting the affairs of the Colony and indirectly throwing blame on the Government at home. The way too, in which reflections are cast upon some of the

Public Functionaries of the Colony and the Colonial Secretary in particular, appear to me to have required some special notice on your part.[10]

Goderich further pointed out that the continuation of Macleay and other officials in employment under the Colonial Office was 'proof that His Majesty's Government had not withdrawn their confidence in them', and that the occasion had been one 'where all bitterness on Public Matters ought studiously to have been excluded'.[11] Several years later, in January 1837, after Macleay had been removed from office, the *Sydney Herald* referred to this first public address by Bourke as a pretty 'specimen of dirty intrigue' and implied that he had been against Macleay from the start.[12] To experience such veiled criticism from his superior in the first days of working with him must have annoyed Alexander.

EXPANSION OF THE PRESS

On 18 April 1831, eight months before Bourke arrived, another newspaper, the *Sydney Herald,* was published by three young men in their twenties: Alfred Stephens, Frederick Stokes and William McGarvie. They had recently arrived in the colony as free immigrants and were keen to capitalise on the opportunity to make money. Stokes's father was a printer in Surrey and his own background was that of a book keeper. Stephens was a clerk. Both men had worked for the *Sydney Gazette.* William McGarvie, whose brother was the Presbyterian Minister, Reverend John McGarvie, had worked briefly for the *Glasgow Herald* and managed the *Sydney Gazette's* library and stationery warehouse since his arrival in 1828.[13] With an emphasis on discussing 'things and principles, not men',[14] this new paper claimed two mottos: 'In moderation placing all my glory, while Tories call me Whig, and Whigs a Tory'; and 'Sworn to no Master, of no Sect am I'. Whilst initially adopting a moderate approach, the *Sydney Herald* was soon disturbed by Bourke's attitude towards convicts, and after an 1832 Act reduced the powers of the magistrates to issue severe sentences, it turned against the Governor.

Unlike Darling, Bourke was not upset by editorial bias in the newspapers and in March 1832 he established a separate *Government Gazette* to publish official announcements that had previously appeared in the *Sydney Gazette*. Under this new arrangement Bourke considered that the 'political combatants' could be left to 'fight their battles as best they could amongst themselves'.[15] In 1833 Mansfield was replaced as editor of the *Sydney Gazette* by Edward O'Shaughnessy, an Irish emancipist transported in 1824, and by William Watt, who held a ticket of leave and had joined the newspaper after working with Hall at the *Monitor* for a short period. The Colonial Office was well aware of the continuing factional harassment by the local press and warned, in September 1832, that the local newspapers were 'highly reprehensible and vile!'[16]

Nevertheless, throughout the period of Bourke's governorship they continued to openly provoke or support public opinion according to the political views of their editors.

NEW POLICIES
INTRODUCED

The directive in January 1831 from Goderich that Crown lands were, in the future, to be sold at public auction for a minimum price of five shillings per acre,[17] caused further friction amongst the colonists. Much land was lying waste as the owners had failed to improve it, quit rents had not been collected and the reservation of prime Crown lands, such as those allocated to the Church and School Corporation under the direction of Bathurst in 1825, had hindered the advancement of colonisation as good land had to be sought further away from existing towns. The encouragement of new immigrants with skills would, according to the Colonial Office, reduce the labour shortage in New South Wales and at the same time relocate England's poor and increase the colony's wealth. Members of the Legislative Council, however, were concerned that this new legislation would immediately increase the price of land to their own detriment.

Alexander was placed in a difficult situation. He disagreed with the policies of the new Governor and was against the moves for constitutional change. Just one month after the arrival of Bourke, Fanny already had reservations about her father's future and she wrote to William:

> Our New Governor is said to be gentlemanly & possessed of some talent. My Father has dined once with him — I do not think that he will succeed to General Darling's place in the affection of my Father — but time will shew.[18]

In this same letter Fanny described her father as 'a kind of *State prisoner*' and bemoaned the fact that, although the Radicals were still 'wreaking their malice upon General Darling and our dear excellent Father', she did not think they would be able to remove him from office. But when Alexander later that year was faced with a directive from Hay in the Colonial Office, to pay rent for the house in Bridge Street, he was most indignant. He spelt out the situation to Bourke:

> when Earl Bathurst did me the honor to propose to me to come to this Colony, His Lordship informed me that I was to have an Official Residence. In consequence of which I have always considered myself as much entitled to this as to any part of my Salary, and have reckoned upon my requiring no other dwelling during the period of my holding my present situation which, at my advanced Age, cannot in the common cause of Nature be of very long duration.[19]

Housing was a major consideration for Macleay as the family mansion at Elizabeth Bay was still only at the planning stage in 1832 and although construction commenced in 1835, it was not occupied until 1839.[20] It was fortunate for Alexander that the Colonial Office later relented on this directive and he was permitted to continue living under existing conditions until he could move into his own house. Forbes was also a victim of the change of government in England and similar cutbacks were applied to him. When salaries in his office were queried, his reply of 28 October 1833 to Stanley was terse:

> The salaries of all the other public officers have been progressively increased, since I came to this Colony, and in some instances to double their original amount. Mine alone has remained stationary, and I feel some confidence, if its duties be examined, that it will not be thought overpaid.[21]

On the question of paying rent he added that he would need a short time 'to build a suitable residence, which I am not aware I could hire at present' and would therefore want a 'convenient piece of ground' assigned to him by the Governor for the purpose.[22] Again it was evident that Forbes, like so many others in the colony, was not averse to seeking out the privileges that he believed went with his office, yet he so often criticised Macleay and, previously Darling, for accepting similar benefits.

CONTINUING COMPLAINTS ABOUT MACLEAY

The complaints about Macleay's salary and pension continued unabated. Stanley eventually decided in 1834, after many years of bitter wrangling, that his pension would be funded from the 'Droits of the Crown' which were raised through 'fines and forfeitures and quit-rents' on Crown lands[23] instead of directly from colonial funding. The *Sydney Gazette* pointed out that as the sale of these Crown lands was 'a branch of the King's ordinary revenue', 'the people here lose nothing to which they have any inherent right'.

Commiserations were also extended in this newspaper article to the Colonial Secretary stating:

> that the continued abuse poured out on Mr. M'Leay in reference to his pension from the British government, was not more violent and undeserved than it was vindictive and senseless.[24]

In August 1835 Macleay decided to defend these issues himself at a Council meeting called to determine the budget for the following year. He understood that the pension for his services in England had been arranged by 'several letters of the successive Secretaries of State on the subject'.[25] And he believed that it was only when the Whigs took over in England that Lord Goderich had complained to Bourke: 'The only gentleman, whose emoluments greatly exceed what I should be inclined to assign as an adequate remuneration for the duties of his Office, is the Colonial Secretary'.[26]

As early as May 1832 Fanny wrote to William that their father 'walks like an old man, his mind is as active and sound as ever but his temper is not what it was, and I think he is become rather deaf'.[27] In January 1833 Fanny poignantly described a visit by her parents to Government House at Parramatta where they 'were received most kindly', and reflected that if both parties were not so politically opposed, they 'would be great friends'.[28] But Anne Bourke did not feel the same way and probably neither did her father. She recorded in her diary that their nearest neighbours, Macleay and Forbes, were both very civil and when they came to dinner in December 1831 Forbes was:

> a tremendous talker but very agreeable, [but] Mr. McLeay is only famous for the immense size of his legs, which Capt. Hunter and I nearly died of yesterday, we laughed so much at them.[29]

Anne was making fun of Alexander's dropsy which, together with the gout that he had suffered for many years, must have been quite painful as well as embarrassing at times.[30] Nevertheless it was Anne who in September 1833 married the future Colonial Secretary, Edward Deas Thomson, with Alexander's son George Macleay as best man at the wedding.

CONFLICT BETWEEN
BOURKE AND MACLEAY

Fanny perceived that Bourke felt threatened by her father's greater knowledge and experience of the local situation and she hinted at this to William as early as May 1832. She suggested that Bourke was not paying 'respect to his opinion or deference to his judgement which as a Person new to the Colony he ought undoubtedly to do'.[31] That same month, however, Bourke's wife died and the Governor grieved deeply over his loss. He was fortunate to still have Anne who took over the household management for the next year and acted as hostess in place of her mother on official occasions. Perhaps it was after his wife's death that Bourke began to suffer the severely debilitating and 'distressing nervous attacks' that he referred to when writing to his son Dick many years later.[32]

With demands being made on him from England for economy in the colony, Bourke complained about the efficiency of the Colonial Secretary's office without comprehending the enormity of the tasks that Macleay had to undertake within the constraints of what was still, primarily, a penal settlement. Even his own son-in-law, Edward Deas Thomson, who succeeded Alexander as Colonial Secretary in 1837, later conceded that Bourke had 'a very erroneous conception' of the Colonial Secretary's duties.[33] Bourke considered that the Colonial Secretary's Department was unnecessarily large when compared with other colonies and inefficient because it could not keep up with the amount of work. In his opinion, Harington's position was unnecessary and his functions should be carried out by the Colonial Secretary, an idea that Thomson later disagreed with.

Another problem in the Colonial Secretary's office was related to the new system of land sales by auction, which led to a dramatic increase in the number of copies of deeds to be prepared. Because these deeds provided the only security over property, they were in great demand and Harington attempted to explain to Bourke in 1833 why there was a delay in issuing them. It was simply a case of too much time-consuming paper work for, as McMartin notes, even under the previous system of land grants:

nine separate sheets of foolscap had to be filled up, signed, folded and dispatched for even the smallest piece of land. Even though some were printed, the amount of clerical labour involved was still large.[34]

Macleay bore the brunt of the Governor's complaints about these delays and Bourke gave him an ultimatum, on 16 April 1834, that 'If the Colonial Secretary cannot find time to do it, I am sure the Collector of Internal Revenue will take the matter in charge'.[35] However, that same year, the Governor complained to his son, Dick, that in all government departments 'Every paper is bundled over to me without report or reference. Every trifling detail left to be adjusted by me or neglected and in weightier matters the Tory faction and Australian party politics offer constant tho' concealed opposition'.[36] Fanny, on the other hand, believed that Bourke had a 'distaste for *sedentary amusements* or reading & writing dry official papers' which made Alexander busier than ever.[37] Christiana also defended her father, writing to Fanny from the Hunter Valley in June 1832 that Mr Blackburn had informed her that Bourke was 'much disliked & that every one pities my Father in having any thing to do with such a Radical — Mr. Jones & the Archdeacon write in the same strain to Col. D'.[38]

Another issue which irritated the Governor was Alexander's handwriting. Not only was it almost illegible but he used pencil rather than ink, Bourke stringently noting in one of his memos to Macleay that 'the Governor relies upon the accuracy of the Col. Secy's observations ... [he] therefore begs that they may in future be written in ink'.[39] Darling, too, had registered a complaint about the way in which Alexander had scrawled over his own 'neat minutes'.[40] Bourke, on the other hand, asserted that the Colonial Secretary's continued use of pencil was due to laziness. But Alexander was not the only person accused of this problem for Brisbane had severe rheumatism and his letters, when he wrote any, were also practically illegible.[41] Even Darling's own handwriting, in 1831, had become shaky because of the gout that he had developed in his right hand.[42] Perhaps Alexander suffered gout in his hands as well as his legs, but more likely it was because anything written in pencil could be easily altered, as in the case of the offending four pence

Stamp Duty written in pencil in the margin of the draft bill sent to Forbes in 1827.

By 1831 it appears that Alexander had decided to ask Harington to copy his original memos, for in the Archives of New South Wales there are two copies of a memo written in May about the need for clerks to work a nine-hour day to catch up on the backlog. One copy is in Harington's neat hand, the other in Alexander's scrawl with a note in the margin to Harington asking: 'Let me have a fair copy of this'.[43] Harington endeavoured to do his best to help Macleay by smoothing over the constant conflict with the Governor. In January 1835, when he extended office hours and introduced a system of fines if work was not completed within 48 hours, Harington stated that he only took this action 'to afford His Excellency that satisfaction which I fear he has never yet felt, that every practical exertion is really made'.[44]

Although trivial, another possibly unconscious reason for discord between the Governor and the Colonial Secretary was Bourke's speech impediment that had been caused by a slight wound to his jaw at the Battle of Bergen in Holland in 1799.[45] This apparent defect prohibited him from entering Parliament though he would have been well qualified to do so. In contrast, Macleay's thick Scottish accent did not detract from his witty public speaking performances as indicated by the numerous society meetings he was called upon to chair and this may have caused further friction with the Governor.

Even though Bourke realised the importance of maintaining mutual respect in his relationship with the Colonial Secretary, by 1835 he concluded that Macleay was not suitable for the position, primarily because he could not work effectively with him. The Governor wrote:

> It must be obvious to your Lordship that the successful administration
> of the affairs of a Colony and the reputation and personal ease of the
> Governor are much influenced by the ability of the Colonial Secretary
> and the confidence, which subsists between that officer and the
> Governor.[46]

POLITICAL DEVELOPMENTS
IN THE COLONY

By the mid-1830s the split between exclusives and emancipists was dying down. Political platforms of property and power were replacing those based on social and legal standing. Wentworth continued to agitate for constitutional reform and drafted several bills for the Australian Patriotic Association which was established in May 1835. Sir John Jamison was installed as its first President, Edward Hall as Secretary and an agent was appointed in London to promote their ideas to parliament. Other members of this body, which advocated liberal reform and representative government, were mostly either property owners, professionals like Dr William Bland, or wealthy merchants such as Alexander Spark. Two Legislative Council members, Richard Jones and Gregory Blaxland, also joined this voluntary organisation as did Ralph Mansfield and Henry Carmichael.[47] Carmichael, a Scotsman with a teaching background, had arrived in the colony in 1831 and became one of the founders of the Mechanics' Institute which aimed to improve the status of all colonists by providing scientific education.

In early 1836 another political group formed in Sydney to counter the arguments of the Australian Patriotic Association. The views they espoused were held by Alexander Macleay, and with his son George on the inaugural committee, there would have been a direct link to the Colonial Secretary. James Macarthur, who later described himself as 'not a Tory, but a moderate conservative, verging on a Whig', became their spokesman and travelled to London to represent them.[48] In 1837 Macarthur published his views under the title, *New South Wales: Its Present State and Future Prospects*. However, whilst the exclusives hoped that transportation to New South Wales would soon end and the numbers of skilled emigrants would increase, they were not ready to accept that emancipists had the unqualified right to be jurors or to vote.

PERSONAL ATTACKS ON
MACLEAY CONTINUE

The Australian Patriotic Association was formed in 1835 but even before then Wentworth had made sure he remained in the limelight. He seized the opportunity to voice his ideas at a meeting of the Benevolent Society in June 1833 but this public occasion backfired on him. At this meeting, which Alexander chaired, Wentworth arrived late and, in a drunken state, vented his spleen against the Colonial Secretary by voicing his objection to the £2,750 paid to 'one Pensioner' when the issue of public funding for the Society was raised. Amidst hisses and cheers from the audience his venom only increased, with the result that Alexander, after observing that several persons had come to the meeting for political purposes, retired with dignity. The meeting ended shortly thereafter.[49] Alexander's opinion in a letter that he wrote in July 1829 to John, Edward Deas Thomson's father, that Wentworth was 'an infamous Blackguard, and in every respect worthy of his birth, his being the Son of an Irish Highwayman by a Convict Whore', was truly reinforced by his behaviour that evening.[50] Harington, who initially tried to speak on behalf of Macleay at the meeting, later challenged Wentworth to a duel on the matter, but such drastic action was quashed before it could take place.[51] Fanny graphically described the events of that evening to William:

> It seems that Mr. Wentworth and a party of radicals (Lawyers) went thither for the purpose of attacking my Father, or rather his salary and pension. Mr. W., being in the habit of drinking more than he ought, was intoxicated and in his speech became so coarse, so ruffianlike, that even his own party, who attended him for the purpose of applauding their Hero, & who expected a complete triumph, became quite shocked & one by one quitted the scene of the action, actually leaving the Patriot roaring like a wild Bull to empty seats, for the friends of the Charity very quickly moved off, not knowing what to make of the affair … A good effect has resulted from the disgraceful scene since that time we have seen scarcely any attacks upon my Father in the vile Newspapers.[52]

Not long after this incident, however, the *Australian* capitalised on an attack at the Colonial Secretary's office to reinforce how unpopular Macleay was in the colony. On 16 August 1833 it reported that a bullet from a musket or some sort of firearm had hit his office on the previous Friday evening and that, whilst there was no injury and only a few glass panes were shattered, the ball 'passed through the window of the room occupied by Mr. Charles Nye, one of the Clerks in that department, and lodged in the wall'.[53] Eight weeks later the *Australian* categorically declared that 'as a public character, Mr. M'Leay is the most unpopular man in New South Wales', not forgetting to add in a letter to the editor on the next page that the Colonial Secretary had absorbed into 'his own personal aggrandisement' upwards of £70,000 'worth of public lands'.[54]

FANNY'S PERSPECTIVE
ON THE SITUATION

In 1834 the relationship between Bourke and Macleay was still ambivalent. Even Fanny was at a loss to explain the situation although she identified the Governor's reliance on Forbes as a part of the problem:

> You ask what is our quarrel with the Govr? Now, I cannot answer
> you, because altho' we are not great friends, we have never quarrelled
> — He has thrown himself so completely — so foolishly into the
> hands of our dishonorable C. Justice, that he cannot act, as I really
> believe he otherwise would, the part of a wise or good Govr — he is
> the governed Governor, and his director is a Man of Talent undoubt-
> edly, but it is sadly perverted, and I believe him to be without a spark
> of truth or uprightness about him — specious, but cruelly deceitful! I
> think I told you that the Govr. has never once had the civility to call
> upon my Father whereas he spends every moment he can with the
> C.J.[55]

Considering this situation, Alexander must have felt some measure of satisfaction when, at the annual dinner of the Agricultural and Horticultural Society on 30 September 1833, the Governor's health and that of the Chief Justice were drunk 'in silence'. But shouts of applause and appreciation accompanied the toast to the Colonial Secretary, much to the annoyance of both the Chief Justice and Wentworth, the latter leaving abruptly.[56] In Fanny's report to William about Wentworth's behaviour, she mentioned that Campbell Drummond Riddell, who had been appointed as Colonial Treasurer by Sir George Murray in 1830, arrived home with her father and announced that 'every Dog has his day!'[57]

MACLEAY PUBLICLY OPPOSES THE GOVERNOR

By 1836 Bourke had sincerely come to believe that there was a 'Cabal amongst the Civil Servants against my government, who had Mr. M'Leay, the first in rank and power, as their leader and model'.[58] His words echoed Forbes's conviction in 1827 that Darling, Dumaresq and Macleay formed the 'real cabinet' of the colony. The events of 1835 had led Bourke to this conclusion, for Alexander openly opposed him on a number of important measures that the Governor attempted to introduce to the Legislative Council. Because he was a member of both the Executive and Legislative Council, the Colonial Secretary was able to do this although it placed him in an awkward position. As early as 1825 James Stephen had recognised the likelihood of trouble arising from this part of the constitution.

> It being the appropriate duty of his office [to] act under the direction of the Governor, and in a character entirely subordinate to his, the incongruity of rendering him in Some Sense the Colleague of his Official Superior, and of enabling him, in his Legislative Character, to counteract the very resolutions which, in his official character, he

is bound to carry into effect, might not improbably prove the germ of discord.[59]

His predictions proved correct. Even Forbes was concerned and unhappy about his own 'dual role as judge and councillor' when he was on both Councils in 1825.[60] Stephen Foster claimed, in relation to the issue of the responsibility of civil officers in the Legislative Council, that 'Although their subordination as executive officers to the governor was stated unequivocally, their relationship to him as legislative councillors remained undefined'.[61] Behind the refusal of the Colonial Office to address this problem was the fact that the colony was still perceived to be in a period of transition from a penal colony and any changes away from that would need to be gradual. Too much dissolution of power too quickly could reap unwanted results such as rebellion and uprisings, especially amongst a convict community. Even Bourke freely admitted to Thomas Spring Rice, who by 1836 had become Chancellor of the Exchequer in the British Government, that the colony was 'like a healthy child outgrowing its clothes — we have to let out a tuck every month'.[62]

TRIAL BY JURY

Probably the most contentious issue during Bourke's time in New South Wales was trial by jury. Should trial by jury be extended and should the right to act as a juror extend to ex-convicts as was the case in England? Under the Act of 1823 trials of civil cases could be carried out by a jury composed of twelve inhabitants, either free or born in the colony, at the request of either party. Criminal cases continued to be handled by military juries of seven officers but in 1828 the Legislative Council was empowered to draw up lists of people who were considered suitable to serve on juries for civil cases. The requirements for eligibility, which applied to ex-convicts who had been pardoned or whose sentences had expired, were that they were aged between 21 and 60,

and had an income of £30 per year from real estate or a personal estate worth
at least £300. In addition, Courts of Quarter Sessions were introduced at that
time under which minor complaints could be handled by Justices of the Peace
four times a year. Both the exclusives and the emancipists were unhappy with
these new arrangements. The emancipists believed that the property qualifications immediately placed unrealistic restrictions upon their eligibility, whilst
the exclusives objected to sitting on juries with possible ex-criminals, even
though they were happy to interact with them when business opportunities
arose. When Harington was fined for not attending jury duty in November
1833, it was more than likely because he did not approve of other jury members on the panel.[63]

The legislation enforcing this new provision was not passed until the 1833
Jury Act under Bourke. In August of that year Fanny informed William that:

> every respectable Person is now anxiously awaiting the decision of
> the Council respecting the Jury Bill — or the right of Emancipists
> & others to sit as Jurors in Criminal Cases instead of the Military
> — the C.J. has frightened the Govr and thus, it is said, into a belief
> that the Engsh Ministers expect this proceeding and that the
> measure is necessary for the prosperity of the colony — All persons
> but those of his party say that the consequences will be dreadful and
> that the life of any respectable man will be liable to be taken from
> him without redress upon slight grounds and a little false swear-
> ing which in this place is thought nothing of by the majority of the
> Inhabitants![64]

Obviously Fanny's ideas reflected those of her father but she did not realise
that, even before he came to Australia, Bourke had promoted the introduction of civil juries to replace military juries for criminal cases on the grounds
that it would 'encourage citizens to take more civic responsibility'.[65] However
Fanny was correct about the English origin of such a directive, as Goderich
had authorised Bourke to propose the extension of trial by jury to criminal
cases to the Legislative Council after he arrived in the colony.[66] In fact, in
June 1830, the then Secretary of State, George Murray, had issued an order

to Darling to provide a jury service for criminal cases when official or military personnel were the prosecutors but the implementation was delayed because of the change in governors.

During his first year in office Bourke, realising that this was a sensitive issue, proceeded cautiously. He was so concerned about the situation in the Legislative Council that he informed the Under-Secretary of State, Viscount Howick, that of the seven members nominated by the Secretary of State, 'five are the principal opponents of the Emancipists and of Trial by Jury, if any of that Class are to be allowed to sit as Jurors'.[67] Because the previous Jury Act was about to expire in 1832, Bourke was obliged to renew it. Existing regulations were maintained, although he managed to introduce one important new element whereby trial by jury could proceed for criminal cases specified by the Governor or government officials.

The following year Bourke felt he could no longer delay matters and in July 1833 he submitted his Jury Bill to the Legislative Council to extend trial by jury to all criminal cases. Despite much objection this bill was passed but only by the Governor's casting vote and with an amendment to allow the accused to nominate either a civil or military trial. These changes remained for another six years until military juries were finally abolished in New South Wales.

Alexander was concerned about the incongruity of serving as Colonial Secretary and as a Councillor. Several years later he pointed out to Bourke that when this legislation was first proposed, he offered to absent himself from Council during the discussions:

> but that, if present, I could not possibly vote in favour of a measure
> which proposed to allow criminals, whose sentences of transpor-
> tation had expired, to become jurors, in a country where so great
> a proportion of the free population consisted of persons of that
> description; but I stated that I was satisfied with the Act passed in
> the present year on the subject, because it invests the magistrates
> with full power to return as pure a list of jurors as could be procured
> in England.[68]

His ideas had not changed since 1830 when he advised Darling that:

Trial by Jury according to the Law of England ought to be extended
to this Colony, as soon as the state of the Population will admit of
this being done without extreme inconvenience, yet I am decidedly of
opinion that it is not expedient at present to make any alteration in the
Law with respect to the Trial of Criminal Cases, or at least those cases
in which the Government is not immediately concerned.[69]

It was not that he was against emancipists acting as jurors in civil cases
but, when it came to criminal cases, Macleay believed that the colony was
not ready for such a change because of the background of such jurors. After
1833 there was still a preference by offenders for military rather than civil
trials which implies a degree of suspicion about the composition of the civilian
juries.[70]

CHANGES FOR THE
MAGISTRATES

In August 1832 Bourke had upset the local establishment by introducing
legislation which more precisely defined the powers and duties of the magistrates. New regulations were instituted and more serious offenders, who had
previously been despatched to Norfolk Island and other isolated settlements,
were now required to work in chain gangs for public works in the colony. The
reasoning behind Bourke's action was that as most of the magistrates, particularly in outlying areas, were friends of those who employed convicts and
brought convictions against them, the sentences they issued could be biased
and unjust. Under this Act, which was drawn up by Forbes, magistrates were
forbidden to inflict punishment on succeeding days and the powers of individual magistrates were considerably reduced. Some sections of the community viewed the Act as evidence of the Governor's lenient attitude towards
convicts which they considered would only increase the incidence of crime.

This opinion was confirmed by a much publicised trial the following year.

The Hunter Valley region, which had only been settled since 1821, had become associated with wealthy free immigrants who had received large land grants from both Brisbane and Darling.[71] Predominantly Tory in their political outlook they were mostly Anglicans and Presbyterians,[72] and because their properties were so remote, pastoralists were faced with numerous problems of safety. Not only was there the continual threat of bushrangers and conflict with Aborigines, but they had to maintain control over their convict servants as well. In early November 1833 convicts on the property of James Mudie rebelled against the cruel treatment they had received from their master. In retribution they stole from the estate and threatened Mudie's daughter and her husband, John Larnarch.[73] Five offenders were subsequently hung. The manner in which the two ringleaders, Anthony Hitchcock and John Poole, were led to their death is reminiscent of how Sudds and Thompson were paraded before their military colleagues. After their conviction in Sydney, these 'miserable men' sailed to Green Hills (renamed Morpeth in 1834) near Maitland where they 'were placed on their coffins in a one horse cart and proceeded' to their death which was to take place 35 miles inland on Mudie's property. The *Sydney Herald* reported that 'It is hoped that this awful exhibition will act as a warning to servants at the Hunter'.[74]

Whilst the convict masters were adamant about their own authority and that they had done nothing wrong, Bourke was not convinced and he ordered an enquiry into how convicts were treated on Mudie's property. Although no firm evidence emerged to justify the withdrawal of convicts from his farm, Mudie was dismissed as a magistrate and vowed to take revenge with the explicit aim of removing the Governor. Enlisting his supporters he proceeded to raise a petition to the King which came to be known as the 'hole and corner petition' because it was secretly passed between households rather than at a public meeting.[75]

Roger Therry's account of the court proceedings, on behalf of the convicts, is poignant. As their barrister, his defence made reference to Mudie's attitude towards convicts which was that once they had committed an offence they should be punished for the rest of their lives. Reformation was out of the question and not only were floggings on his farm 'perpetual and excessive', but he refused to issue tickets of leave. When Hitchcock, 'the most intelligent of the five men', started to announce in court the names of other proprietors where 'floggings were incessant', the Court immediately stopped him from providing such incriminating evidence. And neither was he permitted to display the dreadful lacerations on his back.[76] Hitchcock's testimony in court, as reported by the *Sydney Gazette*, revealed the close connection between masters and magistrates in the area: 'Whatever punishment was threatened by the master to his servant was always sure to be inflicted by the Bench, and this was the way in which justice was administered on the Hunter'.[77]

Although there is no evidence to directly implicate Macleay in the protests against Bourke by the Hunter Valley settlers, he would have followed the Mudie case with great interest especially as his daughter and son-in-law, William Dumaresq, and Dumaresq's brother Henry, held pastoral properties in the area and experienced similar problems with security and personal safety.

EXPANSION OF THE SQUATTERS

The difficulties in maintaining law and order in outlying areas were directly related to the expansion of the squatters during this period. Initially predominantly composed of convicts, they were considered a nuisance by the government and the word 'squatter' was associated with problem makers who occupied illegal lands. Not only were they accused of stealing cattle, sheep and horses, but they were also involved in criminal activities such as hiding bushrangers and selling illegal alcohol to assigned convicts.[78] After free land grants ceased in 1831, and land prices were restricted, land within the settled districts became more expensive in the early 1830s. Consequently wealthy pastoralists and men of respectability now turned to squatting as extra grazing land was badly needed for their rapidly increasing stock. Because wool was such an important contributor to the wealth of the colony, and although the Colonial Office directive was to check the spread of settlement for administrative and financial reasons, the Governor initially ignored the pastoralists' involvement in squatting.

In November 1834 Bourke received notification from England that gaols and police facilities should be funded, in the future, from colonial revenue.[79] The Legislative Council then set up an inquiry into the problems of maintaining law and order in all areas and Alexander was appointed to chair a Police and Gaols Committee. Not only did the results of their enquiry imply that the numbers of free immigrants would fall because monies would be diverted to fund police and gaol facilities, but they also advocated the introduction of legislation to control squatting. The Committee further recommended that the powers of the police should be extended to outlying areas and was adamant that ticket-of-leave men should be prohibited from squatting.[80] Macleay's attitudes concerning convicts and ex-convicts and their unsuitability to be granted full rights were evident in the Committee's report which emphasised that emancipist and ticket-of-leave squatters were the main cause of problems in the interior. But as a leading pastoralist, Macleay also needed extra land for his own stock and was therefore determined to protect the interests of the squatters in general. Even the Colonial Secretary was guilty of 'illegal' squatting. Historian Keith Swan reveals that in 1835 Borambola and Pulletop, the properties that George Macleay managed for his father in the Wagga Wagga region, were listed as pastoral runs beyond the nineteen counties limits of 1829.[81]

After Bourke received permission in 1835 from the Colonial Office for settlement in the Port Phillip district to proceed, and with the Legislative Council pushing for legislation, the Crown Lands Occupation Act, which came to be known as the 'Squatting Act', was introduced in July 1836 to appease the demands of the squatters. Renewable squatting licences of £10 per year were to be issued to persons of good repute and additional Commissioners were appointed to ensure that the law was adhered to on these Crown Lands.[82] From that time on the word 'squatter' ceased to be associated with unruly and illegal activities in the colony and came to represent respectable colonists who now held a licence for the lands they occupied.[83]

RELIGION AND EDUCATION
UNDER BOURKE

Macleay's religious views also came under attack because of the Governor's policies, which led him into an unexpected alliance with the Bishop. William Broughton, who had returned to New South Wales in 1836 after a visit to England, had originally arrived in the colony in 1829 to replace Scott as Archdeacon. He was a friend of the Macleays and had officiated at the weddings of both Christiana in 1830 and Fanny in 1836. Although Broughton was high church and Macleay moderate to low church, the two were brought together in opposition to Bourke's views on religion and education. In both spheres the Church of England, which had hitherto occupied a privileged position, was seriously threatened.

Bourke proposed legislation in 1833 to allocate government funding equitably to clerics and church buildings of all denominations in proportion to the size of their congregations.[84] Catholics had been officially accepted in the colony for some time, even before the Catholic Emancipation Act in England of 1829, and other major denominations such as Methodists and Presbyterians were also represented. The 1836 Church Act ultimately introduced Bourke's ideas of 1833, much to the chagrin of the Church of England.

The education question was much more complex, but again, members of the Church of England were affronted by the perceived challenge to their authority. When Bourke arrived in New South Wales the fact that the education of convict children was scarcely considered, and the children of the growing numbers of immigrants were not well provided for, was of increasing concern. The Church of England offered primary schooling in 35 parochial schools,[85] including two King's Schools that Broughton had established after his arrival in the colony: one at Parramatta and the other in Sydney. In addition, Dunmore Lang had established the Presbyterian Australian College and there were several other small private schools. With the assistance of continued government funding and the Archdeacon's presence in the Legislative Council, the Church of England had sustained its power under the auspices of the Church and School Corporation. But by 1833 it was apparent that this body was unable to continue without further government aid and it was abolished, much to the consternation of Broughton.[86] When it became clear that Bourke's proposed education scheme, which was 'to be supported by the Government in England',[87] would challenge the authority of the Church of England by reducing the importance of religion in education, Broughton was naturally even more angry.

The Governor's education scheme, to be funded by the government, was founded on the Irish National Schools system introduced into that country in 1831. But Macleay and, according to the *Sydney Herald*, 'two-thirds of the inhabitants' were 'conscientiously opposed' to Bourke's education plan.[88] When, in 1835, he moved in the Legislative Council that £3,000 should be put towards the establishment of two or three non-sectarian schools, protests immediately arose. Even Bourke admitted to Lord Glenelg, the new Secretary of State, that he had proceeded cautiously in introducing this measure into the Legislative Council when the estimates for the following year were discussed, as he was 'aware that the Bishop of Australia and Mr. McLeay the Colonial Secretary were opposed to it'.[89]

Summing up objections to Bourke's education bill in relation to Roman Catholics, the *Sydney Herald* reported that:

> It will first of all give an ascendency to the children of the present race of transported Irish papists, at the expence of the Protestant Landowners of this country. It will be a bonus to the Irish Convict population, imprudent and wasteful in a notorious degree. It appears also that compulsory payments will be required to establish the system; which the British Ministry should, and if they please may, pay out of the

British funds. But the Protestant Emigrant colonists should refuse the payment and resist the exaction for their funds, for the education of the children of Roman Catholic Convicts.[90]

Although eight members supported the proposal, four opposed it, including the Colonial Secretary who 'not only cast his vote against the approbation, but spoke against it at length'.[91] In Bourke's written description of this scenario to Glenelg, he wrote that Alexander:

> To the last moment, ... opposed it in Council, and, when no division was likely to take place, he spoke at great length against it. He admitted on that occasion having opposed the Governor on four different questions in Council, and seemed to take credit to himself for his moderation.[92]

In contradiction to Bourke's despatch to Glenelg, Alexander later stressed that the only point on which he had differed with the Governor was over the use of selected scripture passages rather than the whole Bible.[93] His comment elucidates the concern he held about separating education from religion for, according to his beliefs, religion was an integral part of any education. Macleay also complained that as the community was mainly composed of Protestants, why should their taxes have to fund the education of Roman Catholic children? Furthermore, why should any denomination have to pay for the education of illegitimate children of convicts whose education should be paid for by the British Government? And why should Protestants have to sacrifice their beliefs concerning which section of the scriptures should be taught at these schools?

Bourke continued his criticisms about Macleay to Glenelg by accusing him of 'indifferences, delays, and perhaps ... infidelities' in his office, particularly in relation to confidential official information possibly being leaked out to the press. Although Bourke stressed that he had 'sincere respect' for Macleay's private character, he implied that the Colonial Secretary, through his 'intimacy with the principal opponents of my Government may have led the Colonists to believe that its secrets are not best preserved, nor its objects promoted in his office'. He added that he was not prepared to make any charges against Macleay but was merely pointing out to his superior that, because of his lack of confidence in his Colonial Secretary, it was extremely difficult to carry out His Majesty's directives.[94]

Alexander's open opposition to the Governor caused considerable controversy. On 25 July 1836, the day that he opposed the proposal in the Legislative Council, a heated debate continued until 7 o'clock in the evening. The *Australian* reported that the subject had attracted more public attention than any other in the colony for quite some time and that 'speeches of great vehemence against the measure were given by Messrs. M'Leay and M'Arthur'. Deliberately placing himself in an 'ugly predicament' by voting against the Governor and the 'KING'S Government at home', the *Australian* claimed that 'the vote of MR. M'LEAY has naturally excited public surprise!'[95] And when a petition was circulated only two days after Macleay's verbal opposition, the *Australian* declared that its 'manifest aim and object' was:

> to support and sustain the Hon. ALEXANDER M'LEAY and his opinions … friends of Mr. M'LEAY must come to his aid at this time of urgent need — and supply him with the means of vindicating his vote …[96]

This petition emanated from the Protestant Association that Dunmore Lang had established in May 1836 to unite opposition to Bourke's proposed education system. When Broughton returned to the colony the following month, he was promptly recruited to lead this group.[97] He voiced his strenuous objection to only selected scripture passages being read, on the grounds that it was unfair bias towards Catholics, as Protestants had to make sacrifices but not the converse.[98]

Broughton and the Protestant Association then presented this petition to the Legislative Council where it was noted, by Bourke, that Alexander did not sign it even though he did 'divide against the Resolution to pass Bourke's Bill in Committee'.[99] Bourke's despatch to Glenelg on this scenario included details about the Protestant Association including members' names, amongst whom George Macleay was listed on the sub-committee for Camden along with William Macarthur.[100]

On 23 July 1836 Bourke instructed Alexander to issue 'A Circular letter to police magistrates' to encourage them to support the proposed National School system on the basis that they would render 'the means of promoting charity and good will amongst all Classes of the People'.[101] This manoeuvre by the Governor precipitated events which took place over the next few months, leaving Macleay in an untenable position.

Forbes's expressed opinion to Bourke on this subject in October 1835 was:

> I do not think the Aristocracy of N.S.W. are sufficiently in advance
> with the times to understand that poor people have any right to
> education at all — it is considered a very democratic and dangerous
> opinion — tending at once to the dishonour of true religion, and the
> entire subversion of the State.[102]

But society in general was changing, as Forbes pointed out, and even New South Wales was adopting a more liberal approach towards religion and education. However, another thirteen years passed before Bourke's national education system was finally introduced under Governor FitzRoy in 1849.

Because of the publicity given to this bill and the importance Bourke placed upon the idea of religious tolerance, Macleay's opposition was widely touted. The *Australian* took the opportunity to print that the Colonial Secretary led 'His Majesty's opposition on This memorable occasion'.[103] The *Sydney Herald* proclaimed that 'among the zealous Protestant community' there was 'the greatest proportion of respectability and intelligence' and that Alexander was leader of a faction of 'the emigrant gentry of the colony' who were opposed to the Governor.[104] The question inevitably arises as to why Alexander deliberately opposed the Governor so openly on such a controversial issue. He was sensible enough to realise that he was treading on dangerous ground. Why then his vehement outburst in the Legislative Council?

The timing of this incident reveals another dimension in Macleay's life. His eldest and favourite daughter, Fanny, married Thomas Harington on 25

June 1836 but only three weeks later she became seriously ill. This would have been around mid-July and by 25 July Macleay must have been desperately worried about her. In fact three days before she died on 6 August, Fanny herself knew that the end was near. With emotions so strained behind the scenes, it is conceivable that Macleay's angry outburst in Council was related to his personal distress.

MACLEAY'S FATE IS SEALED

Another issue over which Alexander opposed the Governor in the Legislative Council was the proposed Marriage Law of 1834. His objection to this proposal, which would allow Church of Scotland clergymen to marry minors 'of different communions without the consent of parents or guardians', was obviously based on moral grounds.[105] Macleay did later withdraw his opposition to this bill after Forbes advised that these marriages would be legally invalid even without such a law in place.

It was during a discussion about the Post Office Bill in the Legislative Council in June 1835 that Alexander's fate was sealed. This Bill proposed, amongst other issues such as granting free postage to newspapers, the removal of the Colonial Secretary's privilege of having his mail franked whilst the Governor's Private Secretary retained the benefit. Macleay thought that if this practice was introduced, the office of the Private Secretary would appear more important than his which 'he considered to be contrary to the express order of the Secretary of State'. His precise words were, as he later recalled, that he 'had no personal feeling on the subject, as it was not probable that I should be long in office; and that I only made the objection from a sense of what I owed to my successor, whoever he might be'.[106]

At no stage did Macleay officially advise Bourke that he would be retiring. Yet Bourke seized upon his intimation that he might not be in office for much longer and wrote to his son, Dick, who had returned to England, that the Colonial Secretary was retiring. Furthermore, Bourke wrote to Lord Aberdeen, who was Secretary of State for a few months in 1835, regarding the subject of an appointment to the office of Colonial Secretary 'which is, as I suppose, about to take place, Mr. McLeay having publicly announced the probability of his retirement within a year'. In addition, Bourke nominated Deas Thomson as Macleay's successor and William Macpherson, who was Collector of Internal Revenue, to take Thomson's place as Clerk of the Council.[107]

A year later, Bourke was forced to admit to Glenelg:

> I beg to add that the probability of Mr. McLeay's resignation
> appears now to be distant. Accounts having reached the Colony
> through private channels and by the public papers that Mr. Deas
> Thomson is to succeed Mr. McLeay; the latter has stated that he
> has no intention of resigning, and, lately in Council, observed in a
> tone of complaint and anger that many persons were looking for his
> appointment. It was, however, in the same room just one year previ-
> ous that he announced publicly he would not be in office at another
> session or words to that effect. This Declaration, being raised
> abroad, led to the applications from more than one quarter of which
> Your Lordship is aware.[108]

Nevertheless, Forbes wrote to Bourke from London on 6 September 1836, describing how Glenelg had enquired as to whether McLeay had 'resigned before [Forbes] left NSW?' Forbes's guarded response was that he:

> had not nor was I aware of his intention to resign — but that about
> a year ago I had heard him twice say in the Legislative Council, on
> some occasion of his addressing the Council, that in all probability he
> should not be a year longer in office …[109]

By October 1836 the *Sydney Gazette* predicted the demise of the Governor as well:

the Governor we pronounce cannot even with safety venture to remain our ruler much longer; his obstinate determination in enforcing the Irish system down the protestants throats … as well as his notoriously admitted laxity of discipline among the convicts …[110]

On 30 December 1836 it was Macleay who received written instructions from the Governor to relinquish office as Thomson's commission was about to be issued. Yet he still adamantly refused to resign, and it was only after official letters appointing Thomson as Colonial Secretary were released on 2 January 1837 that he was forced to leave. In his own defence, Macleay asserted that he did not 'give a *vote* against the Government, nor did the Council divide'[111] on three of four issues, namely, trial by jury, the Marriage Bill and the Post Office Bill. But, by then, the situation was a fait accompli and far beyond his control.

In January 1837 the headlines in the *Colonist* announced that a 'deserving and talented public officer has been removed from his situation without any just cause'.[112] This newspaper had been established in 1835 by Dr John Dunmore Lang who had arrived in the colony in 1824 to become the first Presbyterian minister. As he was categorically against the policies of Bourke, this statement is not surprising. The *Sydney Herald* sympathetically reported:

Mr. M'Leay, it seems, is to be ousted from his post — not because he was an inefficient public officer — but because he is an honest man and does not agree with Sir Richard Bourke in POLITICS.[113]

The editor claimed that Bourke had plainly told Alexander that 'the fact is, Mr. M'Leay, your POLITICS and mine do not agree; and I must have some one in that office who can agree with me in that respect'. The paper went on to imply that the cabal against Macleay was long standing and that:

misrepresentations as to the expressed wish of Mr. M'Leay to retire, were transmitted home — then, again, statements were made, whereby Mr. M'Leay was made to appear several years older than he really is and it was asserted that his impaired faculties unfitted him for office &c. These were the sort of weapons with which the Whigs worked in the dark to effect their purpose … the Colony will lose the services of a valuable public officer; but he will carry with him into private life the respect and esteem of every honourable mind in the community. As a public functionary, his duties were arduous and multiplied, but they were ever discharged with zeal and efficiency for the public service; as a private gentleman, highly distinguished for urbanity and benevolence, his character requires no eulogium from us.[114]

Even London circles in 1836 had been buzzing with news about Alexander's replacement for some months prior to his departure. In August 1836 Alexander wrote to Bourke stating that he had read of Deas Thomson's appointment to the position of Colonial Secretary in the *London Gazette* of 25 March 1836 'without any reference to my having held that office'. He further requested that Bourke clarify the situation and inform him as to 'the cause of my having been thus unceremoniously superseded, without any intimation having been made to me of such an intention being entertained by His Majesty's Government'.[115]

Bourke did not receive written confirmation of Thomson's appointment until 30 August 1836 although the official document from England was dated 26 February of that year. In his statement Glenelg expressed surprise that he had not received a formal resignation from Macleay and he directed Bourke to consult with the Colonial Secretary as to a convenient time, a 'moderate and reasonable period',[116] for his departure from office. 1 January 1837 was the date Bourke independently decided upon. Later that month he attempted to justify his actions and explain why he had not discussed the matter earlier with Macleay. He wrote: 'if the words [Alexander's remark that he might be out of office within a year] were to bear their natural meaning, Mr. McLeay had already taken steps to vacate his office without thinking it necessary to acquaint the Governor with his intention'.[117] This statement seems insincere under the circumstances and more likely to have been fabricated by Bourke to rectify his reputation and redeem himself in the eyes of the Home Government. The *Sydney Herald* wrote strongly in defence of Alexander that:

The observation made by him in Council was a very natural one. He was 'standing up' for what he considered to be the privilege of his office. He, in substance, stated, that whether he held the office of Colonial Secretary for a long time or a short time — although the measure then under discussion might not come into operation until a time when he would no longer be a public officer, still he felt it a duty to uphold the rights of whoever might succeed him. He 'might not be in office when the Act under discussion came into operation'.[118]

PUBLIC SUPPORT
FOR MACLEAY

In May 1837 Alexander's friends decided to give him a 'piece of plate', for use as 'a centre ornament for a dining table',[119] in recognition of his services to the colony. His friends remitted the 400 guineas required for this gift to England and although it did not arrive in the colony until November 1841,[120] there was a ceremony marking the occasion in 1837.[121] The accompanying speech, which was published in the *Sydney Herald*, was signed by six Council members, 81 magistrates and more than 500 of the 'most respectable Colonists'. Reference was made to Alexander's 'faculties of mind and vigour of constitution' which had enabled him 'through a long series of years, to sustain the fatigues of a most laborious office'. Acknowledgement was also made of his other pursuits which had elevated him 'to a high rank amongst men of science in Europe, as to the advancement of the religion, the morals, and the arts of this growing Community'.[122] In response, Alexander was most gratified and declared:

> Although the loss of office, under the circumstances in which I have
> for some time held it, is, I assure you, no subject of regret to me, yet I
> must confess, that the very uncourteous manner in which I have been
> dismissed, has given me more pain than I have ever before experienced
> during the long course of my public service … It may be expected, that

on this occasion I should state some circumstances connected with my dismissal; but I regret to say that I am still considerably in the dark on this subject, and I have no desire to impute blame where I am not certain of its being merited.

In conclusion he stated that 'I shall proudly appreciate your valuable gift as a proof of my conduct having, under the blessing of Providence, met with the approbation of the most respectable of my fellow Colonists'.[123] Today this magnificent silver epergne is on public display at Parliament House in Macquarie Street, Sydney. Inscribed and standing about one metre high, it is a fine example of exquisite craftsmanship. In addition, the colonists requested that a portrait of Alexander be made at their expense:

> for the purpose of being placed in an appropriate situation in the
> Colony, as a lasting memorial of our regard and esteem for your private
> worth and of the grateful sense entertained by us of the co-operation
> we have always experienced from you in conducting the business of
> our respective departments.[124]

Alexander was flattered with the request for his portrait: 'The mode in which you have chosen to testify your approbation and regard, is one of such proud distinction, that I cannot sufficiently express my sense of the honor which you have done me'.[125] However, he remained convinced that because he had done no wrong he should be compensated. Even before his actual departure from office he had written, in October 1836, to Lord Glenelg asserting:

> It is, I think, impossible for any man to attend more strictly or more
> constantly to the Duties of his Office than I have done. The whole of
> my absence from duty since Sir Richard Bourke's arrival in the Colony
> has not extended to fourteen days, and I have never failed to attend
> him, early or later, in Sydney or Parramatta when called upon.[126]

He further implored Lord Glenelg to seek the opinion of his character from others who were then in England. Identities such as Sir Edward Parry, who was the past Commissioner of the Australian Agricultural Company and had lived in New South Wales between 1829 and 1834, Archdeacon Scott, and James Macarthur, were among the names that Macleay put forward. But he specifically omitted Forbes on the basis that it was the Chief Justice whose 'insidious enmity against me as the Friend of Sir R. Darling' had caused him such considerable annoyance over the past five years.[127] Notwithstanding, his considerable efforts were to no avail as Glenelg believed that Alexander had received enough over the years. Some months later Glenelg attempted to justify his decision by decreeing 'as to the value of your Public Services':

> His Lordship has every reason to believe that you have served the King and H.M. Subjects with undeviating zeal ability, and Public Spirit. No suggestion to the contrary has ever reached his Lordship from any quarter.[128]

WILLIAM SEEKS COMPENSATION FOR HIS FATHER

It was fortuitous that William, planning to retire on a pension of £900 per annum, had arrived back in London in 1836 and could act there on his father's behalf.[129] He promptly challenged Glenelg's decision to appoint a successor whilst his father was still in office and lodged a claim for compensation on behalf of Alexander, even though he had not actually left the position of Colonial Secretary, on the grounds that he appeared 'to have been deprived of his Office through a Mistake, and not for any neglect of duty'.[130] Glenelg, in response, informed William that the superannuation from the Transport Board that his father had continued to receive had 'been treated by the Government with liberality and indulgence of which it would not perhaps be easy to produce another example'.[131] Forbes, upon his return to England, had also spoken of Macleay's pension to Glenelg, which he described as

Silver epergne which was presented to Alexander Macleay in 1842 by a large number of his fellow colonists, in recognition of his distinguished public services to the citizens of the Colony of New South Wales. Today it is on display in the Parkes Room at Parliament House in Macquarie Street, Sydney. Silversmith unknown.
Photograph courtesy of the Parliament of New South Wales Collection

163

'public plunder'.[132] Glenelg explained that the general policy ruling on this situation was that any allowance be discontinued if the officer joined the public service again, but in Macleay's case an exemption was granted and he had been allowed to retain his superannuation upon his appointment as Colonial Secretary.[133]

A couple of years later, in June 1838, Eliza Darling advised her brother, William Dumaresq, that Glenelg was ashamed of his actions and that her husband thought William should have persisted on his father's behalf.[134] Stephen Roberts's comment on Glenelg is pertinent. Not long after Bourke's departure Glenelg was removed from Cabinet 'under particularly ignominious conditions'. Roberts bluntly described him as 'a distinctly weak Minister' who 'did not know his own mind'.[135]

Alexander wrote again to Glenelg in 1838 setting out his side of the story regarding his dismissal in order to vindicate his character against the aspersions of Bourke. He wrote:

> I had myself been most grossly misrepresented — words had been
> ascribed to me which I have never uttered; and there was strong
> reason to believe that I had been described both as incompetent to
> my duties, and above all as hostile to the Government under which I
> served … the first intimidation I had received of any intention to dis-
> miss me had been the announcement of my Successor in the London
> Gazette.[136]

After his dismissal from office, Macleay was keen for his friends in England to be acquainted with circumstances in New South Wales from his own point of view. A pamphlet entitled 'Correspondence between Major-General Sir Richard Bourke, K.C.B., Governor of New South Wales and Alexander M'Leay, Esq., the Colonial Secretary', was circulated, the cover of which was inscribed in Macleay's handwriting. His old friend from the Linnean Society in England, William Kirby, wrote that he had:

> read the pamphlet with great interest, & was sorry to find that you
> had been so unhandsomely treated after your long Services — which

appear to have been duly estimated (though not by the Government) by the inhabitants of Sidney [sic] & its Vicinity, whether private Individuals or persons officially connected with you, as is evident from the addresses presented to you on the occasion, & signed by such a number of individuals, & by the other marks of regard & attachment which you have received.[137]

GOVERNOR BOURKE RESIGNS

Not only was Macleay out of office but Bourke's differences of opinion with other officials had reached such a crisis that within a year he resigned and left New South Wales in early December 1837 to return home to Ireland. Conflict between the Governor and Riddell had erupted over the Colonial Treasurer's election as chairman of the Quarter Sessions in November 1835. Because Riddell was already Treasurer, Bourke did not consider it appropriate for him to hold the two offices let alone take on a position that would require his absence from Sydney for several months each year. After Bourke suspended Riddell as a member of the Executive Council, although permitting him to retain his position as Colonial Treasurer, he wrote to Glenelg to explain his actions, stating that if Riddell was reinstated he would resign because he considered him untrustworthy as a councillor.

When Glenelg ignored Bourke's request and reinstated Riddell, the Governor resigned.[138] That same month the *Sydney Herald* revealed that when Alexander mentioned the fatal words in Council during the debate about the Post Office Bill in 1835 that he might not be long in office, his friend Riddell who was one of the 'Tory party', had 'at once applied to his friends in England, for the purpose of making use of their interest to obtain the situation for him'. To make matters worse he had acted on hearsay 'without ascertaining, as he might have done, from Mr. M'Leay himself', whether the Colonial

Alexander Macleay's eldest son, William Sharp Macleay (1792–1865).
Artist unknown. Mitchell Library, State Library of New South Wales

Secretary really did mean to resign in the near future.[139] With such intriguing manoeuvres also taking place in the background, Macleay must have felt even more maligned.

To think that Bourke resigned so soon after Macleay's departure indicates how personally unhappy he had become surrounded by constant conflict. By then he was 60 years old, alone except for Anne and her family in the colony, and his six-year term was almost over even though an extension had been anticipated.[140] It must have afforded him some degree of recompense to be made a Knight Commander of the Bath in December 1834, just before the Whigs were voted out of office in England.[141]

MACLEAY REMAINS
IN NEW SOUTH WALES

Unlike his predecessor, Goulburn, and the two Governors with whom he had worked, Macleay remained in New South Wales until he died in 1848. And unlike Darling, Bourke and Forbes, who Bourke recommended should receive the award in 1837 in appreciation of his 'public conduct in the colony',[142] Alexander was never knighted. By 1828 Goulburn was living in retirement in England and when, in 1830, Sir George Murray offered him the 'Government of one of the Colonies' he declined, professing a 'hearty disrelish for any office connected with politics'.[143] Goulburn replied to William Huskisson, who was by then Secretary of State, that:

> The lesson which has lately been taught me, that when I quit this
> country I leave not a soul behind me willing and able to protect my
> reputation against the foulest aspersions, obliges me in common
> prudence to decline all proffers of colonial employment until I see
> in operation those new measures for the protection of public officers
> abroad, to which I anxiously look forward.[144]

In the ensuing years Macleay encountered extraordinarily difficult times, primarily because of personal financial problems. Nevertheless he persevered and stayed on in Australia to contribute to the development of the colony, even though he could scarcely have afforded to return to England. In 1837, whatever years he had left lay bleakly ahead, but of one thing he was certain: like his predecessor, he too was 'most anxious to avoid everything like interference with Colonial Politicks'.[145]

REFLECTIONS ON THOSE TURBULENT YEARS

Looking back on those turbulent years which McMartin describes as 'one of the most vicious periods in our history',[146] it is significant that Alexander Macleay was the second longest serving Colonial Secretary in New South Wales, surpassed only by Deas Thomson who held the office from 1837 to 1856. By the time Deas Thomson took over, much of the administrative reform had taken place and the transition from a penal settlement to a colony that could support itself with its own constitution, was well under way. Under Bourke, migration to the colony increased substantially and pastoral wealth flourished as the squatters spread settlement north and south. Both Darling and Bourke were Generals whose military backgrounds had accustomed them to asserting authority through specific orders and regulations. When they were confronted with a colony that was changing away from military control, it was inevitable that they should encounter difficulties.

Historians differ in their opinions about how well Macleay performed his duties under Bourke. Hazel King, in her biography of Bourke, pointed out that the governor could be so pedantic and nitpicking that even the most industrious person could not meet his expectations. Bourke commented on this aspect of his personality himself in a private letter to Macleay in May 1835 when he explained that, whilst he had frequently complained about other matters, he had no wish 'to give offence or to cause pain'. He even admitted in 1835 that his regulations:

> instead of saving … [had] added to trouble in your office as the reports
> and decisions were sometimes transcribed I believe three times, and
> I observed on many occasions that my decisions from errors in the
> Copyists were sometimes rendered quite unintelligible.[147]

Bourke also admitted to an improvement in the efficiency of the Colonial Secretary's office even though he found that his time:

> from which the Public shd. expect better things [was] almost totally
> taken up with matters of insignificant details from much of the labor
> of which a careful examination of the Papers in your Office might
> have relieved me. I have also complained of delays in matters to which
> I attach great importance such as the preparation of Deeds, … of the
> Indents. These last are now proceeding rather more to my satisfaction
> but after <u>two years</u> of renewed importunity.[148]

The tone of this letter reveals that, despite their conflicting opinions, the Governor was sympathetic. He stressed again in his concluding remarks that 'I can only repeat I am most anxious to avoid giving pain or offence and after this I will probably be unwilling to make any further remarks of this kind'.[149] Macleay also wanted to appease the Governor at this time for on 8 May he wrote a letter to him addressed 'My dear Governor' and on 11 May wrote another addressed 'My dear Sir Richard' in which he offered his congratulations to Bourke after receiving the news of his knighthood.[150] Rarely before had he ever addressed the Governor in this way.

Apart from differences in background, temperament and politics, there were other dimensions to the problems that exacerbated the tension between Bourke and Macleay. McMartin believed that 'it was McLeay's misfortune to hold office at a time when new conventions about the role of senior officials and their tenure of office were being established'.[151] This is undeniably true. But McMartin also claims in relation to the Colonial Secretary's Department that 'a well-organised, hard-working and efficient department' had been 'built on the foundations laid by Darling', 'mainly through the efforts of Harington' until the latter resigned in 1838.[152] Yet it was Alexander Macleay, with 22 years of clerical experience and a reputation for efficiency, who retained the position of Colonial Secretary.

Although identified with the Tories, and inclined to resist rapid dramatic changes, Macleay was not totally averse to change in general. His political attitudes were clearly stated in the 1840s when he was elected to a seat in the first partially-represented Legislative Council and became first Speaker in the colony. By that time supporters such as Hannibal Macarthur acknowledged how well he had carried out his duties as Colonial Secretary:

> in the execution of the duties of that office, all would concur that his conduct was at all times most advantageous to the Colony at large. Any gentleman having occasion to see him upon public business was always treated with the greatest consideration by him.[153]

In direct contrast is Roberts's contention in 1935 that:

> He conducted all local correspondence and was really the permanent head of the Government until events forced him to quarrel with Bourke. Darling had not questioned his paramountcy, but a quarrel with Bourke was a foregone conclusion because this testy old man could not brook a rival, even in the Governor. He made no secret of his antagonism and openly opposed the Governor on four important matters in the Council in 1836 alone. Yet he had sworn to be the first officer in the local ship of State![154]

A quotation, originally used by Brisbane, and quoted by Darling in 1827 to Goderich, could well apply to everyone in positions of power in those early colonial days: that not even an 'Angel from Heaven' could get on in New South Wales.[155] Bearing in mind Alexander's future participation in colonial affairs in the 1840s, it is doubtful whether, in retrospect, he would have regretted his time as Colonial Secretary, even though his last days were so bitter.

five

FAMILY AND SOCIAL LIFE IN COLONIAL NEW SOUTH WALES

ALEXANDER'S DISTINCT APPEARANCE

Alexander was immensely fond of his large family and wide circle of friends. Through Fanny's eyes previously unknown, more humane aspects of her father are revealed that he kept well concealed from his official persona. Although her letters to William were obviously coloured by her own prejudices and do contain some factual errors, they are still the most extensive record about the family's daily trials and tribulations.

The few contemporary descriptions of Alexander's physical appearance agree that he was not especially attractive, although opinions differed substantially about his personality. Unlike the tall, handsome William Charles Wentworth, Macleay was short and stout. In 1830 William Riley, who was only 23 at the time, met Alexander at Government House and described him as 'an extraordinary looking but agreeable old man dressed with Council Uniform — but with none of the stiffness of the Staff about him'.[1] The ascerbic diarist Boyes was prejudiced against Scots and so it is not surprising that when he wrote home to his wife in England in 1826,[2] his language was colourful and exaggerated, apart from the fact that he added six years to Alexander's age. He described him as:

> a short corpulent man, about fifty stone of 8 lbs and sixty five years
> of age, somewhat of a bustling body for his time of life, resembling,
> taking the whole together, a chinese Jos or an Amsterdam Burgonmaster of civic Importance ... He is an honest looking man for a Scotchman, good humoured and shakes hands with everybody as if he was
> glad to see them.[3]

With such a distinct appearance, at least his identity could not be mistaken! Judge Dowling, who was appointed second judge in the colony in 1827, described his first impression of Alexander:

> he appeared to be a man of about sixty years of age, bald headed,
> and what hair he had grey. He was short, thick set, square built, and,
> although not absolutely vulgar, he impressed me with the idea of a
> decent shopkeeper of a Scotch Royal Burg. He had quick, intelligent
> eyes but his carriage and look were altogether ungentlemanly and discouraging. I thought he consumed me with a prying curiosity of aspect
> which by no means impressed me. I soon found that he had a vulgar,
> Scotch dialect, neither highland nor lowland.[4]

Dowling was equally unflattering about his first encounter with Chief Justice Forbes. He thought he was 'very unwell' and appeared to be about 55 years old rather than 43, with a cold and 'rather forbidding' manner. However, Dowling excused Forbes on the basis that he may have thought Dowling had arrived to 'supplant him'.[5]

Historians vary in their opinions about Alexander Macleay. To Hazel King his portrait illustrated that he was 'good humoured, benign and intelligent'[6] and Fanny's writings confirm these characteristics. With a slightly regal air, Macleay's face exudes determination and confidence and gives the impression of a man who would not easily be persuaded.[7] Yet the same portrait evokes a certain wistfulness, perhaps in memory of his youth so long ago and so far away in Wick.

A BEVY OF
DAUGHTERS

Having a large family to support was an underlying reason behind Macleay's decision to become Colonial Secretary in New South Wales. At the time of his arrival in Sydney his six daughters were aged between 11 and 32 and, naturally, he would have liked to see them all happily married in due course. The good education and training they had received in England was noticed in the colony and, from London, Barron Field advised Samuel Marsden that they were 'not pretty, but accomplished'.[8] However, Boyes's observations about the girls were not as complimentary:

> The young ladies, as they are all called by courtesy are six in number, the eldest grown in years and desperation under repeated disappoint-ments in matrimonial speculations, endeavour to revenge the neglect and indignity offered by the men to their Charms by doing all in their power to inflict their younger sisters upon them, but I don't think my gallant friends of the Buffs and the 57th. are marrying them, at least without an adequate compensation for the risk, and these girls, as I before said, or meant to have said, have no fortune, and therefore I suspect the business and their hopes will terminate in a little flirta-tion — and besides, under the rose, I hear the military rogues at Mess, quizzing one another upon the subject of love, and such recommend-ing to his friends a McCleay till the whole party have been tried on as it were, and rejected at least half a score times — with the utmost

good humour — a certain sign of there being nothing serious among them.[9]

Boyes described the physical attributes of the Macleay girls in detail:

> They are all short square built women and, I suspect a little
> bowlegged like their Papa — however this is quite entre-nous. The
> colours of their hair vary from sandy to the deep red tone of a half
> vitrified brick — the former Maman calls Auburn, the latter Chest-
> nut. They are very much alike in countenance as well as person, except
> that one looks and speaks as if she was engaged in polishing up the
> old ivory settlers in the interior with a peach stone. They dress too
> with the utmost attention to uniformity, the first time I saw them they
> wore some gauzy Coquelicot stuff over a satin slip, very loose long
> sleeves and brought up close around the neck — covering a
> large bosom, or whatever was inside, of the shape of the Prussian
> soldier, such as we saw caricatured in the print shops after the battle
> of Waterloo.[10]

But he was wrong about the eldest, Fanny, having had repeated matrimonial disappointments, albeit some of his observations were correct. Fanny herself told William in 1814 that her only fault as his sister was being 'a little petite'.[11]

As to the Macleay sisters' dancing skills, Boyes was even more critical:

> They danced Quadrilles most mechanically, with them it was bounc-
> ing and jumping to music. They were restless to persuade their part-
> ners that they danced lightly and without effort — but the exertion
> they made was very obvious — and in spite of it a refractory foot
> would absolutely, now and then refuse to quit the floor and press its
> leaden weight upon the earth when it ought to have been trembling
> in the air. It was also easy to perceive on more than one occasion
> that the lower part of the person was reluctantly quitting the line in
> which it had been impelled while the bust was making considerable
> progress in a very different direction. After the dance they smiled
> upon their partners, hugged their arms, tried to be playful, in short far

gone in Scarletina, and determined to be pleased with everybody and everything save the beauty of Miss Stephen and the music of Miss Powell.[12]

Whilst much of Boyes's writing is scornful, his unflattering images do convey an impression of heavy featured girls, dressed in unstylish clothes. Annabella Boswell, the niece of Archibald and Margaret Innes, attended school in Bridge Street in 1834 and was a regular visitor to the Macleay's house just along the road. Her diary entries, starting from a very early age around eight, are another wonderful personal record of those times. On one visit to the Macleays in 1834 Annabella described how fascinated she was to watch Kennethina's ('dear kind Aunt Kenny') hair being 'dressed in the fashion of the day'. Soft curls framed her face and her tresses, which were 'very red', were massed at the back and held in place with a high tortoise-shell comb. Annabella wrote that Kennethina was 'not pretty, but I admired her very much'.[13]

Although they were not beautiful, they had pleasant personalities and were among the more intelligent young women in the colony at a time when males greatly outnumbered females. Fanny informed William:

> your sisters certainly shine here for really the other Ladies are either very stupid, or ill-tempered or vulgar, so that we receive all the attention of the gentlemen, who, I believe behave so politely to us in order to vex the other poor ladies more than from any approbation of our conduct. I tell my sisters that we shall be treated in the same way presently should there be a fresh importation.[14]

FANNY'S ACCOMPLISHMENTS

In her letters to William, Fanny frequently referred to new literary works or ancient classics and she often wrote phrases in French or Italian. Her aptitude

Kennethina Macleay (1805–1864), returned to England in 1855 after living in New South Wales since 1826. Albumen print c. 1855. Sir William Macarthur Album, Macarthur Collection, Mitchell Library, State Library of New South Wales

for learning and acquiring knowledge, as well as her clarity of insight on a vast range of issues, is evident by the way in which she describes many incidents and reflects on moral and philosophical issues. Even her austere brother acknowledged her as that 'girl of sense & acquirements' in one of his replies,[15] although she was not slow to admonish him about smoking, writing that 'I fear you indulge too freely in the *filthy* habit of smoking — I am certain it must injure the stomach'.[16] In addition, she was artistically talented making her, by far, the most accomplished of all the females in the family.

Whenever she had the opportunity, Fanny liked to draw and in 1824 one of her fine flower paintings was displayed at the Royal Academy of Arts in London as an honorary exhibit.[17] In October 1826 she informed William that she had made 'a *tolerable Daub* ... [of] a beautiful new Species of Hibiscus ... a very splendid large noble superb magnificent flower of a pretty rose colour ... Such beauty you never beheld'.[18] And in 1830 she sent twelve drawings to Robert Brown in England for possible publication in *Curtis's Botanical Magazine,* the leading English naturalist journal.[19] These were not the first 'daubs' she had sent to Brown and, over the years, she forwarded many more to him which she requested to be either sent on to William in Cuba, or submitted to journals. However, it seems that Brown often kept these drawings as William frequently complained that they did not always reach him. Fanny often queried what had happened to them, sending gentle reminders like: 'Have you rec'd my *beautiful* daubs or has Mr. Brown retained them all?'[20] Alexander even wrote to Brown, chasing them, but to no avail.[21] One excuse for Brown is that he appears to have been a poor correspondent, which William referred to in 1832 when he wrote to him from Havana: 'I could ask you a thousand questions, only I know it is of no use, as you never write and therefore will not answer them'.[22] Copies of two of Fanny's exquisite flower masterpieces in elaborate gold frames often grace the drawing room in Elizabeth Bay House today; the originals are owned by family descendants in England.

Fanny also painted landscape scenes and developed an interest in natural history, drawing plants and animals as well as fossil bones with considerable skill.[23] What a great help this would have been to her father and brother William for she was able to perfectly record any new species on paper. In 1830 she wrote 'I am very busy drawing a large piece of Native Plants'[24] and, that same year, sketched the family residence in Bridge Street.[25] One of Fanny's botanical paintings is printed on the back cover of the book, *Fanny to William: The Letters of Leonora Macleay 1812–1836*, and on the front cover is a copy of one of her flower paintings. How proud she would have been to think that her work was used in this way, but how mortified she would have been to realise that her private thoughts, or as she herself described them, her 'precious bundle of nonsense',[26] had been transcribed for the whole world to read.

Now her letters, painstakingly written, often late at night, by candlelight with pens that could scarcely write, and poor fingers that were numb with cold, have unwittingly helped form a picture of her father. Scrawled both across the page and down it at times to save paper, they would also have given the homesick William great comfort when he received them. In 1832 he admitted to Robert Brown that he was 'ashamed to say that every day only increases my anxiety to travel home … I long to return'.[27] How he must have looked forward to receiving the news from home that Fanny sent weekly from England[28] and monthly from Sydney.

The story of how her letters were rediscovered would have appealed to Fanny's imagination. The Australian historian, Malcolm Ellis, was dining one evening at Camden Park and ventured down into the house's extensive cellars for another bottle of wine. Observing six 'big metal uniform cases in a corner', he asked his host, Lady Stanham, if she knew what was in them. Three days later, after working through '120 lbs of keys', Ellis managed to open the cases and found a historical treasure trove which included papers of James Macarthur and George Macleay. Amongst George's papers were Fanny's letters to William, all 600 sheets of them.[29] What an incredible surprise it must have been to see such copious letters which had been forgotten about for nearly 60 years. Probably William kept them in the house at Elizabeth Bay until he died in 1865. George then inherited the house and let it to his cousin, William John as he had returned to live in England in 1859. After George died in 1891, Rosa and Pooley Onslow's grandson, James William Macarthur-Onslow, inherited

Elizabeth Bay House. It was James's mother, Elizabeth, who requested that all Macleay 'family portraits and documents' be transferred from Elizabeth Bay House to Camden Park in 1892[30] and Fanny's letters would have been included in those bundles of family history.

MARRIAGE FOR THE MACLEAYS

Alexander and Eliza eagerly anticipated the day when their daughters were married and financially independent. There was every expectation of this happening after their arrival in Sydney where there were so many prospects. But time decreed otherwise as Fanny recorded in 1831: 'it seems to be the fate of my Father & Mother to have their Married Daughters to provide for, as well as the poor forlorn ones for whom no one cares'.[31]

It is amusing to read in Fanny's letters just how keen her father was to introduce his daughters into the marriage stakes in Sydney. She described the weekly parades around the Obelisk in Macquarie Place, in front of their house, where her father insisted on them all 'sallying forth and parading', and how embarrassing the whole experience was.[32] The *Australian* recorded one such event in February 1827, noting that 'some little degree of public recreation' had been established by the Governor through an evening promenade with music from the 39th and 57th bands playing for a few hours two or more evenings per week, usually on Tuesday and Friday.[33]

The first wedding in the family took place only three years after their arrival in the colony. Margaret, aged 27, married Archibald Innes on her parents' wedding anniversary, 15 October 1829. The wedding was reported to be a splendid affair and even the Governor 'honoured the ceremony with his presence',[34] but Fanny revealed another side to the occasion. She informed William that they had made all the bridesmaids' dresses themselves and that they must have been the first family in the colony to do so.[35] Archibald was a descendant of the Innes family from Thrumster, just a few miles south of Wick in Scotland, and he had arrived in New South Wales in 1823. Their marriage had been delayed as Alexander had reservations about how they would support themselves. Fanny noted this when writing to William in October 1826:

> Marg and Capt. Innis … are much attached to each other & would soon become one if they knew how to manage about money matters [sic] he has not saved any thing since he has been here, so that they would have but poor prospects before them were they to marry.[36]

FAMILY
FINANCES

Alexander's concerns were perceptive and practical. By December 1830 Fanny informed William that Major Innes and his wife had moved back into Alexander's house in Bridge Street as both were 'fond of society & idleness & therefore would rather live here if possible than leave for their farm where something must be done'.[37] Finances must have been very tight in the Macleay family as Fanny complained to William that because she could no longer obtain supplies from the government, she could scarcely afford the paper and pens to write to him, apart from the fact they were so hard to find in the colony.[38] The previous year she had spelt out how Alexander 'quite grudges the expence'[39] of such purchases.

By 1831 Fanny was still complaining that Innes was 'sadly extravagant, and gives my Father much annoyance for people fancy that my father should pay his debts. I know not how this will be'. Yet in 1831, Innes's new job, as police magistrate at Port Macquarie, and his government contract there to manage convict supplies, brought him in £2,000 per year, exactly the same salary as that of his father-in-law.[40] At least by then he was some distance away from Sydney.

Christiana, affectionately more commonly called Susan, was 31 when she married Captain William Dumaresq who had arrived in Sydney at the end of 1825 with his sister and brother-in-law, Governor Darling. His brother, Colonel Henry Dumaresq, who was private secretary to the new Governor, had preceded them by a few weeks. The Dumaresqs were descendants of a family that had migrated to Jersey from France in the 13th century[41] and they had known the Macleays for some years in England. William and Christiana ended up also marrying on Alexander and Eliza's 39th wedding anniversary, 15 October 1830. [42] Manning Clark described Christiana as 'a marvellous, discreet, pious, bulky woman',[43] an impression he no doubt gained from her photograph taken in the 1850s.

Rosa – called 'Roppy' by the family – was supposed to be married at the same time as Christiana but Alexander would not allow her marriage to proceed when he discovered that her intended, Arthur Pooley Onslow, had no money.[44] Onslow, often referred to as Pooley, seems initially to have been an ardent admirer of all the Macleay girls. Fanny wrote with much amusement in 1826 that he paid someone to stand near the family gate to observe when any of the Miss Macleays ventured out on horseback.[45] Rosa finally married Onslow in Madras, India, in 1832 when she was 25. Although Fanny commented that 'Rosa does not love him' but was intent on becoming her own mistress,[46] she ended up living in India for the rest of her life, dying in 1854 at the relatively young age of 47. In 1838, on one of their return visits to Sydney, the couple left two of their children in the good care of their grandparents for several years.[47] Even they, who lived so very far away, were still dependent upon the family for support.

Frugality was not a term that could be applied to any of Alexander's sons-in-law. Onslow had initially caused considerable controversy in November 1828 when he arrived, as an invalid, from India where, the *Sydney Monitor* reported, he held:

> the rank of a writer in the civil service. And [sic] introduction to our
> Colonial Secretary, gave a new turn to his life. He determined on
> becoming a settler, and after being put in possession of a lucrative

Christiana 'Susan' Dumaresq (1799–1866). c. 1858. Alexander's daughter,
Christiana lived in a house called Tivoli at Rose Bay in Sydney in the 1840s.
Her father died there in 1848. Royal Australian Historical Society, Sydney
Inset: William John Dumaresq (1793–1868), husband of Christiana.
Mitchell Library, State Library of New South Wales

office in the Customs protempore with five or six hundred a year, he was finally granted several thousand of the very richest acres of the river Manning, and with the saving of the public money, and his other property, he has established himself there.[48]

In 1829 the *Sydney Monitor* mentioned that Onslow, Macleay's 'intended son-in-law', was 'cribbing all the cedar at the Manning' and further informed its readers that he had been there nearly three years during which time he had been allowed to cut timber from Crown lands above 200,000 feet and that 60,000 trees were still lying around on that land. As this cedar was not on his own land, Onslow was exempt from government tax.[49] In October 1829 he left the colony,[50] and the *Sydney Monitor* blatantly claimed some years later, in 1833, that he had returned to India to resume 'his situation in the Honourable East India Company's service, having received pay for two offices at two different parts of the world at the same moment'.[51] After Onslow's departure, Alexander was still determined that Rosa should be well provided for and he wrote to him in India 'to say that when his debts are all liquidated he may send his Brother for Rosa, as by his coming himself he may risk the loss of his good appointment'.[52] Fanny was more optimistic in 1828 when she described Pooley as:

> about 24 — well educated, very reserved and rather constrained
> in his manners. In appearance he is very well, a handsome resem-
> blance of his intended bride. His sentiments are highly honorable
> and just, so, that excepting in point of money, he is better than
> Roppy had any reason to expect. She will, I hope, make a very good
> Wife. Her temper has improved wonderfully and she is sensible
> and lively.[53]

The next daughter to leave the family home in Sydney was Barbara who married 25-year-old Pieter Laurentz Campbell on 10 September 1834 when she was aged 20. Again Fanny mentioned that this future relative was a man of 'no fortune' and that 'my Father has promised his consent whenever Laurentz Campbell can shew [sic] that he can keep house without incurring debt'.[54]

Only about nine days after they finally married, Fanny recorded that Barbara, who had moved with her husband to Maitland where they were living on Campbell's salary as police magistrate of around £300 per annum, was already complaining 'about a want of money' and 'begins to find what my Father told her was true'.[55]

There were a further five marriages in the family but only two of these took place in New South Wales. In 1833 Alexander Rose married Jane Oliver in Scotland, in 1836 Fanny married Thomas Harington in Sydney and in November 1837 James and Amelia Savage, who was said to have inherited money from properties in Mauritius, were married in London. In 1842 George was married in Sydney for the first time to [56] Barbara St Clair Innes, sister of Archibald, whom Fanny described as 'colourless' and 'vain'. Many years later in Mentone, France, only one year before his death at age 81 in 1891, George married again to Augusta Anne Sams who was 51 years old and chaperone at the time to his Onslow nieces, Elizabeth and Susan.[57]

Family members came back to stay in the Bridge Street house with alarming regularity, often for months at a time. In 1832 Fanny let William know that Margaret and Archibald had been living with them for nearly three months, the Dumaresqs nearly six weeks and furthermore William Onslow, Arthur's brother who was on leave of absence, had taken up residence with them 'like an adopted son'. She was much relieved that soon the house members would reduce from thirteen to five![58]

There was one family member who never came to Australia although he threatened to do so on a number of occasions. In 1828 Fanny wrote to William that 'we are all in alarm lest Alexr should step in upon us … We fear he is in debt. Here, he can do nothing without money, and poor Papa cannot advance him any'.[59] In 1827 Alexander Rose had been transferred from Thurso to remote Stornoway which was situated on the island of Lewis in the Outer Hebrides and he remained there until moving to Dumfries to take up a new position in 1845. Fanny informed William that when Alexander Rose was 21 years old he badly wanted to get into the Army and thought that his father had not helped him enough to achieve this ambition.[60] Many years later, in 1846, Alexander did send him money and his son responded with 'heartfelt thanks' and said that 'the difficulties I have encountered since I left Stornoway I can not recount ... as collector my salary is £300 per an'.[61]

On 16 July 1833, he had married Jane Oliver, the eldest daughter of Captain Benjamin Oliver whom he met through work, as Oliver patrolled smuggling along the coast by boat.[62] They had eight children and when Jane, at the age of 35, died in early January 1848 after losing her ninth child the month before, his recently widowed mother-in-law, Jean Oliver, came to his aid. Her presence must have been most welcome as one of Alexander's legs had been amputated in 1825 following a serious injury. But this did not prevent him, in 1834, from fighting with 'his landlord McIver in Stornoway after a meeting at which he, the Collector attempted to strike Mr. McIver with his stick'.[63] Apparently the source of dispute was over the exorbitant expense of repairs in the house that he rented from McIver. How he must, at times, have envied the family living in comparative luxury in Australia. His last years were even more miserable. In 1856 he moved to Newcastle and his final days were spent in France, presumably having moved there with the assistance of brother George. In 1869 he died a pauper at Tours and was survived by six single daughters and one son who had been declared insane.[64]

DOMESTIC
DUTIES

Although Alexander's daughters helped out wherever they could, undoubtedly they were more of a financial burden than sons. As paid work was not readily available for women, the girls had to assist in other ways as best they could. This entailed some housework and sewing all their own clothes which Fanny complained took up most of their time, as they were always 'making Bonnets or Gowns' because people dressed up so much that their clothes wore out faster, leaving her no time for drawing.[65] She explained the neces-sity to engage in such domestic activity, which she loathed, by saying that she had:

> been occupied with putting the House in a little order and in Needle
> work for people here think of little besides dress & as there are none
> to assist in altering & repairing we shall have enough to do in order to
> 'look like others' as Mama says — This is a monstrous bore to me who
> hates all this folly.[66]

The situation was even worse by 1828 for that year she wrote to William:

> We have scarcely any servants now and are not likely to procure any
> I fear — consequently our House is dirty and we are obliged to do
> more domestic work than is compatible with a neat lady like appear-
> ance and our clothing becomes soon shabby here and we are very idle
> and illhumoured.[67]

But appearances had to be upheld, especially for members of the Colonial Secretary's family, and it was up to Fanny, as the eldest daughter, to set a good example. Furthermore, any marriage in the ranks of high society in Sydney created such good gossip that it was considered essential to put on a grand show. Fanny dutifully recorded that 'People delight in a Marriage — what a feast for the tongues of old & young, Men & Maids!'[68]

PREVIOUS
SUITORS

Boyes's assumption that the Macleays were all desperate for a husband only highlights his ignorance. For, Fanny tells us in her letters, Margaret had a suitor even before she arrived in Sydney and there were quite a number of ardent admirers amongst the colonists. One prominent potential suitor was Sir John Jamison who Fanny really detested; she told William so in October

1826.[69] When he proposed to her a couple of months later, Fanny explained her feelings to William:

> Sir J's house is a very handsome one, by far the best in the Colony & it
> is very tastefully & expensively furnished — He did me the honor to
> request me to become the Mistress of it — but I did not feel inclined
> to share it with such a Being I am sure I could never love & respect
> him … . Every body here, it seems, insists that I am to be Lady
> Jamison which enrages me very often.[70]

The Macleays had known Jamison in England long before they came to New South Wales and in 1817 Fanny had written to William about how he had discovered that the male platypus secreted its poison in spurs from its hind feet.[71] In 1809 he was knighted by King Charles XIII of Sweden for his assistance in curbing 'a serious outbreak of scurvy' amongst sailors in the Swedish navy.[72] Since the family's arrival in Sydney, Jamison had sought to win the hand of one of the Macleay daughters, saying, according to Fanny, that 'he must have one of us'.[73] Prior to Fanny, he had already proposed to Christiana[74] but she had also vehemently rejected this wealthy 'Knight of Regent Ville'.[75] At that time he was 50 years old and Christiana only 27.

Why Fanny had come to despise Jamison's character so much was a direct reflection on the circumstances surrounding his domestic life.[76] Having arrived in Sydney in July 1814, by 1819 he had two daughters with a convict woman, and in 1822 Mary Griffiths, the 'colonial-born daughter of his dairyman' was living with him.[77] He was twenty years older than her and by the time they married in 1844 they had two daughters and five sons. With such a personal history, it is not surprising that the Macleays were reluctant to encourage his attentions. Baron Karl von Hügel (commonly known as Charles) was similarly unimpressed and when he visited Jamison's famous palatial mansion known as Regentville, he recorded in his journal:

> The interior furnishings are ostentatious and uncomfortable and the
> heavy curtains and bed hangings are said to contain, in addition to

the vast quantity of superfluous yardage, a population which does not receive visitors in a particularly friendly fashion.[78]

Fanny's letters included numerous references to romantic episodes. She would have liked Christiana to marry a Mr Condamine who she considered was 'perfection if man can be so'.[79] She also referred to a suitor of the 'gentle Kenny' in 1828, declaring: 'I hear Mr. Icely is attached to her and he is very attentive but I have not heard that he has proposed, neither do I believe he would be accepted were he so to do …'[80] Kennethina's mother, however, was very keen on Icely, especially as he was building a 'Splendid Mansion' near Parramatta,[81] but her hopes proved futile as this daughter remained single for the rest of her life.

In 1829 Fanny advised William that Eliza Darling, the Governor's wife, had been trying to arrange a match for her with her brother Henry Dumaresq.[82] She had noted at the time, in 1826, that her father was very anxious that 'such an affair should take place'.[83] It would have suited Alexander very well as he and Henry were so closely associated with the Governor through their work. In 1826 Fanny was 30 years old and as Eliza was only 25, and her husband of six years was 51 years old, she too would probably have relished the idea of having Fanny as a sister-in-law. Later that year Fanny became Godmother to the 'Governor's little Son'[84] and the two women became good friends, Fanny informing William in 1827 that Mrs Darling was 'very agreeable' and that she was very fond of her.[85]

Astute Fanny realised that neither she nor Henry were really interested in each other and in due course he returned from a trip to England with the attractive Elizabeth Sophia Danvers as his wife. But she was happy when Christiana finally agreed to marry Henry's brother, William, as she considered him to be 'an excellent kind Man of no very great talent, altho' by no means deficient in good common sense & highly honourable feeling', and well suited to the sister who was dearest to her heart.[86] Possibly Fanny also felt some special affiliation with Christiana who she says left behind in England 'poor Mr. Guthrie, the parting from whom cost her so much'.[87]

THOMAS HARINGTON
WEDS FANNY

There was yet another man in the colony who had been admiring Fanny's drawings for some time. In 1830 Fanny had received a brief thank-you note for three 'daubs' she had given Thomas Harington after his request for some of her drawings. At the time she commented to William that:

> This person is much admired by my sisters — I am afraid of him,
> for he is very clever & I think satirical so that I avoid his company as
> much as possible — He is always sending some present or other to my
> Brothers & Sisters — He was one of Susan's admirers & they are great
> friends.[88]

Harington, as Macleay's chief deputy in the Colonial Secretary's office, would have seen a lot of the family after they arrived in Sydney. On 25 June 1836, Thomas, aged 39 years and Fanny 43, were married but within six weeks, on 6 August, the new bride sadly passed away. Sarcely seven months before, Fanny had written a tantalising comment to William describing James's romantic interest in the Miss Savage whom he eventually married, reflecting that:

> This reminds me of my own affair which I regret to say is as little
> likely of fulfilment as it was a year ago truly as you say 'Hope long
> deferred doth sicken the heart' … & my heart is so sick that hope has
> fled and left me no comfort in my sickness![89]

Who was Fanny referring to? In 1830 she found Harington inhibiting and, anyway, he had been one of Christiana's admirers. Yet by 1835 she says she felt the same way about a certain person for a year and now considered her situation hopeless. Why then did Fanny choose to marry Harington and plead to William in February 1836: 'I wish that you *knew* and *loved my Husband* — that is to be I hope! You must love him, my dearest Brother, already he feels affection for you — if he did not I would say nothing to him'.[90]

The honeymoon lasted only three weeks at Alexander's country residence, Brownlow Hill, as Fanny became ill with a cold and complications associated with stomach irritability and heart palpitations. Her weak heart had been a debilitating problem for many years and in her letters Fanny frequently complained about this condition. Before she died Fanny was moved from her new home, which had been freshly painted, to her father's house so that the family could look after her. How devastated Harington must have felt to have lost his talented new wife so suddenly. But Fanny had often been sick and even three months prior to her wedding she recorded that 'I am not so well as I could wish for *palpi* has again commenced to annoy me'.[91]

Did Fanny perhaps have a premonition that she was soon to die and realised time was running out? Was she concerned that her father would soon lose his job and thought that, by marrying, she would relieve the financial burden she imposed on him? Her letters were so often full of worry and concern in this respect, particularly about how her father could meet his debts,[92] that this may well have been the reason. Even in 1827 she had told William that 'I sometimes think I ought to relieve him of one burthen — but then again my courage fails me and I wish myself out of the World'.[93] Perhaps, by 1836, she was so convinced that the family would never return to England, even though they had expected to return in 1832 'to leave our bones',[94] that she finally resigned herself to making the best of circumstances in the colony that she could. Probably the real reason behind Fanny's decision to marry Harington will never be known.

Whilst William may well have approved of the match, as did her father, George was not at all in favour of the marriage. In 1836 he described Harington to William as 'a half-caste Indian, a person of little commonsense and a visionary not qualified to make his way in the world'. He added:

> he is moreover in debt and too scrupulous and peculiar in his
> notions to be any other than a poor man — Fanny who has lived the
> best part of her life in the enjoyment of all kinds of comfort — is
> not the person in my opinion to submit to the inconvenience of
> poverty in a cottage.[95]

How thrilled the Macleays would have been to see this magnificent entrance to Sydney Harbour after so many months at sea. Artist Augustus Earle (1793–1838). The National Library of Australia

The Colonial Secretary's Residence, Macquarie Place, Sydney. When Fanny sent this drawing to William on 14 August 1830, she wrote that it was 'ill done' and explained that the front door was not shown as it was at the back of the house. Artist Frances Macleay (1793–1836). Mitchell Library, State Library of New South Wales

< Portrait of Governor Ralph Darling (1775–1858). Artist John Linnell (1792–1882), 1825. The National Library of Australia

< Eliza Darling (1798–1868), wife of Governor Darling. Their portraits were painted before leaving England for Sydney. Married in 1817, Eliza was herself a talented artist. Artist John Linnell (1792–1882), 1825. The National Library of Australia

St James's Church, Sydney, where
Alexander Macleay worshipped.
Adjoining is the Supreme Court House
in Macquarie Street. Artist Russell
Robert (1808–1900). The National
Library of Australia

< Thomas Cudbert Harington
(1798–1863). This miniature is
believed to date from his school days
in London. Artist P. Henderson, 1816.
Mitchell Library, State Library of
New South Wales

Port Jackson looking east from Sir Richard Bourke's statue, 1843. An inscription on this monument, erected in 1842 by the colonists of New South Wales, describes Bourke's time in government as 'a period of singular difficulty'. Artist George Edwards Peacock (1806–1890?). National Library of Australia

Governor Richard Bourke's (1777–1855) facial disfigurement is barely discernible in this regal image. Artist Martin Archer Shee (1769–1850). Dixson Galleries, State Library of New South Wales

Major Archibald Clunes Innes (1800–1857) arrived in Sydney in 1823. Six years later he married Margaret Macleay. Artist unknown. Dixson Galleries, State Library of New South Wales

EMIGRATION
of
FEMALES
to
SIDNEY.
under
SANCTION
of
GOVERNMENT

London Pub by J. Kendrick 54 Leicester Sqe
Aug. 10, 1833.

EMIGRATION in SEARCH
of a
HUSBAND.

What are you going to Sidney for, pray ma'am.
Vy they says as how theres lots of good husbands to be had cheap there
whereas the brutes in England can't see no charms in a woman unless she's got plenty
of money to keep'em in idleness.

Cartoons such as this commonly circulated in England. Five of the six Macleay daughters who came to Sydney did find a husband. Artist J. Kendrick, 10 August 1833. The National Library of Australia

The botanist Robert Brown (1773–1858). Artist Henry William Pickersgill (1782–1875).
By permission of the Linnean Society of London

Still Life with Flowers of the Northern Hemisphere. Artist Frances Leonora 'Fanny' Macleay, c. 1824, watercolour. Private collection. Reproduction of copy held at Elizabeth Bay House, courtesy Historic Houses Trust of New South Wales

1. Wooloomooloo.	8. St James Church.	15 School of Industry.
2. New Gaol.	9. Botany Bay.	16 Natives.
3. Catholic Chapel.	10. Cooper's Distrillery.	17 Entrance to Government Gardens.
4. Entrance to Government Domain.	11. Road to Paramatta.	18 Gen. Darling & Col. Dumaresq.
5. Prisoners Barracks.	12. New Court House.	19 King Bongaree.
6. General Hospital.	13. Market.	20 Bank of New South.
7. Wesleyan Chapel.	14 Mc. Barnet Levys.	21 Military Barracks.

43 Mc.R.Campbell.	47 Macquarie Fort.	51 Pinchgut Island.
44 Dawes Point & Battery.	48 Government Stables.	52 Garden Island.
45 Phoenix Hulk.	49 Port Jackson	53 North Head.
46 H.M.S. Success.	50 H.M.S. Fly & Volage.	54 South Head.

Panorama of Sydney New South Wales 1829. Artist Robert Burford (1791–1861). Based on 1827
paintings sent to him by Augustus Earle. Mitchell Library, State Library of New South Wales

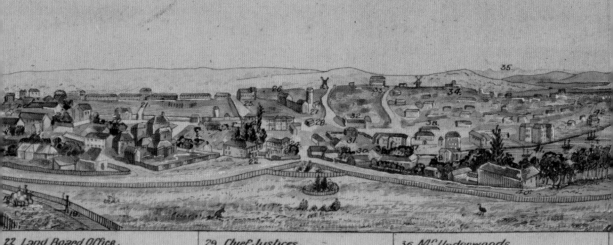

22 Land Board Office.	29. Chief Justices.	36. M.r Underwoods.
23 Sir John Jamieson's.	30. Colonial Secretary's.	37. Bank of Australia.
24 Colonial Treasurer's.	31. Orphan School.	38. Gaol.
25 Scotch Kirk.	32. Sydney Gazette Office.	39. Australian Agricultural Companys.
26 Cockle Bay.	33. Military Hospital.	40 Governor's House.
27 St. Phillips.	34. Fort Philip.	41 Commissariat store Kings Wharf & Dock.
28 Sydney Hotel.	35. Blue Mountains.	42. Naval Office.

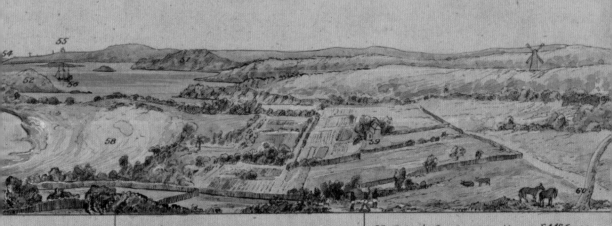

55. Light House.	59. Botanic Gardens & residence of M.r Fraser.
56. H.M.S. Warspite.	60. Native climbing a Gum.
57. Point Piper.	
58. Kangaroo & Dog Dance.	

Aquatic fete on the Governor's Domain in the year 1840. Spectacles such as this were common and the Macleays even had their very own Venetian gondola on Sydney Harbour. Artist W. Gosford. The National Library of Australia

View of Sydney around 1830, when St Mary's Church was the tallest building. Fanny deliberately omitted many buildings from this sketch as they were too difficult to include. Artist Frances Macleay (1793–1836). Mitchell Library, State Library of New South Wales

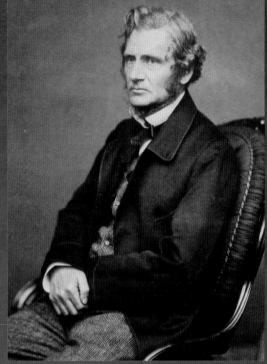

Rosa Roberta Macleay (1807–1854). Fanny's charming depiction of her sister was probably painted while Rosa waited for Arthur's financial position to improve before he could marry her. Artist Frances Macleay (1793–1836). Reproduced with permission from the Stanham Macarthur family, Camden, New South Wales

Arthur Pooley Onslow (1804–1889), husband of Rosa Macleay. It was their grandson, James William Macarthur Onslow, who inherited both Elizabeth Bay House and Camden Park House in 1891. Mitchell Library, State Library of New South Wales

> *Mrs Macquarie's seat, Government Domain, Sydney, N.S.W. Within strolling distance of the Macleays' Bridge Street residence, this promontory would have been regularly visited by family members to enjoy the splendid harbour and watch for approaching ships carrying welcome mail.* Artist Augustus Earle (1793–1838). The National Library of Australia

Interior of St James's Church, Sydney, 1831. The Macleay memorials were later mounted on the right-hand wall of this historic church. Artist William Bradridge, Senior Architect. The National Library of Australia

> *The Female School of Industry 1834. Three female students are depicted in the foreground.* Artist William Wilson. Mitchell Library, State Library of New South Wales

F. WALKER '04

FEMALE SCHOOL OF INDUSTRY, 1834.

Elizabeth Bay, showing Elizabeth Bay House. This watercolour was painted in 1838, the year before the Macleays took up residence in their grand mansion. The artist envisaged how the house would look and added a portico and colonnades that were never built because of financial problems. Artist Conrad Martens (1801–1878). Mitchell Library, State Library of New South Wales

*Saloon, stair and dome
at Elizabeth Bay House.*
Photograph © Ray Joyce,
courtesy Historic Houses Trust
of New South Wales

An incident reported in the *Australian* in 1833 suggests differently. When Harington and Hughes were both fined £1 for not attending jury duty, the newspaper considered that 'the fullest amount ought to have been exacted from these individuals who are rich men'.[96] Why George harboured such reservations about Harington is unclear but, with her own brother so against him, it seems even more surprising that Fanny proceeded. Coincidently, in 1818, Fanny had contemplated visiting India to find a husband. She wrote to William:

> Sir. R. Barclay, who bye the bye has determined to send his niece to
> India this Spring: so, you have lost your chance there, I fear. [sic] I
> really begin to think it would be advisable for me to go to that charm-
> ing place (or market) The expense of the thing alone deters me. I
> assure you.[97]

Harington, by nature and race, also aroused quite different opinions in the local community. When the *Australian* announced in 1826 that he was about to be appointed as Macleay's assistant, it noted that he had 'held the office of Secretary to The Agricultural Company but … quitted that employment on account of a misunderstanding (as it is said) with Mr. John MacArthur'.[98] But Macarthur himself was no easy man to get along with. Even Fanny described him as 'that wicked old Fox MacArthur'.[99] George's description of Harington as 'too scrupulous and peculiar' ultimately proved to contain some truth for, when he resigned from the public service in 1841, it was through a difference of opinion with Governor Gipps.[100] Nevertheless, it was observed in 1830 that there was a proposal for a 'Harrington Street' in Sydney.[101]

When, in 1834 the *Sydney Gazette* sent a messenger to the Colonial Sec-retary's office to check on the authenticity of a story, he was met in a 'most impertinent' manner by Harington, although the newspaper hoped that:

> with the example of urbanity and kindness shown by Mr. M'Leay,
> his superior in office, he would have seen the propriety of putting off
> his Indian austerity, and remembering that Englishmen are not to be

treated like serfs, or like his countrymen who have lost their caste … is this the conduct which you would expect from a man who is, after all, but the chief clerk in a public office.[102]

The *Sydney Gazette* added that it had previously defended Harington but now there were:

obviously just complaints of many whose business, or whose necessities drove them to wait, hot in hand, at the Official threshold of this ephemeral potentate. Even women have complained of his utter disregard of common courtesy.[103]

But fate intervened and Fanny did not have to succumb, after all, to a life of poverty. Not only did Alexander lose his favourite daughter in August 1836, but in June, only twelve days before Fanny's wedding, the *Sydney Herald* repeated February's announcement in London that Alexander had lost his job.[104]

ROBERT BROWN

Before she even arrived in New South Wales, there was another intriguing romantic interlude in Fanny's life involving the famous botanist Robert Brown who was born in Montrose, Scotland on 21 December 1773. This son of a clergyman had originally trained in medicine, and it was through the Linnean and Royal Societies in London that he became a close friend of the Macleay family. One of the saddest letters of all relating to Robert Brown and Fanny is the one that Eliza wrote to William after Brown wrote to her from London saying how upset he was that Fanny had died. It was found amongst papers belonging to William that George gave to the Linnean Society in London and in it Fanny's mother wrote with remorse about her actions:

poor Brown had I thought his love for our dear one had been so great so enduring I would have thrown my weight in the scale but here self interfered [sic] I did not like to part with her and I persuaded myself he was cool, but I cannot help thinking there is a fate in Marriage pray remember me in the kindest manner to Brown tell him that he is near our hearts and that we shall ever regard him.[105]

For the first time Eliza seems to have realised the full implications of taking Fanny with her to New South Wales. Learning from William that Brown was so deeply grieved over Fanny's death must have come as quite a shock to her. Even though Brown was twenty years Fanny's senior, it seems impossible to think that Alexander would not have approved of such a marriage. Was Brown the person who Fanny discreetly referred to in 1835 regarding her 'affair of the heart?' And seemingly there are other letters that have not survived in which Fanny was more explicit about her feelings, like the one she wrote in 1828 in which she emphatically declared:

I shall never marry — I always said so, I always thought that with my particular temper I ought not. This may look like sour grapes and in some degree I have no doubt correctly so — for, I have never yet met with a Person I could have taken for 'better and worse' — Yes! one I have seen, but I could not have him.[106]

Fanny had willingly sacrificed her own future happiness and accepted that Eliza needed help from her eldest daughter to look after the rest of the family. But, realistically, she would have been given no choice in the matter.

In August 1828 Fanny informed William: 'I am told by my friend Mrs. Darling that I am too romantic — perhaps I may be so — I am not sorry for it'.[107] Brown must have been a romantic at heart as well to have kept his affections to himself for so long. David Mabberley, in his definitive book about Robert Brown, took the relationship further and suggested it was possible that the couple became engaged in 1815. His evidence for this is a letter which James Smith, President of the Linnean Society, wrote to Alexander on 15 January 1815 in which he said 'Pray prest. [present] my congratulations to Mr. Brown'.[108] As Brown, 'laid low with rheumatisms', had spent the cold winter Christmas period in 1814 with the Macleays at Tilbuster,[109] perhaps they did indeed announce their engagement. Fanny was then 21 while Brown, aged 41, was only seven years younger than Alexander.

Brown never married and died in London on 10 June 1858. Amongst his papers at the British Museum in London, Annabel Swainston discovered a small gilt-edged farewell note which Fanny had sent, with a drawing, to the French naturalist and explorer, Gaimard, who had visited Sydney on the *Astro-labe* in December 1826.[110] Fanny mentioned this visit at the time to William as she had received a letter of introduction to Gaimard from one of William's friends, a Miss Smith.[111] In May 1828 Fanny again referred to Gaimard in her correspondence with William, mentioning that he 'was a clever intelligent Person' and as he had sent her some books she had felt obliged to send 'him a poor return — a daub of mine — which he most likely may never receive'.[112] Presumably Gaimard passed this daub on to his friend Robert Brown who retained it amongst his personal papers.

TESTIMONY TO FANNY

Eliza advised William in August 1836 that Alexander was overwhelmed when Fanny died as in his heart he was so proud of the daughter who had been 'his Companion in his pursuits',[113] referring to the many hours they spent together studying natural history. Fanny had often assisted her father in classi-fying and identifying different species, and his own vast collection would have been used for reference and comparison. The enormous variety of books in Alexander's personal library, as well as the extraordinary amount of informa-tion that he acquired from contacts during and after his years as Secretary of the Linnean Society in England, would also have helped. Objects collected then had to be either preserved by storage in jars, drawers or cupboards, or else prepared to send away as swaps or donations, all of which involved a massive amount of time and painstaking effort. It was only Fanny who appears to have possessed the intellect and patience required to assist her father in this respect.

The *Sydney Herald's* tribute to Fanny summed up how the community perceived her:

> as Miss M'Leay, she, in common with the other members of her
> family, was distinguished for active benevolence. Whatever were the
> charitable institution in the management of which a lady could take
> part, none was more ready to extend her aid and influence in further-
> ance of its objects.[114]

Fanny's death would have been a terrible loss to all members of the Macleay family as she was the one upon whom they all seemed to rely so heavily, especially in the absence of William. Even after their arrival in New South Wales in 1826, Fanny claimed that they all blamed her 'for their being here'.[115] Quite probably it was Fanny who most strongly supported her father's acceptance of the new position in the colony. She would have comprehended all the extenuating circumstances and considered the opportunity a viable alternative to an unknown future in England, not only for her father, but for the whole family. The beautiful marble memorial inside St James's Church in Sydney describes Fanny's accomplishments and her dedication to the principles of Christian living. Perhaps Thomas Harington helped Alexander write these words for it is surprising that no reference was made to her artistic and scientific talents. She was:

> ENDOWED WITH SUPERIOR TALENTS, EMINENT IN GRACE-
> FUL ACCOMPLISHMENTS, SHE, BY DELIBERATE PREFERENCE
> PARTOOK SPARINGLY OF THE PURSUITS AND AMUSEMENTS OF
> THE SOCIETY SHE WAS QUALIFIED TO ADORN, AND, WITH SELF-
> DENYING UNOBTRUSIVE GOODNESS, DEVOTED HER TIME AND
> FACULTIES TO INSTRUCT THE POOR AND FATHERLESS, IN THE
> PRINCIPLES OF THE DOCTRINE OF CHRIST.[116]

After Fanny's death Eliza mentioned that there was a 'shade they have at Grandmamas of the dear departed',[117] but this has never been found. The only portrait of Fanny that exists today is a painting of three young children who, by family tradition, are believed to be James, Fanny and William. There is a copy of this portrait in *Fanny to William*. Fanny appears to be about six years old.

SOCIAL LIFE IN THE COLONY

Social life, whilst the Darlings were in New South Wales, was particularly active. There was a continual round of balls, suppers, regattas, dinners, family celebrations and parties for visiting ships to attend, apart from the daily visits and calls that had to be made, all of which provided the newspapers with much social gossip. Only three months after her arrival in the colony, Eliza Darling wrote to her brother Edward in Van Diemen's Land, informing him that 'we are very gay'. Weekly dinner parties were held on Thursday and Friday nights with music as well on the Friday night and Eliza was excited that her brother, Henry, had found a fiddler and also two men who could play the Andean pipes.[118] The Macleays themselves gave a ball and supper for about 90 people in April 1826 which Fanny described to William:

> Our rooms were really very prettily ornamented with wreaths of
> flowers &c &c, the doors were taken off the hinges, the window
> sashes removed and their places occupied with lattice work of
> leaves & flowers.[119]

Fanny also mentioned that Eliza Darling was having a ball in honour of the King's birthday and that 'Some of us visit her every day in order to assist her in her preparations'. Eliza described the lavish decorations on this occasion to brother Edward. One side of the room was to be fitted up with

'Bayonets, Flags, and Gun Barrels', the windows removed and a wooden platform built for the band. Furthermore, four large gum trees were to be brought into the room to add to the atmosphere. Eliza added that the Misses Macleay were busy making 'roses, lilies and Golden Crowns' to help celebrate the event.[120] When Annabella Boswell attended a 'grand dinner party' at the Macleay's in 1834, the house was decorated with flowers and the tables laden with food including 'much lovely fruit'. She described being sent for after dinner (the children had their dinner separately in the library) to partake of the sumptuous dessert in the dining-room – and of her pleasure in standing next to 'the kind old gentleman', Alexander Macleay, to enjoy the feast. It seems she was quite a favourite child with the family, Annabella noting in the same journal entry, that Fanny 'wished to adopt and educate me herself'.[121] Whilst Alexander and Fanny would have encouraged Annabella's diary writing, Fanny's interest in taking on her education never eventuated.

In January 1836 the *Sydney Monitor* reported that Alexander Macleay 'gave a splendid fete at his villa at Elizabeth Bay on Saturday last. It was attended by officers of HMS *Beagle* and *Zebra,* many of the military and civil officers and a number of inhabitants'.[122] Charles Darwin was presumably amongst the party who received Alexander's generous hospitality on that occasion. A few weeks later Macleay hosted another large party for about 150 people at Elizabeth Bay House with a 'dejeuné in a sylvan bower, a dance upon the Lawn and fire works … My Father danced a country dance in fine style, I am told',[123] wrote Fanny, who had been too sick to attend.

Sailing on Sydney Harbour was one of the Macleay family's favourite leisure pursuits: how they must have appreciated the temperate climate. The *Australian* informed the community in March 1827 that:

> A handsome pleasure boat has just been brought from the penal settlement of Port Macquarie. It was turned out by the prisoner ship carpenters, and does them great credit. The boat is intended for Mr. Macleay and his family, for whose use it was constructed.[124]

The *Sydney Monitor* described, in 1836, 'Two pleasure barges in the style of the Venetian gondola, ornamented at Wooloomooloo Bay on Sunday last',

Memorial for Frances Leonora Harington (1793–1836) in St James's Church, Sydney. Partially veiled, this elegant marble cenotaph is a beautiful tribute to Fanny who was Alexander's favourite daughter. Photograph courtesy of Historic Houses Trust of New South Wales

adding that 'one of them it is said belongs to Mr. M'Leay'.[125] The Macleay's barge would have been moored at the wharf that had been constructed in the grounds of Elizabeth Bay House in 1835 for the purpose of 'enjoying marine excursions'.[126]

Public entertainment was not forgotten and a theatre was also starting up at this time. The *Sydney Gazette* announced in 1829 that Mr Levey's theatre was to open shortly and reported that two stage boxes had been set aside, one for the Governor and one for the Colonial Secretary.[127] And the Scottish spirit was well and truly alive in New South Wales in the 1830s. An opera about Rob Roy

Fine pewter meat tray, believed to be from a set of seven used in Elizabeth Bay House. To date only three have been found. Reproduced with permission from Bill Perfrement. Photo: Arnold Mitchell

McGregor was performed for the first time in the colony at the Theatre Royal and it was reported that 'the whole of the splendid dresses peculiar to this Piece, and the highlanders of Scotland, have by the great kindness of a Gentleman of the Colony, been presented to Mr. Peat for use on this occasion only'.[128] The 'gentleman' alluded to was possibly Sir John Jamison as he frequently entertained on a lavish scale.

BROTHERS GEORGE, JAMES AND WILLIAM

George arrived in New South Wales in November 1827,[129] and James followed eighteen months later, in May 1829.[130] Both became very popular in the colony and they were favourites of Elizabeth Macarthur who liked to hear all the local gossip as well as the latest English news,[131] which the boys would have gleaned through their father.

Although they spent much of their time at Brownlow Hill, their father's farm situated at Cobbity near Camden south of Sydney, James and George still managed to attend numerous social events in the colony including the magnificent fancy dress ball that Sir John Jamison held at Regentville in 1835. George arrived as a 'Spanish Grandee' and James was dressed as the famous Highland chief, Fergus M'Ivor. Although 600 invitations were sent out, only about half this number turned up because of the dreadful weather and deplorable road conditions. Jamison reigned over the occasion in the 'Court Dress of the time of Charles the 2nd', but he could not prevent the stables catching fire through the negligence of a groom who became drunk.[132]

In appearance George and James were quite different, unlike Alexander who looked so much like his own father.[133] Even Fanny commented on this likeness: 'He has become the very picture of my Grandfather and owing to want of exercise his figure has as close a resemblance to his Father's as his face has attained!'[134] Pictures of the two brothers, James and George, and those of their brother William,[135] show how different the three brothers were. James told William in 1834 that George was 5'6" and had become a 'stout bustling fellow' while he was himself 6' 1½" and had also 'grown stout'.[136] When George arrived in New South Wales Fanny was unimpressed with his physical appearance, lamenting that he looked 'as fat as a pig'. 'He has not grown the least in the world not any taller ... I am sorry to find George so short & thick'. She liked his 'very good manners however — very gentlemanly and pleasing indeed'. And she made a particular point of his whiskers which were 'tremendous in size & colour'.[137]

George also had the family trait of red hair, for Charles Sturt named the River Rufus after him during their journey of exploration together. It was from Brownlow Hill that Sturt's second journey of exploration set off in 1829 to trace the source of the Murrumbidgee River.[138] George apparently was quite a hero on this trip, according to Fanny, for Captain Sturt: '& his Men from fatigue & the effect of want of food were unable to leave the Depot, but the little tough George set off by himself & rode about 3 hundred miles till he reached us'.[139]

At the time, Alexander and Governor Darling differed in opinion as to where the Murrumbidgee would end. Alexander thought that all the inland rivers would merge into one and flow to the south, whilst Darling believed that the Murrumbidgee flowed inland to a huge sea which would have been most useful for developing the interior of the colony. Alexander put his theory forward prior to Sturt's second expedition in 1829. It proved correct.[140]

Fanny reflected on James's character in 1830, stating that he was 'very much beloved by all persons here on acct of his obliging temper & frankness — his little selfishness & simplicity of character'.[141] Such a contrast, she added, from William, who although she adored him, Fanny still considered to be impudent and the 'vainest of the vain'.[142] Although James and George were ostensibly managing the property at Brownlow Hill, and had developed it to the degree that the house and garden were much admired,[143] Alexander refused to give them a salary. Fanny disagreed with her father about this as she felt that they should have monies of their own, but probably Alexander simply could not afford to pay them. When the cottage there was completed in 1829, Alexander requested that two family members should regularly visit for six

James Robert Macleay (1811–1892), Alexander's youngest son. Artist Robert Jenour, 1838. Reproduced with permission from the Stanham Macarthur family, Camden, New South Wales

George Macleay (1809–1891), the second-youngest Macleay son. Reproduced with permission from the Stanham Macarthur family, Camden, New South Wales

At Brownlow Hill, two giant clam shells from the Macleay days are still used as bird baths in the garden. Reproduced with permission from Joan Downes, Brownlow Hill. Photo: Derelie Cherry

The striking sundial at Brownlow Hill, inscribed with the date 1836, remains the central feature of the garden behind the house. Reproduced with permission from Joan Downes, Brownlow Hill. Photo: Derelie Cherry

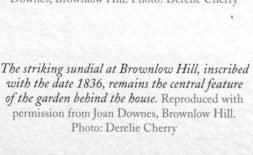

The elegant proportions of the front verandah at Brownlow Hill. Reproduced with permission from Joan Downes, Brownlow Hill

Many original trees still stand at Brownlow Hill. The rear sections of the house were added in the 20th century. Reproduced with permission from Joan Downes, Brownlow Hill. Photo: Derelie Cherry

weeks at a time and Fanny believed that 'the Governor has put this plan into Papa's head for George is a great *favy* of His Excellency's'.[144] But by 1831 George had become disillusioned with the life of a farmer, Fanny observing that:

> George is much disgusted with a Farmer's Life and is very anxious to quit the thing. He has now attained an age when young Men naturally, I suppose desire to distinguish themselves & to possess some pittance however small, which they can call their own — I wish my Father would give both James & him a Salary, but he seems to think they are ever to remain children.[145]

After Fanny died, William came to the colony in 1839 and subsequently played a vital role in the life of his father. Kennethina, in a note to William in 1837, had mentioned how much her father missed his eldest son:

> I have one favour to ask dear William that if you do not come out here soon that you will write to dear Papa by every opportunity [sic] I cannot tell you how much Papa suffers if a ship arrives and brings no letter from you, he says nothing but is ill and loses his appetite.[146]

William was a poor correspondent but exactly how many letters he wrote to Fanny over the years is not known. She scolded him about this frequently and in 1829 wrote that her father was complaining about the very few letters from him and his perceived neglect of the family.[147] Although his original intention was to stay in New South Wales for only three or four years,[148] William ended up remaining there for the rest of his life. After his father's death, William became a well-known local identity and after his own death in 1865 it was said that his 'descriptions and remarks charmed everyone'. According to his friend, Robert Lowe, who knew the 'best talkers in England, ... not one of them was his equal in conversational power'.[149]

It was scarcely surprising that Fanny sought William's advice and opinions for most of her life on so many subjects. How sorely she must have missed his presence and longed for him to come out to New South Wales and how tragic, that by the time he finally did arrive, she had passed away.

ELIZA
MACLEAY

Like her husband, Eliza was overweight. Boyes rudely described her as:

> also fat and square — a very Heidelberg Tun indeed, resembling in
> outline the figure of a hogshead so strikingly, that in the absence of the
> original she would be an invaluable acquisition as a model to an artist
> who had to represent the interior of a Brewer's laboratory.[150]

Furthermore, when Boyes sat down to talk to Eliza, he found that 'she disliked
the country much and the people a little'. Her petty intolerances are evident in
the following passage by Boyes:

> I must tell you that the poultry and Shambles meat of this colony are
> just the finest in the world — but she complained that nothing could
> be procured but skinny fowls, lean ducks, half starved geese, five and
> twenty shillings the three and never a Turkey fit for the spit. The
> beef was poor, and tough as leather and the mutton had no flavour.[151]

Such comments reflect the lifestyle that Eliza had been accustomed to
in England. Other contemporary sources confirm that Eliza was ill-suited
to the position in which she found herself in the colony. In 1838 Elizabeth
Macarthur commented that she wished Eliza Macleay 'was more liberal in
her way of thinking, and more cautious in speaking'.[152] Baron Charles von
Hügel experienced the wrath of Eliza's tongue at the Macleay home in August
1834: 'Mrs. Macleay received me coldly and sarcastically asked me whether
she should congratulate me on my marriage, this is to one of the Misses
Blaxland, with which family she was in a state of open hostility'.[153] No doubt
Eliza was expressing her disappointment that the Baron had not been more
interested in her own daughters as he would have been such a good proposition. Fanny was frequently embarrassed by her mother's inappropriate behaviour although Alexander was apparently not concerned. In March 1826 she
advised William:

You can have no idea of the anxiety of mind my Mother costs me.
Papa leaves her to do & say what she likes here [sic] all eyes, and
those not the most friendly, are directed towards us & I fear we do not
always appear so well as we ought.[154]

Yet it seems Eliza was just as sensitive as her husband. Fanny had noted
this in 1817 when she wrote to William: 'Mama is (you know very well)
very soon *hurt* at anything which appears like a *slight*'.[155] Not surprisingly,
Eliza developed a reputation as an extremely hard and demanding mistress.
In 1839 Governor Gipps implied that it was this attitude that led to the constant problems with her servants which ultimately created negative impressions about the family.[156] In fact, Lady Franklin considered her the 'worst
mistress in the colony'.[157] However, managing convict servants would have
been no easy task, regardless of the person in charge. Fanny spelt this out
to William when describing the workmen who were renovating their Bridge
Street house: 'a parcel of Thieves whom we are obliged to watch as a cat
would a mouse'.[158] Even their own servant, Cox, who had accompanied the
family out from England, proved a disaster as he was more interested in
collecting natural history specimens to sell to the Bristol Institution than
looking after the Macleays. He was sent home a short six months later.[159]
Within twelve months of the Macleays' arrival, 'a Quantity of Plate' comprising eighteen table forks, sixteen table spoons, twelve dessert spoons and two
sauce ladles were stolen from their house and Alexander offered a reward of
£20 for any information about the theft and an additional £10 to recover the
stolen items.[160] In 1829 the *Sydney Monitor* reported that Sampson Fry, who
held a ticket of leave, and his wife Eleanor had been charged with stealing
clothing from Mrs Macleay. Eleanor worked as a domestic for the Macleays
and Sampson had visited her as a suitor; only a month before they were con-
victed Alexander had given them permission to marry.[161]

In April 1835 the *Colonist* reported that two of Alexander's assigned
servants were arrested and in gaol. Whilst off duty for a few hours, they
became drunk and one had stolen the other's clothes while he was asleep.[162]
The *Sydney Monitor* reported more problems in December 1835 when

an assigned servant of Alexander Macleay was sent to post a letter for his Mistress. Four pence was given to him for postage. Several days later another servant found the letter and the accused but not the money; the fellow claimed he had a hole in his pocket, but still received five lashes.[163] Fortunately, in 1836 Eliza obtained the good services of Martha Handcox as her maid and she remained with the family until the end of 1845. Even Martha was a convict, having not long arrived in the colony on a life sentence for stealing jewellery from her long-time employer in London.[164] In the census of 1841, eight domestic servants were listed at Elizabeth Bay House, in addition to 'general labourers and those who worked in the stables and garden'.[165] All these staff would have required supervision and the family would have been constantly on guard, especially considering their previous experience with untrustworthy convicts.

RELIGIOUS AND PHILANTHROPIC DUTIES

As members of the Church of England, the Macleay family regularly wor-shipped at St James's Church in Sydney where they had their own pew. But, in Australia Alexander's religious beliefs crossed denominational boundaries as evidenced by his support for the Methodists in 1845. On 19 March of that year he presided at the Wesleyan Missionary Society's annual meeting. Responding to a vote of thanks for chairing the evening, he claimed that 'he had always esteemed the Methodists; he was perhaps the only one amongst them who had seen John Wesley' frequently in England and added that he had 'always regarded John Wesley as a staunch supporter of the Church of England'.[166] Mr Weiss then pointed out how valuable Alexander's assistance had been especially as, in his 'exalted position', he 'was not likely to be sur-rounded by men very favourable to Methodists — to be associated with whom would once have been deemed a disgrace'.[167] Alexander's comment about

Wesley's support for the Church of England was surprisingly moderate for the time, as the Methodist Church was striving to become a distinct and separate denomination.

Alexander's religious beliefs were publicly channelled in New South Wales through his involvement with numerous charitable organisations and societies. From his earliest days in the colony, utilising the advice of his brother-in-law in Scotland, he became actively involved in the welfare of the community through institutions such as the Benevolent Society, the Sydney Dispensary, the Auxiliary Bible Society and the Auxiliary Missionary Society. Although they were non-government bodies, Macleay's position as Colonial Secretary would have helped all these societies and they would have been honoured that such an important person in the local government had joined their membership. Even before he left London for New South Wales, Alexander had been elected a corresponding member of 'the Adelphi', the Society of Arts which encouraged the development of arts, manufactures and commerce. This Society hoped 'to be favoured with accounts of any useful discoveries or improvements in Science or the Arts which it may be in your power to communicate' after Alexander arrived in Sydney.[168]

In May 1826 the *Sydney Gazette* published a list of annual subscriptions for the Benevolent Society and Alexander was listed, along with Alexander Berry and his business partner Edward Wollstonecraft, as donating the highest amounts of £10 each.[169] A few months later, in July, Alexander took the chair at a meeting of the Benevolent Society which was also attended by Mrs Macleay and their daughters[170] and during the evening he was elected President of that charity.[171] On 25 September 1826 the inaugural meeting of the Sydney Dispensary elected Alexander its President[172] and ten years later, in 1836, he still attended their meetings as President.[173] This society was established to dispense medical assistance to patients who were unable to pay for it, or, as the *Sydney Gazette* described it, for the 'relief of this distressed Multitude of blind, aged, diseased, afflicted and destitute'.[174] Initially, this worthy organisation was funded by subscription but in 1835 it received its first annual government subsidy in recognition of its benefit to the community.

The *Sydney Gazette* reported, in July 1826, a meeting of the Sydney Auxiliary Bible Society at which Alexander was named as the Vice-Patron and the Governor the Patron.[175] And in September 1826 it was also reported that Alexander had taken the chair at the third annual meeting of the Australian Religious Tract Society, where it was announced that more than '62,822 tracts including volumes and detached sheets' had been circulated since their last meeting. Alexander responded to the vote of thanks by saying:

> that he thought it a duty, incumbent on him, from the high office he had the honour to hold, to do all in his power to promote the interests of every Institution having for its objects the good of the Country.[176]

He continued his involvement in all these organisations over the ensuing years and even joined other new societies as well. By September 1829 the *Australian* described Alexander as:

> President of the Benevolent Society, Vice-Patron of an Auxiliary Bible Society ... and a member of the Racing and Jockey Club ... Vice-Patron of a Society called Agricultural and Horticultural — and President of the Subscription Library.[177]

Three days later the *Sydney Monitor* corroborated this opinion when it described Macleay as 'Chairman or President or Vice-President of all the societies and Boards in the colony, religious and prophane'.[178] In 1828 Alexander had taken the chair at the Annual Meeting of the Auxiliary Missionary Society 'with his accustomed regard for the diffusion of religion and morality'.[179] Not only was he a member of these noble and charitable organisations, but he was also Vice Patron of the Australian Racing and Jockey Club which was formed in April 1828,[180] and first President of the prestigious Australian Club which was established on 29 May 1838 in Bent Street at the corner of O'Connell Street.[181] To be elected first President was indeed an honour and the significance of Alexander is acknowledged today through two portraits of him on display in the Macleay Room. Such an appointment contradicted contemporary criticisms made against Macleay as only a true gentleman would have been given the position of President of this esteemed club.

THE MACLEAY WOMEN

All the Macleay women, at one time or another, assisted with various charities and attended meetings of organisations and societies such as the Sydney Dispensary and the Benevolent Society.[182] By all accounts they carried out their duties admirably. It was the Female School of Industry, established by Eliza Darling shortly after her arrival in the colony, that took up most of their time and gave the Macleay girls a worthy cause and one that was appropriate for the daughters of the Colonial Secretary. Funded by subscription, this private school was set up to instruct twenty girls aged between seven and fourteen in 'every Branch of Household Work, Plain Needle Work, Knitting, Spinning, Reading, and the four first rules of Arithmetic'.[183] It was also the responsibility of the school to help find suitable employment for their students. William Dumaresq explained the reason behind its establishment more succinctly. He informed Edward that it was 'to supply the colony with servants and housewives of superior quality'.[184]

Much to her horror, 'and sorely against [her] good will',[185] Eliza Darling appointed Fanny as Treasurer and Secretary on the first Committee. Fanny told William, 'I am very angry — Papa well pleased'.[186] The Macleay sisters, with the exception of Barbara (the youngest), were all on this first Committee.[187] Fanny acted as Secretary over the next ten years and laboriously prepared tedious annual reports, no doubt much to the relief of the other Committee members.[188] Fortunately she was a good delegator and it was not long before Christiana had taken over her role as Treasurer. By the time the School of Industry moved to new quarters in late 1826 (on the site of today's

Mitchell Library), there were 36 permanent boarders and the troops who had previously occupied the barracks on that piece of land had been moved elsewhere.[189]

The Macleay women were also dutifully involved, soon after their arrival in Sydney and again through the auspices of Eliza Darling, with Sunday School public examinations for children at the National Schoolroom, Castlereagh Street. This was an area where the Macleays would have excelled as their own education had been so thorough. The examiners were the Archdeacon and Reverends Marsden, Cowper and Hill, and they tested the children on their knowledge of the Bible. The Macleay women and other ladies who were present at these examinations presumably assisted in a supervisory capacity.[190]

Eliza Macleay became patroness of the Sydney Dorcas Society from 1830 to 1840; her daughter, Margaret Innes, was also a committee member. This Society was formed to help destitute pregnant women in the month prior to the birth of their first child. Eliza was also on the Committee of the Female Friendly Society which was formed, again by Eliza Darling, in 1827 to help sick and elderly female servants and the Macleay daughters were active participants in the work of that Society also.[191]

ALEXANDER'S IMPRESSIVE LIBRARY

Alexander was greatly interested in literature as is evident from the vast subject range in his own library. Only a few days after their arrival in the colony Fanny complained that her poor father's books had to be stored in a coach as there was no room until Goulburn's books were taken away. Unfortunately, about three weeks later, there was a flood and the chests in the coach house were found standing in several inches of water the next morning. She bemoaned to William:

still we comforted ourselves that the books were safe for they were in tin. Alas! … the tin in the most valuable cases was [badly] soldered and the damage immense …. I have been occupied in washing off the sandy stains from them ever since.[192]

When Alexander's 4,000 books were offered for auction in April 1845, the categories listed for sale demonstrated just what an extensive range of reading material he possessed and what a literary environment his children had grown up amongst. There were books on:

History, Biography, Natural History, Zoology, Botany Mineralogy and Geology, natural Philosophy, Chemistry, Medicine & The Arts, Fine Arts and Antiquities, Agriculture Geography and Topography, Voyages and Travels, Divinity, Philology, Education, Belles Lettres, Moral Philosophy, Political Economy, Essays, Novels, Romances etc. Poetry, Drama, Magazines etc. Atlases & Portfolios, Sciences, Mathematics, Every Branch of Polite Literature.[193]

In 1843 Alexander was also one of the Vice-Patrons of the Commercial Reading and Library Room which held periodicals as well as English and Scottish newspapers and provided another important source of information for the developing colony.[194] He had continually encouraged reading by the general public not only in Sydney, but since 1826 Alexander had also been on the inaugural committee to establish a library for the Bathurst Literary Society.[195] The Australian Subscription Library had been established in 1826 and Alexander was a keen supporter of this institution, often taking the chair at meetings.[196] Even this library caused controversy in the community, with the *Sydney Herald* claiming in 1836 that it was not a true public library[197] as admission was by ballot and there was a joining fee and an annual subscription. But these arrangements were necessary in those early years in order to raise purchasing funds and it would also have been essential to ensure that the books remained the property of the library in a penal society. The colony had limited revenue for luxuries such as books, not forgetting too that the first lamp in Sydney's streets was only lit in April 1826. Alexander's brother, Kenneth, had become

President of the Subscription Library in Wick in 1825 and 1826,[198] and his initiative may have encouraged Macleay to inaugurate something similar in Sydney.

It was Alexander who, as President, laid the foundation stone for the Subscription Library's new building at the corner of Bent and Macquarie Streets in 1843 on a land grant made by Darling in 1831.[199] In 1895 this library was renamed the The Public Library of New South Wales and in 1975 it became the State Library of New South Wales. The opening speech on that occasion in 1843 must have gratified Alexander (even more so, perhaps, than attending in the place of the Governor):

> Established in a great measure through your personal influence, the Australian Subscription Library has never failed to enjoy the advantage of your zealous support and enlightened patronage.
> To you, Sir, more than to any other individual, is the Australian Library indebted for the large share of success which has attended its establishment.[200]

MACLEAY, A HIGHLAND LADDIE

The social life of the Colonial Secretary also included attendance at annual dinners to commemorate St George and St Andrew. At one such evening, for St Andrew in 1835, the *Sydney Herald* and the *Sydney Gazette* both reported that Alexander had taken the chair in the absence of Major Innes who had been unable to get a boat from Port Macquarie. Nearly 100 people were present and George Macleay was one of the stewards. Alexander returned thanks in an 'appropriate and amusing speech' and proposed a toast to the memory of Robert Burns.[201] The audience on such occasions would have been entertained by Scottish tunes played on bagpipes, and the tables, decked with Scottish thistle, all contributed to recreating a nostalgic touch of their homeland.

At a St George's dinner in April that same year a toast had been proposed to Alexander Macleay himself, a 'Highland Laddie'.[202] In April 1836, the *Sydney Herald* reported that Alexander had given a most entertaining speech at the recent St George's dinner. On this occasion he was called on to respond, on behalf of the ladies in the colony, to a toast that had been made to them. Alexander's sense of humour is evident in the following passage. He suggested perhaps he was selected because he was:

> about the oldest father of a family present. I can imagine one reason
> why an old man should be selected, which is, because he is most
> like an old woman, or to use an old saying 'Auld wife', and in my
> younger days I paid much attention to the changes that take place
> in the feathered tribe, and as some of you may also have observed
> that an old cock will very often put on the appearance of a hen;
> however, I never had the appearance of a woman in my life, but as
> you have done me the honour to call on me, I have to return you my
> best thanks.[203]

After this eulogy, Mr Manning could not refrain from publicly attesting in a somewhat poetic manner, that Alexander possessed the 'milk of human kindness, with political integrity, and an uncompromising attachment to the institutions of his country, beautifully blended in his composition'.[204] James Macarthur then rose and proposed the official toast to Macleay in which he announced that Alexander had 'commanded the respect of all those whose respect was worth having' in both his private and public life:

> He could speak from his personal knowledge of the extraordinary
> qualifications of the honorable gentleman, who was one of those rare
> characters who could afford to speak disparagingly of himself.[205]

When Alexander replied to James's words, saying that although he 'could not strictly call himself a son of St. George, he was the father of *St. George* (Mr. George M'Leay was present)',[206] the audience responded with laughter and loud cheers erupted.

A DEVOTED
FATHER

How dearly Alexander Macleay loved his family is evident in his attempts to provide for their future. After Fanny's death Eliza wrote to William about what 'a severe trial' Alexander had gone through for someone 'whose happiness you know was in his Children'.[207] Fanny's continual concern for her father is also evident throughout her letters to William and the family kept in close contact after each child married, even if lack of money was the reason.

Bearing in mind the criticisms that Macleay endured from the press and social gossip, Fanny's response written after receiving a batch of letters from England seems apt:

> I can scarcely tell you the strange feelings I have after reading so many
> letters nearly at once — Some full of love & kindness, others colder
> than one has expected some containing melancholy news, others full of
> mirth & wit. I am sure I never succeeded so well as now (altho' I have
> had more practice in former times) in, attaining perfection in the old
> feat Papa used to recommend to us for trial when we were good little
> beings — I mean that of crying with one eye and laughing with the
> other.[208]

Her sentiments reflect Alexander's philosophical approach to the vagaries of life and how his eldest daughter endeavoured to adopt the same attitude.

six

PATRON OF NATURAL HISTORY

THE AGE OF ENLIGHTENMENT

It was through an interest in natural history that Alexander Macleay's name rose to prominence in England long before he came to New South Wales as Colonial Secretary. During his lifetime, the study of natural history became more popular than ever. A major reason for this development was the publication of a book in Sweden called *Systema Naturae*. Written by Carl von Linnaeus, it changed the way the natural world was viewed by providing it with a scientific basis from which to identify and classify new discoveries. Using anatomy as his basis, it was the tenth edition of this book, published in 1758, that presented Linnaeus's nomenclature system of genus and species for the first time. According to the *International Code of Zoological Nomenclature*, '1 January 1758 is arbitrarily fixed' as the date when zoological nomenclature was first introduced.[1]

The British Museum was founded in 1753 and, with Linnaeus's new system of nomenclature firmly established within five more years, interest in the natural world exploded throughout Europe. Emphasis was placed on the usefulness of acquiring knowledge through 'first-hand observations', experience and reasoning, and the additional advantage of 'the possibility of greater wealth and comfort from new products and new lands'.[2] The Age of Enlightenment was at its peak amidst the race to collect and classify in the spirit of progress that could be used to benefit people's lives. And traditional beliefs held by pillars of society such as the Church and State were challenged to introduce more humane social and moral attitudes.[3]

Increased emphasis was placed on voyages of discovery such as Captain James Cook's exploration of the Pacific on the *Endeavour* from 1768 to 1771. Cook's journey was legendary and, thanks to Joseph Banks, a naturalist was appointed to travel on board for the first time in the history of British exploration by sea. Banks was one of the most prominent and enthusiastic advocates of the new Linnean classification system. When he was eighteen years old he inherited landed wealth from his father's estate and, five years later, in 1766, he became a Fellow of the Royal Society which was an exclusive club for patrons of science.[4] A memoir about Joseph Banks, published in a New South Wales newspaper in 1845, summarised his contribution to the development of natural history in the late 18th and early 19th centuries:

> He lived before the taste for natural history had become generally diffused, and it was his pride and his delight to give it that fostering protection it required in his day, from the wealthy and the noble.[5]

Banks's link with Linnaeus was through Linnaeus's 'much-loved pupil',[6] Daniel Solander, who knew well his master's fine collection in Sweden. Banks met Solander at Oxford University in 1760 and recruited him for the *Endeavour* voyage. Solander took up a position at the British Museum (which was closely associated with the Royal Society at the time) and some years later became 'resident librarian and naturalist' for Banks until he died in 1782.[7]

The Rt. Honble. Sir Joseph Banks, Bart., G.C.B., (1743–1820) President of the
Royal Society of London, honorary member of the Horticultural Society of London
& c ... Forever linked with Australia through his association with Captain Cook,
Banks has 80 plant species named after him, including the famous genus Banksia.
Artist T. Phillips; engravers S.W. Reynolds & S. Cousins. Mezzotint by Samuel William
Reynolds, (1773–1835), 1822. The National Library of Australia

THE LINNEAN SOCIETY
OF LONDON

Linnaeus died in 1778 and in that same year Banks became President of the Royal Society, a position he held until his own death in 1820.[8] Subsequently Banks offered to buy Linnaeus's collection for £1,200 pounds but his son rejected what he considered to be a 'cruel offer'.[9] Eventually, after her son died in 1783, Linnaeus's wife Sara offered the collection to Banks. Now it was his turn to refuse. Swainston suggests that 'pique … played a part' in Banks's decision, 'for a refusal to entertain his proposals was not often met with in his experience and the earlier refusal to allow his purchase of the Linnean collections had been more curt than firm'.[10] On the suggestion of Banks, James Smith, who had studied medicine at the University of Edinburgh during the past two years, bought it instead. Smith's father lent him 1,000 guineas[11] and his son subsequently used the collection in October 1784 to establish the Linnean Society in England. Significantly, this price was actually £50 less than the original offer from Banks but wool prices had fallen by then which altered Banks's financial situation, perhaps explaining why he did not buy the collection from Sara. In April 1788 Smith became the first elected President of the new Linnean Society and with a patron like Joseph Banks, and the specimens in Linnaeus's collection providing the basis for comparing and identifying new discoveries, the future was exciting. Membership was exclusively restricted through personal recommendation although it was open to both amateurs and professionals.

PREDOMINANTLY
GENTLEMEN COLLECTORS

Acquiring material from the natural world to build up personal collections became a very fashionable occupation for wealthier members of society during the second half of the 18th century, whether it was butterflies, beetles, mosses or shells. A prerequisite for these so-called 'Gentleman Collectors' was that they had sufficient money to purchase specimens for their collection. It also helped if they had a good network of contacts for exchange wherever possible. Often they paid others to collect on their behalf as they were too occupied with business matters or perhaps too elderly to indulge in such active pursuits. The industrious Banks had followed this course for many years and even Alexander asked Smith in 1800 if he had 'any Butterfly Catchers' near his home as he wanted some 'Papilio Nachaon' specimens.[12]

For some, this habit of collecting extended beyond the natural world. Alexander Macleay was well known for his acquisitiveness, at considerable expense, in a variety of areas. He freely made his collections of books and specimens available to interested parties. Many years later in Sydney, he reflected on the lack of natural history books held in the Subscription Library's collection as they were so expensive. He added: 'I believe it is pretty generally understood that my collection of books on Natural History is tolerably extensive and that my library is accessible to all my friends who study that Science'.[13] Continually adding to the books in his library, he also collected coins. At the end of 1811 William Leach, who collected insects, purchased a collection of coins for Alexander[14] and Fanny noted that a Mr Mantell purchased more coins for both himself and her father from one of William's friends in January 1814.[15]

Although still precluded from membership of any associated club or society, by the 1790s there were movements to encourage interest from women in collecting. Joseph Banks noted this trend in 1796 when he wrote to the Spanish Ambassador that 'botany had become a pursuit ... not of men only but also a large number of the handsomest & most amiable of the English Ladies who have of late years taken this amusing Study under their immediate Protection'.[16]

By 1822 it was more fully accepted that women could offer their opinions on this subject as well as men and Smith wrote to Alexander telling him that he had visited a married couple near Birmingham and that the wife had 'fully and brilliantly attended his lectures'.[17]

One area where females could be of immeasurable assistance was in the compilation of data that accompanied such collections. A famous example of this situation was Joseph Banks's sister, Sarah Sophia, who lived for nearly 50 years with her brother at his Soho residence until her death in 1818.[18] Not only did Fanny help maintain her father's entomological records, but her talents as an artist were most usefully employed. When only seventeen, her skills were acknowledged by her father's friend in the Linnean Society, William Kirby, who requested that she draw 'an outline of the antenna' of two insects for him.[19] It seems Fanny did not take up this offer, for Kirby wrote a couple of years later that he had an artist for his book who could do the antenna drawings if Alexander would lend him the insects selected.[20]

Yet Fanny was not always enamoured with natural history, particularly in New South Wales where William advised her to 'Collect Insects, [as] time spent in this way is a great deal better than Stargazing for believe me you never will set the Thames on fire'.[21] Not that Fanny had any spare time to 'stargaze' in the colony. But such encouragement from her brother did not go unheeded even though she had informed him a few months earlier that she hated insects 'most cordially'[22] because she saw too many of them around her all day. In May 1828 she declared:

> Insects I have no opportunity of collecting, were I so disposed, which I do not admit. You might just as well tell me to fly as to procure Insects in Sydney — a stray Spider or a Mosquitoe, to be sure, I may promise these.

At the end of the letter she capitulated: 'I therefore must promise to collect Insects for you — when I can'.[23] Brother George was more active in Australia. Captain Charles Sturt, whom George accompanied on a voyage of exploration in 1830, recorded in his journal that: 'Macleay, who was always indefatigable in his pursuit after subjects of natural history, shot a cockatoo, a new species hereabouts'.[24]

Robert Barclay (1751–1830). Alexander's father was also painted by this famous Scottish artist, which provides another link between Robert Barclay and the Macleays through Alexander's wife, Eliza (née Barclay). Artist Sir Henry Raeburn (1756–1823), engraver J.D. Harding. By permission of the Linnean Society of London

ALEXANDER JOINS
THE LINNEAN SOCIETY

How, why and when Alexander became interested in natural history is not known but he was keen enough to first attend the 59th general meeting of the Linnean Society in December 1793, only five years after the Society had been established.[25] In April the following year three members of the Society, Robert Barclay, Samuel Goodenough, and Thomas Marsham, who was the Secretary, recommended that Alexander become a member and on 2 July 1794 he officially joined as a Fellow.[26] Robert Barclay may have been related to Alexander's wife, Eliza Barclay,[27] and perhaps it was he who initiated Macleay's entry into the new and fascinating world of natural history. Alexander was actively involved in the Society and in 1798 he became Secretary, a position he held for the next 27 years, right up until his departure for New South Wales in 1825.

The first known reference to Alexander collecting in the field was recorded in 1797 when he and Marsham travelled with Kirby on an entomological excursion. There were some inconveniences and compromises to be made, for when the three friends arrived 'at an old-fashioned wayside inn, they were told that there was only one large room for them, with three beds in it'.[28]

Before Alexander returned to Scotland for a few months in 1802, he wrote to Smith asking: 'What can I do for you in the North of Scotland and the Orkneys?'[29] Despite atrocious weather conditions, Alexander managed to collect over 300 specimens during this time and offered to exchange any duplicates with Kirby and probably made a similar offer to Smith and others upon his return. He also described to Kirby his collecting difficulties in Scotland. His reflections confirm his devotion to the subject, as well as his riding skills, against major impediments. In relation to the district known as Strathnaver, he wrote that it:

> is surely the wildest on the face of the earth. There is no road
> through it, but you are obliged to make the best of your way earlier
> through immense peat-bogs, which are broken up in many places,

and threaten to swallow up horse and rider, or over the sides of
craggy mountains, in which the granite points up in sharp angles, and
above the other, in so rugged a manner, that it is surprising how a
horse attempts to pass. In many places I thought it prudent to
dismount, and more than once I came to the ground involuntarily.
It would, however, take many pages to give you an adequate idea
of this barbarous country.[30]

Alexander must have studied natural history even before he joined the
Linnean Society and was considered quite an expert in the area within a short
period of time. In 1799 William Kirby, who was one of the Society's founding members, asked for editorial input on a paper that he had written about
timber-preying insects.[31] Kirby regularly sent Alexander boxes of insects and
he was an enthusiastic practical collector himself. In 1801 he wrote to Thomas
Marsham:

Give my kindest respects to him [Macleay] and say I hope he will so
manage his business, that while I am in town, we may have a day or
two's hunt together in some spot teeming with all that creeps or runs
or flies, we may take some cold frog of a Post-Chaise and make a long
day.[32]

These days, more than two centuries later, such a hunt scene could be considered quite extraordinary, even comical. Imagine an English Spring with
men in long frock coats and top hats alighting from their chaise to traipse
around the countryside grasping nets on long handles and various other
contraptions. Even if no insects were found or captured it was undoubtedly a good way to catch up with friends and exercise with plenty of fresh
air thrown in! Fanny referred to such a scene in 1829 when she wrote to
William in Cuba that Captain King, son of Governor King who had been
Governor of New South Wales from 1800 to 1806, had written to her father
saying:

that he had heard of your great activity in your pursuits after Natures
beauties and that he understood you had nearly been arrested on one

occasion as a Madman owing to your uncouth dress & queer proceedings in the woods.[33]

Alexander's collecting habits were not as extreme as those of the famous French coleopterist Dejean in his search for insects. Before his triumph at the battle of Alcanizas, the enthusiastic Dejean who later became a general in the army, spotted a:

> *Cebrio ustulatus* (*nomen nudum*) on a flower. He immediately dismounted, pinned the insect, applied it to the inside of his helmet which, for this purpose, was always supplied with pieces of cork, and started the battle. After this, Dejean's helmet was terribly maltreated from cartouche fire; but, fortunately, he refound his precious Cebrio intact on its piece of cork.[34]

THE LETTERS OF JAMES SMITH AND WILLIAM KIRBY

Alexander's interest in natural history, especially insects, grew and he spent an increasing amount of his leisure time on affairs of the Linnean Society. Evidence of his dedication is contained in 40 years' correspondence, housed in the Linnean Society in London, between Alexander and his close friends, James Smith and William Kirby. The 181 Smith letters cover the period 1799 to 1827 and the 104 Kirby letters date from 1799 to 1839. In November 1872 James's widow, who by that time was nearly 100 years old, presented 74 of the Smith letters to the Linnean Society.[35] The Kirby 'manuscripts and correspondence' belonging to Alexander, along with 'a framed water-colour portrait of Kirby', were given to the Linnean Society in December 1866 by Sir George Macleay.[36]

KIRBY RELIES ON
ALEXANDER'S EXPERTISE

Both Smith and Kirby wrote prolifically about natural history during their lives. Smith's major work was *English Botany* whose 36 volumes were published between 1790 and 1814[37] and Kirby became famous for four volumes of entomological work with William Spence, entitled *An Introduction to Entomology,* which were published between 1815 and 1826. In addition Kirby wrote several books on theology. Both authors were keen for constant feedback from Alexander. Smith wrote to him in December 1807 concerning his new work, *Introduction to Physiological and Systematic Botany,* 'I long to hear how you like my book',[38] and Kirby advised him in 1808 that he was entering an 'entomological copartnership' with Spence for a book 'to begin with an Introduction to the study of Entomology, & end in a Synopsis of British Insects'. He wanted Alexander's opinion on the book's viability, especially in view of Thomas Marsham's previous work on the same subject, *Entomologia Britannica,* which was published in Latin in 1802. Kirby thought his work in English would complement Marsham's and that it was 'hard that the entomological door should be forever closed because he [Marsham] has entered in at it'.[39] However, Marsham's work, also published under the title *Coleoptera Britannica,* covered only British beetles and was nowhere near as extensive as that contemplated by Kirby.[40]

Alexander constantly gave Kirby feedback and advice and the project forged ahead. The depth and breadth of Macleay's knowledge on the subject is obvious in the correspondence between the two men in 1809. Kirby even asked, indirectly expressing his own ignorance on the subject, for 'directions for a cabinet & preparing cork & the proper dimensions & depth of the drawers'.[41] Cork and wood were used to line boxes for specimens. The preparation of suitable means of shipment around the world, without incurring damage, was a critical component in building up a collection that was attractively presented and preserved. Macleay's influence on the content of Kirby's book was noted by the author who 'altered that part of the plan of our introduction to

Entomology to which you object & intend saying what an insect is before we give directions how to catch it'.[42]

By July 1810 Kirby acknowledged again that he had acted on Macleay's advice:

> of course we wish it should include every species of information that can be useful to the entomological student: & yet it is not our intention to be unnecessarily minute — I thank you for your caution ....
> & shall attend to it.[43]

But the following year they conflicted in their opinions about the overall aim of the book. Kirby wanted to include 'everything an Entomologist would want to know' whilst Macleay thought it should focus on technicalities. Kirby wrote:

> Indeed a merely technical work, such as you seem to think of, that may be compilized in a few pages would not answer — & though we do not expect to fill our pockets, yet we wish not to empty them —
> & therefore our aim is to make the work as popular & entertaining as we can.[44]

In due course Alexander also assisted in sorting out problems with the publisher. Issues such as the paper stock to be ordered and who held what proportion of the copyright had to be resolved and, whilst their opinions diverged again over the copyright, Alexander pointed out categorically that it was the author's responsibility to ensure that the stock would be available. He advised Kirby: 'When you agreed that B & W should provide the paper, I conclude, that they were told when it would be wanted'.[45]

Kirby also requested Alexander's opinion on the correct terminology for plurals and various other presentation matters and asked him to 'frank the proofs' as he had previously agreed to,[46] presumably a reference to posting them at government expense. He even consulted Alexander on the retail price of the book as he considered the publisher's price injurious to potential sales,[47] even though it was 540 pages long. The publishers did drop the price before the book was released and Alexander played a part in that as well, for Kirby wrote that the publishers had decided to change the price 'in consequence of your suggestions'.[48]

Ultimately Cadell and Davies decided against the work and Longmans, who advanced 'all the necessary cash without charging interest',[49] published it instead. The book was dedicated to Sir Joseph Banks and Kirby checked his proposed wording with Alexander. The dedication referred to how much Banks's 'unrivalled Library & personal communications' had helped the book's content which aimed to show 'the connection that exists between Natural Science and Agriculture'.[50]

Alexander's own cabinet was also a major reference source for the authors which they acknowledged in the preface of their book:

> To Alexander Macleay, Esq., They are under particular obligations for the kind interest he has all along taken in the work, the judicious advice he has on many occasions given, the free access he has indulged to them to his unrivalled cabinet and well-stored Library, & the numerous other attentions and accommodations by which he has materially assisted them in their progress.[51]

THE ROLE OF THE SECRETARY

The Secretary's role was onerous and time-consuming; even more so when it was in addition to a daytime salaried job. In 1801 Alexander informed Smith that he wrote his own private letters, the majority of which would probably have been Linnean Society correspondence, daily after work at the Transport Board and before his evening dinner which was at 5 o'clock.[52] He regularly made practical suggestions for improvement in a variety of areas and in 1800 he agreed with Smith that the collected volumes of papers should no longer be produced annually 'for adhering to any such rule, must inevitably oblige us to print Papers that ought not to be printed'.[53] Needless to say, it was the

Secretary who carried out the laborious work of compilation right through from initially selecting which articles to include and then proofreading them after Smith had provided editorial input.

Alexander came to take on a more executive role than he would have originally envisaged. James Smith's letters to Alexander contain numerous references to his continual health problems which kept him home and therefore unable to attend many of the Society's regular meetings. They note his frequent absences as President since 1797 when he had moved to Norwich from London, and Alexander at times referred to them in his private correspondence. Smith always managed to word his excuses in such a way that Alexander had no alternative but to proceed without him at the meetings and arrange at the last minute for someone else to take the chair. Smith explained in 1810: 'I rather dread a winter journey, & am rheumatic and not strong at present though freer than usual from my teazing autumnal headaches — I am beside very full of business'.[54]

And as there were many meetings, Alexander consequently had even more work to do making alternative arrangements when Smith did not turn up. By 1812 the Society held a dinner on the first Tuesday of each month and regular meetings were held on alternate Tuesdays.[55] Of course Smith was busy writing his own books as well as checking papers for Alexander to include in the volumes that he, as Secretary, was publishing for the Linnean Society. Alexander's patience must have been sorely tried at times although his letters were consistently sympathetic and never resentful or bitter, regardless of how he may personally have felt about Smith's ongoing absences.

But objections were raised to Smith's non-appearance and Alexander taking over in his absence. In 1812 Bishop Goodenough wrote to Smith that he had heard that Alexander and Robert Brown were 'acting for the President' in his absence. He claimed 'Surely they are neither of them capable of giving direction to a Literary Society'.[56] Yet Alexander maintained his position as Secretary for a further thirteen years. Goodenough's haughty attitude was referred to a few years later when Reverend Kirby kindly visited Thomas Marsham who was in financial distress. Marsham wrote to Alexander about how 'gratified' he was by Kirby's visit and reflected 'What a difference between Rector and a Bishop! Which exhibits most the true spirit of Christianity?'[57]

Macleay continued carrying out his duties as Secretary without any financial compensation. His meticulous attention to detail is evident in the type of questions that he asked Smith: what should be included, in what order, should he first list the extracts of meetings to be followed by a list of donations that the Society had received, and should these donations include other gifts such as shells? Should the list be presented alphabetically and should the papers themselves be listed alphabetically? What should appear in the table of contents?[58] Numerous examples survive of his suggestions in relation to printing and publishing the Society's findings. In 1799 he pointed out to Smith that 'It is desirable but certainly not necessary that all our Volumes should be the same size'.[59] Such uniformity would probably have reduced production costs.

The sixth volume of collected papers from the Linnean Society went to press in February 1801,[60] and by January 1823, another eight volumes had been published all of which Alexander would have been responsible for producing.[61] In 1810 he wrote to Smith that volume ten was to be 382 pages long with 21 plates and that he wanted to prepare a general index for all volumes published to date but did not have the time to do so.[62] Smith's reply to this suggestion was non-committal:

> Your idea of an index is an excellt. one, & I would help you if I had not more upon my hands than I can get through. I work almost as hard as you do in your office, — from 9 to 3 every day, & from 7 to 9 almost every eveng.[63]

Such difficulties were compensated for, to some extent, through exciting new discoveries such as the cissus plant which Alexander sent to Smith in 1801.[64] By constantly weighing up the relevance and importance of each new discovery and associated paper, Alexander, in conjunction with the President, was encouraging and influencing the study of natural history in England. For example, in 1817 he advised Smith that Sir Justly Green's paper on ferns was unacceptable for publication:

What are you to expect of a man who has been talking for four or 5 years of publishing a fine Book, and I believe made a finished Drawing of a Frontispiece but has not yet gone on another Step because he cannot make up his mind as to the Title page?[65]

Alexander's contribution to natural history was further enhanced when he was elected a Fellow of the Royal Society in 1809 and in 1824 became a member of Council.[66] His friend Sir John Sinclair was made a Fellow of the Linnean Society in 1811,[67] and that same year Robert Brown also became a Fellow of the Royal Society, Alexander being one of his advocates.[68] Having the support of such close friends on these Societies would have added to his pleasure.

Banks continued to be very much involved and interested in the welfare of the Linnean Society and in 1800 he supported the idea of establishing a Charter for the Society.[69] Possessing a Charter was a turning point in the development of the Society, as thereafter it could legally accept bequests from deceased estates such as Mr Robertson's. In 1801 his grand garden at Stockwell, worth between £80,000 and £100,000, had been left in the hands of Trustees to be set up as a Botanic Garden. As one of the trustees, Alexander reflected 'I regret exceedingly that we did not make the old man a member of our Socy — He would no doubt have left the Garden entirely to us'.[70] Having a Charter in place also made it easier to enforce payment of the annual subscription fee.[71] When incorporation was finally inaugurated in May 1802,[72] the Society then had to choose a 'Coat of Arms' and 'Motto' and Alexander also played a key role in these decisions.[73]

The way in which he described eighteen Lepidopterous insects which had been collected by John William Lewin in 1800 at Botany Bay is evidence of Alexander's great interest, not only in the moths and butterflies that he was studying, but also in their country of origin. He wrote to Kirby in 1805 saying that he had been describing these insects:

with all their changes and natural history. Amongst them there is a most distinct new genus (in my opinion) which I propose to name *Nycter obius* … The caterpillars form for themselves holes in the trunks

Reverend Samuel Goodenough (1743–1827), whose dress and stance in this portrait indicate his powerful position in society. In 1808 he became Bishop of Carlisle.
Artist James Northcote, 1810, mezzotint by H. Meyer. By permission of the Linnean Society of London

of trees, where they hide themselves in the day time: at night, they come out and gnaw off leaves, which they drag to their holes; and when they have provided a sufficiency for the next day's consumption they retire and feed leisurely, with their heads towards the mouth of the hole, which is covered by a curious contrivance ...[74]

John Lewin had sent these specimens, accompanied by drawings, back to England where his brother Thomas arranged for the material to be published in a book entitled *Prodromus Entomology, A Natural History of the Lepidopterus Insects of New South Wales*. It was released in 1805 and the assistance of Dr Smith for the names of food plants was acknowledged, as well as the 'kind observations' of Alexander Macleay, 'for whose abilities as an Entomologist, we have the highest respect, though we cannot avoid differing greatly from him on some points'.[75] However, Alexander revealed another aspect when he wrote to Smith in 1805:

> I took some trouble about describing the Insects, but the Brother here became jealous of my interference and is now to publish the whole in his own way, as he wishes to be considered the author of the Work.[76]

Their difference in opinions was over classifications but probably ego had a part to play as well. Alexander had furthermore provided financial sponsorship for John on the understanding that he would be repaid with insects collected in New South Wales.

THE CABINET OF
ALEXANDER MACLEAY

As early as 1805 Alexander's collection of insects was considered to be one of the finest in England. Edward Donovan, who also possessed a magnificent collection (or cabinet as it was called), published a work that year on the natural history of insects of New Holland, New Zealand, New Guinea, Otaheite (Tahiti) and other islands in the Indian and South Pacific Oceans. In the preface he acknowledged that he had inspected Alexander's cabinet and that of Mr Francillon, and considered them to be cabinets of celebrity in addition to his own and that of Joseph Banks. Drawings of four flies and a butterfly from Alexander's collection were included in two of the plates in Donovan's publication.[77] In May 1805 Alexander was fortunate enough to purchase, for nearly £40, items from the late Dru Drury's (1725–1803) cabinet which included many unique specimens collected over a period of 30 years.[78]

His collection was expanding at an unprecedented rate and on 24 September 1806 Kirby wrote to Spence to tell him the exciting news that 'M'Leay has purchased all Donovan's foreign insects, a most valuable addition to his collection, which, in value, falls not short of Francillon's'.[79] Donovan was a prolific author and in 1807 he opened his extensive collection to the public under the name of the London Museum and Institute of Natural History. And in 1806, Alexander purchased, at auction, the Australian insects that Captain Cook had given to Sir Ashton Lever.[80]

It was remarkable that Alexander built up such an admired collection so rapidly, albeit, as Secretary, he had numerous opportunities for acquisitions. In 1813, for example, Alexander sent a box of fine insects from New Holland and Brazil to Dr Brunmark in Sweden who deposited them with the Royal Academy of Sciences in Stockholm. Olaf Swartz then responded to advise that Brunmark had informed him of Macleay's vast entomological collection and that he was sending a box of insects to him from Mr Schonherr, whose collection 'is at present one of [the] finest in Sweden'. Swartz began his letter in a most flattering manner:

> I congratulate myself by finding an opportunity to address you in this epistolary way, as a Man, whose similar scientific pursuits and generous and amiable disposition towards Cultivation of Natural History — made it one of my foremost wishes, to be introduced into your acquaintance.[81]

Reverend William Kirby (1759–1850). Kirby became one of Alexander's closest friends in the Linnean Society over a period spanning 51 years. A volume of Kirby's work proudly rests on the table next to a prominently placed beetle. Artist F. Bischoff, engraver T. Maguire. By permission of the Linnean Society of London

A year later Alexander was elected a foreign member of the Swedish Royal Academy of Sciences on the basis of the Academy being 'desirous of associating to herself Illustrious Men, distinguishable by their eminent Talents'.[82]

Storage space was possibly becoming a problem for Alexander's expanding collection, or more probably he needed the extra money, because in July 1814 he auctioned some of his own insect duplicates. The sale was described as that of 'the most extensive Entomological Museum in Europe' and included 'an excellent mahogany cabinet, with 23 glazed drawers' for insects.[83] Unfortunately it did not raise as much revenue as had been hoped for,[84] yet Alexander continued to add to his collection. John Francillon died in 1817 and in June 1818 Alexander purchased almost half of his extensive collection at auction, including specimens that Surgeon General John White had collected after he travelled to New Holland with Captain Phillip and the First Fleet in 1788. This auction lasted eight days and the catalogue for it extended to 74 pages. It is assumed that one of the largest wood-boring beetles, the 160 mm long *Titanus giganteus* now housed in the Macleay collection at the Macleay Museum, was bought by Alexander at this time.[85] Other additions to Macleay's collection were gifts. Sir Stamford Raffles gave him a number of insects that he had collected in Sumatra and Sir John Bowring also gave him some that he had collected in Hong Kong.[86]

Actual details of Macleay's acquisitions over the years are difficult to identify. In the library of the Linnean Society in London are copies of catalogues for the sale of the Francillon and Marsham collections with annotations which are believed to represent Macleay's purchases. Other catalogues found in Macleay's collection were dated 1814, 1819 and 1825 and so it is assumed he made further purchases from these as well.[87]

Ornithology was another area of interest for Alexander. He made several donations to the Linnean Society including 34 birds from Berbice in 1811, eleven specimens from New South Wales in 1818 and a third donation in 1822. He obtained all of these from 'undisclosed sources' but whether or not he originally paid for them is not known.[88] Much later, from New South Wales in 1834, Macleay sent back a skin specimen of an unidentified bird to the Zoological Society of London suggesting that 'The white-fleshed Pigeon of the Colony' would be 'A great acquisition in England … far superior to Partridge'.[89] John Gould, the famous American bird painter who visited Australia from 1838 to 1840, acknowledged in the preface of his book, *Birds of Australia*, 'his best thanks for kindness and help during his stay in New South Wales' to several people including Alexander and William Macleay.[90] During his visit Gould made a sketch of a tame brush turkey that had been domesticated by the Macleays but which unfortunately drowned in a well when it mistook its own reflection in the water as a rival.[91]

WILLIAM MACLEAY AND NATURAL HISTORY

William, too, built up his own collection and a vast amount of knowledge on the subject. It was fortunate for William that Alexander had all the right contacts and that he could assist with his father's collection. In 1811, during his second year at Cambridge, he was acquiring specimens and Kirby wrote to Alexander that he was 'very anxious to know whether any bargain has been struck between you & William for your Duplicates'.[92] During William's time in Paris, from 1815 to 1819, he met many famous natural historians. As Paris was so centrally located, many foreigners came to visit with a degree of curiosity that had increased since the days of Napoleon. In December 1815 Charles de Schreibers, from Vienna, wrote to Alexander to advise him that William, whom he had met in Paris, had informed him that his father wished to establish a connection with entomologists in Germany.[93]

Latreille was among the many famous zoologists William met in Paris and from him William received 'a variety of insects … and a good grounding in taxonomy'.[94] He also met Cuvier who was famous for his *Leçons d'Anatomie Comparée 1-5* which were published between 1799 and 1805, and Lamarck who had written *Système des Animaux sans Vertèbres* in 1801.[95] William's mentor from his days at Cambridge, Kirby, visited Paris with his second wife in 1817

M. le CHEVALIER de LAMARCK,
Professor of Botany of the National Institute.

Chevalier de Lamarck (1744–1829). This distinguished botanist, who joined the Linnean Society of London in 1819, was one of many who helped William with his natural history pursuits in Paris. Artist David, engraver J. Hopwood. By permission of the Linnean Society of London

254

during which time they visited Latreille and Dupresne. The following year, William wrote to Kirby:

> my father ... has made his [collection] as brilliant for the amateur as it is instructive for the entomological student ... The French Museum has been prevailed on to let my father have one of the Hexodons; so that now he will have every described genus of Latreille's family of Lamellicornes.[96]

From the late 1700s new schools of thought and classification which challenged the Linnean system began to circulate through journals published in countries such as France and America. Latreille was developing a new theory of classification based on all components of an insect's body rather than just wings as Linnaeus had done, although Latreille still divided them into orders.[97] Another new classification of the natural system of species had been developed by Antoine Laurent de Jussieu in 1789. Joseph Banks encouraged Robert Brown to adopt Jussieu's system when classifying the species Brown had collected during his journey of discovery with Matthew Flinders on *The Investigator* in 1803,[98] and Brown used this system in his ensuing work published in 1810 which was entitled *An Introduction to the Flora of New Holland*.[99] James Smith was also helpful in facilitating introductions for William in Paris. Prior to William's departure Smith advised Alexander: 'If he wants anything from Thouin, Jussieu, Desfontaines, give him full authority to make use of my name'.[100] It must have made Alexander proud to think that his eldest son, aged only 23, was mixing with such great minds and ideas on the continent.

Between 1819 and 1847, William published two books and numerous papers.[101] His most famous book, *Horae Entomologicae; or Essays on the Annulose Animals*, was published in two volumes in 1819 and 1821. In the first volume he referred to the beetles in his father's cabinet which contained 'nearly 1800 species of the Linnean genus *Scarabaeus*; and the study of these, mainly, resulted in his first contribution to knowledge'.[102] These specimens were from 'Northern and Southern Europe, North Africa, Cape of Good Hope, Mauritius, Isle of Bourbon, India, East India, China, Java, North America, Georgia, South America, Brazil, Demerara, Cayenne, Trinidad, Jamaica, Australasia, New Holland, and Van Diemen's Land'.[103] In the second volume, William introduced his renowned Quinary System which was a philosophical system that divided nature into circles composed of five elements based on affinities.[104] When volume one was published, Kirby wrote to Alexander declaring that:

> This work will raise his name as an entomologist of the first class. There are however in it many things which I think will not be generally admitted, & as is the case often with young & ardent writers he seems to me to push his principles too far.[105]

By the time volume two came out Kirby wrote to Alexander to congratulate him 'upon the eminence to which your son is fast rising in Entomology'. He added that despite their differences in opinion, he would always:

> be ready to pay the just tribute of applause to the depth, condition a [&] genius that are so conspicuously displayed in his truly Opus Magnum. It has diffused a new & copious flood of Light over the whole science of Natural History — & whether his system abide the ordeal trial or not, if not the very system of nature it will lead to the discovery of it: & his name will always stand at the head of the Science.[106]

When the fourth and final volume of Kirby's *Introduction to Entomology* was published in 1826, Kirby admitted that he was 'highly influenced' by William's system of higher categories which, like his own ideas, was based on the idea of a Creator.[107] In retrospect, Kirby's initial thoughts were correct. William's system did not stand the test of time and by the 1850s had been abandoned in favour of brilliant new theories such as Darwin's theory of evolution. Smith, on the other hand, offered unreserved congratulations to Alexander on William's achievements in 1825: 'I am delighted with yr. son's most excellt. & learned papers — he indeed is a philosophy naturalist'.[108] After William's death in 1865 his friend Robert Lowe testified to his outstanding ability as:

> an excellent classical scholar, he knew more of modern history and biography, than anyone with whom I was ever acquainted, and in addition to all this he was a profoundly scientific man, thoroughly conversant with Zoology and entomology.[109]

FREE POSTAGE ENDS

Alexander's position at the Transport Board was very useful to his friends in the natural history world. They readily availed themselves of the free postage that was offered by Macleay himself in 1799 when he wrote to Smith: 'I will receive Letters addressed to me at this office free of postage'.[110] Normally the recipient had to pay postage but, being a government office, the Transport Board could both receive and send letters free of charge.[111] His offer was well and truly taken up especially by James Smith who frequently added a postscript to his letters: 'I beg the favour of you to forward the enclosed by Penny Post'.[112] By getting them franked at the Transport Office substantial postal costs must have been avoided. Macleay was happy with this arrangement and in 1816 he even apologised to Smith for holding on to two letters, excusing himself on the grounds that:

> Brown generally brings Letters for you to Queens Square, where I put them into my Pocket, with an intention of forwarding them from the Transport Office, but in the hurry of business here they are forgotten.[113]

He also had the good foresight to recruit Ambrose Serle from the Transport Board to the Linnean Society in 1805. As Ambrose was 'one of the Commissioners of this Board' and a 'very particular Friend' of Alexander's, it was a fortuitous move[114] as undoubtedly tacit approval was obtained from Serle for office privileges, like free postage, to be used in the name of scientific research.

When it seemed that the Transport Board was to be abolished, Smith and Kirby were in a quandary. Smith wrote in November: 'I see every now & then that yr. office is abolished — so I fear to write — But you will warn me in time no doubt'.[115] Alexander replied with a glimmer of hope: 'Notwithstanding what you have seen in the Papers, this office still remains in status quo. Govts. find more difficulty in abolishing the Office than they ever dreamed of, and we are now in as much doubt as to the time of Abolition as we were twelve months ago'.[116] Kirby informed Alexander in January 1817 that he had been meaning to write to William, Latreille and Savignoy in Paris, asking at the same time 'what shall I do with my letters'.[117] Still, he was concerned about Alexander's impending job loss:

> I shall be extremely anxious to know the result of the 10th but hope
> that Government, which cannot be ignorant, will not be insensible
> of your services, but reward them by an ample pension. The present
> outcry for economy I fear is the only great bar to this — should they
> give you what you merit, I hope you will be able to devote yourself
> more to entomology — & give the world that grand desideratum, a
> Genera Insectorum, for which you are so well qualified both by your
> matchless cabinet & your extensive information upon the subject.
> Latreilles Genera is not of half the use it might be from the perplexity
> of his method, & the prolixity & indefiniteness of his characters.[118]

By April 1817 Alexander was forced to advise his friends that he could no longer use the postal services of the Transport Board. He wrote to Smith: 'I forwarded your Notes but I am sorry to tell you that in consequence of the abolition of the Transport Board I no longer receive Letters free of expense'.[119] Smith's reply was amicable enough: 'I know not whether to lament your loss of office — as I hope you will obtain what you so well deserve, & at least as profit-able a place — I am in your debt for postage — & I believe other matters'.[120]

CONCERNS FOR
THE FUTURE

Little did either Smith or Kirby realize that within the space of six years they were to lose Macleay and his wonderful collection forever to the other side of the world. By 1820 Kirby was so concerned about Alexander's immediate future that he wrote to him about their mutual friend, William Elford Leach, who was Assistant Keeper of Natural History at the British Museum: 'If poor Leach should be obliged to quit his situation, or a deputy be appointed — I don't know any one so fitted to succeed him as yourself'.[121] The sympathetic tone in Kirby's letter was because Leach had become 'mentally ill' allegedly as a result of venereal disease.[122] From 1814 to 1817 William Leach had published his *Zoological Miscellany* in three volumes. In these works he referred to specimens in Alexander's collection including *Papilio Macleayanus* which he named after his 'much esteemed friend, Alexander Macleay … to whom I cannot sufficiently express my full sense of his repeated marks of kindness and friendship'.[123]

Over the years both Smith and Kirby regularly sent Christmas turkeys to the Macleay family. Alexander initially responded to the gift of a turkey from Smith by writing: 'I am very much obliged to you for your kind offer of a Norfolk Turkey; but pray why should you send me one? If you have ever eaten a bit of Turkey or even a beef steak in my House the case might be different',[124] he added in jest. Despite their ongoing problems, a great friendship developed between the two and in his role as Secretary Alexander was not only friend and confidant of the President, but also, on occasion his advisor on protocol. For example in 1816 Smith wrote to him asking for a reminder about how he appointed the Vice-President in 1812 saying: 'I know it was by Letter, but when was it sent or read? & can you transmit me a copy, that I may do it in the same form'.[125] Alexander replied with specific instructions:

> I think you ought to address a Letter to the Bishop of Carlisle to be
> read by him after the Elections on Friday referring to the Bye laws
> giving you authority to nominate Vice Presidents, and by virtue of that
> law naming those you intend providing they shall have been chosen
> of the Council on that day — The form is immaterial, but this should
> be the purpose of your Letter which will be insisted [sic] in the Minutes.[126]

When Smith was knighted in July 1814 for founding the Linnean Society and long service as its President to date, he had Alexander to thank. Having asked him six months prior, 'in confidence, what is the right method of applying for this honour',[127] Smith acknowledged in December 1813 that he was 'very much obliged to you for having put the matter in so good a train'.[128]

By comparison, there was much rivalry between Smith and Kirby, especially when both applied for the chair of Botany at Cambridge University, although this did not affect Alexander's friendship with either man. In July 1813 Smith wrote to Macleay that his friend, Professor Thomas Martyn, was going to resign from his position at Cambridge and in so doing would prepare the way for him.[129] But by February 1814 Martyn was still in office and it appeared that the idea of Smith as his replacement was not viewed favourably by the Vice-Chancellor.[130] Two years later Martyn was still at Cambridge and Smith was using all the contacts he could muster to secure the position. Even though he had the support of 'several great people' including 'Lords Spencer, Althorp, John Thynne, Tavistock, Marquess of Bath, Dean of Lincoln',[131] his attempts were in vain. Professor Martyn never did vacate his Chair and after he died in 1825 two years passed before a successor was appointed.[132]

In their rivalry over this position, Smith complained to Alexander that Kirby 'must know that he cannot fill the place with honour or utility as a botanist, however great an entomologist, & that therefore he cheats the public in supplanting me'.[133] Kirby found it difficult to comprehend Smith's attitude but thought some of the opposition against Smith was because he was not a member of the Church of England. Smith retorted that although he was 'a dissenter', he still had the support of 'many other most orthodox clergy'.[134] Although Alexander was surprised that Kirby had come forward on this occasion, he still defended him against Smith's criticisms, declaring that 'I do not believe a more sincere upright man ever drew breath'.[135] An interesting postscript to this scenario was published by *The Statesman* in 1823 which suggested that the main problem with appointing Smith was that it was thought he would place too much importance on lectures rather than practical lessons.[136] There was probably a good deal of truth in this assertion, for how Smith could even consider such a position given his declining health is surprising. As recently as 1812 he had written to Alexander:

> I was just able to go in a one horse chaise yesterday, at foot pace, to dine with my friend Mrs. Crowe, at Lakeham a mile distant, but I could not bear the horse to trot — so I am not likely to bear a journey to London.[137]

Another awkward situation arose for Alexander regarding Thomas Marsham who had borrowed money when he was Treasurer of the Linnean Society that unfortunately he could not repay. Marsham was one of the founders of the Society and, whilst it was painful for Smith and Kirby to witness the events unfolding, it was left to Alexander to take action to retrieve the money. Smith reminded him in 1816 that Marsham had 'failed in business many years ago' and that spending the Society's money was 'a fraud, it having been incumbent on him to lodge it in safety, if not to make interest of it'.[138] Two years later the money still had not been recovered and Alexander wrote to Smith that he had been advised that 'the only thing that can be done is to throw the poor old man into Jail'. He added:

> Surely, my dear Sir James, this must not be. — It must be remembered that he was for many years a most valuable Member of the Society. Indeed I have no hesitation in saying the most valuable, with the exception of yourself alone; and are we to requite such Services, for the sake of such a paltry sum as £350, by throwing an old man of 70 into Prison, and keeping him there for the year or two that he may have yet to live?[139]

Smith replied to Macleay's sympathetic plea: 'As to poor Marsham, you cannot suppose I would for a moment think of such a measure as you mention, even in my char. [character] of Prest. of a Socy.', although he could not refrain from reminding Macleay of Marsham's failings in the business world, adding: 'Did he not fail in the linen trade many years ago?'[140] But before any decision was made to resolve the problem, Marsham died at the end of 1819.

CHANGES AFOOT

The early 1820s saw other changes which made Alexander increasingly frustrated. He had become 'most heartily sick of the Secretaryship' by 1823 and wrote to Smith begging him to consider a replacement.[141] Three years earlier he had intimated to Smith that he was keen to relinquish his duties as Secretary, saying that 'this state of things makes me more anxious than before to relinquish the office of Secretary. — I hope that when you come to Town some arrangement will be made for dispensing with my Services'.[142] Smith's response was a refusal to acknowledge the possibility that Alexander might resign: 'As to your giving us up my dear friend, I sicken at the thought, & cannot bear to write about it'.[143] However, there was a noticeable change in Smith's demands on Macleay when he thought he might lose him. He emphasised that there was no need for Macleay to compile a general index for the Society's publications himself and that he should get someone else to do it for a fee.[144] Smith's sustained hope that Macleay would stay is evident in his sentiment a few weeks later: 'You say nothing abt. your successor — I hope it is a symptom of relenting in you, & of grace towards us'.[145] By then, Smith was 64 years old and after he died only a few years later in 1828, his widow sold his collection to the Linnean Society.

The 'state of things' that Macleay referred to in 1820 was the fact that competing clubs and societies were being established that placed the Linnean Society's monopoly in jeopardy. Macleay expressed his concerns to Smith:

> You have I know heard a great deal about our rival Clubs ... I confess that at first I did not think a second Club would hurt the Society, but I now see with regret that I was mistaken, for, notwithstanding all my poor endeavours to procure peace and quietness, I see symptoms of treachery and ill will that vex me exceedingly.[146]

Complaints were also raised about a request in 1817 from The Horticultural Society to extend their hours of business at the Linnean Society premises which they had used since 1805.[147] Kirby's proposal of a Zoological Society in March 1823, which also requested to use the premises of the Linnean Society, was not well received. And the emerging Asiatic Society was considered to be major threat as the Linnean Society had 'already incurred great expense in publishing descriptions and figures of the Natural Production of Asia'.[148]

It was left to Alexander, as Secretary, to challenge the new Asiatic

Society. He wrote inquiring how much natural history they intended to include and received the reply: 'That although Natural History is not among the direct objects of the Society still they cannot preclude themselves from receiving any communications which may incidentally and consequentially refer to the objects for the promotion of which they are associated'.[149] Alexander's opinion was that if a clause expressly excluding natural history was not included, the Linnean Society Council 'Would feel it to be their Duty to oppose the granting of such Charter'.[150] In due course, other societies were established and flourished and even an Entomological Society was founded in England in 1833.[151] But Macleay was now older and preoccupied with a large family to support and he had no desire to confront further problems. Choosing a suitable replacement was no easy task either because, as he pointed out to Smith, 'Many of the Members seem to consider it quite a sinecure'.[152] Little did they realise the enormous amount of work and tact involved.

ALEXANDER RESIGNS
AS SECRETARY

When Smith finally accepted that Alexander was indeed resigning, his immediate concern was to appoint a replacement as soon as possible. In January 1825 he wrote to Alexander asking 'Would yr. son undertake it? I mention him at random, not knowing his situation or occupation. Would Mr. Brown accept it?'[153] On the same day Smith wrote directly to Brown asking him to consider the office of Secretary, adding that 'Perhaps you will confer with our departing (I could almost say Departed) friend McLeay about it'.[154] Only a few days earlier Macleay had advised Smith in a letter that he had 'asked our Friend Brown if he would accept of the office and although he does not seem to like it much, I think that, if you were to ask him, he would undertake it'.[155]

Brown was an obvious choice as he was by then an eminent botanist. In 1805 he had been elected as clerk, librarian and housekeeper for the Linnean Society,[156] and had retained these positions until 1822. He had also become librarian and curator for Banks's collection at his Soho Square house in 1810 and, after Banks died in 1820, took up residence there as he was bequeathed a tenancy for life. The Linnean Society decided in 1821 to hold its meetings in the drawing room,[157] a convenient arrangement instituted by Brown. After Brown died, Banks's collection was to be transferred to the British Museum, but Brown decided to transfer it in 1827–1828 instead, and as a result the public had access to the first nationally owned botanical collection. Brown remained as caretaker of the collection with the British Museum until 1858.

An interesting reflection on the position of Secretary for the Linnean Society, as well as Alexander's response, is recorded in a letter he wrote to Smith on 25 January 1825:

> Our Friend the Bishop has been pleased to say that he would be
> sorry to see Brown in the office of Secretary, as he considered it
> far beneath him. His Lordship was pleased to compliment me by
> repeating this several times to me, alth' I took some pains to explain
> to him that the acceptance of such a gratuitous office could be no
> debasement to any Member of the society whatsoever his science
> may be.[158]

The Bishop put forward another reason to Smith about appointing Brown: 'I have invincible objection to letting the Linn. society be thrown into the lap of the Horticultural [Society]: this must be the case if Brown is chosen'.[159] Eventually Brown did become Vice-President of the Society from 1828 to 1849 and President from 1849 to 1853, but by that time Alexander had passed away. Smith's reply to Macleay on 27 January 1825 was simple: 'I will bring the Bp. to reason'.[160]

After Alexander penned his letter of resignation to the Linnean Society on 5 January 1825, Smith took nearly three weeks to respond officially and acknowledge his decision. By then it had been determined that James

Ebenezer Bicheno would become the new Secretary. Strangely, there was a later similarity between the careers of Macleay and Bicheno who left the Linnean Society in 1840 to take up the position of Colonial Secretary in Van Diemen's Land. Smith expressed his good wishes to Alexander on his departure by acknowledging:

> I have ever felt the warmest estimation for your character, the most grateful sensibility to your constant active friendship & attention. I have always known where to find you, & was always sure you would do the kindest & most judicious thing. I would not suggest gloomy ideas of your great undertaking, which I trust will be as advantageous, as it is certainly highly honourable. It must on some accounts be delightful to you, & as a naturalist I almost envy you.[161]

Kirby echoed Smith's sentiments: 'Your appointment will form a new Era in the Nat. Hist. of New Holland, & the production of that great country, & the islands of those seas will now be more fully known'.[162] He even added: 'If now you could get me appointed Bishop of Australasia it might be some temptation for me to link my fate & fortune with yours'.[163]

Before he departed from the Society, Alexander wanted three matters settled. He wanted a subscription raised for a bust of Smith, a general index prepared for the 15th volume of the Linnean Papers and thereafter an index for each volume, and he also wanted to improve the funds of the Society.[164] It was a measure of their gratitude that the Linnean Society organised an oil painting of Macleay by Sir Thomas Lawrence before he left England. It was funded by subscription and still hangs amongst other famous portraits in elegant frames on the top floor of the present day Linnean Society headquarters in Burlington House, Piccadilly. At the anniversary meeting of the Linnean Society on 24 May 1825, there was talk of Alexander 'quitting this country for a time' and the minutes of their meeting on 7 June 1825 recorded 'the high estimation in which he is held by them — on account of twenty-seven years of unremitted and unrequited labour devoted to the interests of science'.[165]

NATURAL HISTORY IN
NEW SOUTH WALES

Prior to the Macleays leaving England for New South Wales in 1825, Alexander's insect collection was described as 'the finest and most extensive collection then existing in the possession of a private individual'.[166] It was especially remarkable for its size, range and unique specimens, including many type specimens or holotypes which were used in the preparation of first published descriptions. Other subtypes within the holotypes were known as paratypes. By the 1830s, however, Macleay's collection was surpassed by that of Dejean who through collecting, purchase and exchange held 'the largest private insect collection of his time'.[167] Unlike Macleay, Dejean compiled a series of catalogues for his collection which by 1837 contained more than 22,000 names, but he did have the assistance of a private curator to help him.[168] Dejean also wrote his famous *Species Général des Coléoptères* from 1825 to 1838 which described the species in his own collection and earned him the title of 'the first great coleopterist'.[169] Macleay would never have had the time to take on such an arduous task and even Dejean found he was able to write only five of the anticipated twenty volumes himself and only six were ever published.

Although the Linnean Society had given Alexander permission 'to place his cabinets of insects in one of the attic rooms in the Society's Rooms for preserving during his absence from this Country', he decided to take his cabinet halfway around the world.[170] Perhaps the Linnean Society thought this was one way in which they could retain control over the collection and prevent it from leaving England, thereby enabling it to be accessible for information when required. Smith may also have thought that by leaving his collection behind, Alexander would most certainly return home to claim it and perhaps help out once more at the Linnean Society.

Or such a collection could have been put up for auction, especially considering Alexander was short of money. No, he took it with him on the free passage out to New South Wales, but why? Perhaps it was to enhance his status in the new colony or to benefit directly the development of natural history there. Or was his decision linked to his religious conviction that the natural world was evidence of God's creation? In addition to his insect collection, he also took with him some mounted birds, including a 'Chinese Ringnecked Pheasant, *Phasianus colchicus torquatus*' which was a common game bird.[171] Amongst the furniture that Alexander brought out with him on the voyage to New South Wales was a specimen case in Chippendale style, and there were others that used different types of wood for each drawer.[172] Presumably these cases were housed at the family's first residence in Bridge Street but curiously no mention is made of them. How they fitted into that comparatively small house, with all the family as well, is a mystery. In fact there is some speculation that son William took much of the collection with him to Cuba and later shipped it to Sydney.[173] Feasibly, it was the largest room at Elizabeth Bay House, the library, that eventually became the showroom for the collection. Off this room, in the back left-hand corner, there was an annexe where specimens were dried and mounted. The smell of camphor must have continually pervaded the air in the house. Ten of the original cabinets that Macleay bought with him to Australia, including a magnificent one made with different woods,[174] are now in a laboratory near the Macleay Museum in the grounds of the University of Sydney.

After Alexander's arrival in Australia the *Sydney Gazette* announced that the new Colonial Secretary:

> was well known, not only in this country, but over all Europe as one of the most scientific naturalists and horticulturalists; and the Linnean Society of London, of which he has long been the gratuitous secretary, will deeply lament his absence.[175]

Scarcely six weeks later, the newly appointed Under-Secretary for the Colonies, Robert William Hay, wrote him a letter on 18 February 1826 under directions from Lord Bathurst. This letter, which was only discovered in 1992 by Michael Van Leeuwen, confirms Alexander's input into the development of natural history in the colony. Hay wrote that several British natural historians had requested Bathurst to organise the collection of New South Wales specimens for sending back to England. Acting upon specific instructions from Bathurst, Hay asked Macleay to collect various local natural species including a kangaroo foetus, and eggs of the echidna and platypus.[176]

There was probably some collusion over this request as the group of British natural historians included Edward Barnard and Nicholas Aylward Vigors who were friends of Macleay through the Linnean Society. Edward Barnard had worked in the Colonial Office as agent general for New South Wales and in December 1824 he had written to Alexander about housing for him in the colony.[177] It was Barnard, along with Judge Barron Field, who tried to get William appointed as 'Clerk of the Council' in New South Wales in 1825.[178] Vigors also held Alexander in high regard and in June 1825 he and Horsfield published their paper entitled *Catalogue of the New Holland Birds in the Collection of the Linnean Society*, writing in their introduction:

> the authors express their confident expectation that the deficiency of our knowledge of the habits of the Birds of Australia, will be in great measure supplied by the researches of Mr. A. Macleay during his future residence in that interesting country.[179]

On 16 September 1826, very soon after receiving the letter from Hay, Alexander replied: 'If I had been so fortunate as to have got my eldest son out here with me, I am satisfied that we could have done much in investigating the Zoology of this Country', but as the situation stood he considered that 'there is actually not a single Person in the Colony capable of performing such a job'.[180] Perhaps he still held hopes that a position would be offered, even though William, by then, was working in Cuba. Bathurst had rejected the idea of an appointment for him in New South Wales in January 1825, categorically stating: 'I am afraid that it is quite impossible for many reasons which I would state to you, to make any such Engagement in favour of your son'.[181]

A COLONIAL MUSEUM

Alexander had not underestimated the lack of suitably trained people in the colony. William Holmes, who commenced work as the Colonial Museum's

Zoologist in June 1829, accidentally shot himself dead whilst on a collecting expedition in 1831,[182] the very year that the Colonial botanist, Charles Frazer, died. Just how much input Alexander had into Holmes's appointment is unknown. When Holmes approached Macleay in 1829 in relation to a grant of land, the Colonial Secretary suggested that he delay choosing the actual location 'as he would be travelling about the Colony collecting Natural Curiosities' and would be in a position to choose the most 'advantageous' spot for himself.[183] Whilst Holmes's background as a cabinet-maker was no doubt useful for making display and storage cabinets, his knowledge of natural history was sadly lacking.[184] A salary of £130 per annum was not a very strong incentive either to attract a suitable replacement for him.[185] After Holmes died, William Galvin, an ex-convict, looked after the Museum for several years until Dr George Bennett, an 'eminent surgeon and amateur naturalist',[186] was appointed as curator and secretary in 1836.

In Alexander's reply to Hay in September 1826 he explained that he wanted to 'form a Museum of the Natural Productions of the Colony' for colonists to visit and asked if Bathurst would approve authorisation for convicts to construct a suitable building to house the collection as well as a public library. He recalled that the task of throwing 'some light' on 'interesting subjects of Natural history was no small inducement' for him to come to New South Wales and how 'for thirty years [Natural History] had been [his] favourite Pursuit'. He added that whilst he was disappointed about the lack of encouragement for natural history from the government in England, he was delighted to hear of Bathurst's interest in promoting the colony's flora and fauna. He also reminded Bathurst that if he had not used a subscription for the Linnean Society to purchase a 'large collection of Australian natural history objects' they would have ended up in the Berlin Royal Museum as the British Museum had refused them.[187] His 'competitive nationalism'[188] was even stronger because of increased interest from the French: he would have been aware that the *La Coquille* had already taken away natural history specimens when it visited the colony in January 1824. Macleay stated his case clearly:

I have felt, like most other British naturalists, that it is a disgrace to

our Country, which has more in its power than all the rest of the
world together, that which other countries are doing so much, [sic]
our Government does nothing for natural history.[189]

The letter continued: 'My intention is ... with enough leisure time ... to establish a Society for the pursuit of such Subjects, and I flatter myself that with the
Governor's patronage' such an aim would be successful. He further envisaged
a museum, as part of this Society, that would preserve specimens and duplicates, firstly for their own collection and then to be sent, in precise order, to
the Linnean Society, the British Museum, the College of Surgeons, English,
Scottish and Irish Universities and finally to the Continent of Europe. Significantly, Macleay wanted the best specimens kept in Sydney, affirming his
genuine interest and concern for the welfare and future of his newly adopted
country. He considered such a Museum 'an essential Service to Science as well
as to this Colony'.

Prior to Macleay's arrival in Sydney, the only attempt to establish a local
museum had been in 1821 by 'the colony's first scientific society',[190] the Philosophical Society of Australasia. Based in a small room within the office of
Goulburn, the Colonial Secretary, it closed down in less than twelve months
because of internal dissension amongst its members about the direction it
should take. Barron Field, who had lived in New South Wales since 1817, was
one of the founders and on his return to England in 1824 he met with Alexander to discuss future possibilities for natural history in the colony. More than
likely some of Macleay's ideas for another colonial museum came from Field's
experience with the Philosophical Society.

Van Leeuwen, in 1992, concluded that Macleay was 'the leading man of science to thus far settle in Australia' and that he 'obviously did not feel the need
to demonstrate any kind of educative function for the proposed museum',[191] as
he was more interested in the promotion of science itself. Yet while the focus
was still on maintaining a convict colony, there would not have been a great
deal of interest in natural history and just having items on display would have
been sufficiently educative for those who were interested. A letter to the editor
of the *Sydney Morning Herald* in 1843 voiced a similar opinion, stating that

whilst an individual could acquire a good collection, 'the benefit derived from his industrious and literary pursuits is limited'. A museum on the other hand was for all people as it 'opens its doors to the poor and displays to advantage the contributions of the rich'.[192] The Society that Alexander envisaged was probably along the lines of the Linnean Society with its associated research activities and publications and his nephew, William John, did become involved in the establishment of the Australian Linnean Society some years later. But in 1826, Alexander's vision for a viable society and associated museum accepted that any interest in science in the penal colony was restricted. Even a University was not established in New South Wales until 1850.

After Bathurst received Alexander's reply, on 30 March 1827 he sent word to Governor Darling that he would contribute £200 to assist in the establishment of a museum, including a building in due course, and that he had appointed a young man to be sent out to 'to collect and arrange specimens in the capacity of Zoologist'.[193] Holmes was the person who Bathurst had nominated though it was not until two years later that he arrived in Sydney to take up his new position as the colony's official Zoologist. A few weeks after making the appointment Bathurst was replaced as Secretary of State, but because of Alexander's initiative, plans had been implemented to develop a museum with government support and funding which, in the long term, proved essential for its very survival. At the same time, however, Bathurst chose to ignore Alexander's idea of establishing a scientific society.

There were already encouraging signs of increased interest in natural science in the colony by 1828. The Reverend Charles Wilton, editor of *The Australian Quarterly Journal of Theology, Literature and Science*, which was published in four volumes in 1828, wrote:

The Naturalist, the Botanist and the Geologist — what a vast field is opened and what brilliant prospects offered to the Inhabitant of Australia who will turn his attention to these pursuits. A fifth portion of the world, now, untrodden, unexploited, invites him to examine her curiosities — presents herself in forms so remarkable, so different from those of every other part of the Globe.[194]

In addition Wilton's article emphasised how useful a museum would be to cultivate the mind and refine the manners of such a small population living in seclusion in a sparsely populated country. Wilton had travelled to Australia with Holmes on the barque *Elizabeth* in April 1827,[195] and the two of them no doubt discussed natural history at some length during their voyage.

The actual location of the new Colonial Museum in 1829 is uncertain but possibly occupied the same room that the Philosophical Society had used several years earlier. It was Deas Thomson in May 1834 who suggested to Macleay that the name be changed to 'The Australian Museum'.[196] By early 1830 it was housed in a shed attached to the Judge Advocate's office in Macquarie Place, and in November 1831 moved into the old Legislative Council building in Macquarie Street.[197] In 1840 it relocated again, this time further along Macquarie Street into Thomas Mitchell's old residence, and at the end of 1841 moved once more to the new Court House in Woolloo-mooloo.[198] Finally, in 1849 the North Wing of the new building on the corner of College and William Streets was completed, work having commenced three years earlier on land that had been reserved for the government.

FIRST PRESIDENT OF THE AUSTRALIAN MUSEUM

After George Bennett took up his appointment in 1836, a Committee of Superintendence for the Museum was formed along with a sub-committee. This was the same government-appointed body that was set up simultane-ously to administer the affairs of the Botanic Garden. The first minutes of the sub-committee are dated 8 June 1836 and recorded that Alexander was appointed President and Chairman at that meeting. Following meetings were held weekly until 1838 and thereafter once a month.[199] At some meetings only two or three attended but Alexander was a regular attendee, except during 1843, and his last meeting was on 12 February 1848.

Alexander would have glad to have the 'distinguished zoologist',[200] Dr John Vaughan Thompson, on this inaugural committee. Although Thompson had just arrived in the colony, Alexander had known him for many years as he had contributed papers to the Linnean Society since 1808. George Macleay was also appointed to this Committee of Superintendence but he attended meetings infrequently between 1836 and 1848, presumably as he was so often out of town looking after the family's properties. William, too, joined after he arrived in Sydney but only attended his first meeting in late February 1848. With Alexander becoming increasingly frail, William probably considered it was time to become involved and the following year he was appointed Chairman of the Committee of Superintendence, a position he held until 1853.

On reading the minutes of these meetings it is obvious that Alexander played a major role in the development of policy. At the very first meeting it was resolved that the correspondence of the Museum 'be addressed under cover to the Colonial Secretary',[201] so that for the first six months of its existence Alexander would have known exactly what was going on. In November 1836 it was arranged, with only Alexander and Thompson present at the meeting, that 'duplicate specimens be distributed to various European and other Museums'.[202] Previously, in August, it had been directed that duplicates be sent to British Museums but the later inclusion of European and other Museums implies Alexander's input as he had initially specified such action to Bathurst when proposing to set up a colonial museum. On 30 September 1837 only three members, including Alexander, were present at a meeting which decided that the Secretary should prepare 500 copies of a catalogue to 'be printed and that tenders are to be received from the Atlas and Colonist Printing Office'.[203] Alexander's experience in preparing the Linnean Society Papers for publication would have been indispensable here. When the Reverend William Clarke was appointed as Secretary and Curator in 1841, only Alexander and Clarke were present at the meeting on 4 August 1841 which recorded his appointment. Alexander also seems to have been a prime mover behind building new premises, for on 12 September 1845 it was recorded that:

the application of the sum granted by the Legislative Council for the
erection of a Museum having been brought to the notice of the Meeting by the Honourable Mr. Macleay, the subject of a proper Site for
the building was fully discussed ... [and it was agreed that] east of the
Library ... would be very eligible.[204]

At that meeting it was decided that a deputation of three members, again
including Alexander, should meet with the Governor to gain his approval 'to
make a grant of a sufficient portion of ground in that locality'.[205] At the next
meeting, on 18 November, Alexander informed the other six members present that the Governor's response was to leave it to his successor to decide as
he was soon to leave the colony.[206] But in February 1846 such authority was
granted by Governor Gipps[207] and Alexander must have been satisfied that
the issue was at last resolved although he died before the new building was
completed.

After Bennett resigned in 1841 Clarke, who had come to the colony in 1839
to take up the position of headmaster at the King's School, Parramatta, became
the new Curator and Secretary until 1843, remaining on the Committee until
1874.[208] In late 1843 the decision was made by the Legislative Council to abolish
the position of curator because of a shortage of funds.[209] However, in the minutes of the Museum's Committee on 5 September 1846, the new honorary secretary, Robert Lynd, recorded that William Wall, who was initially appointed in
1840 as 'Collector and Preserver', had 'performed the functions of curator' since
1841, although 'the appointment had not been sanctioned nor had his salary
been increased'.[210] Finally, in 1853, the Museum Act was invoked under which
the Museum, with an annual endowment of £1,000, was to be administered by
24 trustees.[211]

After Alexander's death in July 1848, shells, minerals and coins from his
estate were offered for sale to the Museum by William Dumaresq, who was
one of the executors of the will, but no mention was made of the vast insect
collection which remained in the hands of William Macleay. The minutes of
21 October 1848 record that 'the shells and minerals were refused and a difficulty appeared to exist respecting the value of the coins and Clarke was asked

to prepare a report on their value'. At a later meeting on 24 January 1849, when George was present, the minutes recorded that the shells and minerals were to be auctioned and that William Wall was authorised to purchase amounts for the Museum not exceeding £40.

In 1997 the entrance to the library at the Australian Museum was graced by an enormous portrait of Alexander with the caption 'Sir Alexander Macleay, Founder of the Australian Museum'. This portrait, commissioned by a group of colonists in May 1837 to acknowledge their regard for Alexander, was painted in London in June 1838 by Margaret Carpenter. A letter written by the Honorary Secretary of the Museum, Reverend George Turner, in March 1849, to an unidentified recipient indicates how this portrait ended up with the Museum: 'I was *anxious* it should be placed in some suitable public institution — the property resides in the surviving subscribers of whom I am but one — they would consult I presume the wishes of Mr. Macleay's family'.[212] Presumably surviving members of Macleay's family subsequently gave permission for this portrait to be given to the Museum.

Although such an accolade would no doubt have gratified Alexander, unfortunately he never was knighted. Instead it was his son George who received this honour in England in 1869, and also his nephew William John Macleay, in Australia in 1889, for his public service and benefactions. This error has since been rectified.

The fact that Alexander seems to have added little to his own collection during his time in Australia was due not to lack of interest, but lack of time. When his father's eyesight was failing by 1840 and he could no longer mount specimens, William wrote to William Yarrell that Alexander was 'delighted with you and Professor Bell's joint Fauna. He is still attached to Natural History as ever …'.[213] In their original collection, Alexander and William labelled specimens using only a number on coloured paper but no register has ever been found.[214] Unfortunately, many specimens were re-labelled during the period 1874 to 1912 when George Masters was curator and mistakes inevitably crept in. Masters, who had previously worked at the Australian Museum, had been appointed in 1874 by William John as first curator for the collection.

THE MACLEAY MUSEUM

The Macleay private collection of specimens survived without government intervention or assistance until 1889 when it was bequeathed by William John to the University of Sydney, having been originally offered to them in 1874. It was to be housed in a building specifically constructed for the purpose to be called the Macleay Museum. The government contributed £16,000 towards its cost.[215] It had been directed in William's will that if the collection, which included his own collection as well as his father's, was ever to be disposed of, it should be given to either the University of Cambridge or the University of Sydney. After William's death in 1865, his cousin William John inherited and significantly expanded the collection, particularly after his own famous collecting expedition in the *Chevert* to New Guinea in 1875. In 1876 he built a private museum near the beach in the grounds of Elizabeth Bay House to accommodate the increasing number of specimens. By the time it was transferred to the University of Sydney, the collection consisted of approximately 1,000,000 specimens stored in 936 cabinet drawers.[216]

William John also gave an endowment of £6,000 to the University to pay for a curator for life on the understanding that the Museum should be readily accessible to students of natural history and members of the New South Wales Linnean Society.[217] In 1862 William John founded the Entomological Society of New South Wales and became its first President and he also played a major role in the establishment of the Linnean Society of New South Wales in 1874. His father-in-law, who was especially keen for the collection to stay in Sydney, was none other than Alexander's successor as Colonial Secretary, Deas Thomson, who had become Chancellor of the University of Sydney in 1865. The Macleay Museum opened to the public in 1890. The timing was fortuitous for William John died the following year.

In the 20th century conflicting opinions emerged as to what should be done with the Macleay collection and where it should be housed. As a result, in 1969, type specimens from the three Macleay insect collections were transferred for safe keeping on permanent loan to the CSIRO in Canberra because it was considered that the resources of the Macleay Museum buildings were inadequate for proper preservation and display. As many of these specimens were collected in Europe in the early 1800s and are now extinct, they are valuable records. A few years earlier, in 1965, it was suggested that the whole of the Macleay Museum should be relocated at the University of Sydney into a new building that would also house the School of Biological Sciences, to be called 'The Macleay Laboratories'.[218] In 1982 what remained of the Macleay insect collection was relocated to a small air-conditioned laboratory within the grounds of the university near the Macleay Museum so that it could be 'properly curated'.[219] It is fascinating to see there today examples from Alexander's original collection such as a kangaroo beetle holotype from Brazil and the butterfly *Papilio antinous* which is identified as an 1814 holotype.

THE MACLEAY LEGACY

Many conflicting opinions have been written about Alexander's collecting habits and the overall level of his commitment to science. Ronald Strahan, in his article 'The Dog that did not bark: Alexander Macleay and the Australian Museum', which was published in 1989, put forward the idea that Macleay was more interested in the subject as a suitable hobby for a gentleman, rather than being personally committed himself. Strahan substantiated his claim with the fact that Alexander published nothing at all in the area.[220] His idea is an echo of Lang's in 1843 about Alexander as future Speaker in the Legislative Council. He claimed that he had heard 'many complaints in Europe of the little that gentleman had done in the course of science'.[221] Yet there is ample evidence that Macleay was perfectly capable of publishing material if time had permitted. Perhaps, in his later years, he was content to leave such work to his eldest son. Kirby was especially keen for Alexander to write his own work on insects and as early as November 1817 he had suggested that 'perhaps one day & I hope soon, you will give the society a centuria insectorim it wd. be good amusement for you when at Tilbuster'.[222] Apparently Alexander had considered writing a monograph on genera including *Thynni* and *Paussus* but, much to the disappointment of Kirby, he decided against it, presumably because other concerns were more pressing with the demise of the Transport Board.[223] The obituary notice read at the anniversary meeting of the Linnean Society in London in 1849 also referred to the fact that Macleay had considered a publication:

> As a naturalist, Mr. MacLeay devoted himself almost exclusively to the study of insects ... Of this great class of animals he possessed an intimate knowledge, without, however, having published anything on the subject, although he had made preparations for a monograph of the singular genus Paussus, in which his cabinet was particularly rich.[224]

Whether or not Macleay published material is of trivial concern today when the amount of time and effort he devoted to the promotion of natural history, over 54 years in both England and Australia, is comprehended. Even Banks only ever produced a few sheets of little significance in his time,[225] although he had planned to publish, with Solander, a large book containing 700 plates, about his journey on the *Endeavour*. It was 200 years before this book was finally published in the 1980s.

Unlike many of his colleagues, Alexander remained in Australia. His devotion to natural history and his determination to actively encourage the interests of the colony for which he envisaged a promising future, were sustained by both his son William and nephew William John. Yet Alexander did not leave his collection to the Australian Museum, which would have seemed a natural progression as Banks had done this in England. Instead, William, who no doubt had discussions on the subject with his father before he died in 1848, willed it to a University. Perhaps by that time William had become disillusioned with the way in which the Museum was managed and perceived that the only alternative avenue open to maintain the collection was through a public educational institution such as the university. At least the collection as an entity would be well looked after and accessible within the precincts of a university, or so he hoped.

Alexander has been called 'The Father of Zoology' in Australia,[226] and just after his election as Speaker in the Legislative Council in August 1843, an article about him in *The Register* stated that 'Mr. M'Leay was the founder of the Australian Museum'.[227] Alexander had himself said earlier in 1843, in relation to the Australian Museum, that:

> For some time, I confess, that I felt pride in considering myself the father of that establishment; but now that it is allowed to fall into obscurity, I really am ashamed to own it as my offspring.[228]

He was referring to the fact that the position of curator had been abolished, a move which must have considerably disappointed him, and from 4 January 1843 until 1 February 1844 no minutes at all were recorded by the sub-committee. And, too, there was still no permanent building in which to house the collection. But he would have felt honoured to be called the 'Father of Zoology', especially as Kirby was known as 'the father of entomology in England'.[229]

George Bennett also acknowledged Alexander's contribution to the Colonial Museum which provided:

> An excellent nucleus for a splendid collection, particularly in a country so prolific in rare, valuable, beautiful specimens of natural productions — the commencement of the public Museum is excellent; & Science, I believe, is indebted for it to the Honourable Alexander Macleay, Colonial Secretary & may he see it attain an importance which no one can enjoy or appreciate more than himself, who has devoted the leisure moments of a long & arduous life engaged in other important occupations, to the study of The Natural Sciences.[230]

That the two major scientific bodies Macleay was associated with in England and Australia survived and flourished over time would have pleased him immensely. The Linnean Society of London is now 'the oldest extant

Sir William John Macleay (1820–1891). Alexander's nephew carried on the family tradition of collecting and was elected first President of the Linnean Society of New South Wales in 1874. Mitchell Library, State Library of New South Wales

scientific society in the world devoted to natural history' and there are Linnean Societies in Australia, France and Sweden. From its original membership of seven it has grown to 2,100 members, 'a third of whom live outside the United Kingdom' and 'the Society promotes all aspects of pure biology including anatomy, biochemistry, ecology, genetics, palaeobiology and systematics' as well as 'related disciplines in agriculture, fisheries, forestry, geology, medicine, parasitology and veterinary science, where accurate information is essential to any research'.[231] In 2001 the Australian Museum collection consisted of more than 28,000,000 specimens worth an estimated 4 billion dollars.[232]

A beautiful marble bust of William, bequeathed to the Linnean Society of London under the terms of George Macleay's will, is next to the reception area at the bottom of the stairs in their regal premises near Piccadilly. The Council now consists of twenty members including Biological Secretaries for Botany and Zoology and an Editorial Secretary.[233] In his day Alexander was all of these. Little wonder he grew tired of his responsibilities after 27 years.

The Macleay name has been recognised in the names of birds and insects in Australia and England: the blue kingfisher, *Halcyon macleayii*, the swallow-tail butterfly called *Graphium macleayanus*, a wood moth called *Endoxyla macleayi*, several beetles, a mosquito and a parasitic Wallaby Louse Fly.[234] William Leach named the *Papilio macleayanus* after Alexander and Kirby also referred to two names inspired by Macleay in his letters: *Cerapterus macleaii* in 1808[235] and *Cetonia macleayana* or *macleay* in 1817.[236] As the famous French scientist, Baron Georges Cuvier, author of *Histoire Naturelle* observed in the early 1800s: 'science depends not only on its practitioners, but also on its organisers and entrepreneurs'.[237]

seven

A PASSION
FOR
PLANTS

SURROUNDED BY GARDENERS
AND NURSERYMEN

Alexander Macleay's passion for plants gave him immense pleasure and his horticultural pursuits extended far beyond his own self-interest. Beginning with his youth in Scotland, amidst an environment rich in innovative horticultural practices, he developed a great interest in the area. Richard Clough, in his introduction to Victor Crittenden's book about New South Wales's first nurseryman, Thomas Shepherd, wrote that: 'In the second half of the eighteenth century and through the nineteenth many of the greatest botanists and horticulturists were from Scotland'.[1] In England from 1760 onwards 'a very substantial proportion [of gardeners] consisted of immigrants from Scotland' and 'a very high percentage of all gardeners to the nobility and country gentry were Scots'.[2] Building on his formative years' experience, Alexander built up a vast amount of knowledge, through his association with the Linnean Society in England over a period of 32 years, that would ultimately benefit Australia.

In 1794, only one year after joining the Linnean Society, Macleay moved to live at Stockwell near Lambeth in Surrey[3] where he was surrounded by 'gardeners and nurserymen'.[4] Gardening had become increasingly popular in the 18th century when the industry first developed,[5] and after Macleay became Secretary of the Linnean Society in 1798 new and exciting contacts were opened up. Not only did he meet and correspond regularly with international experts who were interested in plants and new plant discoveries, but he was also placed in the enviable position of being able to obtain and swap whatever plants, cuttings and seeds he desired for his own purposes. He even managed to smuggle *Liliacees*, from the lily family, out of France into England for Sir Joseph Banks during the Napoleonic wars,[6] and in 1824 he swapped insects for some precious tulips with George Milne, another Fellow of the Linnean Society.[7] New species were constantly submitted to Macleay at the Linnean Society from around the world, including the first Chinese wisteria plant which he presented for propagation in England in 1819. He had initially acquired this plant, presumably for identification purposes, from Charles Hampden Turner of Rooksnest in Surrey who had, in turn, received it from Captain Wellbank who had brought it back from Canton in 1816.[8]

THE GARDEN AT TILBUSTER

From 1806 to 1825 Macleay's city residence was at Queen's Square, Westminster. With a backyard that measured about nine metres by seven metres, it was far too small to grow many plants but at his Surrey country house from 1803 onwards, he was able to garden on a much larger scale. Tilbuster, near Godstone, was built in front of a ridge along which other grand country estates stood. It overlooked a wide expanse of rolling English countryside, with a riding track high up behind it in the woods. Swainston, in her research about Alexander, speculated that the view was so expansive, that, if Napoleon had invaded, warning beacons lit on the South Downs could have been seen from this ridge.[9]

Fanny's letters to William include numerous descriptions of the attractive garden at Tilbuster where Alexander developed his interest in growing roses and in 1817 Fanny sent a rough sketch to William updating him on the latest progress with the garden:

> I suppose you have heard from my Father that he has robbed the pad-
> dock once more in order to have rose beds on the western side of your
> rock work to correspond with those on the other side which will have
> an excellent effect from the Drawing room windows.[10]

The roses must have flourished, for a few months later Alexander sent some cuttings to Kirby's second wife[11] and in 1823 Kirby thanked him for his 'very kind and acceptable present of Roses, which arrived safe & will be a great ornament to Charlotte's Garden'.[12] Fanny's black and white drawing portrays an oval lawn in front of the house with a canal below it, presumably where the stream was located. Other sections of the garden beyond this include an abo-retum, an area for shrubs, and eastern and western rose garden beds.[13] Fanny further informed William:

> There is, now, a very good collection of hardy Plants at Tilbuster. I
> am rather surprised that you should ask how we contrive to place our
> plants, because I think you cannot have forgotten the former nakedness
> of our borders which are now very filled & consequently contain all
> that we have very charmingly, without robbing the cattle of much grass.
> Do not, therefore, allow your tender care, of them, prevent your send-
> ing us any plant worth adding to the stock for as yet we have room.[14]

An old photograph of Tilbuster, taken many years after the Macleays had left, but prior to 1850 when the house burnt down, shows a glasshouse at one end of the house and wisteria sprawling along the front verandah which

Tilbuster Lodge near Godstone in Surrey, England was Alexander's country house from 1803–1825. It was more commonly just called Tilbuster by the Macleay family.
Artist unknown. Reproduced with permission from Sarah and Tim Goad, Bletchingley

extends the length of the house.[15] Old floor brickwork from the conservatory can still be seen today. Possibly this was the greenhouse for exotic plants that Fanny mentioned in her letters. The Macleays also had an ice house near the stream on the property which was recorded by the Ice House Society.[16]

As in later years in Australia, a gardener was employed to carry out Alexander's instructions. Fanny told William in 1814 that although the gardener had got rid of the insect infestation in the greenhouse, it had become 'more like a hothouse than a greenhouse'.[17] It was at Tilbuster that Fanny developed her own love of flowers and plants and her artistic talent. She described the white tuberoses in 1815 as having 'a very delightful perfume' and was 'much pleased with the *Althaea Frutex*' that was covered with blossoms in 'the new border'.[18]

No doubt much advice and many plants for Tilbuster were obtained from William Malcolm's famous nursery which was situated at nearby Stockwell. Malcolm was a pioneer of early botanical catalogues, the first edition of which was published in 1771. Owner of a nursery in Kennington until 1788, he then moved south to 50 acres at Stockwell and the following year 'erected a handsome house built with grey stock bricks, which is most delightfully situated; on its south-east side are large hot-houses, conservatories'.[19] It was here that his son, William Malcolm the younger (1769–1835), carried on the Stockwell nursery with various partners until 1815.[20] In August of that year a Harry Malcolm came to spend several days with the family at Tilbuster. Fanny wrote to William that she intended 'if possible to become a complete gardener by learning all I can from him while he is here'.[21]

In 1801 Alexander mentioned a nurseryman named Alexander Malcolm to James Smith, in connection with the late Mr Robertson's estate of which Macleay, Malcolm and five others, had been made trustees.[22] Kirby also made reference to a Mr Malcolm in 1805 when he wrote to Alexander requesting him to obtain a cutting from an *Aloe ferox* plant for him to give to Malcolm when he next saw him.[23] And Robert Brown named a Virginian stock *Malcolmia* in honour of William Malcolm, the 'noted London nurseryman'.[24]

NEW PLANTS FOR NEW SOUTH WALES

By the time Alexander left Tilbuster for New South Wales in 1825 the garden there would have been well established. He would have been keen to take as many cuttings as possible to grow in his new garden on the other side of the world; the first wisteria introduced into Australia came from Tilbuster.[25] Quite a few specimens accompanied him on the journey out and an original notebook in the Mitchell Library, which is described as a 'Register of Plants' that were later 'received at Elizabeth Bay', has over 500 entries.[26] Wisteria tops the list of plants on page one and others include orders that were placed with nurseries such as Loddiges of Hackney before Alexander departed from England. His careful selection of plants also indicates Macleay's expertise in not only how they would travel, but also how they would adapt to a totally different environment.

Included in this list are 34 roses and numerous dahlias and chrysanthemums. The roses are especially remarkable for their diversity: five Gallicas, four Alba, six Damask, six Centifolia, one Moss, two China (Hume's Blush and Parks's Yellow), three Noisette and seven unidentified species.[27] Noisette roses were relatively new, the first having been bred in America in 1811, although there were probably others in Germany as early as 1800. They were considered suitable for a warmer climate and were therefore an excellent and innovative choice for Sydney. With such a mixture of different roses, perhaps Macleay was even hoping to breed some new varieties himself.

Alexander Macleay has been credited with introducing, within a year or two of his arrival, 46 of around 1800 plants that were included in Australia's first census of exotic species. Richard Clough has researched documentation about their origins from records in the Sydney Botanic Garden's library. He examined a plant census by another Scotsman, Charles Frazer, who had been appointed Colonial Botanist by Governor Macquarie in 1817 and was 'the first superintendent of the Sydney Botanic Garden'.[28] Compiled in late 1827 on instructions from Governor Darling, as Bathurst in London had requested regular reports on the Garden,[29] it listed all the plants that were growing in the Botanic Garden at the end of 1827. Some minor errors crept in, as Frazer would have relied on memory as to when they were first planted in the garden. Including an item on the list did not exclude the possibility that it had been in the country for a number of years beforehand, but as no records were previously available, the 1827 census has come to be seen as the first official record of exotic plants in the colony. A catalogue was prepared the following January which Darling used as the basis for reporting to England.[30]

The list was 84 pages long with approximately 30 entries per page. Each plant was given a botanical and common name along with their country of origin and the name, of the person who introduced it into Australia, and the date (where possible) of its introduction. The state of acclimatisation of each plant was also described as well as the bearing state, and category according to possible usage.

Several Chinese plants that Macleay received in 1827 arrived together, suggesting they were received from a single Chinese source, and indicating that it was he who introduced them to Australia from their country of origin.

Those listed as planted in the Gardens in 1825–26 include some Australian natives such as *Dicksonia davalloides*, which is a New South Wales tree fern that would have been either collected by Macleay or given to him, whilst others such as *Sagittaria sinensis*, the Chinese water plant with an arrow-shaped leaf, would probably have been sent to him by contacts in Asia.

The actual list of plants is fascinating in terms of its variety, country of origin and potential usage, either as an edible plant or an attractive bedding plant to add colour and beauty to a garden. The plants in the ornamental list attributed to being introduced by Alexander include:

Genus	Species	Local Name	Origin	Varieties	When
Vitis	Vunefera	Common grape		Grave & Sweet Water	1825
				Calalia Tokay	
				Black Frontignac	
				Roundberried Muscat	
				Seedling from Black	
				Prince	
				Burgundy	
				Tinta	
Olea	Oleafolia	Olive leaved olive			1825
Veronica	Scrophularinae	Speedwell	S. of Europe		1825
Cuminum	Cyminum	officinal cumin	Egypt		1825
Coriandrum	sativum	common coriander	England		1825
Anethum	adanta	sweet scented dill	England		1825
Lilium	japonicum	japon	China		1825
Calla	Aethiopica	Ethiopian Calla	Cape of Good Hope		1825
Epilobium	hirsutum	Willow Herb	Britain		1825
		Codlins & Cream			
Dianthus	sp.	Pheasant Eye	Austria		1825
	fragrans	fragrant	Austria		1825
Euphorbia	officinarum sp.	sp.			1825
Cactus	pusillus	small Indian Fig	S. America		1825
Rosa	canina	Dog rose	Britain		1826
	mobis saligna	smooth willow leaved			
	colmella				
	grandiflora sabine				
Rosa	centifolia	large Chinese	China		1827

The cactus on this list was not the first to be brought to the colony for in 1820 Alexander Berry had brought one with him, as had Chief Justice Forbes in 1824. But the inclusion of the herb cumin, as well as coriander and dill, indicated that Alexander was aware of the growing interest in Asian tastes and flavours. And the number of grape varieties confirms that he had taken up the advice given before he left England about the potential for viticulture in the colony.

The next extract is from the plants listed which were of economic use. Alexander is credited with introducing the following:

Genus	Species	Local Name	Origin	When
Pelargonium		Stork's Bill		1825
	undulatum	wax leaved	CBS	
	radiatum	ray leaved	CBS	
	roseum	rose coloured	CBS	
	olatarium	downy leaved	CBS	
	conduplicatum	curled heart leaved	CBS	
Pelargonium	*dissectum*	jagged leaved	England	1825
Camellia Japonica	*Albo plena*	double white	China	1825
Citrus	*Aurantiaceae*	long leaved Chinese orange	China	1827
		long leaved dwarf Chinese orange		
		seedling Chinese orange		
Caladium	*grandifolium*	great leaved	Canaries	1826
Dicksonia	*Davalloides*	Davalia like	NSW	1827
	Dicksonia			
Trapa	*bicornis*	water caltrops	China	1827
Edwardsia	*tomentosa*	downy Edwardsia	NSW	1827
Magnolia	*tomentosa*	slender	China	1827
	pumila	dwarf	China	1827
	fuscata	brown stalked	China	1827
Passiflora	*sp.*	Passion Flower	NSW	1827
Sagittaria	*Sinesis*	Chinese Arrowhead	China	1828
Anethum	*adanta*	sweet scented dill	England	1825[31]

Again, not all can be confidently credited to Alexander. The camellia listed was not the first one in the colony either, as others had been imported from China in 1823 and 1824. However, Alexander has also been credited with introducing the beautiful blueish-lavender flowered jacaranda into Australia which he grew at Elizabeth Bay 'from seed brought directly from South America'.[32] The *fuscata magnolia*, which is now commonly termed the port wine magnolia because of the power of its fragrance, was of such long-lasting benefit to the colony that it is still considered a prized possession in gardens today. Not so with another later introduction. Lantana, which is a native of South America, was possibly brought into Australia via India by daughter Rosa when she returned home to Sydney for a visit in 1837. By 1839 it was well established in Alexander's garden at Elizabeth Bay. Although the pink and yellow flower is undeniably pretty and dainty, the shrub on which it grows is quite the opposite. Unwieldy and unattractive, it is now classified as a noxious weed in Australia. It still grows on the entrance road to Innes House where it completely covered the ruins in 1950, reaching twelve metres high in some places.[33] Even by 1848 Margaret and Archibald's young niece, Annabella, could write: 'we have been busy tying up the Lantana Bower, but so many young plants have sprung up they quite spoil the place, and are likely to become a nuisance'.[34] Her predictions came true, not only at Innes House, but throughout Australia on an astounding scale!

COLONIAL GARDENING

With his future garden in mind, Alexander not only brought plants with him from England but at the Cape of Good Hope en route to Australia he also enlisted the services of a full-time gardener, 28-year-old Scot, Robert Henderson.[35] Henderson was already known to the family in Wick, as the sister-in-law of John Macleay was married to Captain David Henderson. Crittenden states that Henderson's family lived near the Shepherds in Scotland for many years and suggests that Robert may even originally have worked as a gardener in England with Thomas Shepherd,[36] his future father-in-law and founder of New South Wales's first nursery. 'His whole time being occupied with Government business', Alexander delegated to Henderson the development of the grand garden he envisaged at Elizabeth Bay[37] and in 1827 he built a cottage for him in the grounds so that he could supervise the project. At times there were twenty convicts working in the garden[38] and it was sensible and practical to have the head gardener installed as caretaker to guard the premises, especially at night.

It was no easy task to establish a new garden in the colony and trial and error was often the only way as there was little practical information available. Prior to 1825 only two books of any significance had been published with references to gardening in Australia. George Howe's *New South Wales Pocket Almanack and Rememberancer for the year of our Lord and Saviour 1806* included a twelve-page gardening section entitled 'Observations on Gardening' and Andrew Bent's *The Van Diemen's Land Pocket Almanack,* published in Hobart in 1824, included eleven pages on colonial gardening.[39] In the mid-1820s ornamental gardening, as opposed to vegetable gardening, was still considered an expensive hobby. Fanny succinctly summed up the situation to William:

> The people here seem scarcely to have thought of a garden, but as
> a place where rubbish, cabbages & a few miserable attempts at an
> onion might vie with each other in beauty — Those who are fortunate
> enough to have a purple or red Stock they are said to possess a beauti-
> ful garden.[40]

The Macleay's garden of over 40 plants at their residence in Bridge Street was resurrected, according to Fanny in 1826, from 'a neglected rubbish hole' and it was considered 'the neatest about Sydney'.[41] Flower plantings for their first small garden included iris, lupins, boronia, pelargoniums, antirrhinum, epacris, ericas, daffodils (*Narcissus*), chinese roses, anemones, hyacinthus, gladiolus and dianthus.[42] Probably the dianthus and pelargonium were from their own garden at Tilbuster as examples of these are listed among the plants that Alexander presented to the Botanic Garden. How colourful and homely these flowers must have appeared amongst the drab surroundings. In October 1826 the Macleays were granted permission to build a verandah onto their house[43] which not only offered respite from the scorching summer sun but also provided a framework for climbing plants like roses and *Ipomoea* (Morning Glory).[44] But even by 1832 it was observed that colonial gardens restricted their plantings to the ubiquitous 'blooming rose, as well as the pink, the stock, and other European flowers', with some vegetables.[45] Gardens filled with flowers would have been a luxury when most of the population were struggling just to survive with only limited supplies of water and plant stock.

When work began on the garden at Elizabeth Bay in 1826, long before building of the house there commenced in 1835, Fanny related to William that 'no less than ten prisoners [are] in our service just now — eight of whom are trenching the spot intended for a garden at our pretty little Bay'.[46] Under Henderson's supervision an enormous amount of work was undertaken and other colonists followed these unprecedented developments with great interest. By 1829 Edward Deas Thomson had become involved in developing the grounds as the Engineer. Fanny was impressed with his 'infinity of good taste'. She informed William that Thomson was taking 'an astonishing degree of interest in the improvement of the place', and that he was 'a great favourite' of hers 'because in many things he resembles you'.[47] How Fanny must have missed her beloved brother, especially when Thomson reminded her so much of him.

Fanny and her father would have spent much time identifying all the new plants with an added bonus that Fanny could skilfully draw them. Her eye for detail was excellent and, as many of the plants were native to the Sydney region, they provide a useful historical record of what was growing in the colony in the 1830s. This is the sort of work that she would have sent to Robert Brown in England for publication, although more often Fanny wanted the drawings sent on to William for feedback on her progress.

Many native plants growing around Sydney make up the magnificent composition that it is believed Fanny painted in 1830. They include pale pink *Hibiscus mutabilis* and Macartney Rose (*Rosa bracteata*) from China, *Brumonia australis*, leaf of the Lillypilly tree (*Acmena smithii* or a*ustralis*), waratah, *Hibiscus diversifolius* (yellow), Flannel Flower (*Telopea*), red Christmas Bells (Blandfordia), a pale blue flower called *Conospermum ericifolium*, a trailing yellow flower called *Billardiera scandens*, the small blue fringe flower (*Thysanotus tuberosus*), yellow *Hibbertia scandens*, *Pandorea Jasminiodes* with white flowers and pink centres, and a diminutive blue flower called *Dianella laevis,* all from the Sydney region, lavender morning glory from Asia, red Flanders or Field Poppy from England, *Gardenia globosa* from South Africa and a strand of blowfly grass which was an introduced weed. Her picture even includes in the bottom left-hand corner a superb blue wren which is one of Sydney's beautiful, dainty native birds.[48] Five of these native plants of Australia did not appear in the indexes for *Curtis's Botanical Magazine* or the *Botanical Register* until after 1836.[49]

Throughout his life in Australia Alexander kept abreast of the latest developments in the plant and animal worlds. Although he had left the Linnean Society far behind in England, he maintained regular contact with numerous acquaintances there who kept him up to date. Despite the time delay in reaching him, such correspondence was essential for new information and ideas. Alexander's personal library also provided an extensive reference source and visitors commented on the reading material that was always readily available in his house. In July 1827 Alexander's name was listed, along with only seven others in the colony, as subscribers to a quarterly magazine entitled *The British Farmer's Magazine*. Released for the first time in November 1826, this new publication covered subjects such as the corn laws, and agriculture and rural affairs.[50] When Baron von Hügel visited the Macleays in 1834 he recorded in his diary that there were many newspapers and literary journals on the table in the drawing room.[51]

In 1827, the skilled Scottish-born horticulturist and landscaper, John Claudius Loudon, asked Macleay to find an Australian correspondent for his famous *Gardener's Magazine*.[52] The association between the two men had been long-standing for it was Alexander who had nominated Loudon for membership of the Linnean Society in 1806.[53] After John married Jane in 1828, the Loudons wrote many gardening books which were reprinted in the ensuing decades. Amongst their most famous titles were *Encyclopedia of Gardening* first published in 1822, *Encyclopedia of Agriculture* (1825), *Gardener's Magazine* (1826–1843), *Suburban Gardener* (1838), *Villa Companion* (1838), and *Suburban Horticulturist* (1842). In the 1869 edition of the *Encyclopedia of Gardening*, the garden at Elizabeth Bay was referred to, using a quote from Thomas Shepherd from the 1830s, as a 'notable antipodean' garden.[54]

Even though Loudon died in 1843 and Alexander in 1848, the garden was still considered to be one of the best in Australia.

Von Hügel made a further comment on his visit to the Macleays in 1834. He wrote that Alexander could:

with full reason be described as an intelligent man much versed in Natural History, and I gained knowledge that was rare and new to me in some aspects of this difficult science. Botany is the science with which he seems least familiar and yet he has a great interest in it, and his garden at Elizabeth Bay is said to be the best in the colony.[55]

The Baron reciprocated Alexander's hospitality by giving him some special plants from Western Australia. Always keen to expand his collection, Alexander would have been overjoyed to receive these plants from his visitor, many of which he had probably never seen before. Von Hügel also noted the importance of Henderson's role five years into the project. Although impressed with the position of the garden, he thought the terrain far from suitable:

The garden site is well chosen and some interesting plants are being skilfully cultivated and propagated, only the whole layout is too patchy; not so much because of its unfinished state as because the difficulty of creating a garden on this rocky hillside outweighed the gardener's talent. The splendid *Acrostichum* from Moreton Bay and several New Zealand plants were noteworthy. Pawpaw, guava and many plants from India were flourishing. It was a pleasure to be able to enrich Mr. Macleay's collection with some of the finest plants of Western Australia … His gardener Henderson seems to be a capable man who lives only for his garden. I enjoyed some excellent grapes quite comparable with Europe's finest, but not so the peaches, all that I tasted being hard and bitter, and all from standard trees.[56]

Henderson's role in the development of the garden became such an important one that his opinions were sought elsewhere in the colony. In 1831 it was reported that several gentlemen in the colony were researching the 'selection of situations for future vineyards' as the grapes in the colony had recently

Banksia spinulosa *var.* collina *is a particularly attractive native plant that would have fascinated Macleay.*
Photo: Derelie Cherry

Carl von Linnaeus (1707–1778) in wedding dress. Followers of natural history in the 19th century were keen to own a portrait of Linnaeus. Alexander Macleay's painting showed Linnaeus in the Lapland Dress he wore when collecting specimens. In both portraits Linnaeus holds a sprig of his favourite plant, Linnaea borealis. *1906 copy by J. Hagen of J. Scheffel's portrait, 1739. By permission of* the Linnean Society of London

Sir James Smith (1759–1828), first President of the Linnean Society, is holding a book showing illustrations of the herb Smithia sensitivea *and the fern* Woodwardia radicans. *Artist John Rising, 1793. By permission of the Linnean Society of London*

< *Mallee ringneck,* Barnardius zonarius barnardi *(Vigors & Horsfield, 1827). These parrots vary considerably in colour.* Artist John William Lewin, (1770–1819), 1819. The National Library of Australia

^ *Barron Field (1786–1846). Appointed as judge in New South Wales in 1817, Field helped found Australia's first museum in 1821, although it lasted less than a year. Returning to England in 1824 he encouraged Alexander to work towards the establishment of another colonial museum.* Artist Richard Read, c. 1820. State Library of New South Wales

^ *Several pots of* Macleaya cordata *still grow at Brownlow Hill. The leaf shape is particularly attractive although the small white flower is insignificant.* Reproduced with permission from Joan Downes, Brownlow Hill. Photo: Derelie Cherry

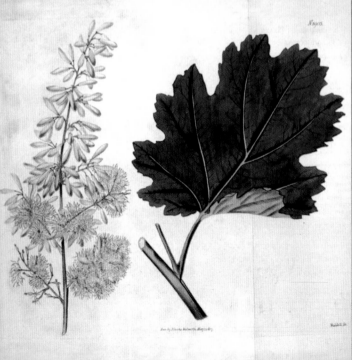

< Macleaya cordata. *Plume poppy that Robert Brown named after his friend Alexander Macleay in 1826.* Lithograph from Curtis's Botanical Magazine, May 1817

Blue Mountain parrots from Sydney. Already well known in England for his landscape paintings, Glover arrived in Tasmania in 1831 where he became even more famous. The Macleays would have been very familiar with his work. Artist John Glover (1767–1849), 1832. The National Library of Australia.

Sir William Jackson Hooker (1785–1865). Alexander's old friend from the Linnean Society, was Director of Kew Gardens for 24 years from 1841. Artist Spinidione Gambardella (1815–1886?). By permission of the Linnean Society of London

The dormant bulbs of dahlias would have been easy to transport out to Australia. Originally from Mexico, dahlias were a relatively recent introduction into Europe at the end of the 18th century where Alexander would have been among the first to grow them. Photo: Derelie Cherry

Looking towards Godstone from the original site of Tilbuster. Photo: Derelie Cherry

Still Life with Flowers of Australia and the Southern Hemisphere. Artist Frances Leonora 'Fanny' Maclea
c. 1830, watercolour. Private collection. Reproduction of copy held by Elizabeth Bay House, courtesy Historic

Plans for Elizabeth Bay House gates by the colonial architect John Verge, 1833. Mitchell Library, State Library of New South Wales

Sweetly scented stocks have been favourites in English gardens since the 16th century. Relatively hardy with long-lasting perfumed blooms, they were a popular choice for colonists, and the Macleays would certainly have included this flower in their garden. Photo: Derelie Cherry

Wisteria, first brought to Sydney by Alexander Macleay, has become one of Australia's most popular climbing plants. This splendid pergola is in the grounds of Derelie and Bob Cherry's garden called 'Paradise' located at Kulnura near Sydney. Each September wisteria adorns the front verandah

Old Government House and part of the town of Sydney, New South Wales, 1828. Even at Government House there were few ornamental plants. Alexander Macleay's Elizabeth Bay House garden rapidly became the best example in the colony of how the landscape could be transformed through careful planning and planting. Artist Augustus Earle, (1793–1838). The National Library of Australia

Gigantic clumps of bamboo still surround the ruins of Innes House near Port Macquarie. Planted not only to shelter the house from the elements, bamboo was used for many purposes, including the construction of gondoliers that once floated on Lake Innes. Reproduced with permission from the National Parks & Wildlife Service. Photo: Derelie Cherry

Brownlow Hill, 1836. Fanny thought this country farm the prettiest in the colony and Martens's early sketch portrays how attractive the setting was. Artist Conrad Martens (1801–1878). Mitchell Library, State Library of New South Wales

This dripstone made of sandstone was used to purify water. Reproduced with permission from Joan Downes, Brownlow Hill. Photo: Derelie Cherry

The pretty flower of Lantana, possibly brought to Australia by Alexander's daughter Rosa, belies its invasive growth habit.
Photo: Derelie Cherry

Le Vésuve is a China Rose that was bred in France in 1825. In Australia's mild climate, China Roses flower for up to ten months of the year, making them an excellent choice for the Macleays to bring out to Sydney. Photo: Derelie Cherry

Behind the entrance to Brownlow Hill some of the original urns still adorn the edge of a lake. Reproduced with permission from Joan Downes, Brownlow Hill. Photo: Derelie Cherry

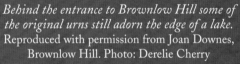

suffered severe blight. The three named were 'Mr. Frazer, the Colonial Botanist, Mr. Henderson, principal gardener of the Honorable, Mr. M'Leay, [and] Mr. Shepherd of the Darling Nursery'.[57] Henderson died on 18 February 1865 and an obituary which appeared in the *Horticultural Magazine and Gardener's Calendar of NSW* in 1865 acknowledged that he had 'superintended the laying out' of the gardens at Elizabeth Bay as well as those at Brownlow Hill, Macleay's country residence.[58] Coincidentally he died just three weeks after William and was buried only a few yards away from the Macleay vault in the Camperdown cemetery which is now in the Sydney suburb of Newtown. Macleay's gardens during the first challenging decade were in reliable hands, although Henderson left his employment at Elizabeth Bay in 1836 before the house was finished.

In 1831 Henderson married Thomas Shepherd's daughter from his first marriage, Elizabeth Joslyn Shepherd. After Shepherd's death in 1835, Henderson, who was one of three trustees of the estate, helped Shepherd's widow, Jane (born a Henderson, she may have been Robert Henderson's cousin[59]) and her two sons run the nursery, finally relinquishing his trusteeship in 1853. In the late 1830s Henderson also established his own nursery called 'Camellia Grove' in Erskineville Lane, Newtown, and by 1841 he lived on the premises with his family.[60]

THOMAS SHEPHERD

In 1827 Thomas Shepherd, who was yet another Scotsman with a passion for plants, arrived in Sydney. He quickly became acquainted with Alexander's mammoth gardening efforts at Elizabeth Bay and his interest and encouragement would have inspired the Colonial Secretary. For the previous eighteen months Thomas Shepherd had been employed as agricultural superintendent for the New Zealand Company which had unsuccessfully tried to propagate flax in that country. Subsequently he sailed for Australia,[61] and opened Australia's first nursery, named the 'Darling Nursery', on 12 February 1827 with the help of Governor Darling. It was located on 28 acres of land in the area of Sydney now within the suburb of Chippendale.

Born in Fifeshire, Scotland in 1776, Shepherd had studied under the well-known landscaper, Thomas White,[62] and had owned a nursery at Hackney for twenty years from which he designed 'nearly a hundred parks, pleasure grounds, and gardens in the neighbourhood of London and also in several counties of England'.[63] Shepherd died aged 56 on 30 August 1835, but by that time, he had written a series of lectures, four on horticulture and seven on landscape gardening. The horticultural lectures, entitled *Lectures on the horticulture of New South Wales delivered at the Mechanics School of Arts, Sydney*, were published in 1835 by William McGarvie who had sold his share as one of the founders of the *Sydney Herald* in 1831 to set up a stationery business.[64] This volume of lectures was 80 pages long and presented in a paper wrapper. The landscape lectures, only one of which was delivered in public before the author's death, were published in 1836 by the same printer.

Shepherd's lectures were the first published books solely devoted to gardening in Australia. The colonists now had access to practical relevant information. The *Sydney Monitor* advertised on 4 March 1835 that the horticulture lectures contained 'some very useful information' and were 'a work which every person in the colony, who has a garden or orchard, should purchase'.[65] Shepherd was especially keen on integrating imported species with native vegetation rather than entirely destroying the native plants as many previous settlers had done. He considered Macleay's garden at Elizabeth Bay a wonderful example of how the two could be successfully grown together and stated that from the beginning, the owner 'never suffered a tree of any kind to be destroyed, until he saw distinctly the necessity for doing so'.[66]

In his 1835 journal, Dr Lhotsky described some of the magnificent native trees that had been left on the property:

> the immense trunks of gum-trees … some of these giants (for instant, in Mr. M'Leay's garden at Elizabeth Bay) measure from six to seven feet in diameter; a dimension like to which I found none others even approaching in my whole tour from Sydney to Pass Britannia (the latter place about forty miles from Bass's Straits.)[67]

In direct contrast was the 'uncommonly ugly sight on a large scale' of Sir John Jamison's house, Regentville, near Penrith, which was described by von Hügel in 1834 as 'looking like a hospital sitting on its hill covered in tree-stumps'.[68] But von Hügel did not appreciate that the scene he gazed upon was because Jamison had been experimenting in extirpating tree roots for some years. In 1830 he had even won a gold award for his successful efforts. Dymphna Clark's article on von Hügel and the Macleays added a note in brackets after her translation from the original journal in German, stating that this 'unflattering account of the Regentville mansion ... seems to have been erased from contemporary pictures of the house'.[69]

All of Shepherd's lectures are scattered with examples and descriptions from two of the most extensive private gardens in Sydney at that time: Macleay's at Elizabeth Bay and Dr James Bowman's surrounding his house named 'Lynd-hurst' which was at Glebe.[70] Bowman, a naval surgeon, married Elizabeth, daughter of John Macarthur, and as his brother-in-law William Macarthur supplied Shepherd with many plants, no doubt he also helped stock the garden at Glebe.

After Shepherd's death, copies of his lectures on landscaping were given to Alexander Macleay, Thomas Barker and 'other gentlemen of skill in Horticulture, to ascertain the propriety of their publication'.[71] The resulting publication, entitled *Lectures on landscape gardening in Australia*, was 95 pages long and also released in a paper wrapper. It was Australia's first book on landscape gardening and it was dedicated to Alexander Macleay.

This dedication was written by the Reverend John McGarvie, brother of William McGarvie, its printer-cum-publisher. John, another Scotsman from Glasgow, had been appointed a trustee of Shepherd's estate along with Robert Henderson and Thomas Barker.[72] He wrote:

> ... it was Mr. Shepherd's ardent desire to dedicate these Lectures to
> you, in admiration of your consummate skill, knowledge, and zeal,
> in Horticultural pursuits. Your high character, long residence in the
> Colony, unwearied efforts to promote its interests, and your extensive
> and successful improvements in Landscape Gardening, independent of

the profound Botanical attainments of yourself and family, will ensure
the favourable reception of these Lectures with the Colonists since it
were difficult to find a more competent judge of their merits or a more
sincere friend to their lamented Author.[73]

McGarvie also pointed out that Alexander had been instrumental in helping Shepherd establish his nursery by importing 'every rare & costly Botanical
production — from all quarters of the world'.[74] Shepherd had collected stock
since 1827 and, referring also to William Macarthur of Camden, wrote that:

> Mr. Alexander Macleay, of Elizabeth Bay, was also a benefactor in
> supplying me with numerous species and varieties of fruit, ornamental
> trees, and flower-roots; and it is to these two gentlemen that the early
> settlers were principally indebted for the numerous varieties of fruit
> and other trees raised in those days.[75]

Even the *Sydney Herald* acknowledged this dedication, announcing that
Macleay's 'botanical acquirements, and profound knowledge of landscape
gardening, were the subjects of his [Shepherd's] esteem and praise'.[76] According to Shepherd, 'the nature of the whole design of the improvements on the
ground' at Elizabeth Bay was 'so correct according to the principles of Landscape Gardening', that, even if 'one had studied for a century', a better example
could not be found.[77]

THE GARDEN AT
ELIZABETH BAY

Shepherd's lectures described the garden at Elizabeth Bay in precise detail,
starting with the physical location where ten acres had been cleared and the
remaining land left covered with rocks and scrub. He mentioned that a lawn
had been laid out in front of the position selected for the house and that the
site itself afforded magnificent views of the harbour. Rocks were dug out,

hollows filled up, and approaches made, including a road about a mile long, that ran through the property. There was a shrubbery near the house which was 'furnished with choice trees and plants from England, China, the Mauritius, the East Indies, North and South America, and from Moreton Bay, Norfolk Island, the Cape of Good Hope and other places. In a few years, therefore, the beauties of Elizabeth Bay will appear unrivalled'.[78] In addition, Shepherd described 'rustic chairs and rustic caves' and a carriage road that led to a river, 'where a convenient wharf has been constructed for enjoying marine excursions'.

The grotto which once formed part of this extensive garden still exists. Inscribed in the rear wall is the date 1835, the year in which the first stone was laid for Elizabeth Bay House. It is an enchanting cave cut into the cliff face and inside it seating is carved out of the natural rock; ferns probably once grew there. Legend has it that a statue of a fairy once resided there, possibly the elusive fairy at the bottom of the garden. With a vista straight out to the harbour, one can contemplate what a beautiful and quiet retreat this would have been in the early days of the colony. A flat square area along from the grotto at the end nearest the house was possibly a landing area for visitors to alight from their carriage and walk to this magical nook. Nearby, a low wall that curves up along the path is reminiscent of the one described by Shepherd that was immediately in front of the house and led down to the water. With decorative 'scroll work' it formed 'an elegant sweep', and was 'bordered by a broad gravel walk: The ground outside of this wall towards the bay falls abruptly down a slope …'[79]

What a charming picture Shepherd painted in words:

Crossing the coach-road you enter through a lattice-work bower, covered with the passion flower, into the botanic garden, laid out in beds and borders of exotic flowers, with elegant sweeping walks and bowers of lattice-work. These are tastefully arranged, imitating Nature in her loveliest form, and creating sensations of exquisite delight in the mind. In walking among these lovely trees, you view on the one side an amphitheatre of lofty woods; and on the other you view a large expanse of water with ships, small vessels, and boats, passing up and down the harbour. The kitchen garden, pits for producing pine apples without fire heat, gardener's cottage, vineyards and terraces sloping to the north, sheltered from the south, and bearing abundance of grapes, follow in succession, and require no particular description.[80]

Every component of fashionable landscape gardening had been incorporated into this extensive garden. Fanny proudly informed William in 1833 that 'The pleasure grounds are really beautiful and the place is considered quite the Lion of Sydney'.[81] With 'turretted stables, cottages, a rustic bridge, terrace walls and grottoes',[82] it was becoming the show-piece of colonial society. With Elizabeth Bay in mind, perhaps, Shepherd wrote prophetically about the future of Sydney:

> I picture [in my] imagination the time when all the land on each side
> of this splendid river, together with its branches and bays, will ... and
> that at no distant date — be ornamented with beautiful marine villas
> and cottages at short distances from each other, forming most pleasing
> parts of the landscape.[83]

It was fortunate that this son of a poor Scottish gardener chose to come to Australia as the next book on landscape gardening in the country was not published for over a century.[84]

In addition to the notebook of plants received at Elizabeth Bay in the Mitchell Library, there is also a seed notebook, listing 3806 seeds which were received at Elizabeth Bay during the period 1836 to 1853.[85] Richard Clough has transcribed this material, too, and wonders why these seed lists only commenced in 1836, the year that Henderson left Elizabeth Bay. Many of these lists were very long; for example, 289 seeds were received from one supplier. It is more than likely that Macleay passed some of these seeds on to friends and the Botanic Garden. Clough hypothesises that perhaps Macleay, in his capacity as a member of the committee formed in 1836 to superintend the Botanic Garden, began to act as a 'post office' because the same plants and seeds arrived each year from the same sources such as Norfolk Island.[86] In his role as Secretary of the Linnean Society in London, Alexander was responsible for a similar distribution of plants and seeds to his international network of contacts. Through the introduction and dispersal of new plants, Alexander was also attempting to achieve his own desire, expressed in 1827, 'to cultivate every plant' that he could obtain.[87]

In 1831 the *Sydney Gazette* noted that the area around Macleay's property, known as Woolloomooloo Hill, was:

> now traversed by an elegant carriage road and picturesque walks,
> decked with respectable mansions, clothed with gardens, and bidding
> for to become the Richmond or the Kensington of the Australian
> metropolis. That these rapid improvements were originated by the
> proprietor of Elizabeth Bay cannot be doubted.[88]

By 1837 it was generally acknowledged that the garden at Elizabeth Bay, being the first to be established in the area, had favourably influenced the growth of ornamental gardening in the surrounding district even if, as the *Sydney Monitor* pointed out, the work had been carried out with mainly convict labour.[89] Such a condescending remark could only have come from the *Sydney Monitor*, but Macleay was fortunate to have the use of convicts to make his impressive garden.

VISITORS TO THE GARDEN

Other visitors recorded their favourable impressions of Alexander's garden. James Backhouse, the Quaker missionary, on a visit to the colony and Elizabeth Bay in 1835 wrote:

> We walked to Elizabeth Bay, and met the Colonial Secretary, at his
> beautiful garden, which is formed on a rocky slope, on the margin of
> Port Jackson, of which it commands a fine view. — Here are cultivated,
> specimens of many of the interesting trees and shrubs, of this Colony,

^ *Charming grotto in the grounds of Elizabeth Bay House.* Photo: Derelie Cherry
ˇ *The date 1835 inscribed on the back wall inside the grotto.* Photo: Derelie Cherry

> *On 13 March 1835 (Mrs Macleay's birthday), the foundation stone for Elizabeth Bay House was laid.*
Four years later the family moved in. Romantic stone steps lead down to the grotto. Photo: Derelie Cherry

along with others from various parts of the world, intermixed with some growing in their native localities. Among the last, is a fine old Rusty-leaved Fig tree, *Ficus ferruginea*, which is an evergreen, and has laurel-like leaves. A noble specimen of *Acrosticum grande*, a fern of very remarkable structure, from Moreton Bay, is attached to a log of wood, and secured by a chain to a limb of this Fig tree. The walks at this place are judiciously accommodated to the inequalities of the sinuous bay, and are continued round a point covered with native bush. Peaches are ripe in the open ground in abundance, and liberty to partake of them freely, was kindly given, by the open-hearted proprietor.[90]

Backhouse had a nursery in York and was very interested in the local flora during his Australian visit,[91] as evidenced by his article 'Indiginous Plants of Van Diemen's Land' which was published in *Ross's Almanack* in 1835. In 1838 Allan Cunningham, who for a brief period was Colonial Botanist, described the silky oak trees at the Botanic Garden and Elizabeth Bay: 'How fine *Grevillea robusta* (forty feet high) is at this time [in the Botanic Garden], and at Mr. Macleay's at Elizabeth Bay, it is a mass of orange blossoms.'[92]

The merchant Alexander Brodie Spark described a happy day in 1838 when he and some friends:

> paid a visit to Mr Mc Leay's house and grounds at Elizabeth Bay. We found the old gentleman there, and though he is now at least 72 he walked over the whole of his beautiful building from the roof to the cellar, and afterwards made the circuit of his garden with us, delighted in having the opportunity of naming the rare and beautiful plants which everywhere ornament the grounds ...[93]

In 1841 the famous British botanist and explorer, Dr Joseph Dalton Hooker, visited Elizabeth Bay and reflected that:

> A long visit to Macleay's gardens proved it to be a botanist's paradise ... My surprise was unbounded at the natural beauties of the spot, the inimitable taste with which the grounds were laid out, and the number and rarity of the plants.[94]

Acrostichum grande *(Elkhorn fern), Elizabeth Bay, New South Wales.*
From Charles Wilkes, *Narrative of the United States Exploring Expedition during the Years 1838 – 1842* (Philadelphia, 1845). Artist Titian Ramsay Peale (1799–1885), 1839, engraver Spittall. Mitchell Library, State Library of New South Wales

Joseph's father, Sir William Hooker, who became Director of Kew Gardens in 1841, was 'a very old and particular friend'[95] of Alexander's and had become interested in mosses since joining the Linnean Society around 1806.[96] When Joseph visited Australia in 1841–42, he declared that 'McLeay has promised to collect for me in New Holland, and knowing him as we do, when one thinks that hardly a dozen mosses have been described from that vast country, there can be no bounds to novelties he may fall in with'.[97] In 1855 Joseph worked as Assistant Director with his father at Kew Gardens, and after William's death in 1865, he became Director himself until 1885 and, also like his father, was knighted for his services to horticulture.

Joseph Hooker also recorded in his 1841 journal that 'beyond the bay' there was 'a rocky precipice christened Sunium, on which it is the intention to build a Temple'.[98] This is believed to refer to the bathing house which was to be constructed at Rushcutter's Bay, with the main building featured in the design sketch 'loosely modelled on the Athenian Tower of the Winds'.[99] Probably it was to be the grandest bathing house in the colony but it was never actually built, presumably because of the cost involved.

Another reference to Elizabeth Bay as paradise was made in 1834 by George Bennett. His observations were perceptive:

> This spot, naturally of the most sterile description, has been rendered, at a great expense and perseverance, in some degree productive as a nursery for rare trees, shrubs, and plants, from all parts of the world. We were much gratified with the valuable and rare specimens the garden contained, and surprised that a spot possessed of no natural advantages should have been rendered, comparatively, a little paradise.[100]

One of the most enchanting of all descriptions about the garden was written around 1843 by Georgina Lowe, first wife of barrister Robert Lowe, who lived in Sydney from 1842 to 1849. She described it as:

> one of the most perfect places I ever saw in my life belonging to Mr. Macleay ... In this garden are the plants of every climate — flowers

and trees from Rio, the West Indies, the East Indies, China, and even England. The bulbs from the Cape are splendid and, unless you could see them, you would not believe how beautiful the roses are here. The orange-trees, lemons, citrons, guavas, are immense, and the pomegranate is now in full flower. Mr. Macleay has also an immense collection of plants from New Zealand.[101]

Georgina was an enthusiastic gardener and an accomplished watercolour artist. When she and her husband moved to a stone house at 'Cugee' (later known as Bronte House) in 1845, she landscaped the grounds which included an orchard, a kitchen garden and a 'picturesque grotto with a small waterfall, a rosery, [sic] [and] a lover's walk'.[102] Robert Lowe's friendship with the Macleays developed whilst he lived in Australia.

Previously a soldier who later became an author, Godfrey Mundy lived in Sydney between 1846 and 1851. In the book published in 1852 about his travels he wrote: 'Elizabeth Bay comprises, beyond compare, the finest house and grounds that I am acquainted with in Australia'. He also mentioned a 'splendid avenue of orange trees, twelve or fourteen feet high and a quarter of a mile in length'. These trees, planted possibly up to twenty years before, would have made a stunning display and provided an abundance of fruit. Mundy observed that the garden had been designed so 'as to command perfect privacy almost within hearing of the hum of Sydney and its 50,000 citizens'.[103] If he had still been alive, how gratified Alexander would have been to read such compliments about the garden he had created on the shores of Sydney Harbour.

BROWNLOW HILL

The Macleay family's country estate at Brownlow Hill near Camden also had a much-admired garden. In addition to the farm, the garden produced 'Oranges, Apples, Loquats, Pears, Plums, Cherries, Figs, Mulberries, Medlars, Raspberries, Strawberries, and Gooseberries, and … Roses are in great profusion'.[104]

Although the appearance of the surrounding landscape has changed dramatically, the cottage at Brownlow Hill still stands on its small hill. The overall original layout and design of the garden remains, too, with a grand driveway leading up to the house which is now overhung with splendid old trees. On the left of the driveway, not far inside the entrance gates, a pretty scene is created by a lake with urns set on the surrounding stone walls. On the opposite side of the lake, some distance from the house, handsome brick stables stand in solitary splendour. Several original features in the garden are directly linked to the Macleays. A sundial inscribed with the words 'George Macleay 1836' is positioned in the middle of the rear lawn and near the back door, adjacent to the cellar entrance, is a sandstone dripstone which was much sought after in the 1830s because it was used to purify water. The property has been preserved with these historic features and buildings by descendants of Jeremiah Downes, who leased the house from George Macleay in 1858 and finally purchased it in 1875. They reside there to this day.

Like Elizabeth Bay, Brownlow Hill was acclaimed for its beauty. When Charles Sturt and his new wife returned to Australia from England in 1835, they reported that the Macleays welcomed them 'most warmly to their paradise of Brownlow Hill'.[105] That same year Fanny proudly informed William that it 'was said to be the prettiest farm in the colony',[106] and even Baron von Hügel acknowledged in 1834 that it 'truly has no equal in New South Wales for cleanliness and orderliness'.[107]

THE SYDNEY
BOTANIC GARDEN

During the 22 years Alexander resided in the colony, he was also actively involved with changes to the Botanic Garden which had been established in 1816 under Governor Macquarie. The colony's first botanist, Charles Frazer, had displayed considerable ability in assisting with the original design. Initially he reported directly to the Governor but from 1821 until 1856 he and his successors reported to the Colonial Secretary. Only a few months after his arrival, Alexander wrote to Hay suggesting that 'a Systematic Arrangement of all our Native Plants' be introduced as he was disappointed to find a lack of indigenous flora in the Garden.[108]

The role of Botanic Gardens throughout the world at that time was also undergoing changes. Sir Joseph Banks, in his capacity as 'de facto' Director of the Royal Botanic Gardens at Kew, had encouraged the introduction of new and useful plants.[109] This trend, incorporating a more scientific approach as well as advocating participation in Botanic Gardens by all sections of the community, rather than as previously 'an appendage to a college or a university',[110] ultimately impacted upon the Botanic Garden in New South Wales. Although it was still a penal colony under the authority of the Governor, there was room to incorporate changes, and a major step was taken when the garden was opened to the public for the first time in 1831. Previously the Botanic Garden had been the main supplier of plants for most gardens in the colony, but that changed with the development of private enterprises like the Darling Nursery.

Yet the *Sydney Herald* voiced its opposition in 1835 claiming that 'A Botanical Establishment, under the auspices of Government, should supply the Colonists free of expense, with ornamental plants and useful agricultural seeds, from all parts of the world'.[111] Furthermore, with the 'recent introduction of nurserymen and gardeners' the public were worse off as they now had to pay for their stock! George Bennett, in 1834, stressed the importance of new plants being grown in the Botanic Garden. He stated that 'exotics are almost entirely confined to the gardens of a few intelligent settlers' and that if the Botanic Garden grew them they would be 'estimable either for timber, fruits, flowers, or dyes, and thus added to the resources of the colony'.[112]

ALLAN CUNNINGHAM

After the unexpected death of 43-year-old Charles Frazer in 1831, Macleay wrote to Hay in England requesting that a botanist as well as a zoologist be sent out, adding that if:

> no Superintendent of our Garden should be appointed before you receive this I beg leave to submit to you whether Mr. Cunningham who passed several years here as Botanical Collector might not be invited to accept of the Situation.[113]

But Allan Cunningham had already been offered the position prior to Macleay's suggestion, and had declined in favour of his brother, Richard. Sons of a Scottish gardener, both brothers had worked for several years at Kew Gardens. On Banks's recommendation, Allan was appointed a botanical collector in 1814 and Richard worked as an amanuensis cataloguing specimens submitted, including those sent in by his brother. In his position as 'collector', Allan was also described as the 'King's botanist',[114] and from 1816 to 1831 he travelled around Australia and New Zealand collecting plants for Kew Gardens. In 1828 he was credited with discovering the rich new pastoral land in Queensland called the Darling Downs and he often accompanied Charles Frazer on exploring and collecting trips.

Strangely enough, Allan did eventually become Colonial Botanist and Superintendent of the Botanic Garden. Richard took up his new appointment in 1831 but four years later he died during an expedition with Thomas Mitchell and, two years later again, Allan took over the position. By then other changes were mooted which Allan opposed. One of the most objectionable arrangements was the idea of building convict barracks in the actual grounds for the workers. Allan claimed that this would require him to not only superintend the garden, but also the convicts, a situation he neither relished nor believed was necessary.[115] And, in his opinion, the future direction of the garden should be on 'Botanical Science' rather than 'practical horticulture and landscape gardening'.

Another bone of contention for Allan was the new committee for the Botanic Garden and Museum that had been formed in June 1836.[116] Even though his friend Alexander was on this committee of eleven members and also the sub-committee of six members,[117] Allan found it difficult to implement his own ideas for the Garden and, at the same time, satisfy the varying ideas of the committee members. From the outset of his appointment, Allan's views conflicted with those of the committee and after only eight months in the job, from February to November 1837, he resigned.

The role of the newly established committee was made clear by Alexander's instructions, given on behalf of the Governor during his last months as Colonial Secretary in 1836. It was to take on the 'Superintendence' of 'the Principal Garden, the New Garden in Farm Cove, and that nearest the Government Stables'.[118] Alexander directed that the kitchen garden and inner Domain be kept under the superintendence of the Colonial Botanist and spelt out, in precise terms, that:

> No Vegetables or Fruit Trees are to be raised in the Botanical Gardens, excepting such as are of so Valuable or Rare a kind, as it may be proper to place there for better preservation. Such of the fruit trees now there are to be removed as the Committee think proper.[119]

Not surprisingly, considering his vast experience with collecting and compiling reports over the years, Alexander also recommended that the committee 'furnish an Annual Report every May, indicating progress 'made towards a Scientific arrangement of the Plants', together with a census of plants actually cultivated, and an account of exchanges made'.[120] Some reorganisation and method was badly needed and even von Hügel had noted in his journal in 1834 that no labels, register of plantings or catalogue existed.[121] Macleay issued these instructions in 1836 but two years later the *Sydney Herald* was still complaining:

> that a Kitchen Garden, under the pretence of being a Botanic Garden, is supported in Sydney at an expense of from £800 to £1,000 a-year! But what care the 'powers that be' for that as long as hungry officials

Allan Cunningham (1791–1839), Colonial Botanist in 1837. This statue on the Lands Department Building in Sydney was sculpted by Tommaso Sani. Statues of other early colonists from Macleay's time, including William Wentworth and Charles Sturt, are also displayed on this stately edifice. Photo: Derelie Cherry

can 'furnish forth' their tables with fruit and vegetables grown at the public cost? We scarcely ever walk through this garden without seeing some servant with a basket carrying off vegetables, or fruit, for Mrs. This or Mrs. That — the wife of some official … It is, in fact, so barefaced that Mr. Cunningham would no longer consent to remain a mere cultivator of official cabbages and turnips; and, accordingly, he has resigned the management of the Botanic Gardens in disgust.[122]

By 1842 there were still complaints about the way in which the garden was administered. The explorer and botanist Friedrich Ludwig Leichhardt declared it was 'a place of public amusement and the kitchen garden of Government House, rather than a place for the students of botany and horticulture'.[123] However, there were extenuating circumstances behind Leichhardt's attitude as his application for the position of Director of the Garden was rejected in favour of Alexander's nominee, Nasmith Robertson, who had been principal gardener for the Macarthurs at Camden Park for many years.[124] In Leichhardt's opinion, Alexander's

… interests proved to be stronger than mine. As a former Colonial Secretary he had acquired a good deal of influence … and as he happened to be the most influential member of the Botanic Gardens Committee, to which the Governor had delegated the authority for appointment, he of course carried the day with ease.[125]

At the time, reservations had been expressed by Governor Gipps about the appointment of Robertson who was aged 58. Two years later this new appointee also died and the committee were once again forced to search for a suitable replacement. Alexander corresponded frequently on the subject with his friend, Sir William Hooker, requesting him to 'recommend a competent person to the Secretary of State'.[126]

By 1845 there was still no permanent head and the acting supervisor, James Kidd, pointed out the 'exhausted state of the Garden'.[127] After Governor FitzRoy arrived in August 1846 he received a despatch from the new Secretary of State, William Gladstone, regretting 'that the Garden has lost the scientific character which it originally had'.[128] To rectify the situation as speedily as possible, the horticulturist John Bidwill, who had arrived in the colony in 1838, was appointed as the new Director of the Botanic Garden. However, unbeknown to FitzRoy, around the same time in England, Gladstone's successor, Earl Grey (formerly Viscount Howick who had been Under-Secretary of State 1830–1834) had appointed 27-year-old Charles Moore to the same position. In the ensuing fiasco, Bidwill held the position from September 1847[129] and Moore took over on 1 February 1848. He remained in the position until 1896. Yet Bidwill's contribution to horticulture in New South Wales was significant as he undertook the first plant breeding near Sydney. His first release was in 1843 – a hybrid hibiscus which he named *Hibiscus Sydneyi*.[130]

Although by the 1840s Macleay had to face numerous personal problems, it must have been frustrating and disappointing to witness firsthand the difficulties that the Sydney Botanic Garden was experiencing, even though there were many positive developments. On 20 June 1848, only a month before Alexander passed away, he took up his last appointment in public life as one of five Vice-Presidents for the new Australian Botanical and Horticultural Society. This Society was established to encourage 'the manufactures and production of the colony' with half-yearly exhibitions of 'flowers, fruits, vegetables, wines and articles of commerce' to be held in the Botanic Garden[131] but, sadly, Alexander did not live long enough to see their first display.

A LASTING
CONTRIBUTION

Alexander Macleay's contribution to the world of horticulture was well-recognised in his own lifetime. In 1826 Robert Brown introduced a new genus of two species which he named *Macleaya cordata*, a plume poppy, and its related *Macleaya microcarpa*. *Macleaya cordata* was 'a handsome hardy plant of stately habit and finely sculptured foliage and, where bold plants are desired, few will be found equal to it'.[132] There is also a *Narcissus macleaii* bulb which Alexander grew at Tilbuster in England,[133] following the common practice of the time to name an introduced plant after the person who first cultivated it. In Australia, the Stringybark or Port Macquarie pine, *Callitris macleayana*, is named after him[134] and there is also an apricot named after him from seedlings which the Macarthurs grew at Camden Park. It was called *McLeay's choice*; two other varieties were named *McArthur's choice* and *Frazer's choice*.[135]

There is even a link between Alister Clark, Australia's most famous rose breeder who died in 1949, and Alexander Macleay. In the 1840s Alister's father Walter, another Scotsman, managed Macleay's rural properties, Kerarbury and Toganmain.[136] He also managed Tubbo, which adjoined Toganmain, and he and John Peter, one of Alexander's most capable managers, were great friends. In 1853 Walter and his second wife Annie built a lovely homestead and garden called Glenara which still exists today adjacent to Melbourne's Tullamarine Airport.

This garden was modelled on the principles that Thomas Shepherd described about Macleay's garden at Elizabeth Bay and, perhaps, some of the plants in Clark's garden came from either Elizabeth Bay or Brownlow Hill as Walter was such a 'close associate' of the Macleays.[137] Many examples of plants common in colonial gardens still thrive at Glenara, for example, the Norfolk Island pine, the bunya pine and the Norfolk Island hibiscus. Alister lived at Glenara from 1888 and began his commercial rose breeding programme around 1910. Some claim that he was the 'greatest horticulturist that Australia has produced',[138] and if this claim is even partly accurate, the connection with the Macleays in the previous century may have helped.

Although the only original features of the garden at Elizabeth Bay that survive today are the grotto and a natural rock cave, which is now incorporated in the small McElhone Reserve in front of the house, Alexander Macleay's name will forever be associated with the development of ornamental and economically useful gardening in Australia. If only the grounds at Elizabeth Bay had been maintained and preserved in the tradition of the grand English estates, it would, without a doubt, still be considered 'The Lion of Sydney'.

eight

AN
APPETITE
FOR ACRES

EXPANSION OF
THE
PASTORAL INDUSTRY

Apart from his official duties as Colonial Secretary, and his interests in his family, gardening and natural history, Alexander Macleay actively participated in the pastoral industry which rapidly developed in New South Wales and prompted the spread of settlement, especially in the 1830s. As Bigge had envisaged in the 1820s, wool exports became a valuable staple and came to meet the demands of the textile industry in England. Cattle, too, improved as the need for meat increased. Alexander arrived in the colony at a most opportune time. Crown land, which was in great demand, was readily available, initially through grants and then by purchase either at public auction or from other settlers.

AGRICULTURAL
REFORM IN SCOTLAND

Tilbuster, the country estate in Surrey that Alexander had purchased in 1803, was not a large holding but there was room for a small farm and when the property was sold in 1825 the prospective buyers, Captain and Mrs Fanshaw, were keen to purchase the stock.[1] By 1804, Alexander had also acquired extensive holdings in the area around Wick, including several mills. He would have been keen to put into practice some of the ideas for improvement in agriculture that emanated from the Age of Enlightenment just as his father had done in Wick. In the second half of the 18th century immense changes in agricultural practices had taken place in Scotland and England. Amongst the leaders of these innovations was Sir John Sinclair, the politician, landlord and agricultural reformer[2] and friend of the Macleay family. After travelling widely throughout Europe from 1776 to 1778, he had returned home with many new ideas for agricultural improvement and helped persuade the British government that it should establish 'a board to promote its agricultural interests'.[3] With the assistance of Henry Dundas, the British Board of Agriculture and Internal Improvement commenced operations in 1793. It collected much data on the state of farming in England between 1793 and 1813,[4] and although it survived only until 1822, its establishment was instrumental in the improvement of agricultural practices throughout the United Kingdom.

Sinclair was also instrumental in forming the Society for Improvement in British Wool in 1791.[5] Moreover, his voluminous *Statistical Account of Scotland*, published between 1791 and 1799, provided an invaluable amount of information based on 166 questions answered by every parish about how people lived at the time. It was hoped that these details would improve overall standards in the community. When Sinclair also published an *Account of the Systems of Husbandry adopted in the More Improved Districts of Scotland* in 1812, Banks declared: 'To have been the cause of imparting to Englishmen the skill of Scots farmers is indeed a proud recollection'.[6] The two men had been corresponding about agricultural reform since 1785 and by 1819 Banks admitted to Sinclair that 'a Scots farmer can get more crop from the earth than an English one seems a fact not to be disputed'.[7]

Six months before Alexander departed for Sydney, Sinclair offered him practical advice on a variety of issues, including personal recommendations for growing grapes and apples in the colony. In an encouraging letter he suggested that the 'great Staple should be Wine':

> all kinds of Vines should be tried there … Not only from Europe, but from the Cape of Good Hope, to see which answers bext [sic] … I would also strongly recommend the Carlisle Codlin, which is among the most prolific and most useful of the apple tribe — I inclose two papers respecting it … I shall probably be in London before you leave it, and we may then discuss together what additional improvements can be introduced in to the colony.[8]

Such useful ideas were implemented by Alexander and his orchards and vineyards became famous in the colony. But Sinclair's idea that the 'true Silver Rabbit … would be an immense acquisition … Its multiplication would be so rapid as to prevent any risk of famine, — its fur is very valuable, and goes into a small bulk' proved to be more of a problem than an advantage as the rabbits bred in plague proportions and ended up eating grass meant for sheep and cattle.

THE ACQUISITION
OF COLONIAL LAND

Along with other recently arrived colonists, Macleay was naturally keen to acquire as much land as he was entitled to and as soon as he could. Under the new regulations administered by the Land Board that Governor Darling had established in 1826, future grants were to be made available to government officers, emigrants and ex-convicts provided 'the Governor is satisfied that the Grantee has both the power and the intention of expending in the cultivation of the lands, a capital equal to half the estimated value of it'.[9] One square mile, or 640 acres, was to be granted for every £500 of capital; the maximum amount per grant was 2,560 acres and the minimum amount 320 acres. As with previous grants that had been operative since 1788, any land granted was subject to the collection of an annual quit rent.[10]

In addition, the territory was to be divided into 'counties, hundreds, and parishes' and further blocks of up to 9,600 acres 'not hitherto granted and not appropriated for public purposes' within a parish could now be purchased at an average price.[11] Darling also continued the practice that had been initiated under Governor Brisbane of issuing a 'ticket of occupation' for temporary grazing on Crown lands. In March 1827, however, he replaced this system by charging two shillings per annum for each 100 acres.[12] In February 1827 Darling rationalised his land policy to Hay:

> A Free Grant would be a Boon, a sort of Heir-loom, which many
> would be proud to hand down to their posterity … There should be
> a distinction in the quantity of land given to the higher officers and
> those of inferior station … It is no doubt beneficial to the colony to
> give Land to those, who have the means of Stocking and improving it,
> and this is insured when the Heads of Departments are Grantees.[13]

Thomas Mitchell described the situation, as he saw it, in 1828:

> All the heads of departments here embark in grazing concerns, and
> have their four square miles of land. Indeed, this quantity is thought
> quite too little for any stock-holder, and many have ten thousand acres
> by grants and purchases. Sheep-farming is the most profitable invest-
> ment of money … You would be astonished at the riches of some who
> have not been more than five or six years here, and who began with
> not more than two or three thousand pounds.[14]

Having left England amidst dire financial circumstances, naturally Macleay aspired to take advantage of such opportunities. Forbes pointed out the advantages of acquiring land to Horton on 25 March 1827:

At present, I am only the farmer of my salary — it all goes in eating, drinking and attendance, and the only control I have is in seeing it justly divided among butchers, bakers, traders, etc. I should have no objection to receive compensation for the time I was detained at home, in Land — altho' I shall never become either farmer or grazier, yet I intend to stock some acres for the future benefit of my children. It will be the only future their poor father can leave them.[15]

A group of wealthy British bankers and merchants also could not resist the opportunity to increase their fortunes and decided in 1824, with the approval of the British Government, to invest in land and sheep in this new country. In June that year they established the Australian Agricultural Company which promised, in return for a grant of 1,000,000 acres, to invest £1,000,000 and employ 1,200 convicts. Shares were rapidly bought in England and by some colonists, including Francis Forbes and Samuel Marsden. It was a good time to start such a company. By 1826 the developing wool industry was starting to bear results and that year the colony sent £1,106,300 worth of wool to England, followed by a dramatic increase in the quantities despatched over the ensuing years.[16] With John Macarthur's improved merino strain of sheep, as well as the introduction of Saxon sheep, cheap freight and minimal duties, the industry, along with the wealth of the pastoralists, began to burgeon.[17] And as investment capital from England poured into the expanding wool industry and some of her surplus labour was sent out to the colony, this new industry became a vital part of the economy for both New South Wales and England.

MACLEAY COMMENCES FARMING

Only a few months after their arrival, in May 1826, Fanny informed William that 'Papa is anxious to have a farm'.[18] By July Alexander had already purchased 300 cattle so his need for land was urgent[19] and in April 1827 he applied for a grant of 1,500 acres at Brownlow Hill.[20] Situated 60 kilometres from Sydney, this region near Camden was previously known as the Cowpastures where government stock had grazed; John Macarthur had been given the first grant in the area of 5,000 acres in 1805. By 1819 the government had built three stockyards, and the one located at Lowe's Hill was renamed Brownlow Hill by Governor Macquarie in 1820.[21] In February 1826, Darling made arrangements to remove the wild cattle belonging to the Government which were still pastured there[22] and the land was opened up for grant and purchase to private individuals. John Oxley, the Surveyor General, explained in a memo to Darling in April 1827, just how the Colonial Secretary acquired this land:

> The Land applied for by Mr. McLeay is the old Government Cattle
> Station known as 'Brownlow Hill' — it has only been open to
> Selection from the Period of the removal of the Government Herds
> about Six Months ago, when Mr. McLeay intimated his intention to
> apply for it; the Land is little known, and, being of so limited extent,
> is probably the reason why no application has been made for it since
> its abandonment by the Government.[23]

When Fanny first visited Brownlow Hill in February 1828 she was impressed and noted that it was:

> about 40 miles hence on one side watered by the Nepean and on two
> other sides it possessed Hunter's Creek and some other … prettily named
> creek … — the land is charmingly undulating, hill and dale, sloping in a
> graceful manner on all sides. The Soil particularly rich, they say … We
> slept at Mr. Oxley's Place about four miles from Brownlow Hill.[24]

In addition to his 300 cattle Alexander had also purchased 'about 800 Sheep and Lambs, and some brood Mares and Fillies',[25] and so he requested a further 'Five thousand acres as a purchase or rather to be rented by me until a Purchase can be made, and a Reserve of Four thousand Six hundred acres more to be ultimately Purchased', as well as 'an additional number of acres, as you may think proper to grant to me … in some other parts of the Colony'.[26] His acquisitions had not ended for in 1828 he purchased the 2,000-acre farm adjoining Brownlow Hill, which was called Glendarual, for £3,000.[27] Fanny's report to William in May 1827 ominously predicted: 'A great source of anxiety our several farms will be for things must be left to the superintendence of Men little interested in our Welfare'.[28] How right she proved to be.

Fortunately, however, on 11 November 1827 George arrived from England and six months later took on the management of Brownlow Hill.[29] His new life would have become less lonely when brother James arrived, nearly eighteen months later, and took up residence with him.[30] Having the Macarthurs nearby at Camden would have been a great help, too, especially in relation to learning about sheep farming. Some years later, in 1867, both families became related when Alexander's grandson, Arthur Alexander Onslow, married John Macarthur's granddaughter, Elizabeth Macarthur. This link continues and today portraits of both Alexander and his mother, Barbara Rose, hang on the walls of the dining room at Camden Park.

DEPRIVATIONS OF A
BUSH LIFE

In the 1820s it was a hard and strange life for new arrivals in the colony. George was only nineteen and James 'a bewildered eighteen; he 'was taken very lightly by the convicts in his charge'.[31] Not only did these boys know virtually nothing about farming practices, especially in such a harsh and alien environment, but their relative youth made the situation even more difficult with a staff of mainly convicts. James endured New South Wales for only eight years until he left and married in London. George, on the other hand, persevered for another 32 years, until he, too, returned to England in 1859. Despite misgivings, they initially settled down well and Fanny advised William in January 1829 that:

> George … is very industrious and attentive to his farming business ….
> My Father says that George's conduct is everything he can wish — The

perfect good humour & contentment with which he bears the great privations of a Bush Life is the admiration of all who know him.[32]

Alexander was satisfied with George's progress and, according to Fanny, expressed surprise that 'one so young could perform and arrange so well, the occupation being quite new to him'.[33] After the trouble he had caused in England by being expelled from Westminster school, George seemed to be adjusting admirably to his new life. Even at that early stage he possessed a good sense of business for, by August 1828, George had decided that his father was too trusting 'of other people's motives'. Fanny informed William that 'Papa is so good himself he suspects no evil in others and he has been overreached by some Persons'.[34] From 1826 to 1829, there was also a severe drought in the colony, and in addition to stock being stolen and dying from lack of food, many contracted disease at the sheep station in the Argyle[35] near Goulburn where Alexander had acquired another sheep run.[36] Adding to their problems was a bushfire which swept through the Cowpastures and Nepean country in 1827.[37] In 1828, George was forced to take stock further afield in search of fodder and Fanny described his venture:

> George has, in consequence, been obliged to act in the style of the Patriarchs of old and to quit his residence and to set off in search of sustenance for his poor Beasts. He was to proceed towards the South, below Shoal Haven — Poor fellow he would find his journey anything but agreeable — cold and comfortable in the extreme. No roads — no places where he could hide his head from the Snows which they say abound in those regions, he has been gone about 3 weeks and we may expect to hear of him in about six weeks hence.[38]

After grants were abolished and Crown lands opened up for sale by auction in 1831, squatting on unoccupied lands rose to immense proportions. Living in these outlying areas was difficult enough, but conditions were made worse by the constant threat of marauding bushrangers and confrontation with Aborigines. In 1830, Fanny recorded that a large gang of bushrangers surrounded James at Brownlow Hill and that their attacks had become so outrageous, murdering and robbing day and night, that a military detachment had been despatched to the area.[39] Fanny claimed that their cattle were 'slaughtered by these *Demons*' and wondered how many 'poor Travellers & lonely stockkeepers' they had murdered.[40] Their sister, Christiana, many miles to the north, suffered similar problems. One evening in 1834 seven armed bushrangers attacked her home at St Aubins in the Hunter Valley and, Fanny informed William, stole items worth about £15, 'wounded one of the men servants and Capt. Dumaresq was shot at'.[41]

The Australian bush was full of other surprises. Annabella Boswell recounted the story of how a woman living in the country trod on a death adder in the dark one evening on the way from the house to the kitchen. Three hours later she was dead.[42] Terrible stories like this circulated rapidly and the Macleays, like the rest of the colonists, would have been aware of the daily need for constant vigilance in such an alien environment.

ABORIGINES

Conflict with Aborigines caused Alexander personal anxiety not only as a landholder but also in his official position as Colonial Secretary. Darling's 'conciliatory and sympathetic' approach towards Aborigines[43] was made clear soon after Alexander took office following an incident in 1828 at the recently established Fort Wellington when several natives were hurt or killed. Instructing Macleay to investigate the affair, the Governor condemned the 'barbarous and inhumane' act. He ordered the commandant in the area to 'take any means and opportunity of inculcating in the people at the settlement generally the danger they will incur by the commission of any acts of cruelty or outrage against the natives'.[44] The annual institution of a special day for Aborigines at Parramatta, which had been sanctioned by Governor Macquarie, was upheld by Darling and Bourke. The Governor and the Colonial Secretary presided over the feast and the distribution of blankets and other gifts during the day's activities. On occasion, Aborigines were also employed as guides or to track bushrangers because it was officially recognised that they possessed 'a most intimate knowledge of the localities of the country'.[45] Therry reflected in 1863, long after these events, that 'a large majority of the squatters were very kind to the Aborigines' and considered that the natives were 'botanists by nature'.[46]

Alexander's personal attitude towards Aborigines is evident in Fanny's comment to William in 1827 after her father sailed south and spent two nights in the bush at Bateman's Bay. She wrote that he:

> had a great deal of fun with some Black Natives — who, by the bye are not the mere brutes they have been represented — they seem to possess great intelligence when not degraded by associating with our civilized people — we teach them to drink and they become worse than brutes in consequence.[47]

But, in October 1838, when Alexander took the chair at a meeting of the New South Wales Auxiliary Bible Society to discuss the protection of Aborigines, he was criticised by the *Sydney Herald* which facetiously claimed that not one Aboriginal soul had, as yet, been saved:

> Many reverend gentlemen addressed the chair, and spoke of the wondrous works that have been done in the way of conversion; but not one convert (although fifty years in that course have now passed) did these gentlemen bring forward as proof positive of their Christian deeds — the whole is but a farce — Why a man like Mr. M'Leay should allow himself to be made the tool of men who, when in the depths of the forest, think more of possessing themselves of wealth than they do of the conversion of the native tribes, I do not know. Do the missionaries wander from place to place as do the natives? Certainly not; but, on the contrary, cast anchor on some snug spot [and] build comfortable houses …[48]

MORE FINANCIAL
PROBLEMS

The vagaries of farming in the colony, which was so much affected by sea-
sonal variations and fluctuating prices, resulted in Alexander not receiving the
revenue he had anticipated as early as he had hoped. Natural disasters such as
drought and floods were only too common and their toll on valuable livestock
was calamitous. In 1838, lightning struck the barns at William Dumaresq's
property, Tilbuster, and all the previous year's wheat and hay was burnt, along
with several adjoining buildings. The following year crops throughout the
entire colony failed causing even more financial hardship.[49]

Despite rapidly increasing debts, Alexander still invested in racehorses,
given the opportunities that arose after Brisbane established the Turf Club in
March 1825 and a racecourse had been built.[50] This pastime of the gentry was
expensive, but the Colonial Secretary did not restrain his spending. Appearances had to be kept up to maintain the family's position in the social hierarchy
of the colony, a fact that Alexander was only too aware of. From time to time
advertisements for Macleay horses appeared in the *Sydney Herald*; for example,
Marmaluke was to 'stand this season – bred by Alexander M'Leay',[51] and in
1835 Fanny wrote to William:

> My Father was well pleased the other day during the Races at
> Parramatta because one of his Horses won & was considered a
> particularly fine Animal. But there appears to be no sale for such fine
> Horses here & the speculation of sending them to India is rather [a]
> bold one if we could only insure their safe arrival there the thing would
> pay exceedingly well. I believe my Father possesses at present some
> very good Horses.[52]

In the late 1840s George did finally succeed in selling stud horses to India but
by that time his father had passed away.[53]

Shortage of money was such a problem at the end of 1827, that Fanny
resorted to borrowing £200 from William's agent. Unfortunately, she had not

sought her brother's permission beforehand, even though William had previously offered to assist her if the need arose. Her excuse was that:

> My Father has been laying out a great deal of money upon stock and in improvements at Elizabeth Bay & at Brownlow Hill, which has left him quite bare and he is in very low spirits, having received some heavy demands upon his purse from some of our London tradepeople. He has now about 2000 Sheep of one kind or another and I know not how many black cattle. — We are to be rich in time, I hope — for truly it is not pleasant to want money even here in this out of the way place.[54]

When he finally heard about this transaction, William became so offended that Fanny was still justifying her behaviour two years later.[55] The 'London tradespeople' she referred to in 1827 included Thomson who had been responsible for handling the affairs of George and James at Westminster boarding school. She described him as 'that vile wretch'[56] so the family must have been very glad when both boys safely arrived in Australia. By November 1829, farming matters had not improved and Fanny complained to William:

> what use is all this but to chain my Father's pockets? since the wool fetches no price and when we have anything to sell we find its value has fallen 70 per cent since we purchased. I am sick of farming ...[57]

By February 1830 Fanny was still in despair and wrote to William:

> we are constantly hearing of some mischance or other at one or other of the Farming Stations. We never should have had but one — I am told enough to think that in having four, my Father has made a great mistake — for the wages of the Overseers would run away with all the profits supposing there was a chance of any, at present, they, and the farming concerns take the money we really require to live respectably in our station ...[58]

In May 1830 Fanny, in one of her rare outbursts of criticism against her father, wrote to William:

Where then goes my Father's salary, how is it spent? Why in paying for expensive farms — to buy which my Father borrowed money at enormous interest — in paying for Horses which have proved to be of no value &c. How much I wish that My Father had not commenced farming when he did every thing then was very dear & now all things have fallen so low that really I see, that unless some change takes place, Farmers must not expect fortunes ... thousands of respectable People were bitten with this mania.[59]

That her father's finances reached a crisis in the 1840s when the colony experienced a severe depression would have come as no surprise to Fanny. Ultimately, Alexander managed to escape bankruptcy but only through the intervention of William who took over his father's financial affairs. Whilst she was alive, and even though she wrote so pertinently to William about the situation, Fanny was in no position to advise her father on money matters. She was merely the onlooker but how frustrated and anxious she would have been to witness the events unfolding.

THE EXPERIENCE
OF JOHN PETER

This state of affairs improved dramatically with the arrival of John Peter, a fellow Scotsman from Glasgow, who initially took up the position of overseer on one of Macleay's properties near Goulburn. Peter recorded the difficulties and problems that he had confronted:

I entered into an engagement with him to take charge of his station, about 150 miles from Sydney, with about 2000 sheep, at a salary of 40/- a year, with one per cent. upon the price of the clip of wool the first year, and an additional one per cent. each succeeding year. I had offers of much higher salary from other gentlemen, but the

kind and fatherly advice I received from Mr. M'Leay, coupled with
the high estimation in which he was universally held, induced me to
prefer his employment to that of others at double the amount of salary,
a resolution which I never had occasion since to regret … in eight or
ten days, I left Sydney for his station, situated between Goulburn and
Yass. On arriving at the station, the person in charge handed over to
me about 2000 sheep, with some stores, and about a dozen of assigned
servants; and he left for Sydney the same day. I now found myself,
without any colonial experience, placed in a position of great
responsibility, alone, and without any one to assist me. In the first
place, I made myself acquainted with the nature of the country, the
sheep, and the servants I had to deal with; and I soon ascertained that
about five years before Mr. M'Leay had lost as large a number of sheep
as were then upon the run. As an illustration of the mismanagement
that had been going on, I was shown by the shepherds piles of bones,
the remains of sheep that had died of scab and starvation. I applied
myself to ascertain the cause of this want of increase, and I found that
it arose from the prevalence of scab among the sheep, and the great
carelessness of the shepherds, who were all assigned servants.[60]

Peter successfully overcame other problems that he encountered as he fully
explained when he:

took up a tract of country with thirty miles of frontage to the
Murrumbidgee river (farther out than any other squatter) for Mr.
M'Leay, and about ten miles of frontage for myself, for which I had
to pay 10/-. a year, and Mr. M'Leay had to pay about 30/- for his stations. These proved excellent and healthy runs, but I found at first
some difficulty with the natives, who were inclined to attack the
shepherds and drive off sheep. By treating them with kindness,
however, I succeeded in making them useful in sheep-washing, and
such-like work. I had also then, being 400 miles from Sydney, great
difficulty in getting up provisions … at the end of twelve years, when I
gave up the management, I counted over for Mr. M'Leay, from whom

I had received the 2000 sheep, above 30,000 thriving, healthy, and well-bred sheep, the gradual increase of the 2000 I had received, exclusive of from 10,000 to 12,000 fat sheep that had been sold during that period. The quality of the wool, and the manner in which it was got up, were so good, that for several years it had fetched the highest price in the London market.[61]

From his early days, Peter had implemented an incentive scheme for his workers based on performance which was similar to the scheme that Macleay had set up for him based on the amount of wool produced each year. This system worked well and in 1833 Macleay received £700 for his fleeces which were sold in England, with a substantial increase in 1834 to around £1,300.[62] His sales reflected the general increase in the colony's production, with wool exports to Britain rising from £175,000 in 1822 to £2 million in 1830, an enormous £10 million pounds by 1840 and £77 million in 1849.[63]

VAST LAND HOLDINGS

Currey, in his biography of Sir Francis Forbes, described Macleay 'as a canny Scott with a prodigious capacity for clerical work and an insatiable appetite for broad acres'.[64] But it was the *Australian*, in 1829, that had first highlighted Alexander's 'appetency for grants of land'.[65]

Not only did Macleay increase his own land holdings as quickly as he could, but he also helped acquire land grants for his daughters. Fanny told William in 1827 that 'Papa is going to apply for grants of land for each of us as there is no difficulty in obtaining them the order against females having grants having been cancelled'.[66] And so under the marriage grant which was introduced in 1828,[67] the four daughters of Alexander who married before September 1831 each received a land grant of 1,280 acres from Darling on their wedding. Other opportunities for obtaining grants were also taken up, as in the case of George who, in 1830, was given 'two square miles of Land free of Quit Rent' in acknowledgement of 'the assistance which he rendered on the late Expedition under Captain Sturt, in discovering the River Murray and Lake Alexandria'.[68] He finally selected his land 'for proximity' near one of his father's properties at Ulladulla in 1832.[69] A couple of years after he left the office of Colonial Secretary, the *Australian* recorded that the sum total of Alexander's grants would by then be worth £30,000, not including the 8,000 acres of land granted to his children.[70]

Macleay's extended family also acquired many acres of land. The largest holding belonged to Captain William Dumaresq who married Christiana in 1830. Today located five miles northwest of Armidale, this property covered a vast 65,000 acres, with 15,000 sheep and 2,000 cattle.[71] It included Christiana's marriage portion acres which she named Tilbuster after her father's Godstone retreat and in 1835 their property was the furthest out-station in New England.[72] Port Macquarie was only 30 miles away and because Archibald Innes was in charge of supplying the government contracts there, a ready market for Tilbuster's crops was assured. Annabella Boswell recounted a visit to Tilbuster in 1838, and noted that a small 'but very pretty' house had been built and that some of the rooms were even panelled with cedar.[73]

Nearby was the property of William's brother, Colonel Henry Dumaresq, who in 1834 took up the largest holding in the area, 100,000 acres which he called Saumarez after his ancestors' home in Jersey.[74] A shop was set up on this property, 'the Saumarez store', which serviced the Dumaresqs' staff and neighbours until Armidale was settled in 1839.[75] Neither brother chose to live in such isolation preferring instead the Hunter Valley. Henry's property there, known as St Heliers,[76] was near Muswellbrook which was first settled in 1827 and proclaimed a town in 1833.[77] William lived on a property named St Aubins near Scone, where he had nearly 16,000 acres[78] in addition to his wife's dower grant.[79] Fanny stayed with her sister on a number of occasions, the first time being an extended visit of five months in 1831 to help Christiana prepare for the birth of her first child. On that occasion the family stayed in Henry's house at St Heliers as St Aubins had not yet been built. Fanny described her living conditions to William:

We are residing in a very well built Stone House consisting of 10
Rooms five of which are really very good & well furnished for a bush
dwelling … it is placed upon a gentle eminence which is in time to be
converted into a lovely spot with ever blooming parterres of Roses, lil-
lies, and daffy down dillies! … We take much time in talking of what
we should like to see & of what we must have — sloping lawns, green
smooth terraces, stone steps …[80]

Major Archibald Innes, who married Margaret in 1829, also had extensive
land holdings in the Armidale area. When they moved to Port Macquarie in
1830 the area had just been opened up to the public as a free settlement replacing the former penal station. In the ensuing years, Innes acquired 'a series of
stations': Waterloo, Kentucky, Furracabad, Dundee and Mole River,[81] in the
vicinity of New England. The town of Glen Innes, established in 1851, is on
the site of his original Furracabad station.[82] Over 170 years later, the burnt
ruins of Innes House still remain and in Port Macquarie's Historical Society's
Museum a miniature model of this Georgian House and its landscaped surroundings conjures up an image of by-gone grandeur.

The most complete record of Alexander's holdings is that compiled by
William in 1843 as he attempted to sort out his father's muddled affairs. Doc-
umenting that by then Alexander possessed seven large properties, William
attempted to reconcile Alexander's assets and liabilities, and prepared a table
with the following details:

Elizabeth Bay: 5 horses, 2 cows, 56 acres;[83] the property at Brownlow Hill
and Glendaruel in the County of Camden then managed by Walter Scott:
130 horses, 600 cattle, 3,663 acres; Ulladulla in the County of St Vincent
managed by James Stewart: 1,050 cattle, 2,560 acres; Byalla in the County
of Argyle managed by Alexander's nephew, John Macleay: 600 cattle, 3,443
acres; a property at Cabramatta in the County of Cumberland: 120 acres; and
stations as follows: Pembrook Station with Mr R. Cook as overseer, 2 horses,
450 cattle, 2,500 sheep, number of acres not listed; and Richmond River
Station managed by William McMasters: 3 horses, 30 cattle, 8,500 sheep,
number of acres not listed; the Murrumbidgee Station with John Peter as

overseer: 5 horses, 90 cattle, 30,167 sheep, number of acres not listed.[84] However, the Murrumbidgee acreage was listed as 104,960 by 1844; perhaps William deliberately omitted these details in 1843.[85] Macleay's several runs in the Murrumbidgee in western New South Wales were Kerarbury, which was taken up by William John Macleay, Mulberrygong, Burrabodgie, Murrumbidgee and Borambola, and there was also Toganmain in the Riverina.[86] Pulletop, in the same region, also managed by John Peter, was adjacent to the Murrumbidgee River between Albury and Wagga Wagga. On 12 August 1836 Macleay bought the Glendiver estate for £2,700[87] but he offered it for sale only a few months later in December.[88] Perhaps Fanny's death on 8 August had diminished her father's desire to build up his empire of acres.

THE AGRICULTURAL
SOCIETY

Only about six weeks after arriving in the colony in 1826, Alexander became Vice-Patron of the Agricultural and Horticultural Society of New South Wales which publicly acknowledged 'that the talents and experiences of this Gentleman, in all the various branches of general science, would be no trifling acquisition to the agricultural interests of New South Wales'.[89] No doubt this was a reference to Macleay's many years with the Linnean Society. Established as the Agricultural Society of New South Wales in 1822, this organisation aimed to improve livestock and husbandry through the application of scientific methods.[90] With increased importation of plants and seeds, as well as livestock, the quality of wool could be improved as well as the yield of meat.[91]

In January 1826, the Society was officially recognised by Governor Darling who became Patron, and the word 'horticultural' was added to its title.[92] To become a member there was an annual subscription fee and applicants

Part of the extensive melancholy ruins of Innes House, Port Macquarie. Reproduced
with permission from the National Parks and Wildlife Service. Photo: Derelie Cherry

were supported by five nominees who were all members themselves.[93] And just like exclusive English societies, it was a very social business too. At their meetings members first of all dined 'together on the best things that Sydney could afford' and afterwards drank wine followed by 'coffee and buttered muffins' before proceeding to business matters.[94] But, according to some colonists, it was more of a private Society for the 'peculiar advantage and amusement of a small group', and unfortunately the people who most needed the information were excluded.[95] By 1838 the *Sydney Gazette* complained that of:

> systems of agriculture we have none, each settler cultivating his
> land as it suits his own fancy. No rotation of crops such as is
> closely adhered to at home is ever thought of, much less attempted
> ... & no 'help of manure of any kind' ... Indeed manure is almost
> unknown ...[96]

Furthermore, most of the cattle were 'the produce of the coarse buffalo brought originally from the Cape of Good Hope' and the small amount of stock breeding taking place was only being carried out privately.[97] As true as that might have been, the colony was still primarily a penal community and to even just survive in the isolated rural environments at that time was difficult enough[98], as Alexander had discovered.

It was the President, Sir John Jamison, who nominated Alexander from amongst the 'principal gentlemen and landholders in the colony',[99] as Vice-President of this Society. Another large landholder, Edward Wollstonecraft, business partner of Alexander Berry, became Secretary. Exhibitions of produce at Parramatta were held annually from October 1824[100] and by September 1826 the awards presented by the Society were suitably inscribed medals in gold or silver[101] as well as cash premiums for cattle, sheep and horse breeding and the best treatise on Australian agriculture and gardening.[102] In 1827, James Atkinson received a gold medal for his 'judicious and ably written treatise', entitled 'An Account of the State of Agriculture and Grazing in New South Wales', which became essential reading for new farmers.[103] It was through this Society that Alexander introduced some of his own ideas for new crops, such as the encouragement of tobacco cultivation which he announced at a meeting very soon after joining the Society in 1826.

The Society had excellent overseas honorary members including Robert Brown, Alexander's long-standing friend from his days at the Linnean Society, Thomas Andrew Knight, President of the English Horticultural Society, and corresponding members such as Robert Barclay of London and William Hooker who by then was Professor of Botany at Glasgow University.[104] Unfortunately, the Society dwindled in the early 1830s as most members were preoccupied with their own affairs and the population had become so geographically scattered.[105] By the end of 1834, regular meetings had ended and did not start again until 1867 after the gold rushes of the 1850s stimulated a healthier economic climate.[106] The popular annual Royal Easter Show which continues in Sydney today originates from the exhibitions first staged by the Agricultural Society in the 1820s.

THE HONORABLE
GRAZIER SECRETARY

In January 1830, Edward Hall in the *Sydney Monitor* referred to Alexander's pastoral activities by addressing him as 'the Hon. grazier Secretary'.[107] His numerous farming undertakings had been regularly noted by the press: the public seemed to consider it their right to know everything about their high profile public servant. In September that year, the *Australian* gave a detailed description of Brownlow Hill. It announced that Macleay:

> now employed on his farm at the Cowpastures, upward of one hundred assigned servants, and amongst them are a great number of picked mechanics of the very best description. He has on this farm two blacksmiths, two carpenters, two shoemakers, two gardeners, two wheelwrights, two tailors, beside divers and sundry other

mechanics that we know not of, and the best gang of reapers in the country …[108]

At a time when new settlers to the colony were finding it extraordinarily difficult to obtain free labour for themselves, such information would have been particularly perturbing. How could they ever hope to compete in growing or selling their produce? The *Australian* had previously aired this complaint and accused the relatives, friends and favourites of Darling and Macleay of coming in 'first for the pick and choice of convict labour'.[109]

William Edward Riley, the son of a settler, stayed at Brownlow Hill for two days in 1830 and his journal notes provide useful insights about activities there:

> A small, but neat building seated on a gentle eminence overlooking a
> fine piece of wheat now ripe and fit for the sickle, and a large paddock
> of lately cleared land. The main body of farm 2 miles beyond cottage.
> It lies in a small and narrow valley, bounded by gently rising grassy
> hills, thinly wooded, and the state of field and crops reflected great
> credit on the young man's management. The farm paid itself, here
> evident marks of a master's eye. In the dairy are 60 to 70 pans of milk
> from as many cows. The garden full of ornamental and useful trees and
> shrubs, while a fine sheet of water beside it formed in a deep ravine
> and the damming up of the creek that runs thro' it shewed how much
> might be done elsewhere by a similar measure.[110]

The press also reported about the quality butter and cheese that Macleay was producing:

> The Honorable the C. S's butter is very fine. A large box of it, about
> 100 lbs. weight, comes to market of a Thursday morning, made up
> principally in rolls of a pound each, to suit purchasers; and the whole
> box soon goes in this way to the tune of two shillings, two shillings
> and twopence, two shillings and threepence, or two shillings and
> sixpence, as the case may be. One hundred pounds sold off at two

shillings, would make 10 pounds, or a cool 500 pounds and more, yearly, to say nothing of private sales; besides the nice cream-tarts, and the good round cheeses — the cheese parings and the candle ends! Why, the very contemplation is transporting. Nothing will go down so glibly by the bye, we expect, as the M'L butter, and the cheese, and the cream-tarts! Why the PLEBIANS who live by the produce of their scanty farms, will be beaten hollow. A few more butter tubs and cheese crates will produce wonderfully long faces. We always had a sneaking idea that our Honorable high functionary was cut out for a farmer — that he could drive the plough as well as the pen. 'O fortunate Senex.' But you, to be sure, have the rich grassy uplands — the fertile meadows — the fattening butter cups … we do not wonder your butter should be good![111]

On 4 July 1829 the *Sydney Monitor* observed:

We are pained to find Mr. M'Leay was so much annoyed at our brother's notice of his very excellent butter. We too have taken to eating it, and we must say, that if Mr. M'Leay's office were conducted as well as his dairy, we and the public would not need to grudge him either his liberal pension, his handsome salary or his still handsomer grants reserves and leases of Crown land.[112]

Extra proof of Macleay's fine butter was that his transport cart was supposed to have been accosted by bushrangers on several occasions en route to Sydney![113] The *Sydney Monitor* added some extra gossip to this story by implying that a 'fine clinker-built gig', built for Macleay by convicts out of 'Government cedar' at Port Macquarie, 'was sent to him freight free in one of the Government vessels'. Implying to its readers that Macleay had overstepped the mark as far as privileges attached to his office of Colonial Secretary were concerned, this editorial suggested that it was this gig that conveyed Macleay's butter to town.[114] Such an allegation would have made Alexander's rivals even more antagonistic towards him.

CONSTANT OPPOSITION
FROM THE PRESS

No matter what Macleay did it seems there was opposition and it is not surprising that he occasionally became angry at the constant criticisms from the
press. The *Sydney Monitor* reported unsurprisingly that he spoke in insulting
language when questioned about his 'privileges'.[115] But he still managed to
retain a sense of humour when asked how he sent his butter to Sydney in hot
weather in those pre-refrigeration days. He replied: 'Oh! quite easily, it *runs* all
the way'.[116]

When Hall at the *Sydney Monitor* announced in 1828 that he had been
refused the privilege of renting grazing lands for his own starving cattle at
Lake Bathurst,[117] he also reminded his readers about Alexander's own herds.
He pointed out that whilst Macleay had dismissed Mackie, the late Superin-
tendent of Works and Postmaster at Newcastle, for pasturing his animals on
Crown lands there, the Macleay herds had been grazing on Crown reserves
in the interior for some time without anyone daring to impound them.[118]
And, suggesting a virtual cartel in 1831, the *Sydney Monitor* alleged that
Alexander had sold off all his corn to the Commissary under another name,
and that Harington had secured a government tender for hay presumably for
Alexander.[119]

Another incident over which Alexander was criticised in the newspapers
related to land in the area of the Pigeon House near Bateman's Bay south of
Sydney. In September 1826, Macleay had written a letter to Wollstonecraft
about this land, requesting that he arrange for Berry, who was the local magistrate, to inform Kendall who was applying for extra land in the same area, that
it was private property, more than 30,000 acres of it. The reason he gave was
that he hoped to have a 'kind of Establishment' there himself before the end of
the month.[120] Court actions were eventually instigated against Macleay on the
issue of reserving this land for himself, but they were abandoned in 1832 on
the basis that there was no precedent for such a case in the colony.[121] In 1833,
however, Governor Bourke declared in retrospect that Alexander had writ-

ten the original letter to Wollstonecraft to prevent the land being trespassed on for cutting cedar and that as he officially applied for a 8,100 acre grant in September 1828 two years after he said he would have a presence there, all other applications thereafter had to be treated as unsuccessful.[122] This whole scenario seems somewhat suspect. Macleay undeniably had an unfair advantage because he was Colonial Secretary, and his stance on the situation was not legally challenged. Wollstonecraft and Berry were both well aware that the coast south of Sydney was one of the richest for cedar in the colony, as in 1822 they had been granted 10,000 acres in the Shoalhaven region by Brisbane. Cedar was in great demand throughout the colony because it was used extensively in the construction of public buildings and, not surprisingly, Alexander probably hoped to secure this perceived opportunity to increase his income from an additional source.

During the 1830s, Alexander's pastoral enterprises, whilst experiencing major setbacks, still managed to provide him with a good income. But with a severe drought from 1838 to 1840 and an economic depression in 1841, the situation altered dramatically in the 1840s, although it took only a few years for the pastoral industry to recover. After Bourke introduced the Squatting Act in 1836, and squatters were offered a licence of occupation for their chosen land, they were well on the way to achieving their aims of wealth and respectability in the colony. Macleay continued to be involved in the advancement of their cause, particularly during his return to the public arena between 1843 and 1848.

nine

FOR THE BENEFIT OF THE COLONY

CHALLENGES STILL AHEAD

Although he was already 70 years old when he left the position of Colonial Secretary in 1836, Macleay's life still held great challenges. The colony ceased receiving convicts in 1840 and Alexander actively participated in the events that ensued as the agitation for self-government grew. Whilst the division between emancipists and exclusives dissolved entirely, other political factions emerged as the squatters sought control over colonial affairs and the new urban middle classes opposed them. When a partly elected Legislative Council was introduced in 1843, Macleay again played a leading role, this time as first Speaker. His active involvement in these exciting and tumultuous events was tainted, however, by a crisis in his personal circumstances that occurred before his death in 1848.

After Alexander officially left the office of Colonial Secretary in January 1837, discussion about the controversial way in which he was removed kept him in the spotlight for some time. More than four months later, the *Sydney Herald* reminded its readers that 'the transaction itself has by no means faded from the public mind' and that the 'pitiful pretence under which Mr. M'Leay was turned out' and 'underhand manner in which the scheme was concocted … is still talked of abroad'.[1]

Edward O'Shaughnessy, the emancipist editor who had worked with Robert Howe at the *Sydney Gazette* and joined the *Sydney Herald* in 1835, now openly supported Macleay. At the time, William Watt, who was sub-editor of the *Sydney Gazette*, implied that O'Shaughnessy 'had been bought over by a promise to pay his debts', but whatever the reason, 'he wrote in an appropriate Tory manner for the next five years'.[2] When Alexander was asked to preside at a meeting in November 1837 to address the new Queen, Victoria, O'Shaughnessy wrote that ex-Sheriff Mackaness considered Macleay was not 'of the rank and standing in the Colony to qualify him to preside' and that the Governor himself should have taken the position. But when Wentworth 'played the lion's part' and 'was wont to roar like the fearfulest wild fowl living', he only ended up sounding like 'any nightingale' as the audience was not responsive. In contrast, O'Shaughnessy wrote, when Alexander was escorted to the chair, the applause was so loud that it 'must have sounded like a funeral knell' to his opponents. Attention was also drawn to the inconsistency in Wentworth's claim that Macleay was unsuitable because he was 'the supposed advocate and supporter of a certain line of local politics'. Yet his own nominee, Sir John Jamison, who he declared was a '*no* party-man', was President of the Patriotic Association.[3]

The continuation of Alexander's pension of £750 a year, even though payment for £500 of it had reverted back to England, was still complained about by his opponents. Similar criticism was raised against the £1,000 pension that Forbes sought after his retirement in England though it was pointed out that, whilst Forbes had left Australia permanently, Alexander was 'a resident amongst us and of what he receives a fair proportion returns into the common stock'.[4]

Tilbuster Station 1846, New South Wales. Artist Conrad Martens (1801–1878). Mitchell Library, State Library of New South Wales

The squatter's first home. Even in their bush dwellings most squatters still had the comfort of domestic animals and a warm fireplace. Artist Alexander Denistoun Lang (1814–1872). The National Library of Australia

Innes House with possibly Archibald Innes on horseback. The gum trees in the foreground helped identify the house which was built in the 1830s. Artist most likely Joseph Backler (1813–1895). Reproduced with permission from Lyn and Arnold Mitchell who were gifted the painting by Jill Ford who discovered it in an English village market.

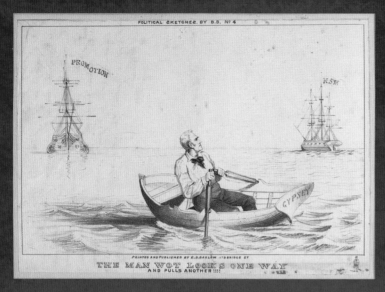

POLITICAL SKETCHES BY B.B. Nº 4

PROMOTION

N.S.W.

GYPSEY

Printed and Published by E.D.Barlow Nº Bridge St

THE MAN WOT LOOKS ONE WAY
AND PULLS ANOTHER!!!!

The Man Wot Looks one Way and Pulls Another!!!! This political sketch illustrates the unpopularity of Governor Gipps in June 1844. Mitchell Library, State Library of New South Wales

Sir George Gipps (1791–1847) was ninth Governor of New South Wales from 1838–1846 but sadly, six months after his return to England, he suffered a fatal heart attack. His failing health in the colony had been exacerbated by the constant strain he was under. Artist probably Henry William Pickersgill (1782–1875). Mitchell Library, State Library of New South Wales

A native family of New South Wales at an English settler's farm. 1826? The house is possibly Charles Throsby's (1777–1828) Glenfield at Casula, which is now a south-western suburb of Sydney. Throsby became a member of the first Legislative Council in December 1825. Artist Augustus Earle (1793–1838). The National Library of Australia

Port Macquarie c. 1841. Artist Joseph Backler. The impressive two storey building in the centre is the Royal Hotel which Archibald Innes opened in 1841. It was on the site of warehouses that he built in 1833 and later converted for public accommodation. Mitchell Library, State Library of New South Wales

The Australian Subscription Library, 1845. It was Alexander Macleay who laid the foundation stone for this new building in 1843 . Mitchell Library, State Library of New South Wales

> *Dunmore Lang addressing the N.S.W. Legislative Council. The importance of the Speaker is shown in this detailed record of the Legislative Council in session. Alexander Macleay was not the only one with white hair. At last the colony recognised the experience and wisdom of its older members.* Artist Jacob Janssen (1779–1856), June 1844. The National Library of Australia

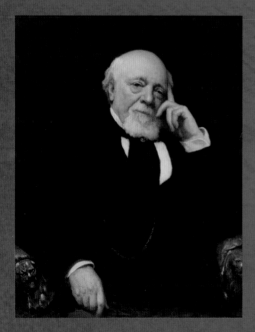

Sir George Macleay 1809–1891. The position George adopted for this portrait was similar to that in his portrait from the 1850s. Only his expression has changed as he perhaps reflects on the years gone by. Artist Sir Hubert von Herkomer (1849–1914). Mitchell Library, State Library of New South Wales

The cemetery at Camperdown where Alexander Macleay is interred, later became part of St Stephen's Church. Artist Conrad Martens (1801–1878) c. 1854. Mitchell Library, State Library of New South Wales

Elizabeth Bay House remains one of Sydney's finest colonial mansions.
Photo: Derelie Cherry

The Macleay and Harington vault is situated next to the Dumaresq vault in the back left corner of the cemetery behind St Stephen's Church. Photo: Derelie Cherry

GOVERNOR GIPPS
ARRIVES

Governor Bourke left New South Wales in December 1837 and when his replacement, Sir George Gipps, arrived in Sydney in February 1838, six colonists presented a welcome address to him. A group of 'Members of Council, Civil Officers, Magistrates, Clergy, Landholders, Merchants and other Colonists'[5] had met on 28 February to appoint this deputation and the inclusion of Macleay could not have been ignored by the new Governor. Despite his background in administration in the West Indies and Canada, Gipps did not fully comprehend the extent of the problems that lay ahead. Faced with economic disaster in the colony only a few years after his arrival, he also had to contend with growing agitation from various factions for self-government and such pressures proved detrimental to his health.

Although Macleay was out of office, Gipps had to deal with issues arising from his period as Colonial Secretary, starting with his Assistant, Thomas Harington. Passed over for the position of Colonial Secretary, and disappointed at the rebuff, he became even more antagonised when the issue of raising his salary arose in the Legislative Council in August 1838. When Gipps queried why the Assistant Colonial Secretary had put up with an inadequate salary while he worked with Alexander, the Governor seemed to be implying that he had only tolerated the situation because of his father-in-law. This slur on both Alexander and Harington was promptly defended by Bishop William Broughton and the Attorney General also defended Harington, claiming he 'would do as much in half an hour, as most other people could do in an hour'. Gipps then revealed that Harington had already asked him for £1,000 (his current salary being £450), arguing that 'the implied rule now is that the deputy is to have two-thirds of the salary of the principal'. At the same time he requested permission for leave to go to England otherwise he would resign. The Governor stated that he was not aware of the existence of any such rule although he did increase Harington's salary, but only by £100.[6] When Harington eventually resigned in 1841 and moved to live permanently in England, his position was finally abandoned, the 'Governor considering that the business of the office can be transacted very well without it'.[7]

MACLEAY CONTINUES TO PARTICIPATE IN COLONIAL AFFAIRS

Out of politics, but still in the public arena, Alexander continued to be very much involved in the numerous colonial societies at whose meetings he was regularly called upon to take the chair. Whilst his participation drew scorn from the *Australian* in February 1838, the *Sydney Herald* denounced their article as 'a drowsy production'.[8] Alexander was grateful for this show of support and appreciated being re-elected as President of the Benevolent Society in July 1837, declaring:

> It might have been supposed that any official influence he possessed hitherto would have benefited the institution; but that having now ceased, the approbation which had been bestowed upon him, and the request that he would continue in the office of President, were doubly gratifying.[9]

In 1837, too, he was again elected President of the Sydney Dispensary, a position he had held since the inception of that society in 1836, and he chaired meetings of the Temperance Society, the New South Wales Auxiliary Bible Society and the Religious Tract Society and attended meetings of the Auxiliary Wesleyan Missionary Society. Not just a figure-head in these societies, he was an active participant and did not hesitate to use his high profile in relation to the controversy surrounding his dismissal. In 1836 he joined the Diocesan Committee which had been established by Bishop Broughton to raise funds, through subscriptions, for Anglican churches and schools.[10] At its meeting in July 1838 he was asked to propose a toast to the health of the Civil Officers but the Stewards had omitted the name of the new Colonial Secretary from their list. Noting this, Alexander announced that 'he felt that he should not be giving justice to his own feelings, if he were to give the toast in the precise words of the Stewards' and thus he toasted 'Mr Thomson and the Civil Officers of the Colony'.[11]

Macleay had lost none of his enthusiasm for public speaking. Responding to a toast to his health at a meeting of the Diocesan Committee in June 1840, he quipped that:

> in his country whenever a person's health was proposed, there is always
> a tune on a bagpipe or some other melodious instrument, which
> always gives him time to think of what he had to say, but here he was
> called upon at once.[12]

Free of official constraints, these public occasions allowed him to express his more personal opinions. In October 1838 he chaired an evening of discussion about the recent voyage of the *Camden*, which had taken a 'Missionary and Exploratory voyage' to the South Sea Islands, for those 'interested in the Commercial, Philanthropic, and Religious enterprises of the present day'.[13] His philanthropic beliefs were evident at a meeting in March 1841 of the Sydney Dispensary when the President's role was acknowledged in relation to his 'many valuable suggestions in the course of their proceedings, ... particularly in regard to the measure taken to procure the Grant of the South wing of the Hospital'. Praise was also given for Macleay's idea, which he had seen 'practised with the best consequences, in Dispensaries and Hospitals in England', that every patient who had recovered should write a note to their minister thanking God, so that the community could be influenced through 'religious feelings and gratitude'.[14] At a meeting of the Bible Society in October 1842, Alexander pronounced that 'All who were interested in their own salvation, must feel the duty which lay upon them of distributing the word of truth among the rest of mankind',[15] a principle upon which he asserted he had based his whole life.

By 1841 Macleay proudly stated that, through the assistance of the Benevolent Society, Sydney 'unlike most towns of the same extent in other countries, had in great measure been as yet kept clear of public begging'.[16] However, the next year, attendance at the meeting he chaired for this Society in July was dramatically down, even though a public appeal pamphlet had been 'left at almost every house in Sydney'.[17] By then, the colony was in the middle of a severe depression and the lack of support was not surprising. This Society had been considered important enough to receive an annual allowance of £3,000 from the Colonial Office but in 1843 that amount was reduced to £2,500 with further reductions in the years to come until all such support finally ended.[18]

Although he maintained his involvement in religious and philanthropic activities, other areas of Macleay's life were changing. On 11 November 1838 William left England to sail for Sydney.[19] He arrived in March 1839, accompanied by cousins William John and John who had decided, after their mother's death in March 1838, to seek their fortunes in a new country with the aid of their Uncle Alexander. Around September 1839 Alexander, Eliza, Kennethina, William, two grandchildren from Rosa and Arthur Onslow and Alexander's two recently arrived nephews all moved into Elizabeth Bay House. Meanwhile, politics was not forgotten by Macleay and he observed with the utmost interest events unfolding as the colony moved towards self-government.

THE MOVE TOWARDS
SELF-GOVERNMENT

The British Government, aware that the end of transportation was imminent, had delayed the replacement of the 1828 Constitution Act which was due to expire in 1837. But no changes could be introduced into New South Wales until after transportation finally ceased in 1840 as a result of the Molesworth Report two years earlier. Nevertheless, between 1835 and 1840, draft proposals for constitutional change, prepared by Bourke, Forbes and other leading colonists such as Wentworth and James Macarthur, were presented to the English authorities.

Their demands were consistent with the demographic changes in the colony. According to a census undertaken by Mansfield in 1841, 64% of the population in New South Wales were free, 15% were emancipists and only 21% were convicts completing their sentences.[20] That year the Tories returned to power in the United Kingdom under Prime Minister Sir Robert Peel and they decided to address the increased agitation for self-government. On 26 May 1842, the Secretary of State, Lord Edward Stanley, introduced the New South Wales Bill into the House of Commons and noted that:

> the bill would considerably extend the popular rights in New South Wales, but not more so than he thought the population, wealth, and importance of the Colony were fairly entitled to.[21]

Details of the new Act filtered through to New South Wales and by October 1842 a copy of the official bill had arrived in Sydney. On the expectation that it would pass unchanged, plans began to be implemented for the colony's first elections. Under the new constitution the Legislative Council would increase to 36 members, two thirds of whom were to be elected, and the remaining twelve nominated by the Crown. Whilst the Legislative Council was given control of funds raised from taxation, monies raised from the sale of Crown lands remained with the Governor, leaving the Executive Council financially independent of the legislature. Because the new Legislative Council was dominated by property owners, it became known as the 'Squatters Council'. With political power now on their side, and the wool industry of such importance to both England and New South Wales, new divisions emerged within colonial society between those who favoured the landed interests and those with an interest in the rising urban middle classes who were against the land monopolisers. The newly-formed Council was to meet for four months each year and the Governor's presence was no longer required at these sessions. As a consequence, political debate could proceed uncensored by the Governor and a president would control their meetings.

Who better, or more experienced, than Alexander Macleay to fill this role of Speaker?

In November 1842 Sydney had a foretaste of what was to come when it carried out its very first election for officers in the newly-formed Sydney City Council. Candidates came from commercial and landowning classes with builders, butchers, publicans and shopkeepers prominent among the successful candidates. Alexander Macleay stood for election for Darlinghurst in the ward of Cook[22] and, although he was unsuccessful, the *Australian* included his name in their own nominations for mayor.[23] Even Governor Gipps was disappointed that some of the wealthier citizens were not represented.[24]

Wealth played more of a role in the Legislative Council election. The franchise and the distribution of seats for the 1843 poll were based on property ownership and 41 men contested 24 seats in eighteen electoral districts.[25] Candidates for election were required to own property that was worth at least £2,000 or earning at least £100 annually in rent.[26] In order to be eligible to vote, colonists had to either own property worth at least £200 or be a householder paying an annual rent of £20. Voting was entirely voluntary and of the 9,300 electors who came forward in 1843,[27] many could vote in more than one electorate if they owned property in each area.

MACLEAY STANDS
FOR ELECTION

On 11 February 1843 Alexander put his name forward to represent the northern counties of Gloucester, Stanley and Macquarie, which extended from Port Macquarie to Moreton Bay. He was nearly 76 years old. In his printed announcement, Macleay stated that encouragement to stand for this electorate in the Legislative Council had come 'from a numerous and highly respectable body of Clergymen, magistrates and others' in the Macquarie county and 'the kind support from influential persons in other parts of the Electoral District'.

He based his claim to stand on the grounds of his 'long public service both in this and our Mother country', his 'straight forward conduct' and his interest in public affairs through his 'connexion with those various Colonial Institutions over which I have the honour to preside'.[28]

There were other reasons why Macleay stood for the northern counties, rather than for Camden or the city of Sydney. It was only after it became apparent that Wentworth and his ally, Bland, were standing for the city and that Roger Therry was to stand for Camden, that Macleay announced his choice of electorate. Not relishing the opportunity to contest seats with such opposition, the northern counties would have seemed an appropriate choice from which to launch a campaign, especially as his daughter Margaret and son-in-law Archibald Innes lived at Port Macquarie. Furthermore, only one candidate came forward to oppose him in the area, namely 63-year-old Charles Windeyer, a police magistrate with a large land holding at Stanley who had arrived in the colony with his family in 1828.[29] With a background as a legal journalist in the Houses of Parliament and law courts of London, he was a formidable opponent, but one whom Macleay could reasonably expect to defeat based on the initial response of the locals.[30]

Five days after his announcement to stand, Macleay declared that there was no need formally to state his 'opinions on religious and political matters' as his 'sentiments on those very important points' were 'well known'.[31] Macleay's political attitudes had changed little since 1802 when he wrote to James Smith in the Linnean Society:

> For my own part I must say that although I may perhaps incline a little to Toryism, yet I highly respect the true old English Spirit of Whigism, and if it were otherwise, I am not [so] illiberal as to condemn a man because he thinks differently from me. Excepting religious Controversy, there is in my opinion no Pursuit so unprofitable as Politics, unless it be to those who professedly make them their business ...[32]

Macleay's opponents argued that he had no land in the electorate and that his conservative Tory political bias was well known whereas Windeyer's 'politics (except that it is understood he is favourable to a protecting duty on imported wheat)' were in favour of liberal reform.[33] But as Windeyer's magisterial salary was paid by the Government, he was not likely to oppose Council policies whereas Macleay was 'totally unconnected with the Government'.[34]

Windeyer announced that he was 'a warm friend to civil liberty, the rights of consciences, and the diffusion of general education' and was interested in promoting 'agricultural and pastoral interests'.[35] His supporters made much of contrasting his character with that of the 'exclusive and self-styled aristocracy, who had ruined the country by their extravagance, credit and paper money' and claimed that:

> M'Leay … had … been too long a servant of the government to turn round now and oppose any of its measures; besides which he was too old and imbecile to attend to the duties which would be imposed upon him.[36]

In response to this accusation Macleay's supporters described him as 'fit and proper' and reminded the public that he had actually lost his job as Colonial Secretary because his opinions conflicted with the Governor at that time, and 'if he would oppose them while he was in office, surely they might presume that he would not hesitate to oppose them now that he was entirely independent of them'.[37]

At a policy speech evening in Port Macquarie, Windeyer recalled from his boyhood days in England that he remembered Macleay as a secretary of war and 'of the two he thought he was the fitter working man'.[38] Yet Windeyer was not young either, the *Sydney Morning Herald* pointing out in May 1843 that both he and Alexander had 'arrived at an honoured old age'.[39]

Not surprisingly, the *Sydney Morning Herald* published a particularly favourable column on why Alexander should be elected. Charles Kemp, previously the paper's parliamentary reporter, and John Fairfax, who had extensive experience working with newspapers in Britain before he arrived in Sydney in 1838, had become owners of this paper in February 1841.[40] In support of Macleay, the article reminded readers how effectively, within a year of his arrival in 1826, he had sorted out the disorder that he inherited in the Colonial Office. The editor asserted that as Macleay was experiencing 'a green and vigorous old age' he would be good for the colony's 'political freedom' and that he would contribute to Council:

> his eminent skill in the conduct of business, his thorough acquaintance with every branch of our colonial interests, and his extensive connexion with the most influential circles in the mother country.[41]

The dates for polling were from 12 June to 3 July 1843 and the nomination day for Macleay's electorate was held on 12 June. As the show of hands on this occasion was indecisive, it was determined that the election day should be on 23 June. In the interim, Alexander obviously decided it was essential that his policies be more widely circulated and he sent George to speak on his behalf at a public meeting at Raymond Terrace near Newcastle. Announcing that because his father was sick he would endeavour to explain his principles in his absence,[42] George declared that his:

> father was a strenuous supporter of the church; he would promote education founded on religion; he was independent of government, and had a great stake in the country. He had arrived at an age when most people would feel disposed to enjoy those comforts which a life devoted to the service of his country had gained for him, but it was not his case; while he saw that he could be useful to his adopted country he could not remain inactive, but would devote the last hours of his life to its service. He was a Conservative, not an opposer of free trade, and would defend the agricultural interests of the country, and he begged to remind the electors that there would be but very few in the new council who would feel so great an interest in the agricultural interests of the country, as the major part of them would be large sheep and cattle holders.[43]

In the *Sydney Morning Herald*'s report on this speech, Mansfield (or perhaps Charles Kemp) maintained that George had expressly said of free trade that 'his father was doubtful of the advantages, even in England, with all its different and conflicting interests but to this colony he thought those principles *entirely inapplicable*'.[44] In direct contrast to Macleay's statement, the article declared that free trade had flourished very well in the colony until now and any thought of 'protective taxes' would be similar to 'the national curse' of a Corn Law.

When George was asked whether or not his father would now oppose measures that he had previously approved when in office, he replied 'he certainly would' and explained that he had previously acted 'wisely and judiciously under the existing circumstances of the colony … as it was then supposed that this colony would remain a penal settlement'. However, 'the present position of the colony would call for an opposite line of policy, and his father would be the first to adopt it'.[45]

By the end of the year there were several new regional newspapers, including the *Windsor Express and Richmond Advertiser* in May 1843, and the *Parramatta Chronicle* in December 1843. On 7 January 1843 the *Maitland Mercury and Hunter River General Advertiser* began publication under the management of Thomas William Tucker, a former reporter for the *Sydney Herald*, and the printer Richard Jones. Promoting 'moderately liberal and sometimes reticent politics' it was widely read amongst the squatters[46] and, with the coming election, all these new papers had plenty to write about. The inauguration of the Maitland newspaper was excellent timing for Alexander. Its support in the months to come lasted right up to the time of him being elected first Speaker.

VICTORY AT THE POLLS

Six days before polling day Alexander arrived in Port Macquarie via the *Maitland* steamer from Sydney to deliver his election speech. A luncheon had been organised by friends for 21 June to be held at the Royal Hotel which was one of the many business ventures that Archibald Innes either owned or was connected with. It must have been a rough journey, for Annabella Boswell reported that the steamer had to 'lay off the port all night' and Alexander and his party only landed in the morning in a boat that 'narrowly escaped being swamped'.

She described how bagpipes played under Mr Macleay's window every morning for his enjoyment, and how he showed them the 'old country dance' called 'the Country Bumpkin'.[47] She wrote that her aunt 'asked us if we had pink sashes, as pink was her father's colour, and she wished us very much to wear pink'.[48] Apparently Alexander had 'by mere chance'[49] chosen pink as his electoral colour but it was used extensively and effectively. The verandah posts were bedecked with pink streamers, some of which had mottoes printed on them, such as 'Macleay for ever', and even the local Aborigines wore pink calico on polling day.[50]

The evening before election day the extended family and friends held a dinner at home in style. Young Annabella described that the table, set for eighteen, 'presented a splendid appearance' and that 'Bruce [the bag-pipe player] and the butler waited, and we had four footmen in livery'. 'I felt quite dazzled, as I had never been at so splendid an entertainment before'.[51]

On 21 June, two days before voting began, approximately 60 people attended the lunch in Port Macquarie at which Alexander spoke. In line with the changing circumstances of the colony, he had adapted his views and was keen that his electorate fully understood the reasoning behind his political opinions. With regard to free trade, he clarified his belief that the 'necessaries of life — such as bread and meat — were entitled to a protective duty', but for all other items he was happy to live with the existing free trade arrangement. In response to the accusation that he was a Tory, he announced that he 'Was not; he was what might be termed a Moderate conservative' as he did not really see that the distinction between Whig and Tory applied to Australia where every-one had the same aims. On religion, he declared that although he belonged to and was a staunch supporter of the Protestant church, 'he was a firm advo-cate for the liberty of conscience' as evidenced through his involvement in the colony over the years. His choice of the word Protestant, encompassing as it did in the colony the Church of England, Presbyterian, Congregational,

Baptist and Wesleyan denominations, reinforced his tolerant attitude towards other religions with the conspicuous exception of Roman Catholicism.

On education he believed that there should be a state system, but that religious education should be left with local clergymen and he reminded his audience that this was the very subject on which he had clashed with Governor Bourke. Another issue which he raised was the existing insolvency law which he considered 'caused ruination to all concerned', especially during the severe economic depression that the colony had recently experienced. Under this law, when parties were declared insolvent their property was immediately seized and put on the market.[52] Alexander affirmed that he would try to have this law altered for the obvious benefit of landed people.

By the evening of 23 June, it was apparent that Macleay was in the winning seat. Votes for Port Macquarie were 75 for Macleay and 2 for Windeyer.[53] When voting for the other counties was completed, Macleay scored an outright victory with a total of 142 votes to Windeyer's 36.[54] In a preliminary victory speech at a dinner in Port Macquarie that evening, he made special reference to the argument that had been put forward that he was too old for such an office: 'He was happy in saying he did not belong to a very short-lived family, his mother had only died the last year at the advanced age of 103 years'.[55]

The very next day Macleay turned 76 and his birthday was celebrated extravagantly in the light of his victory at the polls. Pink was again the prevailing colour chosen for the decorations and, as there were so many pink China roses in the garden, Annabella arranged some in an epergne on the breakfast table which pleased Alexander immensely.[56] And when the victor triumphantly paraded around Port Macquarie all the onlookers wore a pink flower to help celebrate the victory.[57] Alexander's success would have been even sweeter after he learned later that day that his son-in-law, William Dumaresq, was the winning candidate, with a margin of only four votes, for the counties of Hunter, Brisbane and Bligh.[58] In 1840 Dumaresq had relocated his family to Rose Bay in Sydney. Like Alexander, he would be an absentee although he continued to hold extensive property in his electorate.

Peter Bruce 'The Piper' was also overseer at Innes House. Reproduced with permission from the Port Macquarie Historical Society

MACLEAY ELECTED AS
FIRST SPEAKER

The new Legislative Council met on 1 August 1843 and its first task was to choose a Speaker. William Duncan, editor of the *Weekly Register* which was established in July 1843, reported on the three candidates for the position, namely, Alexander Macleay, Edward Hamilton and William Charles Wentworth. Originally a schoolmaster in the colony where he had arrived in 1829, and a well-known Catholic advocate, the 'markedly liberal and literary'[59] Duncan claimed that:

> of the first we must say that his known habits of order and regularity
> — habits so necessary for the office — go far to balance against his old
> school politics to which we have the most decided dislike.[60]

The *Maitland Mercury* on 5 August 1843 believed that it would not have been a good idea to have Wentworth, who was originally the only candidate for the position, because he was such a good debater and would be denied this role if elected Speaker. It made reference to the '*general* deference and respect which it is so highly essential the Speaker should always command'.[61] The *Sydney Morning Herald*'s opinion on the subject was that 'the SPEAKER should be habitually cool and collected: everybody who knows Mr. WENTWORTH is aware that he is exactly the reverse ... His blood is constitutionally hot ... His temper is like gunpowder'.[62] Furthermore, 'habits of strict punctuality, of patient plodding, of persevering industry' were required for the position and not only did the Speaker have to be present on each day that sessions were held, but he also had to 'superintend the clerical details of the Council office; for he will be the head of the department, and be responsible to the house and to the country for the efficient and economical conduct of its business'.[63]

Under such criteria, the *Sydney Morning Herald* considered Wentworth quite unsuitable for the position, whereas Macleay was 'a man of shrewd common sense, well versed in the rules of business'. The fact that Wentworth was still averse to Macleay and could not 'mention his name without snarling and showing his teeth' was not overlooked. This article discussed the issue of whether or not the Speaker was in a position to voice his own opinion, concluding that he was not able to but, rather, had 'the right of enforcing order, of putting questions, of deciding on majorities, and of giving the casting vote'. Nearly a week later, the *Sydney Morning Herald* concluded that because Macleay's oratory skills were lacking, he would fit this new role perfectly.[64] It was ironic and rather contradictory that this support came because Macleay was perceived as not being a good speaker, making him perfect therefore for the role of Speaker!

It was not too long before Wentworth withdrew his candidature and on the day of selection the Commander of the Forces, Lieutenant-General Maurice O'Connell, nominated Alexander and Hannibal Macarthur seconded the motion. The latter expanded upon his friend's 'long tried abilities as a government officer, his attainments in literature and science, and the advantage which age and experience would give him'.[65] And the *Sydney Morning Herald's* Mansfield reminded its readers that Macleay had held 'for many years the highest official situation in the colony'.[66]

Roger Therry, the newly elected member for Camden, proposed Edward Hamilton as Speaker and emphasised the 'energy and preserverance [sic] which would be required' and that Macleay's former experience would not help him in the position. Moreover, he was too old for consideration, whereas Hamilton was 'in the full enjoyment of all his faculties',[67] even though he had only arrived in the colony in 1839. Therry implied that because Macleay had been superannuated for many years, he was not fit for such a demanding position. But at the end of his speech Therry admitted that he was only 'but slightly acquainted with Mr. Hamilton' and in fact had only been asked to nominate him upon entering the meeting that very morning. As to who made this request, Stephen Roberts claims that it was Governor Gipps.[68] This idea probably came from the report in the *Sydney Morning Herald* on 1 August that Hamilton owed 'his seat to the circumstance of his being one of the Governor's private friends'.[69] In seconding the motion in favour of Hamilton, Bland said how fortunate it was that his favourite candidate, Wentworth, had not come forward as he was too closely aligned with 'the interests of a party'. He suggested this was also the case with Macleay, making him unsuitable for the office, whereas Hamilton was not 'identified with any particular party'.[70] The *Maitland Mercury* pointed out that the choice of Speaker was certainly not based on the political 'opinions of the members of Council, as both candidates professed themselves Conservatives'.

Soon afterwards Hamilton admitted to the Council that he had not come forward of his own volition but because he had received two letters, one from the Colonial Treasurer and another from Wentworth, both informing him that ten members of the Council had met and decided to approach him to consider the position. Hamilton added that he had 'decided opinions' and that 'he had always been a Conservative, and he thought he should remain so'.[71]

In another follow-up speech, Wentworth reminded the Council how closely associated Macleay had been with Darling's policies, especially in relation to restricting the freedom of the press, and also claimed that Macleay was:

> the means of organising that disgraceful system of espionage which existed in those days of oppression and which made the office of the colonial secretary a rendezvous for every dirty spy.[72]

Wentworth continued his vitriolic attack on Macleay by saying that he never doubted his scientific abilities and that if the appointment had been as president of a scientific board, he 'would have been a great recommendation'. He also pointed out two major objections to Alexander, namely, 'his want of distinct utterance [presumably his Scottish accent] and his deafness'. In conclusion he insinuated that Macleay wanted the position for the money, not for the honour. Considering Alexander's dire financial situation at that time, this may have been true even though the Speaker's salary was to be only £500.

Wentworth's spy accusation was an indirect reference to an episode in August 1830 when Matthew Gregson, a clerk in the Colonial Secretary's office, was accused of informing by Hall in the *Sydney Monitor*.[73] In response to Wentworth's suggestion, Alexander categorically 'defied any man to say that he had ever employed a spy in his life'.[74] The *Weekly Register* also made a pertinent observation about Wentworth's criticisms of Macleay's large grants of public lands, announcing that Wentworth 'two years ago, did his best to possess himself of 1,000,000 of acres of such lands — the most monstrous attempt at public robbery, on the part of an individual ever heard of since the creation of the world!'[75] This reference was to Wentworth's attempt to buy vast acres of land from the Maoris, including virtually all of the south island of New Zealand, for a nominal amount. Gipps's rejection of his claim and his recommendation that Wentworth be withdrawn from nomination to the Legislative Council, had made Wentworth rile even more against Macleay.[76]

As the debate continued about the future Speaker, William Foster, who had been elected unopposed in the county of Northumberland, claimed that in relation to the 'pensions and salaries and grants of land ... no one would have been so silly as to refuse them, had they been offered to him'. Instead of Macleay being too old for the position, he would 'add weight and dignity to the office' whereas Hamilton was too young.[77] Mansfield added in the *Sydney Morning Herald* that Foster had taken the opportunity to repay a 'debt of gratitude' for, upon his arrival in New South Wales, he had met with 'great kindness' from Alexander. It was perfectly natural 'that a man should accept the [emoluments] which properly belonged to his office' and, questioned Foster, 'was it likely that he would refuse what was offered him, and say "Oh, that is too much!"'[78]

Later on in Council proceedings, the controversial Reverend Dunmore Lang, Member for Port Phillip, sneeringly claimed in relation to Macleay that 'the only points of natural history to which he seemed to have turned his attention had been attended to by other gentlemen with equal effect, viz. the rearing of sheep and cattle'.[79] However, the *Sydney Morning Herald* recognised his 'high scientific attainments which have rendered his name known throughout the civilised world' as well as 'his unblemished reputation'.[80] Nicholson further defended Macleay by observing that:

> With respect to the measures of government with which Mr. M'Leay had been concerned, though they might now appear oppressive, if the true state of the case was known they might, when adopted, have been actually necessary.[81]

In his own defence, Macleay claimed that his conduct in association with

Darling 'would be found blameless' and that his pension and land grant at Elizabeth Bay had been handled in the appropriate manner. In relation to Bathurst, the only request he had ever made of him was that 'his furniture should be sent back to London at the expense of the government'.[82] In the end, Alexander won the day and was elected Speaker by the small majority of four.[83] When he took the chair, 'after thanking his friends and attributing personal motives to his opponents, [he] expressed a hope that they should now all be friends'.[84] Some of the colonists, too, now changed their opinions. Although Deas Thomson and Campbell Riddell, the Colonial Treasurer, had initially voted against Macleay, they agreed to fully support him after he was elected.[85]

The second of August 1843 was a proud and memorable day for Macleay as Council members escorted their new Speaker in a procession of carriages from the new Legislative Chambers in Macquarie Street to Government House. Not surprisingly, Wentworth and Richard Windeyer, Charles Windeyer's son who had won the electorate of Durham adjacent to Macleay's electorate, absented themselves. The *Weekly Register* noted that 'we have got at all events, a sufficiently Conservative Council',[86] presumably implying that the presence of Alexander as Speaker would have a significant effect on proceedings. Deas Thomson proposed that the Governor stand next to the Speaker at the formal opening of the Council the following day. Inevitably, Wentworth objected but Thomson's suggestion was implemented. The next day 'the unbecoming expressions' in debate were commented on by the outspoken Lang in his *Colonial Observer* newspaper:

> We trust also the Speaker will abstain from such language as 'A book which I have not seen for ten years, I'll swear' and 'Mr. Wentworth abused me like a fish-wife.' Honourable members must remember that the New Council is the Colonial School for the study of Oratory, and they would surely not willingly offer such models as these to their Colonial pupils.[87]

The *Weekly Register* marked the events of that week by reporting that the first debate in the new Council was:

Singular, on account of the strange anomalies it presented, for here we had a 'Whig-radical' representative of a radical constituency proposing as speaker an avowedly 'staunch conservative', which staunch conservative was seconded by the almost republican Bland ... & he supported by out & out radical, Mr. Windeyer, & Mr. Wentworth, who from a 'rascally Whig' to use his own designation has recently become a conservative of the first order.[88]

Opening of the Legislative Council in Sydney 29 July, 1845. Friends and relatives wait nearby to enter the building after the arrival of the Governor who was to open proceedings. Alexander Macleay, as Speaker, met him at the door. This drawing appeared in *The Illustrated London News* in 1846. The National Library of Australia

On 12 August 1843 the *Weekly Register* commenced a new weekly series of articles which continued until October. Entitled 'Heads of the Australian People', their first profile, with an accompanying drawing, was about Alexander Macleay. Depicted as a peculiarly diminutive man in an over-sized chair, lampooning his inadequacy for the Speakership, this portrait is one of the least flattering of the whole series.[89] Perpetuating the Tory connection, the *Weekly Register* wrote on 19 August that:

> His political character has often and recently been brought unfavourably before the public. It is unnecessary in this place to say more, than that he is a staunch Tory of the old school, and that while in office, he was understood to be a supporter of the arbitrary measures of General Darling, and an opponent of the more enlightened policy of Sir Richard Bourke.[90]

The Speaker (Alexander Macleay). Even though he had been elected Speaker, the opposition papers still could not resist making fun of Alexander Macleay. The *Weekly Register* 12 August 1843. State Library of New South Wales

Despite such assertions, Macleay's appointment as first Speaker in the colony was a great honour. During his three years in the chair, Macleay was rigid on matters of punctuality and decorum and, in December 1844, he adjourned the session when only ten members turned up, not enough for a quorum.[91] The first session of Council ran for 86 sitting days from 1 August to 28 December 1843. During that time it passed 24 public acts, 22 of which were approved by the Governor with the other two requiring the Queen's approval. The second session sat from 5 March to 20 May 1844, a period of 85 days, and approved 24 acts, including three which needed royal assent. And the third session sat for 61 days, from 29 July 1845 to 13 November 1845, during which time 30 public acts were passed, two of which required royal approval.[92] Although he was approaching 80, Macleay's pace of life had certainly not slowed down.

DEMANDS FROM THE SQUATTERS

Within the colony the squatters were becoming a formidable body but the Colonial Office was determined to keep control of Crown lands and their revenues. Nevertheless, because of the importance of the pastoral industry, growing sympathy for the cause of the squatters led Stanley to concede that the 'circumstances of widespread and urgent distress among their constituents' resulting from the 1840s depression justified the Council's emphasis on 'putting back public expenditure in aid of local revenue'. Furthermore, he wrote to Gipps:

> While I agree with you that the tone and temper of some of the proceedings of the Legislative Council in this their first session are to be regretted, I am unwilling to make them the subject of any comment, which could be misconstrued as a failure in the respect and confidence due to that Body. Meeting as they did for the first

time with no practical experience of the inconvenience of insisting on extreme rights and doubtful claims, a large allowance is due for any such discretion.[93]

However, the *Sydney Morning Herald* reported a distinct rift between the Legislative Council and the Governor claiming that there were 'two branches of the Legislature of New South Wales' and that:

> between these co-ordinate powers there had been several sharp conten-
> tions, and almost a total want of sympathy; the one being, in all its aims
> and objects, in all its prepossessions and antipathies, essentially colonial,
> and the other essentially British; one studying, as its paramount duty,
> the interests of the country placed especially under its charge, and the
> other the good graces of the Minister in whose smile it officially exists.[94]

Rather than hand over Crown lands to what he considered was a monopoly of 'land-grabbers', Gipps sought to make them available for everyone to use. His new occupation regulations of 2 April 1844, which incorporated an annual licence fee in proportion to the 'size and stock of their runs',[95] created an outcry amongst the squatters.[96] The Governor followed up this proposal in May with purchasing regulations which afforded the squatters some security of tenure, as they could either purchase or move after five years' occupancy. But this additional measure was viewed as another tax, especially as land prices were so high at £1 an acre and the colonists were still recovering from the disastrous economic conditions of the earlier 1840s. So they held out for long leases, which would effectively give them control of the land, and also sought compensation for improvements if the land was sold and a right of first purchase if the government wanted to sell their leasehold.[97]

Macleay's intense interest in all these proceedings related as much to his own pastoral concerns as to his political hope that the landed classes could take control of the colony's affairs through the introduction of responsible government. He was a key supporter of the Australian Pastoral Association which was formed in England to voice the demands of the squatters. In August 1843, the Legislative Council resolved to appoint an Agent for this Association in

London, on a salary of £500 per annum, to act on their behalf, and without 'official influence' to advocate the colony's interests to the British Parliament and press.[98] After an initial delay, Francis Scott was appointed in 1844 and a Committee of Correspondence was established. Even before Gipps had granted official permission, Macleay was given the task of enlisting Scott and he spelt out that he 'would be asked to ventilate the agricultural and the pastoral grievances, of which that connected with the squatting regulations was the most important'.[99]

A few weeks' later, in December 1844, Macleay wrote again to Scott, informing him that the:

> repeated collisions between the executive and legislative authorities of
> this colony must doubtless be regarded as circumstances to be deeply
> regretted, and must afford an unanswerable reason for the necessity of
> responsible government.[100]

In another letter to Scott in September 1845, Alexander openly sided with the elected members of the Council against the Governor, by categorically defining the Legislative Council's objectives:

> The Committee [of Council] wished you distinctly to understand that
> your appointment was quite independent of the executive government
> of this colony, upon which, indeed, it is intended to operate as a check
> ... not only are His Excellency's views sometimes far different from
> those of the Council ... His Excellency and the Council are occasion-
> ally at issue even upon matters of fact ... the Council must have some
> independent organ of communication with Her Majesty's government,
> who shall truly represent their views and wishes, according to their
> own interpretation of them.[101]

As Alexander's opponents had frequently pointed out, both personal and political reasons continued to motivate his actions. To advise that the body paid for by the legislature could openly oppose the Governor as the Crown representative, was inviting controversy. But having been appointed Speaker and once again back in the public eye, Macleay seems to have not been as concerned as he once was about likely repercussions from his outspoken directives. His own finances were at stake.

ECONOMIC
DEPRESSION STRIKES

As a pastoralist with vast acreage, Alexander would have been personally affected by the new land policies under Gipps. It was bad enough when the Governor raised the price of Crown land to 12 shillings per acre in 1838 but when it was increased to £1 in 1842, sales fell dramatically. In 1840 revenue from land sales was £316,626 and in 1842 it reached a low of £7,541.[102] Adding to the squatters' problems was the effect of a severe drought from 1839 to 1841. Wool prices fell dramatically and by the start of the 1840s the colony was in deep depression. The *Sydney Morning Herald* summarised the situation in May 1843:

> The fast growing embarrassments of 1841, and the six hundred insolvencies of 1842, have been crowned in the first third of the year 1843, by the explosion at the Bank of Australia, then by the minor explosion of the Sydney Bank, and last of all by the run on the Savings Bank.[103]

Interest rates escalated, in some instances to as high as 20%,[104] and 'doubt, suspicion, and fear' replaced 'confidence and trust' in investment.[105] All sections of the community were affected, especially those with extensive mortgages. Because the squatters did not own their runs they were unable to obtain mortgages from the colonial banks and were forced to borrow from merchants who acted as intermediaries between banks and agents in London. When the supply of wool fell because of the drought, the colony was left with a shortage of capital which, combined with large borrowings and exorbitant interest rates, resulted in many bankruptcies. Sheep and cattle were almost worthless but in

1843 a new industry of boiling down sheep carcasses for candles and soap was introduced which offered some consolation.

By late 1844 rumours were circulating in the colony that Alexander Macleay was in such dire pecuniary trouble that he would be forced to resign his position as Speaker. When Gipps was asked to provide the Colonial Office with the names of individuals who he considered eligible to receive a local merit award, as such honours were to be introduced for the first time, the Governor could only come up with nineteen names. Second on his list was Alexander Macleay, but in his despatch to England, Gipps noted that Macleay 'is, I regret however to say, understood to be in pecuniary embarrassment'.[106]

Lang, in an unusual show of support for Macleay, wrote in November 1844:

> One would have thought that honourable members, under such circumstances, would have hesitated to the last in believing such a report; that previous to its absolute confirmation they would have taken no step in the matter; and that even then delicacy and good taste would have prevented them from anticipating the act of resignation by any selfish act of their own. But no nice scruples of this sort guide the representatives of the people of New South Wales. Though we have no very particular regard for the present Speaker as a public man, we do sincerely hope that he may yet keep his place, to laugh at and 'call to order' the gentlemen who now seek to pull away his chair and pocket his salary.[107]

Three council members had already begun canvassing for his position: Wentworth, Charles Nicholson and Charles Cowper. The *Australian* and the *Register* also recorded this turn of events and the *Maitland Mercury* reported on 'The discourtesy and indelicacy of asking for Mr. M'Leay's office before he had resigned it, and took occasion to rap the hon. members over the knuckles for the eagerness they displayed to live by their country, rather than for it'.[108] Treating Macleay's resignation as a fait accompli, these councillors were behaving in exactly the same manner as the adversaries of the Colonial Secretary in 1836. However, by 30 November 1844, the *Colonist* reported that 'after all, the anticipated vacancy is not likely to occur, Mr. M'Leay having, it is said, obtained a settlement of his affairs'.[109]

MACLEAY'S
TROUBLED FINANCES

Yet the newspaper reports about Alexander's financial circumstances were correct and it was only because of the intervention of William, and the assistance of several friends from outside the Legislative Council, that he did not become bankrupt. By 1841 Alexander was so desperately short of money that he was forced to advertise 44 allotments for sale at his Elizabeth Bay Estate,[110] although only eight sold during this time of economic depression.[111]

In July 1841, the *Sydney Morning Herald* announced that the Australian Trust Company would open for business on 2 August. This new enterprise had been initiated in London around 1838 with the specific aim of lending money and investing in the flourishing wool industry in the colony. A similar organisation had been established in America and the Australian venture was an attempt to duplicate the American example which had 'been acted upon with great success … that of receiving deposits in England at a moderate fixed rate of interest on the credit of a large invested capital, and laying them out on real security at the rate of interest current in Australia'. By means of a 'Charter obtained from the Crown' in London, the Trust was 'authorised to receive Deposits to four times the amount of its paid up capital' but its operations were limited to mortgage loans on 'real security in Australia' and it was 'expressly prohibited from banking, discounting, or trading in any way whatever'.[112] With a starting capital of £1,000,000 in 10,000 shares of £100 each, and the power to increase the capital to £2,000,000, the express purpose was to assist landowners when land values were at a premium.

Unfortunately, Macleay had decided to take out a substantial mortgage with this new company and it was to his detriment that the local board, to which he had been appointed, was given so much flexibility in its dealings. Even the *Sydney Herald* commented on this aspect:

> The advances will be made at the interest of ten per cent per annum in
> all cases, and in such proportions to the value of the property offered

as security and for such periods as the Colonial Board of Directors and the applicants may agree upon in each case.[113]

In 1843 Robert Morehead wrote to the directors of the Scottish Australian Company in Aberdeen that the Australian Trust Company's financial troubles were due to the local board lending great sums of money to themselves from the start. The 'worst offender' in this respect was Alexander Macleay. But as the historian David Macmillan reflects, whilst Macleay 'brought himself and his family into near ruin in this period … he was not doing anything illegal'.[114] Becoming part of this new company would have seemed a viable proposition and a way for Macleay to raise money within a fairly short period of time. Even the Chairman, Hastings Elwin, who had arrived in New South Wales in 1840 to direct the affairs of this new company, appeared to be a capable business administrator with an impressive background in finance and law.[115]

Alexander's situation was so critical by 1843 that William took complete control of the family finances. In April that year he documented Alexander's assets and liabilities, including the 21 loans that he had transferred to his father's account since 1824. Commencing with the first transfer of £550, they had escalated over nearly twenty years and by 10 April 1843 Alexander owed his son £12,369 without factoring in interest at 5% per annum.[116]

The anticipated family income that William recorded was still substantial considering the depressed economic climate: £1,000 received for wool sales in 1843, £1,500 projected for wool if sold in Sydney in 1844, books and plate £1,500, horses from India £230, station at Richmond £1,500, cattle and land at Ulladulla £2,000, cattle horses and land at Byalla totalling £3,500, 13 acres at Elizabeth Bay £13,000 pounds (this acreage was the 8 allotments sold since 1841) and an additional unidentified £3,000 pounds.[117] Yet this total income scarcely covered the interest due, let alone discharged the capital debts.

As a result of his calculations, William devised a plan whereby he would pay off his father's creditors in Australia and England from his own pension and assume himself the Trust Company mortgage for Elizabeth Bay House.

There was one overriding condition for these arrangements: William would stay living in Elizabeth Bay House but Alexander must leave. This was the only viable solution to avoid Alexander losing his home and various other properties. To justify his actions, William wrote a letter to his father on 26 October 1844, explaining that he would 'try and live as economically as possible … to prove that we are ready to make sacrifices', but that he would not enter any agreement whereby Alexander could end up in the Insolvent Court. He concluded that he knew of 'no other way of paying' off his father's debts except to sell up,[118] and that, although everything he said was 'viewed with a prejudiced eye', he had 'no other anxiety in this matter than as speedily as possible to be allowed to settle with your creditors. This can never be done if we continue to live on in the way we have been doing'.[119]

Under these circumstances, especially being evicted from his own beautiful house, it was not surprising that Alexander could not understand William's behaviour. William further enunciated:

> I have never yet said or written a word to hurry you from the house but with your own solicitor I am convinced that in the peculiar cir-cumstances — you ought to leave it as soon as possible. Of course My Mother and Kenny will take away their own property, and as for the other things you mention what you and they wish to take away is com-pletely at your Service. Only I shall thank you for a list of the various articles removed, and on my part I shall attend to your every wish as to the things you may desire should be retained. However with regard to selling the books in London that would not meet our object which is to realize for this immediate demand of your Creditors. If possible therefore I shall avoid selling the books.[120]

Considering the urgent state of his finances, to even contemplate sending the books in his library to London to sell was quite unfeasible, a fact which Alexander seems to have not comprehended.

MACLEAY LEAVES
ELIZABETH BAY HOUSE

So, according to William's instructions, the family moved out to Brownlow Hill although, during Council sessions, Alexander stayed with Christiana at Tivoli, her house at Rose Bay. Despite his aim to avoid such a sale, William was unable to save his father's library. Lasting over five days from 23 April 1845, the sale of his 'extensive and valuable library of nearly four thousand volumes' was described as *'forming decidedly the largest and most valuable collection of Book*s ever brought to the hammer in New South Wales'.[121] In addition, Alexander's furniture was sold to help William pay the creditors' immediate demands as devised in his plan of 26 October 1844.

Alexander felt so ostracised by his son's behaviour in 1843 that he asked Thomas Barker, Robert Lowe and Charles Nicholson to act on his behalf. Barker, who was Director of the Commercial Bank of Australia and a wealthy landowner and successful entrepreneur, had widespread knowledge and experience on financial matters. He proposed a plan of specific action after receiving all the liabilities and asset details from William, Alexander even referring to his friend as 'Chancellor of the Exchequer' in one of the many letters that were subsequently exchanged between them.[122] The tone of these letters is poignant, with Macleay often pleading to Barker that he honestly believed he had paid the various bills that were still outstanding.

Barker lived near Elizabeth Bay House and was a long-standing friend of Alexander, as was Robert Lowe who was also a friend of William and 'lifelong' friend of George.[123] It was his expertise in law that would have assisted Barker and Nicholson in sorting out the technicalities involved as they drew up an agreement between father and son. Lowe had arrived in Sydney in October 1842 with a background as a lawyer and teacher at Oxford University. Originally nominated by Gipps as a member of the new Legislative Council in 1843, Lowe developed an increasing hostility towards the Governor's policies and eventually resigned his seat in August 1844. Three months later, with funding 'coming primarily from a group of wealthy colonists, including

Wentworth and Nicholson',[124] he established *The Atlas* newspaper which was initially closely aligned with the views of the squatters. Although he was only in the colony for six years and returned to England in 1850, Lowe had a bright future ahead of him, culminating in his appointment as Chancellor of the Exchequer in 1868 and a peerage.[125] Macleay would have been impressed when Lowe spoke for the first time in the Legislative Council, for his oratory skills surpassed even those of Wentworth. Charles Nicholson was a graduate from Edinburgh University and one of the members elected for the Port Phillip region in 1843 where he held substantial land. Wealthy and with a 'natural dignity' about him, he was esteemed in the community,[126] and someone who could be relied upon. After Macleay resigned as Speaker it was Nicholson who filled the position. Although his friends tried to alleviate the situation, they were unable to save Alexander from leaving his home which would have been the hardest thing of all to accept.

Others in the colony did not rally so readily to Alexander's cause. Alexander Berry, when approached by Barker to help his old friend, was in the same predicament as Alexander. Berry replied in a candid manner about his own embarrassing financial situation which he claimed had been brought about by over-investment in sheep, 'a precarious and dangerous investment, and their management is a matter of great expense and trouble'.[127]

By August 1845, Byalla was advertised for sale in the *Sydney Morning Herald*. Comprising 4,263 acres and situated on the Lachlan River ten miles from Gunning and about 35 miles from Goulburn, it included 'a comfortable slab cottage of 3 rooms with store and kitchen detached, a stable, barn and dairy' at the head station and a couple of other portions of land as well. On the main property there was also a good fenced garden which had numerous fruit trees 'and a stockyard, recently put up, capable of holding 3,000 head of cattle'.[128]

Barker managed to juggle Alexander's financial affairs and his experience in banking was useful in allaying some of the debts. In an undated statement which Barker compiled of Alexander's debts and the amounts paid off, it was recorded that Alexander's debts had been reduced from £42,429 to £11,170.[129] William's figures differed substantially. According to him, by 8 October 1844, his father's total debts with interest amounted to £36,965.[130]

By way of paying off this loan, William agreed to give his father £400 per annum for board at Elizabeth Bay House and also paid for a cabinet of insects that his father had given him in 1835. The remainder of Alexander's collection seems not to have been accounted for though, obviously, it was retained by William. In addition, William effectively sold Elizabeth Bay House to himself for £12,000. He agreed to take 5% simple interest instead of 10% in repayment on one account over a period of 20 years and reduced the interest on the gross sum due to him from 8% to 5%, payable half yearly. By these means the total sum payable to Alexander was reduced to £13,500 which had to be paid back with 5% interest each half year within two years.[131] In his meticuluous manner, William documented all these details in book form with the title, 'Papers connected with my Father's debt to me'. By August 1845 the 36 allotments that had previously not sold at Elizabeth Bay in 1841 were again placed on the market. Alexander still could not understand William's actions and in September 1845 he wrote to Thomas Barker stating that he hoped:

> the arbitration with William is going on — you cannot be in any
> doubt, as to the concern of his hostile feelings towards you … [for you
> to have] … rescued his Parents from his clutches must be in his eyes
> an unpardonable offence.[132]

William, as the oldest son, felt it was his responsibility to solve the crisis as best he could, whilst Alexander would have found the situation insufferable. Even George eventually agreed with William's actions. Around 1844 he described three letters from William about their father's affairs as 'the most unwelcome' that he had ever received in his life. He told William that he had written to his father 'in the strongest language informing him, if it be not too late, to save himself from destruction'. George left Sydney, 'pledged' to look after Brownlow Hill, and 'believing that my Father would in the end follow the course I had so strongly urged'. Of Alexander's belief that one of his bills was a forgery which he did not see the need to pay, George wrote to William that 'my father's memory must fail him'. George, however, was financially dependent himself on William who was paying the family bills, including his brother's expenses. He even had to ask William for 30 shillings to cover the expense of coming to Sydney and ended one letter to his brother declaring he was 'in the deepest state of distress, in fact, half mad'. Alexander must have felt similar emotions.[133]

BANKRUPTCY
ALMOST UNIVERSAL

It was not only Alexander who was in dire financial straits. By 1841 a regular list of insolvents in the Debtor's Court was published in the *Sydney Herald*. Disaster struck everywhere. Richard Jones, member of the Legislative Council from 1828 to 1843, and one of the founding members of the Australian Club in 1838, was declared insolvent in November 1843, his demise directly linked to his position as director of the Bank of Australia.[134] George Hobler who lived in Aberglasslyn House near Maitland in 1840 described the local situation in his diaries:

> Bankruptcy is almost universal and confidence in mercantile matters lost entirely — I consider Dickson, Dee & R.P. Cumming the only three solvent men left in Maitland — so valueless has property of all kinds become that no monied engagement can be met but at most dreadful sacrifices — Sheep are sold at 6d and 7d each, stations etc. given with them — The whole Community seems horror struck and nothing that can be now foreseen can avert general bankruptcy.[135]

Hobler, too, became insolvent, having to put his property of 700 acres including his house 'with twelve apartments besides cellars, closets and every convenience for a gentleman's family — plus garden and orchard' up for sale in June 1844.[136] Hobler's tale is but one of many. There is a connection between Hobler and Macleay for in 1840 Macleay's architect, John

Verge, replaced Henry Robertson as the architect of Aberglasslyn.[137] As a result, there is a striking similarity in the exterior appearance between Elizabeth Bay House and Aberglasslyn whose interior also has a dome and a spiral staircase.

Alexander's family dealings added to his financial burdens. On 27 November 1845 a mortgage was taken out by Archibald Innes with Alexander, George Macleay and William Dumaresq in the form of 25 promissory notes amounting to £31,609.[138] Even before Archibald took his wife to live in Port Macquarie, he was 'deeply in debt' and owed hundreds of pounds.[139] All those years later he was still dependent on his father-in-law even though Alexander's own finances were in turmoil. Ultimately, in 1852, Archibald was declared bankrupt.

THE SQUATTERS ACHIEVE SUPREMACY

Amidst the state of general financial collapse and Alexander's own personal financial crisis, rumours surfaced once again about him leaving the political arena. In April 1846 the *Sydney Morning Herald* published a letter from 'A Colonist' on their front page which said they were sorry to hear that Alexander Macleay thought of resigning as Speaker and recommended either Wentworth, Cowper, Hannibal Macarthur, Colonel Gipps, Captain O'Connell or Dumaresq (presumably William) to replace him.[140]

New regulations proposing long-term leases for the unsettled lands, with the option to purchase at any time, arrived from the Colonial Office after William Gladstone replaced Stanley in December 1845. But the Legislative Council was concerned that Gipps would oppose these new proposals and so they adjourned the session.[141] Ultimately Gipps left Sydney in July 1846 and it was left up to Governor Charles FitzRoy, who arrived on 2 August 1846, to reintroduce the new legislation. This bill, which was officially passed in March 1847 by Earl Grey, ensured the squatters' supremacy. The colony was divided into three zones with leases in the outlying areas increased to 14 years, eight-year leases for the second zone and yearly leases in the inner, settled areas. And the squatters were given the first right to buy the land they occupied. The efforts in England of Francis Scott, on behalf of the Pastoral Association, in enlisting the support of 'merchants, manufacturers and bankers' as well as the press and parliament, had been successful.[142] Gipps did not live long enough to see these changes introduced. Unwell even before he departed from Sydney, he passed away in England in February 1847 at the relatively young age of 56.

MACLEAY RESIGNS
AS SPEAKER

Three months prior to the arrival of Governor FitzRoy, Alexander officially resigned as Speaker on 14 May 1846 on the grounds of failing health although he retained his electoral seat. He thanked the house for the 'kind and gentle manner in which he had always been treated' and said that although it was the general wish of Council that he should stay on, his health prevented him from doing so. On this point it was reported that he was surprised at their reaction as he had expected that the news of his resignation 'would have been received with pleasure'. He declared that 'To have been elected the first speaker of the first Representative Assembly of New South Wales, was the summit of honour to which his ambition had ever aspired'.[143] Even Wentworth had acknowledged on the opening day of session in 1843 that the position of Speaker was 'the highest honour the Colony had to bestow'.[144] Alexander also conveyed to Council members 'his high sense of the talent, care, and industry by which their deliberations had been characterised and which had rendered the Council an honour to themselves and to the land of their adoption'.[145] He added that he had only one complaint about the Council:

> which he deeply regretted — which was, the omission of hearing
> divine service previous to the despatch of business. He could have

wished to have seen them adopt this practice, so universally followed in similar British assemblies, and he trusted yet they would reform the only fault which seemed to him to reflect discredit on the proceedings of the first representative council of New South Wales.[146]

The *Sydney Morning Herald* added that he 'betrayed strong symptoms of emotion during his address' and several months later the *Colonial Gazette*, in England, commented that Alexander had 'tendered his resignation in a very feeling speech'.[147] Wentworth's admission that Macleay's conduct as Speaker was 'unimpeachable'[148] would certainly have not gone unnoticed. But most surprising of all was Wentworth's praise for the abilities of the Speaker:

> especially as he had given him most strenuous opposition at his election; he did so from conscientious motives, for he did not then think the present Speaker was the most proper person to fill the office; but he was glad to say he had been most agreeably disappointed.[149]

This previous bitter opponent of Macleay pronounced his 'deep and unfeigned regret' that Alexander was retiring and that 'Perhaps, indeed, this expression of regret would come better from him than from any other member of the House'. And he referred to the 'strictest impartiality' and the 'strictest integrity' that marked Macleay's decisions not only as Speaker but as a 'member of the House in ordinary business'.[150] With the passing of years and the development of a mutual interest in pastoral concerns, both men had found a common denominator. Alexander's response to Wentworth's comments a few days later evinced his pleasure: 'Particularly was he grateful to the honorable and learned member for Sydney for the open, courteous, and generous manner in which he had awarded him so full a meed of praise'.[151]

Subsequently, Nicholson was the only candidate to come forward to replace Macleay as Speaker. The *Maitland Mercury* recorded that he possessed a 'tolerably even temper, an average share of intellect, and a fair stock of general information and common sense along with the ability to apply himself to the role in a systematic manner', all of which were considered requisites for the position.[152] This journalist, however, did not rank Alexander amongst those such as Wentworth, Windeyer, Lowe, Robinson, Lang and Cowper, who led public opinion in the colony. Rather than lose these men of extraordinary 'mental qualities', he considered that it was 'men of second-rate intellect, but who combine weight of character with good business qualifications, who are generally elected Speakers in the House of Commons'.[153]

Nicholson, in his acceptance speech reported in the *Colonial Gazette* in London, acknowledged the esteem with which Macleay was held. He stated that he:

> regretted as much as any the circumstance which called his late venerable predecessor from the chair, and he also felt that the qualifications of that honourable member connected with his experience during a long official career, his well-known private virtues, and the abilities he had displayed on all occasions in the exercise of the functions of the office he had just vacated, served to cause him to feel more sensibly the responsibility of the position in which he had just been placed.[154]

FINAL DAYS

In August 1846 Alexander suffered a severe accident when the carriage in which he was travelling collided with a stone pillar at the entrance gates to Government House in Macquarie Street.[155] In a strange recurrence of events, William John Macleay was killed in a carriage accident at the gates of Government House in 1891 and George Masters, curator of the Macleay Museum, was also killed in a carriage accident on the way to Government House in 1912. On 1 September 1846 Christiana wrote to Alexander Rose in Dumfries, Scotland, informing him of the bad news and he replied on 4 February 1847 saying how much he was grieved by his father's 'dreadful accident', and hoped that he was making a good recovery even though he did not expect to ever see him again in this world'.[156] Catherine, Alexander's sole surviving sister in Wick, also wrote on 24 April 1847 after she heard the news about his accident, and hoped that her brother's 'health had been as good as before the accident'.[157]

Despite his political reputation coming under attack, continuing conflict with William and increased frailty, Alexander retained his seat in the Council right through until the end of session on 12 June 1848. By then, however, his supporters had become dissatisfied with his representation, claiming they were 'somewhat unfortunate in their choice of a representative'. In November 1847, the *Sydney Morning Herald* published in a 'News from the Interior' column on Port Macquarie that 'during the five years Mr. M'Leay has been in the House he has but twice alluded to this district'. The first occasion was in 1846 'on the vote for the Police Magistrate' and the other time was in 1847 when he presented a petition to the House requesting that a Court of Quarter Sessions be established in Port Macquarie and:

> although that petition was got up at the suggestion of the honorable gentleman, he neither proposed that it be printed or that it be taken into consideration of the House, or even that it be laid before the Select Committee on Police.[158]

What they were most disappointed about was the fact that nothing had been done to improve the road between Port Macquarie and New England. His constituents complained that Alexander had not requested that part of the monies set aside in the colony for road repairs be allocated to that portion of road.[159] On 1 November 1847, the *Sydney Morning Herald* proclaimed:

> A greater indifference to the interests of his constituents no represen-tative could be guilty of, and we think that if the honourable gentle-man should come forward at the next election he will meet with but a poor reception.[160]

But at Macleay's advanced age of 80, and with continuing concerns over financial matters, he was unlikely to stand again. Eliza Macleay, his wife of 55 years, had died on 13 August 1847 at the age of 78. Yet he continued his active involvement in the colony's social life and on 14 January 1848 he chaired the annual meeting for the Australian Subscription Library[161] and later that month the annual meeting of the Sydney Infirmary and Dispensary.[162] In March he chaired the annual meeting of the Auxiliary Bible Society and was once again voted in as President for the following year.[163]

In early February, although unable to attend in person, Alexander sent a letter to be read out stating his views on the issues for discussion at a public meeting of residents in the Camden area. An official despatch had recently been received from England advocating, amongst other matters, that Port Phillip separate into a distinct province to be called Victoria, that a local parliament be established to make laws for 'Australian colonial matters generally', and that two legislative chambers should replace the mixed Council of part-representative and part-nominee members. Alexander was 'in favour of having two houses, which he deemed safer and certainly more analogous to the constitution of the empire than that they now possessed'.[164] But he did not live long enough to see them finally introduced in 1856.

However, the differences in opinion between Broughton and Macleay came to a head in 1847 when the Bishop disapproved of Macleay's support for denominations other than the Anglican church in the colony and bitterly opposed his nomination as chairman of the Bible Society. Subsequently he arranged for Alexander to be removed as chairman and from 'other duties' of the Diocesan committee. Lowe explained in *The Atlas* just how the Bishop managed to achieve this:

> Some of the clergymen who signed this document, called afterwards upon the venerable old gentleman, and pleaded in their defence that they were compelled to sign the requisition for fear of offending the Bishop .... Do you [Bishop Broughton] really consider the chairmanship of a Bible Society to be incompatible with the chairmanship of the Diocesan Committee? ... The crime of presiding at a meeting of those whose only aim is to disseminate as widely as possible the truths contained in the sacred volume you profess to regard as your authority, is in your eyes unpardonable. And why? Because those who are members of this society recognise no sect in particular ....[165]

Lowe described Broughton's High Church attitudes as 'rampant', making them, so different from members of the Bible Society who did not confine 'their Christian zeal' to solely one denomination.

A LONG LIFE OF
USEFULNESS

Alexander died 'as if in his sleep' at half past nine on the evening of Thursday 18 July 1848, at age 81. In April and again in June that year William Dumaresq had written to his brother Edward in Van Dieman's Land about Alexander's deteriorating health and mentioned that his breathing was seriously affected by dysphemia. After his father-in-law passed away William advised Edward that 'He is a great loss to us and to all his family'.[166] Aware that the end was near, Alexander recorded 'his most affectionate dying remembrances to his dear friend Robert Brown'.[167] Fifty carriages attended his funeral which left Christiana's house at Rose Bay at 10 o'clock on Tuesday 25 July. Catherine, the last of Alexander's siblings, had died only a few months earlier on 15 April in Wick.

The farewell ceremony was held in St James's Church at midday and the congregation included:

> the Commander of the Forces, the three Judges, and nearly the whole
> of the Government Officers, and a large number of old colonists of
> all classes. The pall-bearers were the Colonial Secretary, the Colonial
> Treasurer, Colonel Gordon, Mr. Barker, the Attorney-General, Mr.
> Macpherson, Mr. Mitchell, and Mr. Campbell.[168]

The church service was read by the Reverend Robert Allwood of St James's, who had arrived in Sydney in 1839 and some years later became Vice-Chancellor of the University of Sydney. Bishop Broughton, in an ironic twist of fate, conducted the service at the graveside. A fitting tribute to Alexander in the *Sydney Morning Herald* listed his active participation:

in the management of colonial institutions; he was President of the
Australian Subscription Library, of the Benevolent Society, and
the Infirmary; and was the founder of the Australian Museum. Mr.
M'Leay was a man almost universally respected, and has descended
into the grave full of years and full of honors; and from his consistent
Christian character, we may feel assured he has gone to his reward.[169]

Alexander was interred in ground only recently consecrated, at the Camperdown Cemetery which was situated on one of the highest parts of Sydney
with views extending to the Blue Mountains. Over 150 years later a leaflet
about the St Stephen's Church which was opened in 1849, notes that this
historic cemetery contains the 'graves of some of the people who were famous
in the building of this country'.[170] Prominent in the grounds is the grave of
Alexander Macleay.

In St James's Church in central Sydney there are further reminders of the
Macleay family. In addition to the cenotaph for Fanny, a memorial for Alexander and Eliza is mounted on the interior walls and a smaller memorial for
William is nearby. The descriptive leaflet for this church states that as a 'fashionable church in Sydney in the earlier 19th century St James was considered
a most suitable place to commemorate prominent members of colonial society'.[171] Alexander's memorial details all aspects of his life:

ENTERING IN EARLY YOUTH

THE CIVIL SERVICE OF HIS COUNTRY,

OCCUPIED DURING ONE OF THE MOST EVENTFUL PERIODS

OF ITS HISTORY,

SUCCESSIVE POSITIONS OF DISTINCTION AND HIGH TRUST:

WAS SELECTED IN 1826 TO PROCEED

TO NEW SOUTH WALES AS COLONIAL SECRETARY:

AND ULTIMATELY CLOSED A LONG CAREER OF VARIED USEFULNESS.

AS FIRST SPEAKER

OF THE FIRST REPRESENTATIVE ASSEMBLY OF THE COLONY.

DEVOTING THE INTERVALS OF DUTY TO SCIENCE.

AND THE PROMOTION OF CHARITY, EDUCATION, AND RELIGION, WITH A

NUMEROUS FAMILY

AND A CIRCLE OF FRIENDSHIPS CONTINUALLY ENLARGING.

HE SO FULFILLED THE OBLIGATIONS OF EVERY OFFICE,

AND EVERY RELATION OF A LIFE

EXTENDED BEYOND LIFE'S ORDINARY TERM:

AS HIS ABILITY AND PUBLIC ZEAL,

HIS PROBITY, BENEVOLENCE AND UNAFFECTED KINDLINESS.

TO WIN THE PRAISE OF THOSE WHOSE PRAISE WAS HONOR.

TO SECURE THE RESPECT AND REGARD OF HIS FELLOW CITIZENS.

AND TO ENDEAR HIMSELF MOST WHEREVER MOST INTIMATELY KNOWN.

BUT IN AND ABOVE ALL IT WAS HIS AIM AND END.

LOOKING HUMBLY TO THE AUTHOR AND FINISHER OF HIS FAITH

TO OBTAIN THE TESTIMONY THAT, IN CHRIST,

'HE PLEASED GOD'.

Alexander's will, dated 27 April 1846, gave his address as Brownlow Hill and for understandable reasons omitted any reference to William except for the following terse statement:

> I do hereby declare that in consequence of the rapacious
> ungrateful unnatural and cruel conduct of my eldest Son William
> Sharp Macleay towards me, his mother and all the rest of his family
> it is my will and determination that he shall not in any way participate
> in the Real or personal property which shall belong to me at the time
> of my decease.[172]

Although the conflict with William split the family, it was also reunited to some degree during the last year of Alexander's life. Alexander retained his will from 1846, although he must have implemented sister Catherine's plea in 1847

ALEXANDER MACLEAY, Esq.
F.R.S. L.S. ETC
ELDEST SON OF WILLIAM MACLEAY ESQ.
OF CAITHNESS, SCOTLAND,
BORN 24TH JUNE 1767, DECEASED 18TH JULY 1848.

ENTERING IN EARLY YOUTH
THE CIVIL SERVICE OF HIS COUNTRY,
OCCUPIED, DURING ONE OF THE MOST EVENTFUL PERIODS
OF ITS HISTORY,
SUCCESSIVE POSITIONS OF DISTINCTION AND HIGH TRUST,
WAS SELECTED IN 1825 TO PROCEED
TO NEW SOUTH WALES AS COLONIAL SECRETARY,
AND ULTIMATELY CLOSED A LONG CAREER OF VARIED USEFULNESS,
AS FIRST SPEAKER
OF THE FIRST REPRESENTATIVE ASSEMBLY OF THE COLONY.
DEVOTING THE INTERVALS OF DUTY TO SCIENCE,
AND THE PROMOTION OF CHARITY, EDUCATION, AND RELIGION,
WITH A NUMEROUS FAMILY,
AND A CIRCLE OF FRIENDSHIPS CONTINUALLY ENLARGING,
HE SO FULFILLED THE OBLIGATIONS OF EVERY OFFICE,
AND EVERY RELATION OF A LIFE
EXTENDED BEYOND LIFE'S ORDINARY TERM,
AS BY HIS ABILITY AND PUBLIC ZEAL,
HIS PROBITY, BENEVOLENCE, AND UNAFFECTED KINDLINESS,
TO WIN THE PRAISE OF THOSE WHOSE PRAISE WAS HONOR,
TO SECURE THE RESPECT AND REGARD OF HIS FELLOW CITIZENS,
AND TO ENDEAR HIMSELF MOST WHEREVER MOST INTIMATELY KNOWN.
BUT IN AND ABOVE ALL IT WAS HIS AIM AND END,
LOOKING HUMBLY TO THE AUTHOR AND FINISHER OF HIS FAITH,
TO OBTAIN THE TESTIMONY THAT, IN CHRIST,
"HE PLEASED GOD."

ELIZA,
HIS WIFE, DAUGHTER OF JAMES BARCLAY, ESQ. OF LONDON,
THE HONORED MOTHER OF SEVENTEEN CHILDREN, OF WHOM NINE SURVIVED
TO MOURN THE LOSS OF HER CONSTANT LOVE AND MATRONLY EXAMPLE,
BORN 13TH MARCH, 1769; DECEASED 13TH AUGUST, 1847,
PRECEDING HER HUSBAND BY A FEW MONTHS ONLY, AFTER A HAPPY UNION
OF MORE THAN FIFTY YEARS.

Memorial to Alexander Macleay (1767–1848) in St James's Church, Sydney.
These profound words were probably mostly scribed by Alexander's
son-in-law, William Dumaresq. Photograph courtesy of Historic Houses
Trust of New South Wales

to place his relationship with William on a 'friendly footing' after Eliza's death. Catherine urged such a reconciliation as a 'comfort to their parents'.[173] After Alexander died, George wrote to Robert Brown to inform him that whilst his father had forgiven William when Eliza died in 1847 he had 'seen little of him until a week before his own death'. George's letter continued: 'Since my parents forgave him we all have done so. I speak to him when we meet. His association is not sought'.[174]

The nominated executors of the will were Alexander's wife, Eliza, son George, sons-in-law William Dumaresq and Archibald Clunes Innes, and his trusted friend Thomas Barker. With Eliza's pre-decease, only four executors remained to administer and unravel the complicated financial affairs of Alexander's estate. Under the terms of the will, Alexander's outstanding debts were all provided for, a wish that Alexander expressed to George and William Dumaresq only a few days before his death when he confirmed that 'the Estate should be carried on as hitherto until the debts were paid after which the provisions of the Will were to be carried out'.[175]

Brownlow Hill and the surrounding lands in Camden were left to Eliza during her life and then to George subject to the mortgage on them with an annuity of £100 a year each for George and Kennethina. It was understood that Brownlow Hill should pass to George after Eliza's death 'in fulfilment of my promise to him at the time of his marriage', and provisions were also made for the residue of the estate and its revenues to be divided equally between sons Alexander Rose, George and James as well as daughters Christiana, Margaret, Kennethina, Rosa and Barbara.[176] In a statement issued after his father's death, George declined the legacy of Brownlow Hill once the debts were paid off. Instead he suggested a complicated, but no doubt more advantageous idea, whereby he managed and superintended the estate for twenty years at £200 a year set against the mortgage of £4,000. It was no surprise that the executors agreed to this arrangement as George was one of them. Ultimately the executors paid the mortgage which left Brownlow Hill in George's possession encumbered only with the annuity of £100 to Kennethina.[177]

TRIUMPH OF A MODERATE CONSERVATIVE

Looking back on the last decade of Macleay's life, it is to his credit that he took on an electorate and the position of first Speaker in the Legislative Council with such alacrity at his advanced age. Enduring unfortunate personal circumstances during the same period, he again held a leading role in public life that culminated in approval from former adversaries. As the colony advanced towards full responsible government, Macleay's alignment with the squatters' cause caused him to overlook some of the social and moral evils of squatting that Gipps had been so concerned with. He became an important mediator in achieving the squatters' aims for control of the land, although such notions were finally dispelled by the British Government when responsible government was granted in 1856. Emerging as a moderate conservative, rather than a Tory, Macleay's successful return to public life for the benefit of the colony after being dismissed as Colonial Secretary, was both a personal triumph and a triumph for the conservative spirit. Many years later, even Dunmore Lang doubted whether the first Legislative Council in the country had ever been surpassed 'by any legislature out of England in the British Empire' for 'general ability, for extent and variety of information available for the business of legislation, for manly eloquence, for genuine patriotism, and for energetic and dignified action'.[178]

Such acknowledgement was high praise coming from the critical Lang and reflects the ability of those who participated, especially the Speaker who was responsible for running each session. Macleay would have applauded when responsible government was finally granted to the colony in 1856 with the two houses he had envisaged: a Legislative Assembly as well as the Legislative Council. However, at the same time, he would have been disappointed that the additional powers the squatters sought in the new constitution were rejected by the British Government in their aim to satisfy the aspirations of the expanding urban middle class rather than landed interests. George and William John Macleay and William Dumaresq were all actively involved in this constitutional change. From 1856 to 1859 George was a member of the Legislative Assembly and was succeeded there by his cousin, William John. The Macleays would be permanently recorded in the history of Australia and most prominent of all would be the name of Alexander Macleay.

Epilogue

Although the history of Australian conservatism, charted in part by Professor John Manning Ward, has still to be written, it is clear from Ward's biography of James Macarthur that conservatism made an important contribution to Australian life. Connected with that group of colonists whose conservative views have received unfavourable attention from historians in the past, the complete life and career of Alexander Macleay has been neglected. Yet his unique attributes bear comparison with any of the legendary figures who lived in Australia's early colonial days.

As an administrator Macleay proved diligent and hardworking, and although he displayed little initiative of his own as Colonial Secretary, when it came to other areas of his life he stood out as a man of inspiration and creativity. During the period under Darling, foundations were laid for the public service and Macleay carried out his official routine orders implicitly. Even under Bourke, as the struggle for constitutional rights amongst the settlers escalated, the Colonial Secretary strictly adhered to his administrative duties and it was only in the area of personal principles, especially in relation to education and religion, that he came into conflict with the Governor.

His attitudes and views were directly linked to the Scottish Enlightenment.[1] Encouraged in the first instance by his enterprising father, Alexander grew up surrounded by agricultural and commercial progress and it was a particular vision for the pursuit of these values that he brought with him for the lasting benefit of the colony. Furthermore, his interest in the arts and his high moral standing impacted on colonial life in New South Wales, especially in relation to the encouragement of the study of literature and natural history. His many terms as President of numerous institutions also exemplifies these aspects of his character and the title of 'Father of Australian Zoology' is fitting in relation to his devotion towards this subject.

Hawthorns School, Bletchingley, Surrey. George Macleay purchased this estate, called Pendell Court, in 1878. It was described as 'the finest and most important mansion in the parish'. Photo: Derelie Cherry

Allegations that have circulated over the years about Macleay as a reckless spendthrift should be set in the wider context of the circumstances of the time. During his period of unemployment in England after the demise of the Transport Board it was only too apparent, as we see through Fanny's letters, that he was most concerned about the future and considered a number of alternative solutions to his predicament. His later period of acute financial embarrassment in New South Wales was not singular as so many other colonists at that time experienced similar problems.

Notwithstanding, the Macleay name has been honoured from Scotland to Sydney: Macleay Street in Wick, Macleay Island in Scotland, Macleay Island in Queensland, Point Macleay at Lake Alexandria in South Australia, Macleay Street in Sydney and the Macleay River and Macleay Ranges in New South Wales.

Direct descendants of Alexander live in England and Australia. Although he had no children of his own, George's life after returning to England in 1859 was quite illustrious. Apart from purchasing a steam yacht and regularly sailing around the Mediterranean in his later years, he purchased Pendell Court in 1878. Described in 1893, as 'the finest and most important mansion in the parish' of Bletchingley, it was located just a few miles from Godstone.[2] Robert Lowe lived nearby and often visited George, observing that there was a 'fine bust' of brother William in the library at Pendell Court and a 'beautiful picture of his house and grounds at Elizabeth Bay' in the hall.[3] Built in 1624 on what is believed to be the site of a Roman villa, the original manor house now forms part of the prestigious Hawthorns School. Alexander's aspirations towards becoming part of the landed gentry were ostensibly fulfilled by George back in England.

Martin, in his biography of Robert Lowe, wrote in 1893 that:

the Macleays were a most distinguished as well as most worthy family. No less than four of them have left their mark on the history of New South Wales. We note in all these Macleays alike the highest mental and moral qualities coupled with great capacity for public affairs, and each with an inborn love of scientific research.[4]

With the help of Fanny's letters and a detailed analysis of all the complicated facets of Macleay's extraordinary life, there is no doubt that Alexander Macleay was a major figure in the development of colonial New South Wales. It was Governor Darling's son who penned the words: 'one looks to history to make amends'[5] in relation to his father's experience in the Antipodes. His words could just as easily apply to the life of Alexander Macleay.

Notes

INTRODUCTION

1   M. Steven, *Merchant Campbell 1769–1846: A Study of Colonial Trade*, Melbourne, 1965, p. 8.

2   B. Earnshaw, J Hughes, L. Davidson, *Fanny to William: The Letters of Frances Leonora Macleay 1812-1836*, Sydney, 1993.

3   Ibid, introduction.

4   Ibid, foreword.

5   A. Swainston, 'William Sharp Macleay 1792-1865', *The Linnean Newsletter and Proceedings of the Linnean Society of London*, Vol. 1, No. 5, 1985.

6   A. Swainston, 'Background to a Caithness Bank, *The Three Banks Review of National and Commercial Banking Group Limited*, No. 108, 1975.

7   H. King, 'Man in a Trap: Alexander Macleay, Colonial Secretary of New South Wales', *JRAHS*, Vol. 68, Pt. 1, 1982, p. 47.

8   S. Foster, 'A Piece of Sharp Practice? Governor Bourke and the Office of Colonial Secretary in New South Wales', *Historical Studies*, Vol. 16, No. 64, 1975.

9   D. Clark, 'Baron Charles von Hügel and the Macleays', *JRAHS*, Vol. 75, Part 3, 1989.

10 M. Van Leeuwen, 'The Plan of a Museum — Alexander Macleay's proposal for the Australian Museum', *JRAHS*, Vol. 78, Parts 3 & 4, 1992.

11 R. Strahan, 'The Dog that did not bark: Alexander Macleay and the Australian Museum', *JRAHS*, Vol. 75, Part 3, 1989.

12 J. Fletcher, 'The Society's Heritage from the Macleays', *Proceedings of the Linnean Society of New South Wales*, Vol 45, Sydney, 1920.

13 L. Gilbert, 'Plants, Privileges and Power: Some Glimpses of Elizabeth Bay and Sydney's Botanical Community 1825-1865', M.A., University of Sydney, 1989.

14 C. M. Clark, *A History of Australia The Beginnings of an Australian Civilization 1824-1851*, Vol.3, Melbourne, 1973, p. 141.

15 S. Roberts, *The Squatting Age in Australia 1835-1847*, Melbourne, 1935, p. 31.

16 J. Iltis to D. Pike, 8 January 1965, *Australian Dictionary of Biography* file on Alexander Macleay, Australian National University, Canberra.

17 Swainston to Pike, 5 March 1965, *Australian Dictionary of Biography* file.

18 Ibid.

19 Pike to Swainston, 18 March 1965, *Australian Dictionary of Biography* file.

20 R. Phin to A. Macleay, 12 April 1825, Linnean Society, London.

CHAPTER 1

1   *Swainston Papers.*

2   Ibid.

3   The only evidence for this conclusion is the 1841 census in Wick which records that Alexander's

youngest sister, Catherine, was not born in Wick. She died on 15 April 1848 at age 75, however ages for this census were rounded to the nearest 5, hence it is difficult to establish exact dates.

4   *Collins Guide to Scots Kith and Kin A Guide to the Clans and Surnames of Scotland*, Glasgow, 1989, p. 35.

5   Ibid, p. 84.

6   *Swainston Papers.*

7   *Collins Guide to Scots Kith and Kin*, p. 84.

8   G. Black, *The Surnames of Scotland - their origin, meaning and history*, New York, 1962, p. 533.

9   D. Alston, *Ross and Cromarty A Historical Guide*, Edinburgh, 1999, p. 59.

10 *Collins Guide to Scots Kith and Kin*, p. 81.

11 A. Shaw & C. Clark (editors), *The Australian Dictionary of Biography*, 1788–1850, *Vol. 2*, Melbourne, 1967, p.178.

12 F. Foden, *Wick of the North The Story of a Scottish Royal Burgh*, Wick, 1996, p. 234.

13 J. Gascoigne, *Joseph Banks and the English Enlightenment*, Cambridge, 1994, pp. 188-189.

14 Foden, *Wick of the North*, pp. 228 & 234.

15 Alexander's brothers were Kenneth who was born in 1765 and died in 1826, John who died in 1821, William who was born in 1770 and died in 1802, and his sisters were Margaret Elizabeth who died in 1822, Barbara who died in 1836 and Catherine who died in April 1848.

16 Earnshaw, Hughes, Davidson, *Fanny to William*, p. 24.

17 *Collins Guide to Scots Kith and Kin*, p. 82.

18 *Swainston Papers.*

19 Mormon International Genealogical Index from Old Parochial Registers pre 1855 for Caithness, *North Highland Archives.*

20 *Collins Guide to Scots Kith and Kin*, p. 82.

21 Swainston, 'Background to a Caithness Bank', p. 37.

22 *John O'Groat Journal*, 27 May 1842.

23 Caithness Index to Names and Persons to Abridgments of the Registers of Seisins 1781–1928, 2 March 1790, *North Highland Archives.*

24 Ibid, 22 November 1809.

25 Foden, *Wick of the North*, p. 427.

26 D. Macmillan, *Scotland and Australia 1788–1850*, Oxford, 1967, p. 109.

27 *Swainston Papers.*

28 *Collins Guide to Scots Kith and Kin*, p. 83.

29 W. Sutherland, *Wick 1794*, A reprint from the First Statistical Account of Scotland (drawn up from the Communications of the Ministers of the different parishes, by Sir John Sinclair, Bart; Edinburgh, William, Creech, 1794), Thurso, undated, p. 31.

30 A. Wight, *Present State of Husbandry in Scotland: extracted from reports made to the Commissioners of the Annexed Estates, and Published By Their Authority*, Vol. 1V, Part 1, Edinburgh, 1784, p. 325.

31 Ibid, pp. 326-327.

32 Ibid, pp. 324-325.

33 Ibid, pp. 326-327.

34 Wick Town Council Minute Books 1788–1818, *North Highland Archives.*

35 Foden, *Wick of the North*, p. 235.

36 Ibid, p. 695.

37 Slater's Directory 1852–1882, *North Highland Archives.*

38 Swainston, 'William Sharp Macleay, 1792–1865', p. 11.

39 Sutherland, *Wick 1794*, p. 29.

40 Ibid, p. 32.

41 *Swainston Papers.*

42 *Sydney Gazette*, 25 February 1826, p. 4.

43 Foden, *Wick of the North*, p. 96.

44 Sutherland, *Wick 1794*, p. 30.

45 Ibid, p. 32 & Foden, *Wick of the North*, p. 172.

46 D. Williamson to J. Horne, 7 June 1787, Caithness Manuscripts and Letters of Various Notables 1787–1911, *North Highland Archives.*

47 Swainston, unpublished chapter 'New Worlds for Alexander', p. 6, *Swainston Papers.*

48 Swainston, unpublished chapter, 'The Anchor of Hope', *Swainston Papers.*

49 *Collins Guide to Scots Kith and Kin*, p. 4.

50 P. Stanbury and J. Holland (editors), *Mr. Macleay's Celebrated Cabinet: The History of the Macleays and their Museum*, Sydney, 1988, p. 17.

51 Barclay Descendants, England, June 2002.

52 Swainston, unpublished chapter, 'New Worlds for Alexander', p. 4, *Swainston Papers.*

53 The Macleay children were William Sharp, born 31 July 1792, died 1865; Frances Leonora, born 9 November 1793, died 1836; James, born 13 December 1794, died 1810; Alexander Rose, born 14 February 1796, died 1869; Barbara, born 1 May 1797, died 1812; Elizabeth, born 28 July 1798, died 1800; Christiana Susan (twin) born 12 October 1799, died 1866; Catherine (twin), born 1799, died 1813; Elizabeth Catherine, born 13 November 1800, died 1814; Margaret, born March 1802, died 1858; Johanna, born July 1803, died 1820; Kennethina (twin), born 1805, died 1856; twin of Kennethina, stillborn 1805; Rosa Roberta, born 1807, died 1854; George, born 1809, died 1891; James Robert, born 1811, died 1892 and Barbara Isabella who was born in 1814 and her year of death is unknown.

54 *Swainston Papers.*

55 Kirby to Macleay, 9 November 1805, Linnean Society, London.

56 *Swainston Papers.*

57 Earnshaw, Hughes, Davidson, *Fanny to William*, 19 January 1818, p. 36.

58 S. Carlin, *Elizabeth Bay House A History and Guide*, Sydney, 2000, p. 1.

59 Gascoigne, *Joseph Banks and the English Enlightenment*, p. 191.

60 *Swainston Papers.*

61 Miscellaneous Correspondence Concerning the Escape, Exchange and Relief of Prisoners-of-War, 1807–1818, *Public Records Office*, ADM/97/130.

62 King, 'Man in a Trap', pp. 38-39.

63 Ibid, p. 37.

64 Macleay to Smith, 30 March 1805, Linnean Society, London.

65 King, 'Man in a Trap', p. 37.
66 Ibid.
67 M. Falkus & J. Gillingham (editors), *Historical Atlas of Britain*, London, 1981, p. 119.
68 King, 'Man in a Trap', p. 38.
69 Ibid.
70 Ibid.
71 Ibid, p. 37.
72 Kirby to Macleay, 9 November 1805, Linnean Society, London.
73 King, 'Man in a Trap', p. 37.
74 Miscellaneous Correspondence Concerning the Escape, Exchange and Relief of Prisoners-of- War, 1807–1818, *Public Records Office,* ADM/97/130.
75 Macleay to Smith, 27 September 1803, Linnean Society, London.
76 Foden, *Wick of the North*, p. 218.
77 Ibid, p. 223.
78 Ibid, p. 292.
79 Macleay to Smith, 24 November 1802, Linnean Society, London.
80 Fletcher, 'The Society's Heritage from the Macleays', p. 571.
81 Freeman, *Life of William Kirby*, p. 221.
82 Piggott & Company Trade Directories 1825, *North Highland Archives.*
83 Foden, *Wick of the North*, p. 298.
84 Caithness Index to Names and Persons to Abridgments of the Register of Seisins 1781–1928, 22 June 1812, *North Highland Archives.*
85 Ibid, 20 May, 1824.
86 Iain Sutherland, Wick Heritage Centre, Wick, June 2002.
87 Ibid.
88 Caithness Index to Names and Persons to Abridgments of the Registers of Seisins 1781–1928, 22 June 1812, *North Highland Archives.*
89 Swainston, 'William Sharp Macleay 1792–1865', p. 11.
90 Earnshaw, Hughes, Davidson, *Fanny to William,* 18 May 1813, p. 3.
91 Ibid.
92 Ibid, 8 February 1814, p. 11.
93 Kirby to Macleay, 3 July 1810, Linnean Society, London.
94 Ibid, 1812 (undated).
95 Ibid, 7 October 1814.
96 Earnshaw, Hughes, Davidson, *Fanny to William,* 8 February 1814, p. 11.
97 Ibid, 19 September 1815, p. 15.
98 Kirby to Macleay, 7 January 1813, Linnean Society, London.
99 Earnshaw, Hughes, Davidson, *Fanny to William,* 9 December 1816, p. 22.
100 Ibid, p. 12.
101 Kirby to Macleay, 11 November 1811, Linnean Society, London.
102 Macleay to Smith, 14 December 1811, Linnean Society, London.
103 *Swainston Papers.*
104 Ibid.
105 Earnshaw, Hughes, Davidson, *Fanny to William,* p. 24.
106 Ibid, 15 August 1817, p. 35.
107 Ibid, 15 August 1817, pp. 34-35.
108 Ibid, 10 October 1820, p. 40.
109 Ibid, 15 August 1817, p. 35.
110 M. Coventry, *The Castles of Scotland,* Aberdeen, 2001, p. 228.
111 Foden, *Wick of the North,* p. 125.
112 Caithness Index to Names and Persons to Abridgments of the Registers of Seisins 1781–1928, 3 August 1813, *North Highland Archives.*
113 Earnshaw, Hughes, Davidson, *Fanny to William,* 10 October 1820, p. 40.
114 Ibid, 30 September 1820, pp. 38-39.
115 Ibid, p. 39.
116 Piggott & Company Trade Directories 1825, *North Highland Archives.*
117 Macleay to Smith, 22 May 1824, Linnean Society, London.
118 Foden, *Wick of the North,* p. 302.
119 Swainston, 'Background to a Caithness Bank', p. 33.
120 *Swainston Papers.*
121 Caithness Index to Names and Persons to Abridgments of the Registers of Seisins 1781–1928, 3 October 1804, *North Highland Archives.*
122 Earnshaw, Hughes, Davidson, *Fanny to William,* 8 February 1814, p. 11.
123 Ibid, 7 March 1817, p. 31.
124 Ibid, 28 January 1817, p. 26.
125 Ibid, 20 August, 1816, p. 20.
126 Ibid, 20 February 1813, p. 2.
127 Ibid, 13 December 1813, p. 5.
128 Ibid, January 1814, p. 8.
129 Ibid.
130 *Swainston Papers.*
131 *Sydney Morning Herald,* 23 February 1844, p. 3.
132 Swainston, unpublished draft preface to Fanny's letters, *Swainston Papers.*
133 M. Herman (editor), *Annabella Boswell's Journal,* Sydney, 1965, p. 53.
134 S. Goodenough to A. Macleay, 15 December 1805, Linnean Society, London.
135 Stanbury & Holland, *Mr. Macleay's Celebrated Cabinet*, p. 20.
136 Kirby to Macleay, 27 September 1811, Linnean Society, London.
137 Ibid, 17 December 1811.
138 Earnshaw, Hughes, Davidson, *Fanny to William,* September 1816, p. 21.
139 Ibid, 9 December 1816, p. 22.
140 Swainston, 'William Sharp Macleay 1792–1865', p. 12.
141 King, 'Man in a Trap', p. 39.
142 Official Letter Book of Second Earl, 11 June - 5 October 1812, *Lord Liverpool Papers,* Vol. CXXXIX, f. 38.
143 Earnshaw, Hughes, Davidson, *Fanny to William,* 5 August 1816, p. 19.
144 Ibid, 7 March 1817, p. 31.
145 Ibid, 22 September 1815, p. 16.

146 Ibid, 4 February 1817, p. 33.
147 Ibid, 4 August 1827, p. 85.
148 Ibid, 6 April 1828, p. 95.
149 *Swainston Papers*.
150 J. Jaques, *Bygone Godstone*, Chichester, 1992, illustrations 65 & 66.
151 Alexander's daughters buried in Godstone cemetery are Barbara, aged 15, Catherine aged 14, Elizabeth aged 13, Johanna aged 16 and Kennethina aged 58.
152 E. Beaton, *Caithness An Illustrated Architectural Guide*, Edinburgh, 1996, p. 31.
153 Kirby to Macleay, 27 November 1817, Linnean Society, London.
154 Ibid, 30 November 1817.
155 *Sydney Morning Herald*, 23 February 1844, p. 3.
156 Earnshaw, Hughes, Davidson, *Fanny to William*, 19 January 1818, p. 36.
157 Ibid.
158 Ibid, 28 January 1817, p. 25.
159 Kirby to Macleay, 10 May 1819, Linnean Society, London.
160 Stanbury & Holland, *Mr. Macleay's Celebrated Cabinet*, p. 18.
161 Macleay to Bathurst, 28 December 1824, Linnean Society, London.
162 Earnshaw, Hughes, Davidson, *Fanny to William*, 4 August 1827, p. 86.
163 King, 'Man in a Trap', p. 41.
164 Earnshaw, Hughes, Davidson, *Fanny to William*, p. 40.
165 *Sydney Gazette*, 25 February 1826, p. 4.
166 J. Sinclair to R. Peel, General Correspondence, 21 December 1834, *Peel Papers*, Vol. GGXXVII, ADD 40407, p. 249.
167 Ibid, 3 December 1834, p. 161.
168 Foden, *Wick of the North*, p. 327.
169 Sinclair to Macleay, 30 January 1825, Linnean Society, London.
170 Ibid, 30 June 1825.
171 Caithness Index to Names and Persons to Abridgments of the Registers of Seisins 1781–1928, 30 September 1813, *North Highland Archives*.
172 Ibid, 2 December 1816.
173 Ibid, 23 February 1818 & 23 March 1818.
174 Ibid, 21 February 1815.
175 Caithness Index to Names and Persons to Abridgments of the Registers of Seisins 1781–1928, 30 September 1813, *North Highland Archives*, 29 September 1815.
176 Ibid.
177 Ibid.
178 Ibid, 20 October 1817.
179 Foden, *Wick of the North*, p. 83.
180 Caithness Index to Names and Persons to Abridgments of the Registers of Seisins 1781–1928, 27 July 1820, *North Highland Archives*.
181 Ibid, 30 October 1820.
182 Ibid.
183 Ibid, 26 November 1814, & 15 November 1815.
184 Ibid, 25 January 1819.
185 Ibid, 24 March 1820.

186 Ibid, 23 December 1820.
187 Ibid.
188 King, 'Man in a Trap', p. 40.
189 R. Phin to Macleay, 30 April 1825, Linnean Society, London.
190 Ibid.
191 Ibid, 25 June 1825.
192 Ibid.
193 Swainston, 'Background to a Caithness Bank', p. 41.
194 Kirby to Macleay, January 1825, Linnean Society, London.
195 Ibid, 8 February 1825.
196 Will of James Henderson, 24 February 1894, Bilbster, Wick.
197 Interview with Ian Stewart, Bilbster, Wick, June 2002.
198 Piggott & Company Trade Directories 1825/26, *North Highland Archives*.
199 A. Johnston & J. Hope, *Gloag and Henderson's Introduction to the Law of Scotland*, Edinburgh, 1968, p. 264.
200 Caithness Index to Names and Persons to Abridgments of the Registers of Seisins 1781–1928, 19 June 1826, *North Highland Archives*.
201 Ibid, 28 September 1829.
202 Ibid, 20 May 1824.
203 Ibid.
204 Ibid, 5 July 1825.
205 Kirby to Macleay, January 1825, Linnean Society, London.
206 Ibid.
207 Ibid.
208 Earnshaw, Hughes, Davidson, *Fanny to William*, 29 May 1827, p. 83.
209 Phin to Macleay, 12 April 1825, Linnean Society, London.
210 D. McArthur to Macleay, 7 January 1825, Linnean Society, London.
211 J. Loch to Macleay, 9 January 1825, Linnean Society, London.
212 Foden, *Wick of the North*, p. 71.
213 Ibid, p. 82.
214 Earnshaw, Hughes, Davidson, *Fanny to William*, 30 September 1820, p. 39.
215 Macleay to Smith, 5 January 1825, Linnean Society, London.
216 Macleay to Horton, 26 May 1825, *Public Records Office*, CO 201/67, London.
217 Bathurst to Macleay, 5 January 1825, Linnean Society, London.
218 Earnshaw, Hughes, Davidson, *Fanny to William*, 11 September 1826, p. 64.
219 Ibid, 4 August 1827, p. 85.
220 Will of James Henderson, 24 February 1894.
221 Ibid.
222 Confirmations and Inventories 1928, A-L, *North Highland Archives*.
223 Earnshaw, Hughes, Davidson, *Fanny to William*, 23 February 1831, p.131.

CHAPTER 2

1 Earnshaw, Hughes, Davidson, *Fanny to William*, p. 41.
2 Ibid, 20 October 1825, p. 46.
3 Ibid, 6 September 1825, p. 42.
4 Ibid, 20 October 1825, p. 46.
5 Ibid, pp. 47-48.
6 L. Rose, 'The Administration of Governor Darling', *JRAHS*, Vol. 8, Part 2, 1922, p. 57.
7 G. Forbes (ed.), *Sydney Society in Crown Colony Days (Being the Personal Reminiscences of the late Lady Forbes)*, Sydney, 1914, p. 13.
8 The Colonial Secretary's Papers 1788-1825, Information Leaflet No. 40, *AONSW*, 1990, p. 5.
9 J. Ritchie, *The Wentworths Father and Son*, Melbourne, 1997, p. 115.
10 J. Ritchie, 'John Thomas Bigge and His Reports on New South Wales', *JRAHS*, Vol. 60, Pt. 1, 1974, p. 18.
11 A. McMartin, *Public Servants and Patronage The Foundation and Rise of the New South Wales Public Service, 1786-1859*, Sydney, 1983, p. 67.
12 B. Fletcher, *Ralph Darling A Governor Maligned*, Melbourne, 1984, p. 88.
13 Ritchie, 'John Thomas Bigge', p. 12.
14 T. Perry, *Australia's First Frontier, The Spread of Settlement in New South Wales, 1788-1829*, Melbourne, 1963, p. 34.
15 J. Ritchie, *Punishment and Profit The Reports of Commissioner John Bigge on the Colonies of New South Wales and Van Diemen's Land, 1822-1823; their origins, nature and significance*, Melbourne, 1970, p. 233.
16 Ibid, p. 233.
17 Rose, 'The Administration of Governor Darling', p. 67.
18 Fletcher, *Ralph Darling*, p. 80.
19 Ritchie, 'John Thomas Bigge', p. 24.
20 A.C. Melbourne, *Early Constitutional Development in Australia*, Oxford, 1934, p. 99.
21 McMartin, *Public Servants and Patronage*, p. 69.
22 C. Liston, 'NSW Under Brisbane 1821-1825', Ph. D., University of Sydney, 1980, p. 66.
23 Melbourne, *Early Constitutional Development*, p. 113.
24 Ritchie, *Punishment and Profit*, p. 253.
25 Ibid.
26 B. Fletcher, *Colonial Australia Before 1850*, Melbourne, 1998, p. 75.
27 H. King, 'Frederick Goulburn: The Man and His Office', *Australian Journal of Public Administration*, Vol. 38, No. 3, 1979, p. 234.
28 McMartin, *Public Servants and Patronage*, p. 71.
29 Liston, 'NSW Under Brisbane', p. 20.
30 McMartin, *Public Servants and Patronage*, p. 68.
31 King, 'Frederick Goulburn', p. 236.
32 J. Stephen to G. Arthur, 31 July 1824, *Sir George Arthur Papers*, Vol. 4.
33 Brisbane to Bathurst, 1 May 1824, *HRA*, Series 1, Vol. XI, p. 256.
34 Liston, 'NSW Under Brisbane', p. 20.
35 J. Bennett, *Some Papers of Sir Francis Forbes First Chief Justice in Australia*, Sydney, 1998, p. 39.
36 Ibid.
37 Ibid, p. 40.
38 Bathurst to Darling, 14 July 1825, *HRA*, Series 1, Vol. XII, pp. 18-19.
39 Swainston, 'William Sharp Macleay, 1792-1865', p. 13.
40 Fletcher, *Ralph Darling*, p. 73.
41 B. Fletcher, 'Administrative Reform in New South Wales Under Governor Darling', *Australian Journal of Public Administration*, Vol. XXXVIII, September 1979, p. 248.
42 Fletcher, *Ralph Darling*, p. 12.
43 *Sydney Gazette*, 1 February 1826, p.2.
44 Fletcher, *Ralph Darling*, p. 74.
45 *Sydney Gazette*, 1 February 1826, p. 2.
46 J. Macarthur Junior to J. Macarthur, 27 December 1824, *Macarthur Papers*, A2911, pp. 234- 236.
47 Ibid. p. 304.
48 Fletcher, *Ralph Darling*, p. 77.
49 McMartin, *Public Servants and Patronage*, p. 149.
50 Darling to Bathurst, 16 November 1826, *HRA*, Series 1, Vol. XII, p. 691.
51 Darling to Hay, 2 February 1826, *HRA*, Series 1, Vol. XII, p. 149.
52 Fletcher, *Ralph Darling*, p. 89.
53 McMartin, *Public Servants and Patronage*, p. 151.
54 Fletcher, 'Administrative Reform in New South Wales Under Governor Darling', p. 247.
55 McMartin, *Public Servants and Patronage*, p. 151.
56 Ibid, p. 161.
57 Ibid, p. 213.
58 Enclosure No. 3, Darling to Huskisson, 15 May 1828, *HRA*, Series 1, Vol. XIV, p. 186.
59 Darling to Bathurst, 20 May 1826, *HRA*, Series 1, Vol. XII, p. 299.
60 McMartin, *Public Servants and Patronage*, p. 218.
61 Fletcher, *Ralph Darling*, pp. 94 – 95.
62 McMartin, *Public Servants and Patronage*, p. 218.
63 Darling to Macleay, 6 July 1826, *HRA*, Series 1, Vol. XII, p. 370.
64 Darling to Bathurst, 8 September 1826, *HRA*, Series 1, Vol. XII, p. 552.
65 R. Crawford, *Young and Free – The Letters of Robert and Thomas Crawford 1821-1830*, Canberra, 1995, p. 188.
66 Hay to Darling, 13 July 1827, *HRA*, Series 1, Vol. XIII, p. 445.
67 Fletcher, 'Administrative Reform in New South Wales Under Governor Darling', p. 252.
68 McMartin, *Public Servants and Patronage*, p. 72.
69 A. McMartin, 'Born Bureaucrat, Thomas Cudbert Harington', *Australian Journal of Public Administration*, Vol. XXXVIII, No. 3, September 1979, p. 264.
70 Enclosure No.1, Bourke to Aberdeen, 1 September 1835, *HRA*, Series 1, Vol. VIII, p. 89.
71 McMartin, *Public Servants and Patronage*, p. 153.
72 Goderich to Darling, 16 June 1827, *HRA*, Series 1, Vol. XIII, p. 420.
73 Earnshaw, Hughes, Davidson, *Fanny to William*, 28 May 1826, p. 56.
74 McMartin, 'Born Bureaucrat', pp. 263-264.

75 Harington to Macleay, No. 44, 22 June 1836, Administrative & Domestic Papers of Colonial Secretary, 2/1844, *AONSW.*
76 *Australian*, 16 December 1829, p. 3.
77 McMartin, *Public Servants and Patronage*, p. 155.
78 Ibid, p. 155.
79 Harington to Macleay, February 1827, Administrative and Domestic Papers of Colonial Secretary, 2/1844, *AONSW.*
80 Ryan to Harington, 17 February 1827, Administrative and Domestic Papers of Colonial Secretary, 2/1844, *AONSW.*
81 Fletcher, 'Administrative Reform in New South Wales', p. 253.
82 Governor's Minutes, No. 81, 10 October 1827, 4/991, *AONSW.*
83 Ibid.
84 McMartin, *Public Servants and Patronage,* p. 158.
85 Ibid, p. 164.
86 Fletcher, *Ralph Darling*, p. 93.
87 Governor's Minutes, No. 81, 10 October 1827, 4/991, *AONSW.*
88 Goderich to Darling, 28 January 1828, Governor's Minutes, No. 16, 4/992, *AONSW.*
89 Macleay to Darling, 7 July 1829, *HRA*, Series 1, Vol. XV, p. 69.
90 Darling to Hay, 7 July 1829, *HRA*, Series 1, Vol. XV, p. 69.
91 Macleay to Darling, 7 July 1829, *HRA*, Series 1, Vol XV, p. 69.
92 Darling to Hay, 23 February 1831, *HRA*, Series 1, Vol. XVI, pp. 97-98.
93 McMartin, *Public Servants and Patronage*, p. 157.
94 *Sydney Monitor*, 24 July 1830, p. 2.
95 Ibid, 9 July 1831, p. 2.
96 Greville to Macleay, 19 September 1829, Administrative and Domestic Papers of Colonial Secretary, 2/1844, No. 65, *AONSW.*
97 Administrative and Domestic Papers of Colonial Secretary, 3 July 1829, 2/1844, *AONSW.*
98 Darling to Bathurst, 16 November 1826, *HRA*, Series 1, Vol. XIII, p. 692.
99 Earnshaw, Hughes, Davidson, *Fanny to William*, 21 April 1826, p. 52.
100 C. Currey, *Sir Francis Forbes*, Sydney, 1968, p. 300.
101 *Australian*, 14 October 1826, p. 2.
102 Fletcher, 'Administrative Reform in New South Wales Under Governor Darling', p. 262.
103 Fletcher, *Ralph Darling*, p. 83.
104 Ibid, p. 82.
105 Ibid, pp. 81-82.
106 Ibid, p. 84.
107 List of Magistrates, 31 January 1827, *HRA*, Series 1, Vol. XIII, p. 59.
108 Currey, *Sir Francis Forbes*, p. 307.
109 Bennett, *Some Papers of Sir Francis Forbes*, pp. 97-98.
110 Ibid, p. 100.
111 Foster, 'A Piece of Sharp Practice?', p. 404.
112 *Australian*, 9 May 1827, p. 3.
113 Rose, 'The Administration of Governor Darling', pp. 162-163.

114 G. Richardson, 'The Archives of the Colonial Secretary's Department of NSW 1788-1856', M.A., University of Sydney, 1951, p. 23.
115 Ibid, p. 30.
116 McMartin, *Public Servants and Patronage*, p. 164.

CHAPTER 3
1 Liston, 'NSW Under Brisbane 1821–1825', p. 411.
2 *HRA*, Series 1, Vol. X, Note 90, p. 825.
3 Liston, 'NSW Under Brisbane 1821–1825', p. 407.
4 Ibid, p. 414.
5 Ibid, p. 413.
6 R. Walker, *The Newspaper Press in NSW 1803–1920*, Sydney, 1976, p. 6.
7 Ibid, p. 6.
8 J. Ritchie, *The Wentworths Father and Son*, p. 144.
9 Ibid, p. 135.
10 Ibid, p. 211.
11 Ibid, p. 181.
12 Ibid, p. 223.
13 Walker, *The Newspaper Press in NSW*, p. 8.
14 Fletcher, *Ralph Darling*, p. 240.
15 L. Stephens (ed), *Dictionary of National Biog-raphy*, Vol. XI, London, 1887, pp. 142-145.
16 R. Lochore, Diaries of Baron Karl von Hügel, Sydney, New Zealand and Norfolk Island from 17 February to 16 April 1834, translation, *D. Clark Papers*, uncatalogued, p. 50.
17 S. Proctor, 'Henry Dumaresq on the Sydney Press in 1827', *JRAHS*, Vol. 57, Pt. 2, 1971.
18 Governor's Minutes, No. 132, 18 August 1826, 4/990, *AONSW.*
19 Rose, 'The Administration of Governor Darling', p. 128.
20 Walker, *The Newspapers Press in NSW*, p. 5.
21 Ibid, p. 3.
22 Forbes, *Sydney Society in Crown Colony Days*, p. 84.
23 Fletcher, *Ralph Darling*, pp. 239-240.
24 *Sydney Gazette*, 7 May 1827, p. 2. & 16 May 1827, p. 2.
25 *Australian*, 3 February 1829, p. 3.
26 Ibid, 23 October 1829, p. 2.
27 Ibid.
28 Walker, *The Newspaper Press in NSW*, p. 11.
29 J. Hogue, 'Governor Darling, the Press and the Collar', *JRAHS*, Vol.2, Pt. 12, 1929, p. 313.
30 Governor's Minutes, No. 1, 12 January 1826, 4/990, *AONSW.*
31 Bathurst to Darling, 4 August 1825, *HRA*, Series 1, Vol. XII, p. 48.
32 *Sydney Monitor*, 10 November 1828, p. 5.
33 King, 'Frederick Goulburn', p. 237.
34 McMartin, *Public Servants and Patronage*, p. 162.
35 Downing Street to Brisbane, Governor's Minutes, No. 11, 1826, 4/990, *AONSW.*
36 Bennett, *Some Papers of Sir Francis Forbes*, p. 137.
37 Earnshaw, Hughes, Davidson, *Fanny to William*, 8 October 1826, pp. 66-67.
38 Ibid, 4 December 1826, p. 69.
39 W. Dumaresq to A. Macleay, 1 February 1828, *HRA*,

Series 1, Vol. XIV, pp. 46-47.

40 *Monitor*, 2 February 1828, p. 8.

41 *Sydney Monitor*, 18 January 1837, p. 2.

42 *Sydney Gazette*, 16 February 1827, p. 2. Unfortunately the number of acres listed is illegible on the microfilm copy in the Mitchell Library.

43 Ibid, 26 October 1827, p. 2.

44 *Sydney Monitor*, 20 December 1828, p. 3.

45 Darling to Murray, 22 December 1830, *HRA*, Series 1, Vol. XV, p. 854.

46 Darling to Huskisson, 26 March 1828, *HRA*, Series 1, Vol. XIV, p. 41.

47 Bennett, *Some Papers of Sir Francis Forbes*, p. 185.

48 Ibid, pp. 97-98.

49 *Australian*, 9 September 1829, p. 2.

50 Ibid, p. 3.

51 *Sydney Monitor*, 22 May 1830, p. 2.

52 *Monitor*, 27 April 1827, p. 5.

53 *Australian*, 21 August 1829, p. 3.

54 Ibid, 6 February 1829, p. 2.

55 *Sydney Monitor*, 10 November 1828, p. 5.

56 Earnshaw, Hughes, Davidson, *Fanny to William*, 22 February 1830, p. 117.

57 W. Wood, *Dawn in the Valley: The Story of Settlement in the Hunter Valley River Valley to 1833*, Sydney, 1972, p. 175.

58 *Australian*, 30 August 1833, p. 2.

59 Ibid, 23 August 1833, p. 2.

60 Ibid, 30 August 1833, p. 2.

61 Ibid, 25 October 1833, p. 2.

62 Wood, *Dawn in the Valley*, pp. 264-266.

63 Darling to Hay, 9 February 1827, *HRA*, Series 1, Vol. XIII, pp. 97-98.

64 *Monitor*, 22 December 1826, p. 5.

65 Darling to Horton, 15 December 1826, *HRA*, Series 1, Vol. XII, pp. 747-748.

66 Ibid, p. 748.

67 Ibid, p. 749.

68 Ibid p. 763.

69 Ritchie, *The Wentworths*, p. 226.

70 Darling to Hay, 9 February 1827, *HRA*, Series 1, Vol. XIII, pp. 99-100.

71 Ibid.

72 Ibid.

73 Bathurst to Darling, 12 July 1825, *HRA*, Series 1, Vol. XII, p. 17.

74 Ibid.

75 Darling to Hay, 9 February 1827, *HRA*, Series 1, Vol. XIII, p. 97.

76 Bennett, *Some Papers of Sir Francis Forbes*, p. 160.

77 Fletcher, *Ralph Darling*, p. 257.

78 Bennett, *Some Papers of Sir Francis Forbes*, p. 163.

79 Forbes to Horton, 31 May 1827, Private Letters to Horton, p. 195.

80 Bennett, *Some Papers of Sir Francis Forbes*, p. 170.

81 Fletcher, *Ralph Darling*, pp. 253-254.

82 Bennett, *Some Papers of Sir Francis Forbes*, p. 163.

83 Ibid, p. 164.

84 Forbes to Horton, 31 May 1827, Private Letters to Horton, p. 195.

85 Ibid, p. 198.

86 Bennett, *Some Papers of Sir Francis Forbes*, p. 164.

87 Forbes to Horton, 20 September 1827, Private Letters to Horton, pp. 250-251.

88 Proctor, 'Henry Dumaresq', p. 177.

89 Ibid, p.178.

90 Ibid, p. 175.

91 Bennett, *Some Papers of Sir Francis Forbes*, p. 164.

92 Ibid, p. 161.

93 Ibid, p. 176.

94 Forbes to Horton, 29 April 1827, Private Letters to Horton, p. 346.

95 Earnshaw, Hughes, Davidson, *Fanny to William*, 4 August 1827, p. 85.

96 Bennett, *Some Papers of Sir Francis Forbes*, p. viii.

97 Melbourne, *Early Constitutional Development*, p. 157.

98 *Sydney Monitor*, 10 November 1828, p. 4, & Rose, 'The Administration of Governor Darling', p. 156.

99 *Sydney Monitor*, 13 January 1830, p. 2.

100 Earnshaw, Hughes, Davidson, *Fanny to William*, 27 April 1831, p. 134.

101 Forbes to Horton, 22 March 1827, Private Letters to Horton, p. 117.

102 Bennett, *Some Papers of Sir Francis Forbes*, p. 136.

103 Fletcher, *Ralph Darling*, p. 84.

104 Bennett, *Some Papers of Sir Francis Forbes*, p. 136.

105 Ibid, p. X.

106 Forbes to Horton, 1 June 1827, Private Letters to Horton, p. 188.

107 Ibid, 22 March 1827, p. 121.

108 Ibid, 1 June 1827, p. 188.

109 Ibid, 22 March 1827, p. 136.

110 Bennett, *Some Papers of Sir Francis Forbes*, p. 167.

111 Ibid, p. 169.

112 Ibid, p. 167.

113 Fletcher, *Ralph Darling*, p. 257.

114 Ibid.

115 Darling to Forbes, 9 March 1827, Private Letters to Horton, p. 263.

116 Darling to Hay, 5 July 1827, *HRA*, Series 1, Vol. XVIII, p. 430.

117 Bennett, *Some Papers of Sir Francis Forbes*, p. 181.

118 Melbourne, *Early Constitutional Development*, p. 146.

119 Bennett, *Some Papers of Sir Francis Forbes*, p. 119.

120 Fletcher, *Ralph Darling*, p. 417.

121 Bennett, *Some Papers of Sir Francis Forbes*, p. 171.

122 Earnshaw, Hughes, Davidson, *Fanny to William*, 31 July 1830, p. 122.

123 Melbourne, *Early Constitutional Development*, pp. 152-153.

124 Murray to Darling, 31 July 1828, *HRA*, Series 1, Vol. XIV, pp. 265-266.

125 Melbourne, *Early Constitutional Development*, p. 157.

126 *Sydney Gazette*, 9 April 1829, p. 2.

127 Fletcher, *Ralph Darling*, p. 287.

128 *Sydney Gazette*, 25 April 1829, p. 2.

129 *Sydney Monitor*, 16 January 1830, p. 1.

130 *Australian*, 16 September 1831, p. 3.

131 Ibid, 12 November 1830, p. 3.

132 Fletcher, *Ralph Darling*, p. 288.

133 *Sydney Monitor*, 21 September 1831, p. 2.

134 Liston, 'NSW Under Brisbane', p. 466.
135 Earnshaw, Hughes, Davidson, *Fanny to William*, 11 November 1831, p. 138.
136 Ibid, 21 July 1831, pp. 136-137.
137 *Sydney Monitor*, 21 September 1831, p. 2.
138 Ibid.
139 Ibid.
140 Rose, 'The Administration of Governor Darling', p. 176.
141 Fletcher, *Ralph Darling*, pp. 292-293.
142 *Australian*, 21 October 1831, p. 3.
143 *Sydney Gazette*, 25 October 1831, p. 2.
144 *The Weekly Register*, 2 September 1843, p. 2.
145 *Sydney Gazette*, 25 October 1831, p. 2.
146 Ibid.
147 Currey, *Sir Francis Forbes*, p. 173.
148 R. Therry, *Reminiscences of Thirty Years' Residence in NSW and Victoria*, facsimile ed., Sydney, 1974, p. 55.
149 *Australian*, 1 April 1831, p. 2.
150 Currey, *Sir Francis Forbes*, p. 307.
151 Bennett, *Some Papers of Sir Francis Forbes*, p. 41.

CHAPTER 4

1 H. King, *Great Australians Richard Bourke*, Melbourne, 1963, pp. 3 & 7.
2 Roberts, *The Squatting Age*, p. 22.
3 King, *Richard Bourke*, pp. 145 & 212.
4 Ibid, p. 166.
5 Ibid, p. 155.
6 Bourke to Stanley, 25 December 1833, *HRA*, Series 1, Vol. XVII, p. 303.
7 J. Manning Ward, *James Macarthur Colonial Conservative 1798-1867*, Sydney, 1981, p.59.
8 *Australian*, 21 October 1831, p. 2.
9 It is assumed that this is meant to read 'cormorant' defined by *The Concise Oxford Dictionary* as a 'large lustrous-black voracious sea-bird'.
10 Goderich to Bourke, 13 May 1832, *HRA*, Series 1, Vol. XVI, p. 646.
11 Ibid.
12 *Sydney Herald*, 2 January 1837, p. 4.
13 G. Souter, *Company of Heralds A century and a half of Australian publishing by John Fairfax Limited and its predecessors 1831-1981*, Melbourne, 1981, p. 18.
14 Ibid, p. 19.
15 Therry, *Reminiscences of Thirty Years' Residence*, pp. 132-133.
16 Earnshaw, Hughes, Davidson, *Fanny to William*, 23 September 1832, p. 149.
17 Governor's Minutes, No. 93, 30 September 1831, 4/995, *AONSW*.
18 Earnshaw, Hughes, Davidson, *Fanny to William*, 8 January 1832, p. 141.
19 Macleay to Bourke, 19 September 1832, *HRA*, Series 1, Vol. XVI, p. 753.
20 Carlin, *Elizabeth Bay House*, pp. 1 & 3.
21 Bennett, *Some Papers of Sir Francis Forbes*, p. 214.
22 Ibid.
23 Stanley to Bourke, 30 April 1833, *HRA*, Series 1, Vol. XVII, p. 88.
24 *Sydney Gazette*, 26 June 1834, p. 2.

25 *Colonist*, 17 September 1835, p. 3.
26 Goderich to Bourke, 29 September 1831, *HRA*, Series 1, Vol. XVI, p. 383.
27 Earnshaw, Hughes, Davidson, *Fanny to William*, 6 May 1832, p. 144.
28 Ibid, 7 January 1833, p. 153.
29 P. Clarke, D. Spender, (editors), *Life Lines Australian Women's Letters and Diaries 1788-1840*, Sydney, 1992, pp. 76-78.
30 Foster, *Colonial Improver*, 1978, pp. 20 & 48.
31 Earnshaw, Hughes, Davidson, *Fanny to William*, 6 May 1832, p. 144.
32 King, *Richard Bourke*, p. 246.
33 Foster, *Colonial Improver*, p. 48.
34 McMartin, *Public Servants and Patronage*, p. 167.
35 Bourke to Macleay 16 April 1834, No. 22, Administrative & Domestic Papers of Colonial Secretary, 2/1844, *AONSW*.
36 R. Bourke to D. Bourke, 26 October 1834, *Bourke Papers*, Vol. VI, f. 49.
37 Earnshaw, Hughes, Davidson, *Fanny to William*, 8 January 1832, p. 140.
38 Ibid, 18 June 1832, p. 147.
39 Foster, 'A Piece of Sharp Practice?', p. 406.
40 Fletcher, *Ralph Darling*, p. 88.
41 Liston, 'New South Wales Under Governor Brisbane', p. 71.
42 Fletcher, *Ralph Darling*, p. 223.
43 21 May 1831, No. 61, Administrative and Domestic Papers of Colonial Secretary, 2/1844, *AONSW*.
44 23 January 1835, No. 29, Administrative and Domestic Papers of Colonial Secretary, 2/1844, *AONSW*.
45 King, *Great Australians*, pp. 1-2.
46 Bourke to Aberdeen, 1 August 1835, *HRA*, Series 1, Vol. XVIII, p. 57.
47 Manning Ward, *James Macarthur*, p. 59.
48 Ibid, p. 76.
49 *Australian*, 7 June 1833, p. 2.
50 Foster, *Colonial Improver*, p. 21.
51 *Australian*, 7 June 1833, p. 2.
52 Earnshaw, Hughes, Davidson, *Fanny to William*, 16 August 1833, pp. 156-157.
53 *Australian*, 16 August 1833, p. 2.
54 Ibid, 18 October 1833, pp. 2-3.
55 Earnshaw, Hughes, Davidson, *Fanny to William*, 25 January 1834, p. 161.
56 Ibid, 1 October 1833, p. 158-159.
57 Ibid, p. 159.
58 King, *Richard Bourke*, p. 233.
59 Richardson, 'The Archives of the Colonial Secretary's Department', p. 24.
60 Forbes, *Sydney Society in Crown Colony Days*, p. 45.
61 Foster, 'A Piece of Sharp Practice?', p. 409.
62 Bourke to Spring Rice, 11 October 1836, *HRA*, Series 1, Vol. XIII, p. 270.
63 *Australian*, 22 November 1833, p. 3.
64 Earnshaw, Hughes, Davidson, *Fanny to William*, 16 August 1833, p.157.
65 King, *Richard Bourke*, p. 157.
66 Ibid, p. 156.

67 Bourke to Howick, 28 February 1832, *HRA*, Series 1, Vol. XVI, p. 544.

68 A. Macleay, Macleay to Bourke, 3 September 1836, *Correspondence with his excellency Sir R. Bourke and other documents relative to the removal of A. M'Leay from the office of Colonial Secretary of New South Wales*, Sydney, 1838.

69 Macleay to Darling, 11 October 1830, *HRA*, Series 1, Vol. XV, p. 777.

70 Melbourne, *Early Constitutional Development*, p. 197.

71 Ward, *Dawn in the Valley*, pp. 21-29.

72 B. Fletcher, 'Christianity and free society in New South Wales 1788-1840', *JRAHS*, Vol. 86, Pt. 2, 2000.

73 King, *Richard Bourke*, pp. 163-164.

74 *Sydney Herald*, 26 December 1833, p. 2.

75 King, *Richard Bourke*, pp. 163-164.

76 Therry, *Reminiscences of Thirty Years' Residence*, pp. 167-168.

77 *Sydney Gazette*, 12 December 1833, p. 2.

78 B. Fletcher, 'Governor Bourke and Squatting in New South Wales', *JRAHS*, Vol. 74, Pt. 4, 1989, p. 271.

79 Melbourne, *Early Constitutional Development*, p. 181.

80 Roberts, *The Squatting Age*, p. 79.

81 K. Swan, *A History of Wagga Wagga*, Sydney, 1970, p. 20.

82 Roberts, *The Squatting Age*, p. 79.

83 P. Burroughs, *Britain and Australia, 1831–1855: A Study in Imperial Relations and Crown Lands Administration*, Oxford, 1967, p. 151.

84 Bourke to Stanley, 30 September 1833, *HRA*, Series 1, Vol. XVII, p. 227.

85 G. Shaw, *Patriarch and Patriot William Grant Broughton 1788-1853 Colonial Statesman and Ecclesiastic*, Melbourne, 1978, p. 79.

86 B. Kaye (ed.), *Anglicanism in Australia A History*, Melbourne, 2002, p. 17.

87 A. Austin, *Australian Education 1788-1900 Church, State and Public Education in Colonial Australia*, Melbourne, 1972, p. 35.

88 *Sydney Herald*, 1 August 1836, p. 2.

89 Bourke to Glenelg, 8 August 1836, *HRA*, Series 1, Vol. XV111, pp. 466-467.

90 Soutar, *The Company of Heralds*, p. 22.

91 Austin, *Australian Education 1788-1900*, p. 40.

92 Bourke to Glenelg, 8 August 1836, *HRA*, Series 1, Vol. XVIII, p. 477.

93 Macleay to Bourke, 3 September 1836, *Correspondence with his excellency Sir R. Bourke*.

94 Bourke to Glenelg, 8 August 1836, *HRA*, Series 1, Vol. XVIII, p. 477.

95 *Australian*, 29 July 1836, p. 2.

96 Ibid.

97 Shaw, *Patriarch and Patriot William Grant Broughton*, pp. 108-109.

98 Ibid, p. 88.

99 Bourke to Glenelg, 8 August 1836, *HRA*, Series 1, Vol. XVIII, p. 468.

100 Ibid, pp. 468 & 473.

101 *HRA*, Series 1, Vol. XVIII, p. 472.

102 Bennett, *Some Papers of Sir Francis Forbes*, p. 238.

103 *Australian*, 29 July 1836, p. 2.

104 *Sydney Herald*, 1 August 1836, p. 2.

105 King, *Richard Bourke*, p. 7.

106 Macleay to Bourke, 3 September 1836, *Correspondence with his excellency Sir R. Bourke*.

107 Bourke to Aberdeen, 1 August 1835, *HRA*, Series 1, Vol. XVIII, pp. 58-59.

108 Bourke to Glenelg, 8 August 1836, *HRA*, Series 1, Vol. XVIII, p. 478.

109 Bennett, *Some Papers of Sir Francis Forbes*, p. 244.

110 *Sydney Gazette*, 29 October 1836, p. 2.

111 Macleay to Bourke, 3 September 1836, *Correspondence with his excellency Sir R. Bourke*.

112 *Colonist*, 19 January 1837, p. 2.

113 *Sydney Herald*, 2 January 1837, p. 4.

114 Ibid.

115 Macleay to Bourke, 24 August 1836, *Corres-pondence between Major-General Sir Richard Bourke and Alexander Macleay*.

116 Glenelg to Bourke, 26 February 1836, *HRA*, Series 1, Vol. XVIII, p. 298.

117 Bourke to Glenelg, 3 January 1837, *HRA*, Series 1, Vol. XVIII, p. 638.

118 *Sydney Herald*, 10 April 1837, p. 2.

119 G. Abbott & G. Little, *The Respectable Sydney Merchant A.B. Spark of Tempe*, Sydney, 1976, pp. 98-99.

120 *Sydney Herald*, 6 November 1841, p. 2.

121 In an ironic twist of fate this piece of plate was eventually returned to England, but in 1943 it was given to the NSW State Government by the widow of Sir Ronald Macleay, one of Alexander's great grandsons. War delayed its despatch and it arrived back in Australia in 1947.

122 *Sydney Herald*, 4 May 1837, p. 2.

123 Ibid.

124 Ibid.

125 Ibid.

126 Macleay to Glenelg, 15 October 1836, *Public Records Office,* CO 201/258.

127 Ibid.

128 Glenelg to Macleay, 31 July 1837, *Public Records Office,* CO 201/258.

129 Pike, *Australian Dictionary of Biography*, Vol. 1, p. 182.

130 W. Macleay to Glenelg, 1 September 1836, *Public Records Office*, CO 201/258.

131 Glenelg to W. Macleay, 9 September 1836, *Public Records Office*, CO 201/258.

132 Bennett, *Some Papers of Sir Francis Forbes*, p. 246.

133 Ibid.

134 P. Stanbury, Summary of Swainston Notes, *Swainston Papers*, p. 85.

135 Roberts, *The Squatting Age*, p. 32.

136 Macleay to Glenelg, 20 March 1838, *Public Records Office*, CO 201/282.

137 Kirby to Macleay, 1839, Linnean Society, London.

138 Bourke to Glenelg, 30 January 1837, *HRA*, Series 1, Vol. XVIII, p. 661.

139 *Sydney Herald*, 9 January 1837, p. 2.

140 Foster, *Colonial Improver*, pp. 46-47.

141 King, *Richard Bourke*, p. 247.

142 Bennett, *Some Papers of Sir Francis Forbes*, p. 244.

143 *Sydney Gazette*, 24 August 1830, p. 2.
144 King, 'Frederick Goulburn', p. 245.
145 Richardson, 'The Archives of the Colonial Secretary's Department', p. 31.
146 McMartin, *Public Servants and Patronage*, p. 147.
147 Bourke to Macleay, 9 May 1835, *Bourke Papers*, Vol. XI, folios 333-334.
148 Ibid.
149 Ibid.
150 Macleay to Bourke, 8 & 11 May 1835, *Bourke Papers*, Vol. XI, f. 335.
151 McMartin, *Public Servants and Patronage*, p. 171.
152 Ibid, p. 174.
153 *Weekly Register*, 5 August 1843, p. 5.
154 Roberts, *The Squatting Age*, p. 31.
155 Darling to Goderich, 1 November 1827, *HRA*, Series 1, Vol. XIII, p. 587.

CHAPTER 5
1 *William Riley Papers 1830–1831*, p. 128.
2 Carlin, *Elizabeth Bay House*, p. 3.
3 P. Chapman (ed), *The Diaries and Letters of G.T.W.B. Boyes, Vol. 1, 1820–1832*, Melbourne, 1985, p. 255.
4 Currey, C., *Sir Francis Forbes: The First Chief Justice of the Supreme Court of New South Wales*, Sydney, 1968, p. 307.
5 J. Dowling, *Journal 1827–1828 and other papers 1800–1903*, p. 65.
6 King, 'Man in a Trap', p. 40.
7 The portrait referred to here is in Earnshaw, Hughes, Davidson, *Fanny to William*, p. 13.
8 B. Field to S. Marsden, 2 March 1825, *Marsden Papers*, p. 437.
9 Chapman, *The Diaries and Letters of Boyes*, p. 255.
10 Ibid, p. 256.
11 Earnshaw, Hughes, Davidson, *Fanny to William*, 8 February 1814, p. 10.
12 Chapman, *The Diaries and Letters of Boyes*, p. 256.
13 M. Herman, *Annabella Boswell's Journal*, Sydney, 1953, pp. 3-4.
14 Earnshaw, Hughes, Davidson, *Fanny to William*, 21 April 1826, p. 53.
15 Ibid, 15 August 1817, p. 34.
16 Ibid, 6 April 1828, p. 95.
17 A. Graves, *The Royal Academy of Arts: A complete dictionary of contributors and their work from its foundation in 1769 to 1904*, London, 1906, Painting no. 520.
18 Earnshaw, Hughes, Davidson, *Fanny to William*, 4 December 1826, p. 71.
19 E. Windschuttle, *Taste and Science Women of the Macleay Family 1790–1850*, Sydney, 1988, p. 68.
20 Earnshaw, Hughes, Davidson, *Fanny to William*, 8 January 1832, p. 142.
21 Ibid, 25 January 1834, p. 162.
22 Correspondence of Robert Brown 1760–1858, Vol. 11, 1836–1858, 20 September 1832, f.178.
23 Earnshaw, Hughes, Davidson, *Fanny to William*, 14 August 1830, p. 125.
24 Ibid, 2 December 1830, p. 128.
25 Ibid, 1830, p. 107.

26 Ibid, 9 December 1816, p. 22.
27 Correspondence of R. Brown 1760–1858, Vol. 11, 1826–1858, 20 September 1832, f.178
28 Earnshaw, Hughes, Davidson, *Fanny to William*, 22 September 1815, p. 16.
29 De Berg Tapes, Malcolm Ellis, 7 November 1967, National Library.
30 Carlin, *Elizabeth Bay House*, pp. 48–49.
31 Earnshaw, Hughes, Davidson, *Fanny to William*, 15 March 1831, p. 132.
32 Ibid, 15 February 1828, p. 92.
33 *Australian*, 1 February 1828, p. 3.
34 *Sydney Gazette*, 17 October 1829, p. 4.
35 Earnshaw, Hughes, Davidson, *Fanny to William*, 19 October 1829, p. 113.
36 Ibid, 4 December 1826, p. 69.
37 Ibid, 2 December 1830, p. 127.
38 Ibid, 31 July 1830, p. 123.
39 Ibid, 21 November 1829, p. 115.
40 Windschuttle, *Taste and Science*, p. 18.
41 Fletcher, *Ralph Darling*, p. 25.
42 Earnshaw, Hughes, Davidson, *Fanny to William*, 13 October 1830, p. 126.
43 Clark, *A History of Australia Vol. 2*, p. 103.
44 Earnshaw, Hughes, Davidson, *Fanny to William*, 19 October 1829, p. 113.
45 Ibid, 11 September 1826, p. 65.
46 Ibid, 19 October 1829, p. 113.
47 Windschuttle, *Taste and Science*, p. 20.
48 *Sydney Monitor*, 29 November 1828, pp. 5 & 7.
49 Earnshaw, Hughes, Davidson, *Fanny to William*, 28 November 1829, p. 4.
50 Ibid, 24 October 1829, p. 2.
51 *Sydney Monitor*, 23 March 1833, p. 4.
52 Earnshaw, Hughes, Davidson, *Fanny to William*, 2 December 1830, p. 127.
53 Ibid, 29 August, 1828, p. 99.
54 Ibid, 12 March 1834, p. 162.
55 Ibid, 24 October 1834, p. 167.
56 A. Atkinson, *Camden Farm and Village Life in Early New South Wales*, Melbourne, 1988, p. 4.
57 *Swainston Papers*.
58 Earnshaw, Hughes, Davidson, *Fanny to William*, 8 January 1832, p. 141.
59 Ibid, 6 April 1828, p. 95.
60 Ibid, p. 141.
61 Alexander Rose Macleay to Alexander Macleay, 14 December 1846, *Thomas Barker Papers*, National Library of Australia.
62 *Swainston Papers*.
63 Letter from Thomas Knox at Seaforth Lodge, Stornoway, 31 October 1834, Old Register House, Edinburgh, *Swainston Papers*, 3.49.
64 J. &. N. Underwood, 'Alexander Rose Macleay', unpublished article, December 1987, *Swainston Papers*.
65 Earnshaw, Hughes, Davidson, *Fanny to William*, 8 November 1828, p. 103.
66 Ibid, 5 March 1826, pp. 51-52.
67 Ibid, 15 February 1828, p. 92.
68 Ibid, 22 May 1830, p. 120.

69 Ibid, 8 October 1826, p. 67.
70 Ibid, 4 December 1826, p. 71.
71 Ibid, 7 March 1817, p. 31.
72 B. Fletcher, 'Sir John Jamison in New South Wales 1814 – 1844', *JRAHS*, Vol. 65, Part 1, June 1979, p. 1.
73 Earnshaw, Hughes, Davidson, *Fanny to William*, 11 September 1826, p. 64.
74 Ibid, 31 January 1826, p. 50.
75 *Australian*, 3 September 1830, p. 3.
76 Earnshaw, Hughes, Davidson, *Fanny to William*, 31 January 1826, p. 50.
77 Fletcher, 'Sir John Jamison in New South Wales 1814–1844', p. 10.
78 S. Ducker, Diaries of Baron Karl von Hügel, Sydney New Zealand and Norfolk Island from 17 February to 16 April 1834, *D. Clark Papers*, uncatalogued. *Karl von Hügel was commonly known as Charles.*
79 Earnshaw, Hughes, Davidson, *Fanny to William*, 25 March 1827, p. 77.
80 Ibid, 29 August 1828, pp. 99-100.
81 Ibid, 6 June 1829, p. 109.
82 Ibid, 17 July 1829, p. 112.
83 Ibid, 21 April 1826, p. 53.
84 Ibid, 4 December 1826, p. 71.
85 Ibid, 25 March 1827, p. 77.
86 Ibid, 2 December 1830, p. 127.
87 Ibid, 5 March 1826, p. 51.
88 Ibid, 16 December 1830, p. 130.
89 Ibid, 26 December 1835, p. 174.
90 Ibid, 10 February 1836, pp. 176-177.
91 Ibid, 9 March 1836, p. 177.
92 Ibid, 27 October 1835, p. 172.
93 Ibid, 4 August 1827, p. 85.
94 Ibid, 8 January 1832, p. 141.
95 G. Macleay to W. Macleay, 1836, *Macleay Papers*, A4303, p. 17.
96 *Australian*, 22 November 1833, p. 3.
97 Earnshaw, Hughes, Davidson, *Fanny to William*, 19 January 1818, p. 36.
98 *Australian*, 16 August 1826, p. 3.
99 Earnshaw, Hughes, Davidson, *Fanny to William*, 26 July 1826, p. 61.
100 A. McMartin, 'Born Bureaucrat: Thomas Cudbert Harington', *Australian Journal of Public Administration*, Vol. 38, No. 3, September 1979, p. 277.
101 *Sydney Monitor*, 7 July 1830, p. 2.
102 *Sydney Gazette*, 29 November 1834, p. 2.
103 Ibid.
104 *Sydney Herald*, 13 June 1836, p. 2.
105 Ibid, 31 July 1837, pp. 180-181.
106 Ibid, 29 August 1828, p. 100.
107 Ibid.
108 D. Mabberley, *Jupiter botanicus: Robert Brown of the British Museum*, London, 1985, p. 242.
109 Ibid, p. 194.
110 Swainston, unpublished preface to Fanny's letters, *Swainston Papers*.
111 Earnshaw, Hughes, Davidson, *Fanny to William*, 4 December 1826, p. 71.
112 Ibid, 28 May 1828, p. 96.

113 Ibid, Eliza to William, 20 August 1836, p. 179.
114 *Sydney Herald*, 15 August 1836, p. 2.
115 Earnshaw, Hughes, Davidson, *Fanny to William*, 31 January 1826, p. 49.
116 Memorial for Fanny Macleay, St James's Church, Sydney.
117 Earnshaw, Hughes, Davidson, *Fanny to William*, Eliza to William, 31 July 1837, p. 181.
118 E. Darling to E. Dumaresq, 9 March 1826, *Dumaresq Family*, 953/1/309.
119 Earnshaw, Hughes, Davidson, *Fanny to William*, 21 April 1826, p. 53.
120 E. Darling to E. Dumaresq, 18 April 1826, *Dumaresq Family*, 953/1/309.
121 Herman, *Annabella Boswell's Journal*, pp. 3-5.
122 *Sydney Monitor*, 27 January 1836, p. 3.
123 Earnshaw, Hughes, Davidson, *Fanny to William.*, 10 February 1836, p. 176.
124 *Australian*, 24 March 1827, p. 2.
125 *Sydney Monitor*, 21 November 1836, p. 2.
126 Carlin, *Elizabeth Bay House*, p. 89.
127 *Sydney Gazette*, 23 July 1829, p. 2.
128 *Sydney Monitor*, 3 October 1834, p. 1.
129 Earnshaw, Hughes, Davidson, *Fanny to William*, 12 November 1827, p. 86.
130 *Sydney Gazette*, 9 May 1829, p. 2.
131 R. S. Macarthur Onslow, (ed) E. Macarthur to Edward, 27 December 1830, *Some Early Records of the Macarthurs at Camden*, Adelaide, 1914, p. 462.
132 *Sydney Gazette*, 17 March, 1835, p. 2.
133 Stanbury & Holland, *Mr Macleay's Celebrated Cabinet*, pp. 13-14.
134 Earnshaw, Hughes, Davidson, *Fanny to William*, 12 November 1827, p. 87.
135 Ibid, pp.175 & 179.
136 J. Macleay to W. Macleay, 10 February 1834, *Macarthur Papers*, A4303, p. 23.
137 Earnshaw, Hughes, Davidson, *Fanny to William*, 12 November 1827, pp. 86-87.
138 *Australia The Beautiful Great Gardens*, Sydney, 1983, p. 235.
139 Earnshaw, Hughes, Davidson, *Fanny to William*, 2 May 1830, p. 119.
140 E. Beale, 'Anticipation of the River Murray', *JRAHS*, Vol. 73, Part 1, June 1987, pp. 3-24.
141 Earnshaw, Hughes, Davidson, *Fanny to William*, 2 December 1830, p. 128.
142 Ibid, 8 February 1814, p. 10.
143 Ibid, 19 May 1834, p. 164.
144 Ibid, 25 February 1829, p. 106.
145 Ibid, 15 March 1831, p. 132.
146 K. Macleay to W. Macleay, 23 December 1837, *Macleay Papers*, A4304.
147 Earnshaw, Hughes, Davidson, *Fanny to William*, 10 October 1829, p. 40.
148 Fletcher, 'The Society's Heritage from the Macleays', p. 606.
149 Martin, *Life and Letters of the Right Honourable Robert Lowe Viscount Sherbrooke, Vol. 1*, London, 1899, p. 283.
150 Chapman, *The Diaries and Letters of G. Boyes*, p. 256.

151 Ibid.
152 E. Macarthur to daughter E. Macarthur, 1830, *Macarthur Papers*, A2906.
153 Clark, 'Baron Charles von Hügel and the Macleays', p. 221.
154 Earnshaw, Hughes, Davidson, *Fanny to William*, 5 March 1826, p. 51.
155 Ibid, June 1817, p. 33.
156 J. Franklin, Gipps to Lady Franklin, Journal of a Journey from Port Philip to Sydney 1839, Ms. 114.
157 Carlin, *Elizabeth Bay House*, p. 75.
158 Earnshaw, Hughes, Davidson, *Fanny to William*, 31 January 1826, p. 50.
159 Ibid, 26 July 1826, p. 60.
160 *Sydney Gazette*, 22 November 1826, p. 1.
161 *Sydney Monitor*, 3 January 1829, p. 8.
162 *Colonist*, 16 April 1835, p. 5.
163 *Sydney Monitor*, 30 December 1835, p. 3.
164 Carlin, *Elizabeth Bay House*, p. 75.
165 Ibid, p. 77.
166 *Sydney Morning Herald*, 19 March 1845, p. 4.
167 Ibid.
168 A. Aitkin, Letter to Alexander Macleay, 6 April 1825, *Swainston Papers.*
169 *Sydney Gazette*, 20 May 1826, p. 1.
170 *Monitor*, 7 July 1826, p. 2.
171 *Sydney Gazette*, 31 July 1826, p. 2.
172 Ibid, 27 September 1826, p. 2.
173 *Sydney Herald*, 7 April 1836, p. 3.
174 *Sydney Gazette*, 14 October 1826, p. 1.
175 Ibid, 22 July 1826, p. 2.
176 Ibid, 16 September 1826, p. 2.
177 *Australian*, 9 September 1829, p. 2.
178 *Sydney Monitor*, 12 September 1829, p. 4.
179 *Sydney Gazette*, 6 October 1828, p. 2.
180 Ibid, 23 April 1828, p. 2.
181 J. Angel, *The Australian Club 1838–1988 The First 150 years*, Sydney, 1988, p. 126.
182 Windschuttle, *Taste and Science*, p. 78.
183 *Sydney Gazette*, 22 March 1826, p. 1.
184 W. Dumaresq to E. Dumaresq, 23 March 1826, *Dumaresq Family*, 953/1/321.
185 Earnshaw, Hughes, Davidson, *Fanny to William*, 21 April 1826, p. 53.
186 Ibid, 21 April 1826, p. 53.
187 Windschuttle, *Taste and Science*, p. 82.
188 Earnshaw, Hughes, Davidson, *Fanny to William*, 27 April 1831, p. 133 & *Sydney Monitor*, 6 April 1827, p. 4.
189 *Sydney Gazette*, 26 March 1826, p. 2.
190 *Monitor*, 18 May 1826, p. 5.
191 Windschuttle, *Taste and Science*, pp. 76 & 78.
192 Earnshaw, Hughes, Davidson, *Fanny to William*, 31 January 1826, p. 50.
193 J. Blackman, *A Catalogue of an Extensive and Valuable Library of nearly 4,000 Volumes … Comprising the Major Part of the Well Selected Library of Alexander McLeay, Esq.*, Sydney, 1845.
194 *Sydney Morning Herald*, 18 December 1843, p. 1.
195 *Sydney Gazette*, 5 April 1826, p. 2.
196 *Australian*, 13 January 1829, p. 3.
197 *Sydney Herald*, 25 January 1836, p. 2.
198 Piggott & Company Trade Directories, 1825, 1826, *North Highland Archives.*
199 *Sydney Morning Herald*, 15 February 1843, p. 2.
200 Ibid, p. 3.
201 *Sydney Herald*, 3 December 1835, p. 2.
202 Ibid, 27 April 1835, p. 2.
203 Ibid, 23 April 1836, p. 2.
204 Ibid.
205 Ibid.
206 Ibid.
207 Earnshaw, Hughes, Davidson, *Fanny to William*, 20 August 1836, p. 179.
208 Ibid, 11 September 1826, p. 64.

CHAPTER 6

1 *International Code of Zoological Nomenclature*, International Trust for Zoological Nomenclature in association with British Museum (Natural History) London, 1985, p. 338.
2 J. Gascoigne, *Joseph Banks and the English Enlightenment*, Melbourne, 1994, p. 32.
3 Ibid, p. 31.
4 Ibid, p. 10.
5 *The Southern Queen*, 8 January 1845, p. 4.
6 Gascoigne, *Joseph Banks*, p. 105.
7 Ibid.
8 Ibid, p. 10.
9 C. Lyte, *Sir Joseph Banks 18th Century Explorer, Botanist and Entrepreneur*, Sydney, 1980, p. 240.
10 Swainston, untitled chapter, p. 5, *Swainston Papers.*
11 M. Walker, *Sir James Edward Smith 1759-1828 First President of the Linnean Society of London*, London, 1988, p. 8.
12 A. Macleay to J. Smith, 18 October 1800, Linnean Society, London.
13 *Sydney Morning Herald*, 15 February 1843, p. 2.
14 W. Leach to A. Macleay, 10 December 1811, Linnean Society, London.
15 Earnshaw, Hughes, Davidson, *Fanny to William*, 9 January 1814, pp. 6-7.
16 Gascoigne, *Joseph Banks*, p. 108.
17 Smith to Macleay, 21 September 1822, Linnean Society, London.
18 Gascoigne, *Joseph Banks*, p. 24.
19 W. Kirby to A. Macleay, 1810, Linnean Society, London.
20 Ibid, 8 November 1812.
21 Earnshaw, Hughes, Davidson, *Fanny to William*, 29 August 1828, p. 98.
22 Ibid.
23 Ibid, 28 May 1828, p. 97.
24 Blue Folder, Vol. 21, *Swainston Papers.*
25 General Minute Book 1788-1802, Linnean Society, London.
26 Ibid.
27 Earnshaw, Hughes, Davidson, *Fanny to William*, p. 185.
28 Freeman, *Life of William Kirby*, p. 221.
29 Macleay to Smith, 1 July 1802, Linnean Society, London.

30 Freeman, *Life of William Kirby*, p. 221.
31 Kirby to Macleay, 2 December 1799, Linnean Society, London.
32 T. Marsham to A. Macleay, 27 May 1801, Linnean Society, London.
33 Earnshaw, Hughes, Davidson, *Fanny to William*, 6 June 1829, p. 109.
34 R. Smith, T. Mittler, C. Smith (editors), *History of Entomology*, Palo Alton, 1973, p. 126.
35 Fletcher, 'The Society's Heritage from the Macleays', p. 578.
36 Ibid, p. 579.
37 Walker, Sir James Edward Smith, p. 19.
38 Smith to Macleay, 22 December 1807, Linnean Society, London.
39 Kirby to Macleay, 29 October 1808, Linnean Society, London.
40 Smith, Mittler, Smith, *History of Entomology*, p. 125.
41 Kirby to Macleay, 1809, Linnean Society, London.
42 Ibid, 5 July 1809.
43 Ibid, 3 July 1810.
44 Ibid, 17 December 1811.
45 Ibid, 11 February 1814.
46 Ibid, 6 December 1814.
47 Ibid, 12 June 1815.
48 Ibid, 20 June 1815.
49 Ibid, 6 December 1814.
50 Ibid, 29 April 1815.
51 Ibid, 19 April 1815.
52 Ibid, 10 December 1801.
53 Ibid, 25 February 1800.
54 Smith to Macleay, 3 December 1810, Linnean Society, London.
55 Macleay to Smith, 14 December 1811, Linnean Society, London.
56 Walker, Sir James Edward Smith, p. 40.
57 Marsham to Macleay, 12 March 1818, Linnean Society, London.
58 Ibid, 27 December 1799.
59 Macleay to Smith, 28 June 1799, Linnean Society, London.
60 Smith to Macleay, 23 February 1801, Linnean Society, London.
61 Macleay to Smith, 6 January 1823, Linnean Society, London.
62 Ibid, 17 November 1810.
63 Smith to Macleay, 20 November 1810, Linnean Society, London.
64 Macleay to Smith, 12 December 1801, Linnean Society, London.
65 Ibid, 8 January 1817.
66 Fletcher, 'The Society's Heritage from the Macleays', p. 578.
67 Council Minute Book 1802-1826, Linnean Society, London.
68 Mabberley, *Jupiter botanicus*, p. 178.
69 Smith to Macleay, 10 June 1800, Linnean Society, London.
70 Macleay to Smith, 16 February 1801, Linnean Society, London.
71 Ibid, 19 July 1800.
72 Ibid, 8 May 1802.
73 Ibid, 24 November 1802.
74 Fletcher, 'The Society's Heritage from the Macleays', p. 572.
75 Ibid, p. 573.
76 Macleay to Smith, 30 March 1805, Linnean Society, London.
77 Stanbury & Holland, *Mr Macleay's Celebrated Cabinet*, pp. 11-12.
78 Fletcher, 'The Society's Heritage from the Macleays', p. 572.
79 Ibid, p. 574.
80 Stanbury & Holland, *Mr Macleay's Celebrated Cabinet*, p. 129.
81 O. Swartz to A. Macleay, 14 October 1813, Linnean Society, London.
82 Royal Academy of Sciences to A. Macleay, 6 January 1814, Linnean Society, London.
83 Stanbury & Holland, *Mr Macleay's Celebrated Cabinet*, p. 17.
84 Kirby to Macleay, 7 October 1814, Linnean Society, London.
85 *Macleay Museum News*, No. 2, September 1993, Sydney, p. 4.
86 J. Anderson, 'The Macleay Museum at the University of Sydney', *Australian Natural History*, Vol. 15, 1965-67, Sydney, p. 48.
87 Fletcher, 'The Society's Heritage from the Macleays', p. 576.
88 Ibid, p. 577.
89 Ibid, p. 581.
90 Ibid, p. 608.
91 G. Bennett to R. Owen, 6 April 1840, *George Bennett Papers 1833-1840*.
92 Kirby to Macleay, 27 April 1811, Linnean Society, London.
93 C. de Schreibers to A. Macleay, 30 December 1815, Linnean Society, London.
94 D. Horning, 'The Macleay Insect Collection', *Antenna — Royal Entomological Society of London 1983-1985 Commemoration*, 1985, p. 173.
95 Smith, Mittler, Smith, *History of Entomology*, p. 122.
96 Fletcher, 'The Society's Heritage from the Macleays', p. 575.
97 Smith, Mittler, Smith, *History of Entomology*, p. 122.
98 Gascoigne, *Joseph Banks*, p. 106.
99 Ibid.
100 Smith to Macleay, 15 January 1815, Linnean Society, London.
101 Stanbury, 'The Gentleman Scientist', p. 47.
102 Fletcher, 'The Society's Heritage from the Macleays', p. 577.
103 Ibid.
104 J. Holland, 'W. S. Macleay Special Feature', *Historical Records of Australian Science*, 2, 1996, p. 101.
105 Kirby to Macleay, 18 September 1819, Linnean Society, London.
106 Ibid, 27 December 1821.
107 Smith, Mittler, Smith, *History of Entomology*, p. 123.
108 Smith to Macleay, 13 March 1825, Linnean Society, London.

109 Fletcher, 'The Society's Heritage from the Macleays', p. 613.
110 Macleay to Smith, 28 June 1799, Linnean Society, London.
111 *Swainston Papers.*
112 Smith to Macleay, 23 February 1801, Linnean Society, London.
113 Macleay to Smith, 22 January 1816, Linnean Society, London.
114 Ibid, 30 March 1805.
115 Smith to Macleay, 28 November 1816, Linnean Society, London.
116 Macleay to Smith, 9 December 1816, Linnean Society, London.
117 Kirby to Macleay, 25 March 1817, Linnean Society, London.
118 Ibid, 13 January 1817.
119 Macleay to Smith, 29 April 1817, Linnean Society, London.
120 Smith to Macleay, 3 May 1817, Linnean Society, London.
121 Ibid, 24 September 1820.
122 Mabberley, *Jupiter botanicus*, p. 244.
123 Fletcher, 'The Society's Heritage from the Macleays', p. 577.
124 Macleay to Smith, 16 February 1801, Linnean Society, London.
125 Smith to Macleay, 21 May 1816, Linnean Society, London.
126 Macleay to Smith, 22 May 1816, Linnean Society, London.
127 Ibid, 13 July 1813.
128 Smith to Macleay, 10 December 1813, Linnean Society, London.
129 Ibid.
130 Ibid, 28 February 1814.
131 Ibid, 26 January 1816.
132 Walker, Sir James Edward Smith, p. 48.
133 Smith to Macleay, 4 February 1816, Linnean Society, London..
134 Ibid, 4 February 1816.
135 Macleay to Smith, 2 February 1816, Linnean Society, London.
136 The Statesman, 4 June 1823 (article attached to letter from Smith to Macleay, 26 January 1816), Linnean Society, London.
137 Smith to Macleay, 15 June 1812, Linnean Society, London.
138 Ibid, 28 October 1816.
139 Macleay to Smith, 31 January 1818, Linnean Society, London.
140 Smith to Macleay, 1 February 1818, Linnean Society, London.
141 Macleay to Smith, 6 January 1823, Linnean Society, London.
142 Ibid, 3 April 1820.
143 Smith to Macleay, 9 April 1820, Linnean Society, London.
144 Ibid, 8 January 1823.
145 Ibid, 1 February 1823.
146 Macleay to Smith, 3 April 1820, Linnean Society,

147 Ibid, 12 February 1817 & 30 March 1805.
148 Council Minute Book 1802-1826, 23 June 1823, Linnean Society, London, p. 295.
149 Ibid, 10 June 1823, p. 268.
150 Ibid.
151 Fletcher, 'The Society's Heritage from the Macleays', p. 570.
152 Macleay to Smith, 6 January 1825, Linnean Society, London.
153 Smith to Macleay, 8 January 1825, Linnean Society, London.
154 Smith to Brown, 8 January 1825, Correspondence of R. Brown 1760-1858, Vol. 11, 1813- 1825, Folio 387.
155 Macleay to Smith, 5 January 1825, Linnean Society, London.
156 Council Minute Book 1802-1826, 17 December 1805, Linnean Society, London.
157 Macleay to Smith, 27 April 1821, Linnean Society, London.
158 Ibid, 25 January 1825.
159 Mabberley, *Jupiter botanicus*, p. 241.
160 Smith to Macleay, 27 January 1825, Linnean Society, London.
161 Ibid, 13 March 1825.
162 Kirby to Macleay, January 1825, Linnean Society, London.
163 Ibid, 8 February 1825.
164 Macleay to Smith, 6 January 1823, Linnean Society, London.
165 Fletcher, 'The Society's Heritage from the Macleays', p. 580.
166 Ibid, p. 570.
167 Smith, Mittler, Smith, *History of Entomology*, p. 126.
168 Ibid, p. 127.
169 Ibid, p. 126.
170 Council Minute Book 1802-1826, 10 May 1825, Linnean Society, London.
171 Stanbury & Holland, *Mr Macleay's Celebrated Cabinet*, p. 132.
172 Ibid, p. 76.
173 W.S. Macleay, Miscellaneous accounts and receipts 1825–1842, *Macarthur Papers*, A4308.
174 Macleay Museum, February 2002.
175 *Sydney Gazette*, 1 February 1826, p. 1.
176 Van Leeuwen, 'The Plan of a Museum', p. 44.
177 E. Barnard to A. Macleay, 25 December 1824, Linnean Society, London.
178 Field to Marsden, 18 May 1825, *Marsden Papers*, p. 442.
179 Fletcher, 'The Society's Heritage from the Macleays', p. 580.
180 Macleay to R. Hay, 16 September 1826, Miscellaneous Papers to the Colonial Office Relating to New South Wales, *Public Records Office* C.O. 201/179, pp. 179-182.
181 Bathurst to Macleay, 5 January 1825, Linnean Society, London.
182 R. Strahan, *Rare and Curious Specimens — An Illustrated History of the Australian Museum 1827-1979*, Sydney, p. 10.

183 Ibid, p. 10.
184 Strahan, 'The Dog that did not bark: Alexander Macleay and the Australian Museum', p. 225.
185 Strahan, *Rare and Curious Specimens*, p. 10.
186 Gilbert, *The Royal Botanic Gardens*, Sydney, p. 59.
187 Van Leeuwen, 'The Plan of a Museum', p. 47.
188 Ibid, p. 44.
189 Ibid, p.47.
190 Strahan, *Rare and Curious Specimens*, p. 3.
191 Van Leeuwen, 'The Plan of a Museum', pp. 42 & 48.
192 *Sydney Morning Herald*, 26 April 1843, p. 2.
193 Van Leeuwen, 'The Plan of a Museum', pp. 49-50.
194 Rev. C. Wilton, (ed), *The Australian Quarterly Journal of Theology, Literature and Science*, Vol.1, Sydney, 1828.
195 Strahan, *Rare and Curious Specimens*, p. 9.
196 Strahan, 'The Dog that did not bark', pp. 226-227.
197 Strahan, *Rare and Curious Specimens*, p.11.
198 Ibid, p. 18.
199 Minutes of the Sub-Committee of the Australian Museum, 8 June 1836, Sydney, *Australian Museum Archives*.
200 Fletcher, 'The Society's Heritage from the Macleays', p. 626.
201 Minutes of the Sub-Committee of the Australian Museum, 8 June 1836.
202 Ibid, 16 November 1836.
203 Ibid, 20 September 1837 & 4 October 1837.
204 Ibid, 12 September 1845.
205 Ibid.
206 Ibid, 18 November 1845.
207 Ibid, 4 February 1846.
208 Ibid.
209 Strahan, *Rare and Curious Specimens*, p. 18.
210 Ibid, pp. 19-20.
211 Ibid, p. 21.
212 Rev. Turner, 2 March 1849, Reference A40.49.1, *Australian Museum Archives.*
213 C. Anderson, 'The Macleay Museum', pp. 47-51.
214 W. S. Macleay to Yarrell, 12 January 1840, Papers re business matters and land 1810-1841, *Macarthur Papers*, Part V, p. 21.
215 Horning, 'The Macleay Insect Collection', p. 175.
216 Anderson, 'The Macleay Museum', p. 50.
217 'Type Specimens in the Macleay Museum, University of Sydney, VIII: Insects: Beetles (Insecta Coleoptera)', *Proceedings of the Linnean Society of NSW*, 105(4), 1980, 1981, Sydney, p. 241.
218 Anderson, 'The Macleay Museum', pp. 49-50.
219 Ibid, p. 51.
220 Stanbury & Holland, *Mr. Macleay's Celebrated Cabinet*, p. 128.
221 Strahan, 'The Dog that did not bark', p. 227.
222 *The Weekly Register*, 5 August 1843, p. 8.
223 Ibid, November 1817.
224 Kirby to Macleay, 27 November 1817, Linnean Society, London.
225 Fletcher, 'The Society's Heritage from the Macleays', p. 570.
226 Gascoigne, *Joseph Banks*, p. 2.

227 C. Anderson (ed.), 'Early Days', *The Australian Museum Magazine*, Vol. 111, No. 3, July – September 1927, Sydney, p. 75.
228 *Weekly Register*, 19 August 1843, p. 4.
229 *Sydney Morning Herald*, 15 February 1843, p. 2.
230 Smith, Mittler, Smith, *History of Entomology*, p. 123.
231 J. Fletcher, The Macleay Memorial Volume, p. IX, Sydney, 1893.
232 Leaflet of the Linnean Society of London, London, 1998.
233 *Sydney Morning Herald*, 9 March 2001, p. 14.
234 Leaflet of the Linnean Society of London.
235 Gilbert, *Mr McLeay's Elizabeth Bay Garden*, p. 1.
236 Kirby to Macleay, 29 October 1818, Linnean Society, London.
237 Ibid, 18 August 1817.
238 Gascoigne, *Joseph Banks*, p. 2.

CHAPTER 7

1 V. Crittenden, *A Shrub in the Landscape of Fame*, Canberra, 1992, introduction.
2 J. Harvey, *Early Nurserymen*, Chichester, 1974, p. 11.
3 P. Stanbury, Summary of Swainston Notes, *Swainston Papers*, p. 56.
4 Harvey, *Early Nurserymen*, p. 87.
5 Ibid, p. 12.
6 Swainston, 'William Sharp Macleay, 1792-1865', p. 13.
7 G. Milne to A. Macleay, 1 May 1824, Linnean Society, London.
8 P. Valder, *Wisterias A Comprehensive Guide*, Sydney, 1995, p. 42.
9 *Swainston Papers.*
10 Earnshaw, Hughes, Davidson, *Fanny to William*, June 1817, p. 33.
11 Macleay to Kirby, 3 October 1817, Linnean Society, London.
12 Kirby to Macleay, 1823, Linnean Society, London.
13 Earnshaw, Hughes, Davidson, *Fanny to William*, 4 February 1817, p. 28.
14 Ibid, p. 27.
15 Ibid.
16 Ibid.
17 Ibid, 9 January 1814, p. 7.
18 Ibid, 28 August 1815, p. 14.
19 Harvey, *Early Nurserymen*, p. 88.
20 Ibid.
21 Ibid.
22 Macleay to Smith, 16 February 1801, Linnean Society, London.
23 Kirby to Macleay, 9 November 1805, Linnean Society, London.
24 Mabberley, *Jupiter botanicus*, p. 186.
25 Valder, *Wisterias*, p. 44.
26 List of plants 1835-1843 and seeds 1836-1853 received at Elizabeth Bay House, *Linnean Society of Australia Papers*, Mitchell Library.
27 H. Le Rougetel, *A Heritage of Roses*, Maryland, 1988, p. 69.
28 R. Clough, 'Charles Fraser's Record of Plants in the Sydney Botanic Garden in 1827-28', *Australian*

Garden History, Vol. 8, No.3, 1996, p. 14.
29 L. Gilbert, *The Royal Botanic Gardens, Sydney A History 1816-1985*, Melbourne, 1986, p. 43.
30 Ibid, & Clough, 'Charles Fraser's Record of Plants', p. 14.
31 Catalogue of plants cultivated in The Botanic Garden, Sydney, Parts 1 & 11, January 1828, & List of fruits cultivated in The Botanic Garden up to November 1827, Botanic Garden Library.
32 Crittenden, *A Shrub in the Landscape of Fame*, p. 50.
33 Archibald Clunes Innes: photographs and paper cuttings [compiled by Newcastle Region Public Library].
34 M. Herman, *Annabella Boswell's Journal*, p. 162.
35 Carlin, *Elizabeth Bay House*, p. 40.
36 Crittenden, *A Shrub in the Landscape of Fame*, p. 81.
37 Fletcher, 'The Society's Heritage from the Macleays', p. 584.
38 T. Shepherd, *Lectures on Landscape Gardening in Australia*, Sydney, 1836, p. 88.
39 V. Crittenden, *A History and Bibliography of Australian Gardening Books 1806-1950*, Canberra, 1986, p. 178.
40 Earnshaw, Hughes, Davidson, *Fanny to William*, 11 September 1826, p. 65.
41 Ibid.
42 Ibid.
43 Ibid, 8 October 1826, p. 67.
44 Ibid, 25 February 1829, p. 106.
45 G. Bennett, *Wanderings in New South Wales, Batavia, Pedir Coast, Singapore and China, Vol. 1*, London 1834, p. 53.
46 Earnshaw, Hughes, Davidson, *Fanny to William*, 8 October 1826, p. 67.
47 Ibid, 25 February 1829, p. 106.
48 Interview with Robert Cherry, Kulnura, 2000.
49 Windschuttle, *Taste and Science*, p. 94.
50 *Sydney Gazette*, 23 July 1827, p. 1.
51 Clark, 'Baron Charles von Hügel and the Macleays', p. 214.
52 M. Martin, 'Digging for Garden Treasures', *Insites, Newsletter of the Historic Houses Trust of NSW*, Issue 22, 2000, p. 8.
53 Council Minute Book 1802-1826, Linnean Society, London.
54 P. Stanbury, 'The Gentleman Scientist', *Australian Natural History*, Vol. 19, No. 2, 1977, p. 47.
55 Clark, 'Baron Charles von Hügel and the Macleays', p. 215.
56 Ibid.
57 *Sydney Herald*, 20 June 1831, p. 2.
58 *Horticultural Magazine and Gardener's Calendar of NSW, Vol. III*, No. 15, 1865, p. 68.
59 Crittenden, *A Shrub in the Landscape of Fame*, p. 81.
60 A. Aitken & M. Looker, *The Oxford Companion to Australian Gardening*, Melbourne, 2002, p. 295.
61 *Sydney Herald*, 10 September 1835, p. 2.
62 Crittenden, *A Shrub in the Landscape of Fame*, p. 81.
63 W. Hazlewood, *Australia's First Nurseryman Thomas Shepherd*, Sydney, 1953, p. 1.
64 G. Souter, *The Company of Heralds*, p. 18.
65 *Sydney Monitor*, 4 March 1835, p. 1.
66 Shepherd, *Lectures on Landscape Gardening in Australia*, p. 89.
67 *Sydney Monitor*, 17 January 1835, p. 4.
68 Clark, 'Baron Charles von Hügel and the Macleays', p. 217.
69 Ibid.
70 Shepherd, *Lectures on Landscape Gardening in Australia*, p. 87.
71 Ibid, preface.
72 Crittenden, *A Shrub in the Landscape of Fame*, pp. 101 & 108.
73 Shepherd, *Lectures on Landscape Gardening in Australia*, preface.
74 Clark, 'Baron Charles von Hügel and the Macleays', p. 217.
75 J. Fletcher, 'The Society's Heritage from the Macleays', p. 591.
76 *Sydney Herald*, 10 September 1835, p. 2.
77 Shepherd, *Lectures on Landscape Gardening in Australia*, p. 89.
78 Ibid.
79 Ibid.
80 Ibid.
81 Earnshaw, Hughes, Davidson, *Fanny to William*, 12 December 1833, p. 159.
82 Carlin, *Elizabeth Bay House*, p. 3.
83 Shepherd, *Lectures on Landscape Gardening in Australia*, p. 86.
84 Crittenden, *A Shrub in the Landscape of Fame*, p. [vii].
85 Fletcher, 'The Society's Heritage from the Macleays', pp. 587-588.
86 Interview with Richard Clough, Sydney, 1999.
87 Earnshaw, Hughes, Davidson, *Fanny to William*, 25 March 1827, p. 78.
88 *Sydney Gazette*, 28 May 1831, p. 3.
89 *Sydney Monitor*, 18 January 1837, p. 2.
90 J. Backhouse, *Narrative of a Visit to the Australian Colonies 1832-1838*, London 1843, pp. 239– 240.
91 Gilbert, 'Plants, Privileges and Power', p. 7.
92 Gilbert, *Mr McLeay's Elizabeth Bay Garden*, p. 11.
93 Abbott & Little, *The Respectable Sydney Merchant*, p. 98.
94 Stanbury, 'The Gentleman Scientist', p. 47.
95 Macleay to Thomson, 14 June 1843, *HRA*, Series 1, Vol. 22, p. 794.
96 *Dictionary of National Biography, Vol. XXVII*, London, 1891, pp. 296-297.
97 J. Stackhouse, 'Mr Macleay's Garden', *Historical Houses Trust of New South Wales*, Sydney, 1981, p. 3.
98 Carlin, *Elizabeth Bay House*, p. 88.
99 Ibid, pp. 88-89.
100 Bennett, *Wanderings in New South Wales*, p. 71.
101 Martin, *Life and Letters of the Right Honourable Robert Lowe Viscount Sherbrooke, Vol. I.* p. 163.
102 J. Winter, *Robert Lowe*, Toronto, 1976, p. 43.
103 G. Mundy, *Our Antipodes, Vol.III*, London, 1852, pp. 12-13.
104 Backhouse, *Narrative of a Visit to the Australian Colonies 1832-1838*, p. 447.
105 Fletcher, 'The Society's Heritage from the Macleays', p. 198.

106 Earnshaw, Hughes, Davidson, *Fanny to William*, 13 April 1835, p. 169.
107 Clark, 'Baron Charles von Hügel and the Macleays', p. 217.
108 Macleay to Hay, 16 September 1826, Miscellaneous Papers to the Colonial Office Relating to New South Wales, *Public Records Office* C.O. 201/179, p. 182.
109 Gascoigne, *Joseph Banks and the English Enlightenment*, p. 33.
110 Ibid.
111 *Sydney Herald*, 10 October 1835, p. 2.
112 Bennett, *Wanderings in New South Wales*, p. 335.
113 Macleay to Hay, 5 June 1832, Miscellaneous Papers to the Colonial Office Relating to New South Wales, *Public Records Office* C.O. 201/179, p. 252.
114 Gilbert, *The Royal Botanic Gardens, Sydney*, p. 29.
115 Ibid, pp. 61 & 71.
116 *NSW Government Gazette*, Vol 1, 15 June 1836, p. 451.
117 Gilbert, *The Royal Botanic Gardens, Sydney*, pp. 58-59.
118 Ibid, p. 60.
119 Ibid.
120 Gilbert, 'Plants, Privileges and Powers', p. 15.
121 Lochore, Diaries of Baron Karl von Hügel, *D. Clark Papers*, p. 31.
122 Gilbert, *The Royal Botanic Gardens, Sydney*, p. 63.
123 M. Aurousseau, *The Letters of F.W.L. Leichhardt, Vol. III*, Cambridge, 1968, p. 492.
124 Gilbert, *Mr McLeay's Elizabeth Bay Garden*, p. 27.
125 Aurousseau, *The Letters of F.W.L. Leichhardt*, p. 470.
126 Gilbert, *The Royal Botanic Gardens, Sydney*, p. 68.
127 Ibid, p. 70.
128 Ibid, p. 71.
129 Ibid, pp. 72-73.
130 Aitken & Looker, The Oxford Companion to Australian Gardening, pp. 87-88.
131 B. Fletcher, *The Grand Parade A History of the Royal Agricultural Society of New South Wales*, Sydney, 1988, p. 43.
132 F. Chittenden, *The Royal Horticultural Society Dictionary of Gardening — A Practical and Scientific Encyclopaedia of Horticulture*, Vol. III, London, 1965, p. 1227.
133 Stackhouse, 'Mr Macleay's Garden', p. 3.
134 Gilbert, *Mr McLeay's Elizabeth Bay Garden*, p. 1.
135 *Sydney Monitor*, 11 May 1831, p. 3.
136 T. Garnett, *Man of Roses Alister Clark of Glenara and His Family*, Sydney, 1990, p. 12.
137 T. Garnett, 'Alister Clark — Horticulturist and Celebrated Rose and Daffodil Breeder', *Australian Garden History*, Vol. 8, No. 3, 1996, p. 20.
138 Ibid, p. 21.

CHAPTER 8
1 Rev. C. Hoare to Macleay, 3 February 1825, Linnean Society, London.
2 Sutherland, *Wick 1794*, foreword by J. Bramman.
3 Gascoigne, *Joseph Banks*, pp. 191-192.
4 Fletcher, *The Grand Parade*, p. 16.
5 Gascoigne, *Joseph Banks*, p. 189.
6 Ibid, p. 196.

7 Ibid.
8 Sinclair to Macleay, 30 January 1825, Linnean Society, London.
9 J. Atkinson, *An Account of the State of Agriculture and Grazing in New South Wales*, London, 1826, facsimile edition, Sydney, 1975, p. 125.
10 T. Perry, *Australia's First Frontier The Spread of Settlement in New South Wales 1788–1829*, Melbourne, 1963, pp. 47-48 & 51.
11 Atkinson, *An Account of the State of Agriculture*, p. 125.
12 Fletcher, *Ralph Darling*, pp. 153-154.
13 Darling to Hay, 6 February 1827, *HRA*, Series 1, Vol. XVIII, p. 78.
14 Rose, 'The Administration of Governor Darling', p. 171.
15 Bennett, *Some Papers of Sir Francis Forbes*, p. 147.
16 Roberts, *The Squatting Age*, p. 42.
17 G. Abbott, *The Pastoral Age — A Re-examination*, Melbourne, 1971, pp. 52-54.
18 Earnshaw, Hughes, Davidson, *Fanny to William*, 10 May 1826, p. 55.
19 Ibid, 26 July 1826, p. 61.
20 Macleay to Darling, 16 April 1827, *HRA*, Series 1, Vol. XIV, p. 389.
21 Ibid, p. 17.
22 Darling to Macleay, 16 February 1826, Governor's Minutes, No. 38, *AONSW*.
23 Oxley to Darling, 18 April 1827, *HRA*, Series 1, Vol. XIV, p. 390.
24 Earnshaw, Hughes, Davidson, *Fanny to William*, 15 February 1828, p. 91.
25 Macleay to Darling, 16 April 1827, *HRA*, Series 1, Vol. XIV, p. 389.
26 Ibid.
27 Earnshaw, Hughes, Davidson, *Fanny to William*, 8 November 1828, p. 103.
28 Ibid, May, 1827, p. 82.
29 Ibid, 28 May 1828, p. 96.
30 *Sydney Gazette*, 9 May 1829, p. 2.
31 Atkinson, *Camden Farm and Village Life*, p. 20.
32 Earnshaw, Hughes, Davidson, *Fanny to William*, 1 January 1829, p. 104.
33 Ibid, 25 February 1829, p. 106.
34 Ibid, 29 August 1828, p. 100.
35 Ibid, 21 November 1829, p. 114.
36 Ibid, 6 June 1829, p. 109.
37 J. Ker, 'The Macarthur Family and the Pastoral Industry', *JRAHS*, Vol. 47, Pt. 3, 1961, p. 142.
38 Earnshaw, Hughes, Davidson, *Fanny to William*, 29 August 1828, p. 100.
39 Ibid, 2 May 1830, p. 119.
40 Ibid, 31 July 1830, p. 123.
41 Ibid, 30 July 1834, p. 166.
42 Herman, *Annabella Boswell's Journal*, p. 164.
43 Fletcher, *Ralph Darling*, p. 189.
44 Ibid, p. 188.
45 Atkinson, *An Account of the State of Agriculture*, pp. 137 & 141.
46 Therry, *Reminiscences of Thirty Years' Residence*, pp. 284 & 295.

47 Earnshaw, Hughes, Davidson, *Fanny to William*, May 1827, p. 81.
48 *Sydney Herald*, 29 October 1838, p. 2.
49 Herman, *Annabella Boswell's Journal*, p. 117.
50 Fletcher, *Ralph Darling*, p. 263.
51 *Sydney Herald*, 25 September 1840, p. 4.
52 Earnshaw, Hughes, Davidson, *Fanny to William*, 27 October 1835, p. 172.
53 Atkinson, *Camden Farm and Village Life*, p. 90.
54 Earnshaw, Hughes, Davidson, *Fanny to William*, 12 November 1827, p. 87.
55 Ibid, 1 January 1829, p. 104.
56 Ibid, 12 November 1827, p. 87.
57 Ibid, 21 November 1829, p. 115.
58 Ibid, 22 February 1830, p. 116.
59 Ibid, 22 May 1830, p. 121.
60 Therry, *Reminiscences of Thirty Years' Residence*, pp. 260-261.
61 Ibid, pp. 261-262.
62 Earnshaw, Hughes, Davidson, *Fanny to William*, 24 October 1834, p. 168.
63 G. Greenwood, *Australia: A Social and Political History*, Sydney, 1955, p.89.
64 Currey, *Sir Francis Forbes*, p. 173.
65 *Australian*, 8 April 1829, p. 2.
66 Earnshaw, Hughes, Davidson, *Fanny to William*, 9 February 1827, p. 75.
67 *Sydney Gazette*, 25 July 1829, p. 2.
68 Governor's Minutes, No. 135, 13 September 1830, 4/994, *AONSW*.
69 Earnshaw, Hughes, Davidson, *Fanny to William*, 6 July 1832, p. 146.
70 *Australian*, 17 August 1838, p. 2.
71 J. Campbell, 'Discovery and Early Pastoral Settlement of New England', *RAHS*, Vol. 111, Part V, p. 239.
72 Ibid, p. 240.
73 Herman, *Annabella Boswell's Journal*, pp. 116-117.
74 Ibid, pp. 231, 235 & 239.
75 A. Philp, *The Ladies of Saumarez*, Sydney, 1988, p. 14.
76 P. Cox, H. Tanner, M. Walker, *The Hunter Valley*, Melbourne, 1978, p. 57.
77 R. Walker, *Old New England*, Sydney, 1966, p. 12.
78 Windschuttle, *Taste and Science*, p. 19.
79 Campbell, 'Discovery and Early Pastoral Settlement', p. 259.
80 Earnshaw, Hughes, Davidson, *Fanny to William*, 21 July 1831, p. 136.
81 R. Champion, 'Major A.C. Innes, 3rd Regiment of Foot', *JRAHS*, Vol. XXI, 1936, pp. 103-16.
82 J. Moyes, G. Mant, *A Town Called Port A Port Macquarie-Hastings Valley Walkabout*, Port Macquarie, 1986, p. 65.
83 Official Grant Indexes record that approval for Alexander's grant of 54 acres at Elizabeth Bay was given on 19 October 1831 but a later survey revealed that the acreage was 56 in total.
84 W.S. Macleay, Papers concerning estates and liabilities of Alexander Macleay 1837–1845, including notes of land grants and purchases, January 1837 and August 1839, stock returns, 1843-44 and papers re settlement of debts and management of estates

1844–45, *Macarthur Papers*, A4310, pp. 21-22.
85 *Macarthur Papers*, A1239, p. 229.
86 T. Garnett, *Man of Roses Alister Clark of Glenara and His Family*, Sydney 1990, p. 12.
87 *Sydney Herald*, 15 August 1836, p. 3.
88 *Sydney Monitor*, 26 December 1836, p. 3.
89 *Sydney Gazette*, 25 February 1826, p. 2.
90 Fletcher, *The Grand Parade*, p. 13.
91 H. Somer, 'First Agricultural Society of New South Wales An Historical Sketch', *RAS Annual*, Sydney 1906, p. 6.
92 Ibid, p. 14.
93 Fletcher, *The Grand Parade*, p. 18.
94 *Australian*, 13 September 1826, p. 1.
95 Fletcher, *The Grand Parade*, p. 32.
96 *Sydney Gazette*, 25 September 1838, p. 2.
97 Ibid.
98 Fletcher, *The Grand Parade*, p. 34.
99 *Sydney Gazette*, 25 September 1838, p. 2.
100 Somer, 'First Agricultural Society of New South Wales', p. 10.
101 Fletcher, *The Grand Parade*, p. 29.
102 *Australian*, 13 September 1826, p. 1.
103 Atkinson, *An Account of the State of Agriculture*, p. 15.
104 Ibid, 26 September 1828, p. 3.
105 Fletcher, *The Grand Parade*, p. 31.
106 Somer, 'First Agricultural Society of New South Wales', p. 17.
107 *Sydney Monitor*, 9 January, 1830, p. 2.
108 *Australian*, 23 September 1831, p. 2.
109 Ibid, 8 July 1831, p. 2.
110 J. Jervis, 'Journals of William Edward Riley', *JRAHS*, Vol. 32, Pt. 4, p. 252.
111 *Australian*, 23 June 1829, p. 3.
112 *Sydney Monitor*, 4 July 1829, p. 3.
113 Atkinson, *Camden Farm and Village Life*, p. 91.
114 *Sydney Monitor*, 18 July 1829, p. 3.
115 Ibid, 22 May 1830, p. 2.
116 Atkinson, *Camden Farm and Village Life*, p. 91.
117 *Sydney Monitor*, 20 December 1828, p. 3.
118 Ibid, 1 December 1828, p. 1.
119 Ibid, 21 May 1831, p. 2.
120 *Sydney Monitor*, 12 May 1832, p. 2 & *Australian*, 18 May 1832, p. 2.
121 *Australian*, 15 June 1832, p. 3.
122 *Sydney Monitor*, 24 March 1834, p. 3.

CHAPTER 9
1 *Sydney Herald*, 10 April 1837, p. 2.
2 Walker, *The Newspaper Press*, pp. 20-21.
3 *Sydney Herald*, 20 November 1837, p. 2.
4 Ibid.
5 Ibid, 1 March 1838, p. 2.
6 Ibid, 24 August 1838, p. 2.
7 Ibid, 18 February 1841, p. 3.
8 Ibid, 8 February 1838, p. 2.
9 Ibid, 20 July 1837, p. 2.
10 Shaw, *Patriarch and Patriot*, pp. 104-105.
11 *Sydney Herald*, 25 July 1838, p. 2.
12 Ibid, 26 June 1840, p. 2.
13 Ibid, 1 October 1838, p. 2.

14 Ibid, 11 March 1841, p. 2.
15 *Sydney Morning Herald*, 25 October 1842, p. 2.
16 *Sydney Herald*, 29 July 1841, p. 2.
17 *Sydney Morning Herald*, 28 July 1842, p. 2.
18 Ibid, 1 August 1843, p. 3.
19 *Sydney Herald*, 11 March 1839, p. 2.
20 M. Thompson, *The First Election The New South Wales Legislative Council Election of 1843*, Goulburn, 1996, p. 12.
21 Ibid, p. 13.
22 *Australian*, 31 October 1842, p. 2.
23 Ibid, 7 November 1842, p. 2.
24 Thompson, *The First Election*, p. 15.
25 Ibid, p. 15.
26 Ibid, pp. 88-89.
27 Roberts, *The Squatting Age*, p. 219.
28 *Sydney Morning Herald*, 11 February 1843, p. 1.
29 Ibid, 7 February 1843, p. 3.
30 Thompson, *The First Election*, p. 68.
31 *Sydney Morning Herald*, 16 February 1843, p. 1.
32 Macleay to Smith, 31 December 1802, Linnean Society.
33 *Sydney Morning Herald*, 16 February 1843, p. 2.
34 Ibid, 27 May 1843, p. 2.
35 Ibid, 20 February 1843, p. 1.
36 *Maitland Mercury*, 15 June 1843, p. 2.
37 Ibid, 17 June 1843, p. 2.
38 Ibid.
39 *Sydney Morning Herald*, 27 May 1843, p. 2.
40 Walker, *The Newspaper Press*, p. 36.
41 *Sydney Morning Herald*, 15 February 1843, p. 2.
42 *Maitland Mercury*, 17 June 1843, p. 2.
43 Ibid.
44 *Sydney Morning Herald*, 20 June 1843, p. 2.
45 *Maitland Mercury*, 17 June 1843, p. 2.
46 Walker, *The Newspaper Press*, p. 44.
47 M. Herman, *Annabella Boswell's Journal*, Sydney, 1965, pp. 60-61.
48 Ibid, p. 62.
49 Ibid, p. 63.
50 Ibid, pp. 64 & 67.
51 Ibid, p. 63.
52 Fletcher, *Colonial Australia Before 1850*, p. 122.
53 *Sydney Morning Herald*, 27 June 1843, p. 2.
54 *Maitland Mercury*, 15 July 1843, p. 4.
55 *Sydney Morning Herald*, 27 June 1843, p. 2.
56 Herman, *Annabella Boswell's Journal*, p. 65.
57 *Voice of the North*, 10 July 1931.
58 Thompson, *The First Election*, p. 115.
59 Walker, *The Newspaper Press*, p. 37.
60 *Weekly Register*, 29 July 1843, p. 2.
61 *Maitland Mercury*, 5 August 1843, p. 2.
62 *Sydney Morning Herald*, 4 July 1843, p. 2.
63 Ibid.
64 Ibid, 10 July 1843, p. 2.
65 *Maitland Mercury*, 5 August 1843, p. 2.
66 *Sydney Morning Herald*, 2 August 1843, p. 2.
67 *Maitland Mercury*, 5 August 1843, p. 2.
68 Roberts, *The Squatting Age*, p. 221.
69 *Sydney Morning Herald*, 1 August 1843, p. 2.
70 *Maitland Mercury*, 5 August 1843, p. 2.

71 Ibid.
72 Ibid.
73 *Sydney Monitor*, 7 August 1830, p. 4.
74 *Sydney Morning Herald*, 2 August 1843, p. 3.
75 *Weekly Register*, 5 August 1843, p. 2.
76 Thompson, *The First Election*, p. 24.
77 *Maitland Mercury*, 5 August 1843, p. 2.
78 *Sydney Morning Herald*, 2 August 1843, p. 2.
79 Ibid, 5 August 1843, p. 2.
80 Ibid, 1 August 1843, p. 2.
81 *Maitland Mercury*, 5 August 1843, p. 2.
82 *Sydney Morning Herald*, 2 August 1843, p. 3.
83 Ibid.
84 Thompson, *The First Election*, p. 132.
85 *Maitland Mercury*, 5 August 1843, p. 2.
86 *Weekly Register*, 5 August 1843, p. 1.
87 Thompson, *The First Election*, p. 133.
88 *Weekly Register*, 5 August 1843, p. 1.
89 Ibid, 12 August 1843, p. 4.
90 Ibid, 19 August 1843, p. 4.
91 *Sydney Morning Herald*, 13 December 1844, p. 2.
92 Ibid, 6 December 1845, p. 2.
93 Stanley to Gipps, 29 March 1844, *HRA*, Series 1, Vol. XXIII, pp. 505-506.
94 *Sydney Morning Herald*, 14 November 1845, p. 2.
95 B. Dyster, 'Support for the Squatters, 1844', *JRAHS*, Vol. 51, Pt. 1, 1965, p. 41.
96 W. McMinn, *A Constitutional History of Australia*, Melbourne, 1979, p. 38.
97 Ibid.
98 Melbourne, *Early Constitutional Development*, p. 325.
99 Ibid, p. 326.
100 Ibid.
101 Ibid, p. 327.
102 McMartin, *Public Servants and Patronage*, p. 230.
103 *Sydney Morning Herald*, 6 May 1843, p. 2.
104 Thompson, *The First Election*, p. 91.
105 *Sydney Morning Herald*, 9 September 1843, p. 2.
106 NSW Governor's Despatches, 4 December 1844, 11 December 1844, p.1918, *Public Records Office 359-360*. Microfilm no. CY POS 696, 1844-1846. Mitchell Library.
107 *The Colonist*, 16 November 1844, p. 1.
108 *Maitland Mercury*, 7 December 1844, p. 2.
109 *The Colonist*, 30 November 1844, p. 2.
110 *The Australian*, 26 June 1841, p. 2.
111 Gilbert, *Mr Macleay's Elizabeth Bay Garden*, p. 30.
112 *Sydney Herald*, 23 July 1841, p. 1.
113 Ibid.
114 D. Macmillan to A. Swainston, 28 April 1965, *Swainston Papers*.
115 Thompson, *The First Election*, p. 7.
116 W. S. Macleay, Papers concerning estates & liabilities of Alexander Macleay 1837-1845, *Macarthur Papers*.
117 Ibid.
118 Ibid.
119 Ibid.
120 Ibid, p. 169.
121 *Sydney Morning Herald*, 23 April 1845, p. 4.
122 A. Macleay to T. Barker, 22 September 1846, *Barker Papers*, National Library.

123 Martin, *Life and Letters of the Right Honourable Robert Lowe, Vol. I*, p. 162.
124 Walker, *The Newspaper Press*, p. 37.
125 Pike, *Australian Dictionary of Biography, Vol. I*, pp. 134-136.
126 Thompson, *The First Election*, p. 82.
127 Alexander Berry to Thomas Barker, 7 January 1845, *Barker Papers*, National Library.
128 *Sydney Morning Herald*, 14 August 1845, p. 4.
129 *Barker Papers*, National Library.
130 W. S. Macleay, Papers concerning estates & liabilities of Alexander Macleay 1837-1845, *Macarthur Papers*.
131 Ibid.
132 A. Macleay to T. Barker, 29 September 1845, *Barker Papers*, National Library.
133 W. S. Macleay, Papers concerning estates & liabilities of Alexander Macleay 1837–1845, *Macarthur Papers*.
134 Abbott & Little, *The Respectable Sydney Merchant*, p. 163.
135 *The Diaries of 'Pioneer' George Hobler, Vol. I*, (transcript), 1992, Sydney, p. 281.
136 *Sydney Morning Herald*, 5 June 1844, p. 1.
137 *The Diaries of 'Pioneer' George Hobler*, p. XXVII.
138 Book 5, General Register of Deeds, No. 473. Register of Mortgages, Registrar General's Department, Sydney.
139 Earnshaw, Hughes, Davidson, *Fanny to William*, 31 July 1830, p. 123.
140 *Sydney Morning Herald*, 27 April 1846, p. 1.
141 Roberts, *The Squatting Age*, pp. 268-269.
142 Fletcher, *Colonial Australia Before 1850*, pp. 116-117.
143 *Maitland Mercury*, 16 May 1846, p. 3.
144 Thompson, *The First Election*, p. 132.
145 *The Colonial Gazette*, 19 September 1846, p. 7.
146 *Sydney Morning Herald*, 15 May 1846, p. 2.
147 *Colonial Gazette*, 3 October 1846, p. 7.
148 *Sydney Morning Herald*, 15 May 1846, p. 2.
149 Ibid.
150 Ibid.
151 Ibid, 20 May 1846, p. 2.
152 *Maitland Mercury*, 6 May 1846, p. 2.
153 Ibid.
154 *Colonial Gazette*, 3 October 1846, p. 7.
155 Fletcher, 'The Society's Heritage from the Macleays', p. 582.
156 *Barker Papers*, 1828-1873, MSS380, Mitchell Library.
157 Ibid.
158 *Sydney Morning Herald*, 1 November 1847, p. 2.
159 Ibid.
160 Ibid, 1 November 1847, p. 2.
161 Ibid, 14 January 1848, p. 2.
162 Ibid, 27 January 1848, p. 3.
163 Ibid, 21 March 1848, p. 1.
164 Ibid 9 February 1848, p. 2.
165 *The Atlas*, 23 October 1847, p. 10.
166 W. Dumaresq to E. Dumaresq, 22 July 1848. *Dumaresq Family*, 953/1/321.
167 Mabberley, *Jupiter botanicus*, p. 378.
168 *Maitland Mercury*, 29 July 1848, p. 3.
169 *Sydney Morning Herald*, 29 July 1848, p. 3.
170 St James's Church leaflet, *A Guide to the Church*, Sydney.
171 Ibid.
172 Alexander Macleay's Will, Macleay Museum.
173 *Barker Papers*, MSS380, Mitchell Library.
174 G. Macleay to R. Brown, 7 August 1848 & 4 February 1849, *Swainston Papers*.
175 A Statement in Substance of Mr McLeay's Will, undated, *Barker Papers*, National Library.
176 Ibid.
177 Ibid.
178 Thompson, *The First Election*, p. 129.

EPILOGUE
1   G. Melluish, 'Justifying Commerce: The Scottish Enlightenment Tradition in Colonial New South Wales', *JRAHS*, Vol. 75, Pt. 2, 1989, p. 122.
2   D. Moore, 'The Hawthorns School', *Bletchingley Conservation & Historical Society*, June 1995.
3   Martin, *Life and Letters of the Right Honourable Robert Lowe*, Vol. 2, p. 407.
4   Ibid, Vol. 1, p. 162.
5   Rose, 'The Administration of Governor Darling', p. 176.

Bibliography

OFFICIAL DOCUMENTS

ARCHIVES OF NEW SOUTH WALES, SYDNEY
Administrative and Domestic Papers of Colonial
Secretary
Colonial Secretary's Archives 1826–1836:
Colonial Secretary, Letters Received 1826–1836
Governor's Minutes and Memoranda 1826–1859
Colonial Secretary's Special Bundles 1826–1859

DEPARTMENT OF INFORMATION AND TECHNOLOGY, SYDNEY
Grant Index 1839–1847, Land Titles Office

MITCHELL LIBRARY, SYDNEY
New South Wales – Governors' Despatches to the
Secretary of State for Colonies A1267-8 CY Reel
696

Returns of the Colony (Blue books) 1826–1829
Microform 442-449

NORTH HIGHLAND ARCHIVES, WICK
Caithness Index to Names and Persons to Abridgments of
the Registers of Seisins 1781–1928
Calendar of Confirmations and Inventories 1928, A-L
Census of 1841
Extracts from Abridgments and Registers of Sasines
(Caithness) 1646–1968
Mormon International Genealogical Index from Old
Parochial Registers pre 1855 for Caithness

Wick Town Council Minute Books 1788–1818

PUBLIC RECORD OFFICE, KEW (now The National Archives)
Admiralty Medical Department Minutes 1810–1816
ADM 99/280
Admiralty Minutes 1796–1816 ADM 99-276-279
Colonial Office Papers in the Public Record Office C.O.
201/213-282, C.O. 202/21-38, C.O. 204/1-6
Miscellaneous correspondence concerning the escape,
exchange and relief of prisoners-of-war 1807–1818
ADM 97/130
Sick and Hurt Board Minutes ADM 99/266-275

REGISTER OF MORTGAGES, REGISTRAR GENERAL'S DEPARTMENT, SYDNEY
General Register of Deeds

MANUSCRIPTS

AUSTRALIAN MUSEUM ARCHIVES, SYDNEY
Bennett, G., Papers 1833–1840
Minutes of the Sub-Committee of the Australian
Museum, 1836

BOTANIC GARDEN LIBRARY, SYDNEY
Catalogue of plants cultivated in the Botanic Gardens,
Part 1 and 11, January 1828
List of fruits cultivated in the Botanic Gardens up to
November 1827

BRITISH LIBRARY, LONDON

Correspondence of Robert Brown 1760–1858, Vol. II, 1836–1858
Lord Liverpool Papers
Peel, R., Papers

LINNEAN SOCIETY, LONDON

Council Minute Book 1802–1826
Macleay Correspondence
Miscellaneous Papers

MACLEAY MUSEUM, SYDNEY

Kirby, W., Letters to A. Macleay, (transcript by D. Horning)
Smith, J., Letters to A. Macleay, (transcript by D. Horning)
Swainston, A., Papers
International Code of Zoological Nomenclature, International Trust for Zoological Nomenclature in Association with British Museum (Natural History), London, 1985

MITCHELL LIBRARY, SYDNEY

Arthur, Sir, G., Papers, Vol. 4
Barker, T., Papers
Bourke, R., Papers, Vols. VI and XI
Dowling, Sir J., Journal 1827–1828 and other papers 1800–1903
Ducker, S., Diaries of Baron Karl von Hügel, Sydney New Zealand and Norfolk Island from 17 February to 16 April 1834, translation, *D. Clark Papers,* uncatalogued
Harington, F., Papers of W.S. Macleay, *Macarthur Papers,* Part V
Linnean Society of Australia, Papers
Lochore, R., Diaries of Baron Karl von Hügel, Sydney New Zealand and Norfolk Island from 17 February to 16 April 1834, translation, *D. Clark Papers,* uncatalogued
Macarthur Papers, A4310, A2899, A2911, A4300, A2931
Macleay, A., *Correspondence between Major-General Sir Richard Bourke and Alexander Macleay,* Sydney, 1836
Macleay, A., *Correspondence between Major-General Sir Richard Bourke and Alexander Macleay and other Documents relative to the removal of Alexander Macleay Esq., from the office of Colonial Secretary of New South Wales,* Sydney, 1838
Marsden, S., Papers
Riley, W., Journals 1829, 1830 and Papers 1829–1831
Spark, A., Diary of A.B. Spark 1 January 1836–22 September 1856

NATIONAL LIBRARY, CANBERRA

Barker, T., Papers

NEWCASTLE REGION PUBLIC LIBRARY

Archibald Clunes Innes: Photographs and paper cuttings (compiled by Newcastle Region Public Library)
Voice of the North (Periodical) 1931

STATE LIBRARY OF TASMANIA

Dumaresq Family NG 953 [Records] (Manuscripts)

NEWSPAPERS

All titles published in Sydney, New South Wales, unless otherwise stated:
Howe's Weekly Commercial Express
Maitland Mercury and Hunter River General Advertiser
*Monitor (*later *Sydney Monitor)*
Morning Chronicle
New South Wales Government Gazette
Sydney Gazette
*Sydney Herald (*later *Sydney Morning Herald)*
The Atlas
The Australian
The Colonial Gazette
The Colonial Observer
The Colonist
The Currency Lad
The Southern Queen
The Sydney Times
The Weekly Observor
The Weekly Register

OTHER PRIMARY SOURCES

MACLEAY MUSEUM

Will of Alexander Macleay, 27 April 1846

MITCHELL LIBRARY

Historical Records of Australia, New South Wales 1788–1848, Series 1, Volumes 9–36, Sydney, 1917–1922
Minutes of Proceedings of the Legislative Council 1824–1831 and Votes and Proceedings of the Legislative Council of New South Wales 1832–1837, Sydney, 1847
Sainty, M., and Johnson, K. (editors), Census of New South Wales, November, 1828, Sydney, 1980
Wilton, Rev. C. (ed.), *The Australian Quarterly Journal of Theology, Literature and Science,* Vol. 1, Sydney, 1828

NATIONAL LIBRARY, CANBERRA

Hazel de Berg Tapes, Canberra, 1967 (transcript)
Franklin, J., Journals of a Journey from Port Phillip to Sydney, 1839

NATIONAL LIBRARY OF SCOTLAND, EDINBURGH

Sutherland, W., *Wick 1794,* A reprint from the First Statistical Account of Scotland (drawn up from the Communications of the Ministers of the different parishes, by Sir John Sinclair, 1794), Thurso, undated
Wight, A., *Present State of Husbandry in Scotland: extracted from reports made to the Commissioners of the Annexed Estates and Published By Their authority,* Vol. 1V, Pt. a, Edinburgh, 1784

NORTH HIGHLAND ARCHIVES, WICK

Piggott & Company Trade Directories 1825,1826,1837

Slater's Directory 1852–1882

PRIVATE PAPERS
Will of James Henderson, 24 February 1894, Bilbster House, Wick

ST JAMES'S CHURCH, SYDNEY
Memorials for Alexander Macleay, Fanny Macleay and William Sharp Macleay

BOOKS

Abbott, G., *The Pastoral Age — A Re-examination*, Melbourne, 1971

Abbott, G. and Little, G. (editors.), *The Respectable Sydney Merchant — A.B. Spark of Tempe*, Sydney, 1976

Aitken, R. and Looker, M. (editors), *The Oxford Companion to Australian Gardens*, Melbourne, 2002

Alston, D., *Ross and Cromarty A Historical Guide*, Edinburgh, 1999

Angel, J., *The Australian Club The First 150 Years 1838–1988*, Sydney, 1988

Atkinson, A., *Camden Farm and Village Life in Early New South Wales*, Melbourne, 1988

Atkinson, J., *An Account of the State of Agriculture and Grazing in New South Wales*, London, 1826, facsimile edition, Sydney, 1975

Aurousseau, M., *The Letters of F.W.L. Leichhardt*, Cambridge, 1968

Austin, A., *Australian Education 1788–1900: church, state and public education in colonial Australia*, Melbourne, 1972

Australia The Beautiful Great Gardens, Sydney, 1983

Backhouse, J., *Narrative of a Visit to the Australian Colonies 1832–1838*, London, 1843

Baker, D., *The Civilised Surveyor Thomas Mitchell and the Australian aborigines*, Melbourne, 1997

Baker, H. (ed.), *Elizabeth Bay House*, Sydney, 1967

Barnard, M., *Macquarie's World*, Melbourne, 1961

Beaton, E., *Caithness An Illustrated Architectural Guide*, Edinburgh, 1996

Bennett, G., *Wanderings in New South Wales, Batavia, Pedir Coast, Singapore and China — Being the Journal of a Naturalist in those countries during 1832, 1833 and 1834*, Vol. 1, London, 1834

Bennett, J.M. (ed.), *Some Papers of Sir Francis Forbes First Chief Justice in Australia*, Sydney, 1998

Black, G., *The Surnames of Scotland — their origin, meaning and history*, New York, 1962

Blackman, J. A (ed.), *A Catalogue of an Extensive and Valuable Library of nearly 4,000 volumes — Comprising the Major Part of the Well Selected Library of Alexander McLeay, Esq.*, Sydney, 1845

Boswell, A., *Further Recollections of my early days in Australia*, Canberra, 1992

Braim, T., *A History of New South Wales from its settlement to the close of the year 1844*, Vols. 1 and 2, London, 1846

Broadbent, J., *The Australian Colonial House: Architecture and Society in Colonial New South Wales 1788–1842*, Sydney, 1997

Brunet, B., *Australian Insects A Natural History*, Sydney, 2000

Burroughs, P., *Britain and Australia 1831–1855: A Study in Imperial Relations and Crown Lands Administration*, Oxford, 1967

Butlin, N., *Forming a Colonial Economy Australia 1810–1850*, Melbourne, 1994

Butlin, S.J., *Foundations of the Australian Monetary System 1788–1851*, Melbourne, 1953

Carlin, S., *Elizabeth Bay House A History and a Guide*, Sydney, 2000

Chanin, E., *Book Life The Life and Times of David Scott Mitchell*, Melbourne, 2011

Chapman, P. (ed.), *The Diaries and Letters of G.T.W. Boyes*, [Vol. 1, 1820–1832] Melbourne, 1985

Checkland, S.G., *Scottish Banking: A History 1695–1973*, Glasgow, 1975

Clark, C.M.H., *A History of Australia New South Wales and Van Diemens Land 1822–1838*, Vol. 2, Melbourne, 1968

Clark, C.M.H., *A History of Australia The Beginnings of an Australian Civilization 1824–1851*, Vol. 3, Melbourne, 1973

Clark, D. (ed.), *New Holland Journal, The Journal of Baron Charles von Hügel, November 1833–October 1834*, Melbourne, 1994

Clarke, P. and Spender, D. (editors), *Life Lines Australian Women's Letters and Diaries 1788 to 1840*, Sydney, 1992

Chittenden, F., *The Royal Horticultural Society Dictionary of Gardening — A Practical and Scientific Encyclopaedia of Horticulture*, Vol. III, London, 1965

Cochrane, P., *Colonial Ambition Foundations of Australian Democracy*, Melbourne, 2006

Cohen, L., *Elizabeth Macquarie Her Life and Times*, Sydney, 1979

Collins Guide to Scots Kith and Kin A Guide to the Clans and Surnames of Scotland, Glasgow, 1989

Coventry, M., *The Castles of Scotland*, Aberdeen, 2001

Cox, P., Tanner, H., Walker, M., *The Hunter Valley*, Melbourne, 1978

Crawford, R., (ed.), *Young and Free — Letters of Robert and Thomas Crawford 1821–1830*, Canberra, 1995

Crittenden, V., *A History and Bibliography of Australian Gardening Books 1806–1950*, Canberra, 1986

Crittenden, V., *A Shrub in the Landscape of Fame*, Canberra, 1992

Cumpston, J., *Charles Sturt: His Life and Journeys of Exploration*, Melbourne, 1951

Cumpston, J., *Thomas Mitchell Surveyor General and Explorer*, Melbourne, 1954

Cunningham, P., *Two Years Residence in New South Wales*, Vols. 1 and 2, London, 1827

Currey, C.H., *Sir Francis Forbes: The First Chief Justice of the Supreme Court of New South Wales*, Sydney, 1968

Dawson, W. (ed.), *The Banks Letters – a calendar of the manuscript correspondence of Sir Joseph Banks preserved in the British Museum (Natural History) and other collections in Great Britain*, London. 1958

Bibliography

Dictionary of National Biography, Vol. XXVII, London, 1891

Dowd, B. (ed.), *Squatting on Crown Lands in NSW*, (by J.F.Campbell), Sydney, 1968

Dyster, B., *Servant and Master: Building and Running the Grand Houses of Sydney 1788–1850*, Sydney, 1989

Earnshaw, B., Hughes, J., Davidson, L, *Fanny to William: The Letters of Frances Leonora Macleay 1812–1836*, Sydney, 1993

Ellis, E., *Conrad Martens: Selected Sketches 1835–1872*, Sydney, 1994

Ellis, M., *John Macarthur*, Sydney, 1955

Ellis, M., *Lachlan Macquarie: His Life, Adventures and Times*, Sydney, 1947

Falkus, M. and Gillingham, J. (editors), *Historical Atlas of Britain*, London, 1981

Ferry, J., *The Royal Hotel, Port Macquarie*, Armidale, 2000.

Field, B. (ed.), *Geographical Memoirs on New South Wales by various hands*, London, 1825

Fletcher, B., *Colonial Australia before 1850*, Melbourne, 1976

Fletcher, B., *Ralph Darling A Governor Maligned*, Melbourne, 1984

Fletcher, B., *The Grand Parade A History of the Royal Agricultural Society of New South Wales*, Sydney, 1989

Fletcher, H., *The Story of the Royal Horticultural Society 1804–1968*, London, 1969

Fletcher, J. (ed.), *The Macleay Memorial Volume*, Sydney, 1893

Foden, F., *Wick of the North The Story of a Scottish Royal Burgh*, Wick, 1996

Forbes, G. (ed.), *Sydney Society in Crown Colony Days (Being the Personal Reminiscences of the late Lady Forbes)*, (typescript) 1914

Foster, S.G., *Colonial Improver Edward Deas Thomson 1800–1879*, Melbourne, 1978

Freeman, J., *Life of William Kirby*, London, 1852

Garnett, T., *Man of Roses Alister Clark of Glenara and His Family*, Sydney, 1990

Gascoigne, J., *Cambridge in the Age of the Enlightenment, Science, religions and politics from the Restoration to the French Revolution*, Cambridge, 2002

Gascoigne, J., *Sir Joseph Banks and the English Enlightenment*, Cambridge, 1994

Gilbert, L., *Mr. Macleay's Elizabeth Bay Garden*, Canberra, 2000

Gilbert, L., *The Royal Botanic Gardens, Sydney A History 1816–1985*, Melbourne, 1986

Goddard, R., *The Life and Times of James Milson*, Melbourne, 1955

Godstone Rober Scouts, (H. Fairall, ed.), *Glorious Godstone*, London, 1934

Graves, A. *The Royal Academy of Arts: A complete dictionary of contributors and their work from its foundation in 1769 to 1904*, London. 1906

Greenwood, G. (ed.), *Australia: A Social and Political History*, Sydney, 1955

Gregson, J., *The Australian Agricultural Company 1824–1875*, Sydney, 1907

Harvey, J. H., *Early Nurserymen*, Chichester, 1974

Hawker, G., *The Parliament of New South Wales 1856–1965*, Sydney, 1971

Hazlewood, W.G., *Australia's First Nurseryman Thomas Shepherd*, Sydney, 1953

Heaton, Sir J., *Australian dictionary of dates and men of the time, containing the history of Aust-ralasia from 1542 to May 1879*, Sydney, 1879

Herman, M., *Annabella Boswell's Journal*, Sydney, 1965

Hirst, J., *Convict Society and its enemies: A history of early New South Wales*, Sydney, 1983

Horticultural Magazine and Gardeners' Calendar of New South Wales, Vol. 3, No. 15, Sydney, 1865

Huxley, L, *Life and Letters of Sir Joseph Dalton Hooker, based on material collected and arranged by Lady Hooker*, Vols. 1 and 2, London, 1918

Inglis, K., *Australian Colonists*, Melbourne, 1993

Jacques, J., *Bygone Godstone*, Chichester, 1992

Johns, F., *An Australian Biographical Dictionary*, Melbourne, 1934

Johnston, A. and Hope, J., *Gloag and Henderson's Introduction to the Law of Scotland*, Edinburgh, 1968

Kaye, B. (ed.), *Anglicanism in Australia A History*, Melbourne, 2002

Kelly, M., *Sydney City of Suburbs*, Sydney, 1987

King, H., *Richard Bourke Great Australians*, Melbourne, 1963

King, H., *Richard Bourke*, Melbourne, 1971

Lang, J.D., *An Historical and Statistical Account of New South Wales*, Vols. 1 and 2, London, 1834

Le Rougetel, H., *A Heritage of Roses*, Maryland, 1988

Lee, S. (ed.), *Dictionary of National Biography*, Vol. XXXV, 1893

Loudon, J., *Encyclopaedia of Plants*, London, 1836

Lyte, C., *Sir Joseph Banks 18th Century Explorer, Botanist and Entrepreneur*, Sydney, 1980

Mabberley, D., *Jupiter botanicus: Robert Brown of the British Museum*, London, 1985

Macarthur, James, *New South Wales, Its Present State and Future Prospects*, London, 1837

Macarthur-Onslow, R.S. (ed.), *Some Early Records of the Macarthurs at Camden*, Adelaide, 1914

MacDonnell, F., *Before Kings Cross*, Melbourne, 1967

Macleay Museum News, No. 2, Sydney, 1993

Maclehose, J., *The Picture of Sydney and stranger's guide in New South Wales for 1838: embellished with forty three engravings of the public buildings and picturesque land and water views in and near Sydney*, Sydney, 1838

Macmillan, D., *A Squatter Went to Sea, The story of Sir William Macleay's New Guinea Expedition (1875) and his life in Sydney*, Sydney, 1957

Macmillan, D., *Scotland and Australia 1788–1850*, Oxford, 1967

Macmillan, D., *The Debtor's War — Scottish Capitalists and the economic crisis in Australia 1841–1846*, Melbourne, 1960

Madgwick, R.B., *Immigration into Eastern Australia 1788–1851*, Sydney, 1969

Mander-Jones, P. (ed.), *Manuscripts in the British Isles Relating to Australia, New Zealand, and the Pacific*, Canberra, 1972

Mansfield, R., *Analytical View of the Census of New South Wales for 1841*, Sydney, 1841

Martin, A., *Life and Letters of the Right Honourable Robert Lowe, Viscount Sherbrooke*, Vols. 1 and 2, London, 1893

McCulloch, S., *George Gipps Great Australians*, Melbourne, 1966

McKay, Mitch, and others, *If I Could Just See Your Face: Port Macquarie's Second Burying Ground*, Port Macquarie, 2007

McMartin, A., *Public Servants and Patronage, The Foundation and Rise of the New South Wales Public Service, 1786–1859*, Sydney, 1983

McMinn, W., *A Constitutional History of Australia*, Melbourne, 1979

McNaught, J. (ed.), *Index and Registers of Land Grants — Leases and Purchases 1792–1865*, Sydney, 1998

Melbourne, A.C.V., *Early Constitutional Development in Australia*, Oxford, 1934

Moyes, J., Mant, G., *A Town Called Port A Port Macquarie — Hastings Valley Walkabout*, Port Macquarie, 1986

Mudie, J., *The Felonry of New South Wales*, London, 1837

Mundy, G., *Our Antipodes*, Vol. III, London, 1852

Murray, D., *The West Indies and the Development of Colonial Self-Government 1801–1834*, Oxford, 1965

Norst, M., *Ferdinand Bauer The Australian Natural History Drawings*, London, 1989

O'Farrell, P., *The Irish in Australia*, Sydney, 1993

Perry, T., *Australia's First Frontier The Spread of Settlement in New South Wales, 1788–1829*, Melbourne, 1963

Philp, A., *The Ladies of Saumarez*, Sydney, 1988

Pike, D. (ed.), *The Australian Dictionary of Biography 1788–1850*, Vol. 1, Melbourne, 1966

Port Macquarie Historical Society, *Raise Your Glass: A Brief History of the Pubs of Port Macquarie*, Port Macquarie, 2011

Prentis, M., *The Scots in Australia A Study of New South Wales, Victoria and Queensland 1788–1900*, Sydney, 1983

Retter, C., Sinclair, S., *Letters to Ann: The love story of Mathew Flinders and Ann Chappelle*, Sydney, 1999

Ritchie, A., *Punishment and Profit The Reports of Commissioner John Bigge on the Colonies of New South Wales and Van Diemen's Land, 1822–1823; their origins, nature and significance*, Melbourne, 1970

Ritchie, J., *The Wentworths Father and Son*, Melbourne, 1997

Roberts, S., *The History of Australian Land Settlement 1788–1920*, Melbourne, 1935

Roberts, S., *The Squatting Age in Australia 1835–1847*, Melbourne, 1935

Roxburgh, R., *Early Colonial Houses of New South Wales*, Sydney, 1974

Salmon, M., *The Aurelian Legacy British Butterflies and their collectors*, Colchester, 2000

Searle, C., *Elizabeth Bay House Case Study*, Sydney, 1989

Serle, P., *Dictionary of Australian Biography*, Vol. 2, Sydney, 1949

Shaw, A. G. L., *Convicts and the Colonies: A Study of Penal Transportation from Great Britain and Ireland to Australia and other parts of the British Empire*, London, 1966

Shaw, A. G. L., *Heroes and Villains in History: Governor Darling and Bourke in New South Wales*, Sydney, 1966

Shaw, A.G.L., *Ralph Darling Great Australians*, Melbourne, 1971

Shaw, A., *The Story of Australia*, London, 1955

Shaw, A. and Clark, C. (editors), *The Australian Dictionary of Biography 1788–1850*, Vol. 2, Melbourne, 1967

Shaw, G.P. , *Patriarch and Patriot: William Grant Broughton 1788–1853, Colonial Statesman and Ecclesiastic*, Melbourne, 1978

Shepherd, T., *Lectures on Landscape Gardening in Australia*, Sydney, 1836

Shepherd, T., *Lectures on the Horticulture of New South Wales*, Sydney, 1835

Smith, R., Mittler, T., Smith, C.(editors), *History of Entomology*, California, 1973

Souter, G., *Company of Heralds A century and a half of Australian publishing by John Fairfax Limited and its predecessors 1831–1981*, Melbourne, 1981

Stanbury, P. and Holland, J. (editors), Mr. *Macleay's Celebrated Cabinet: The History of the Macleays and their Museum*, Sydney, 1988

Stanbury, P. and Phipps, G., *Australia's Animals Discovered*, Sydney, 1980

Stephen, L. (ed.), *Dictionary of National Biography*, Vol. XI, London, 1887

Steven, M., *Merchant Campbell 1769–1846: A Study of Colonial Trade*, Melbourne, 1965

Strahan, R., *Rare and Curious Specimens — An Illustrated History of the Australian Museum 1827–1979*, Sydney, 1977

Swan, K., *A History of Wagga Wagga*, Sydney, 1970

The Diaries of 'Pioneer' George Hobler, Vol. 1 (transcript), Sydney, 1992

Therry, R., *Reminiscences of Thirty Years' Residence in New South Wales and Victoria*, London, 1863, facsimile edition, Sydney, 1974

Thompson, M., *The First Election The New South Wales Legislative Council Election of 1843*, Mittagong, 1996

Tink, A., *William Charles Wentworth Australia's Greatest Native Son*, Sydney, 2009

Tomasson, K., and Buist, F., *Battles of the '45*, London, 1967

Valder, P., *Wisterias A Comprehensive Guide*, Sydney, 1995

Waldersee, J., *Catholic Society in New South Wales 1788–1860*, Sydney, 1974

Walker, M., *Sir James Edward Smith M.D., F.R.S., P.L.S. 1759–1828 First President of the Linnean Society of London*, London, 1988

Walker, R., *Old New England*, Sydney, 1966

Walker, R., *The Newspaper Press in New South Wales 1803–1920*, Sydney, 1976

Ward, J., *James Macarthur Colonial Conservative 1798–1867*, Sydney, 1981

Waterhouse, R., *Private Pleasures, Public Leisure, A History of Australian Popular Culture since 1788*, Melbourne, 1995

Watson, S., *The Oxford History of England, The Reign of George III, 1760–1815*, Oxford, 1960

Williams, J., *The Australian Club Centenary*, Sydney, 1938

Windschuttle, E., *Taste and Science The Women of the Macleay Family 1790–1850*, Sydney, 1988

Windschuttle, E. (ed.), *Women, class and history: feminist perspectives on Australia 1788–1978*, Melbourne, 1980

Winter, J., *Robert Lowe*, Toronto, 1976

Wood, W., *Dawn in the Valley: the story of settlement in the Hunter River Valley to 1833*, Sydney, 1972

Woodward, L., *The Oxford History of England, The Age of Reform 1815–1870*, Oxford, 1962

ARTICLES

Anderson, J., 'The Macleay Museum at the University of Sydney', *Australian Natural History*, Vol. 15, Sydney, 1965-67

Anderson, C. (ed.), 'Early Days', *The Australian Museum Magazine*, Vol. 3, No. 3, Sydney, 1927

Beale, E., 'Anticipation of the River Murray', *JRAHS*, Vol. 73, Part 1, 1987

Buckley, K., 'Gipps and the Graziers of New South Wales 1841–1846, Pts. 1 and 2', *Historical Studies*, Vol. 6, No. 24, 1955, and Vol. 7, No. 26, 1956

'Butterflies, Beetles and the Bizarre — the Macleays as Gentlemen Scientists', *Historic Houses Trust Newsletter*, Sydney, undated

Campbell, J., 'Discovery and Early Pastoral Settlement of New England', *JRAHS*, Vol. 8, Pt. 5, 1992

Champion, R., 'Major A. C. Innes, 3rd Regiment of Foot', *JRAHS*, Vol. 21, Pt. 2, 1935

Clark, D., 'Baron Charles von Hügel and the Macleays', *JRAHS*, Vol. 75, Part 3, 1989

Clough, R., 'Charles Fraser's Record of Plants in the Sydney Botanic Garden in 1827-28', *Australian Garden History*, Vol. 8, No. 3, 1966

Dyster, B., 'Support for the Squatters 1844', *JRAHS*, Vol. 51, Pt. 1, 1965

Ferguson, J. A., 'Edward Smith Hall and the Monitor', *JRAHS*, Vol. 17, Pt. 3, 1931

Fletcher, B., 'Administrative Reform in New South Wales under Governor Darling', *Australian Journal of Public Administration*, Vol. 38, No. 3, 1979

Fletcher, B., 'Biography and the History of Colonial New South Wales', *Teaching History*, July, 1981

Fletcher, B.. 'Christianity and Free society in New South Wales 1788–1840', *JRAHS*, Vol. 86, Pt. 2, 2000

Fletcher, B., 'Elizabeth Darling: Colonial Benefactress and Governor's Lady', *JRAHS*, Vol. 67, Pt. 4, 1982

Fletcher, B., 'Fetters to Federation', *Insites: Newsletter of the Historic Houses Trust of New South Wales*, Autumn 2001

Fletcher, B., 'Governor Bourke and Squatting in New South Wales', *JRAHS*, Vol. 74, Pt. 4, 1989

Fletcher, B., 'Sir John Jamison in New South Wales, 1814–1844', *JRAHS*, Vol. 65, Pt. 1, 1979

Fletcher, J. J., 'The Society's Heritage from the Macleays', *Proceedings of the Linnean Society of New South Wales*, Vol. 45, Sydney, 1920

Foster, S., 'A Piece of Sharp Practice? Governor Bourke and the Office of Colonial Secretary in New South Wales', *Historical Studies*, Vol. 16, No. 64, 1975

Foster, W., 'Education in New South Wales Under Governor Sir Richard Bourke', *JRAHS*, Vol. 47,

Pt. 5, 1961

Garnett, T., 'Alister Clark — Horticulturist and Celebrated Rose and Daffodil Breeder', *Australian Garden History*, Vol. 8, No. 3, 1996

Gilbert, L., 'Plants, Politics and Personalities in Nineteenth Century New South Wales', *JRAHS*, Vol. 56, Pt. 1, 1970

Hartwell, R., 'Australia's First Trade Cycle, Boom, Crisis, Depression and Recovery in NSW 1820–1832', *JRAHS*, Vol. 42, Pt. 2, 1956

Hogue, J., 'Governor Darling, The Press and the Collar', *JRAHS*, Vol. 2, Pt. 12, 1929

Holland, J., 'W. S. Macleay Special Feature', *Historical Records of Australian Science*, 2, Sydney, 1996

Horning, D., 'The Macleay Insect Collection', *Antenna — Royal Entomological Society of London 1983–1985 Commemoration*, 1985

Information Leaflet, Linnean Society of London, 1998

Jervis, J., 'The Journals of William Edward Riley', *JRAHS*, Vol. 32, Pt. 4, 1946

Ker, J., 'The Macarthur Family and the Pastoral Industry', *JRAHS*, Vol. 47, Pt. 3, 1961

King, H., 'Frederick Goulburn: The Man and His Office', *Australian Journal of Public Administration*, Vol. 38, No. 3, 1979

King, H., 'Man in a Trap: Alexander Macleay, Colonial Secretary of New South Wales', *JRAHS*, Vol. 68, Pt. 1, 1982

King, H., 'Pulling Strings at the Colonial Office', *JRAHS*, Vol. 61, Pt. 3, 1975

King, H., 'Villains All?' *JRAHS*, Vol. 53, Pt. 1, 1967

Maiden, J., 'History of Sydney Botanic Gardens', *JRAHS*, Vol. 17, Pt. 3, 1931

Martin, M., 'Digging for Garden Treasures', *Insites: Newsletter of the Historic Houses Trust of New South Wales*, Issue 22, 2000

McCulloch, S., 'Unguarded Comments on the Administration of New South Wales, 1839-46, The Gipps — La-Trobe Correspondence', *Historical Studies*, Vol. 9, No. 33, 1959

McMartin, A., 'Aspects of Patronage in Australia 1786–1836', *Australian Journal of Public Administration*, Vol. 18, No. 4, 1959

McMartin, A., 'Born Bureaucrat: Thomas Cudbert Harington', *Australian Journal of Public Administration*, Vol. 38, No. 3, 1979

Melluish, G., 'Justifying Commerce: The Scottish Enlightenment Tradition in Colonial New South Wales', *JRAHS*, Vol. 75, Pt. 2, 1989

O'Grady, F. 'Archibald Clunes Innes', *JRAHS*, Vol. 53, Pt. 3, 1967

Proctor, S., 'Henry Dumaresq on the Sydney Press in 1827', *JRAHS*, Vol. 57, Pt. 2, 1971

Ritchie, J., 'John Thomas Bigge and His Reports on New South Wales', *JRAHS*, Vol. 60, Pt. 1, 1974

Robertson, J., 'The Australian Agricultural Company and the Port Stephens Fiasco', *JRAHS*, Vol. 50, Pt. 3, 1964

Rose, L.N., 'The Administration of Governor Darling', *JRAHS*, Vol. 8, Pts. 2 and 3, 1922

Shaw, A., 'Heroes and Villains in History Governors

Darling and Bourke in New South Wales', *The Fifth George Arnold Wood Memorial Lecture*, Sydney, 1966

Somer, H., 'First Agricultural Society of New South Wales A Historical Sketch', *RAS Annual*, Sydney, 1906

St James's Church leaflet, *A Guide to the Church*, Sydney, undated

Stackhouse, J., 'Mr Macleay's Garden', *Historic Houses Trust NSW Newsletter*, Sydney, 1981

Stanbury, P., 'The Gentleman Scientist', *Australian Natural History*, Vol. 19, No. 2, 1977

Strahan R., 'The Dog that did not bark: Alexander Macleay and the Australian Museum', *JRAHS*, Vol. 75, Pt. 3, 1989

Swainston, A., 'Background to a Caithness Bank', *The Three Banks Review National and Commercial Banking Group Limited*, No. 108, 1975

Swainston, A., 'William Sharp Macleay 1792–1865', *The Linnean Newsletter and Proceedings of the Linnean Society of London*, Vol. 1, No. 5, 1985

Tilley, A., 'Brave Men and Fit Governors: The Recall of Governor Darling from New South Wales', *JRAHS*, Vol. 61, Pt. 4, 1975

'Type Specimens in the Macleay Museum, University of Sydney, V111: Insects, Beetles (Insecta Coleoptera)', *Proceedings of the Linnean Society of NSW*, 105 (4), Sydney, 1980, 1981

Underwood, J. and N., 'Who was Captain Oliver', *Eilean an Fhraoich, Stornoway Gazette Annual*, December 1987

Van Leeuwen, M., 'The Plan of a Museum — Alexander Macleay's proposal for the Australian Museum', *JRAHS*, Vol. 78, Pts. 3 and 4, 1992

Walkam, A., 'Portrait of Alexander Macleay', *The Australian Museum Magazine*, Vol. V11, No. 10, 1941

Ward, J. M., James Macarthur, Colonial Conservative, 1798–1867, *JRAHS*, Vol. 66, Pt. 3, 1980

UNPUBLISHED THESES, WRITINGS AND INTERVIEWS

Australian Dictionary of Biography File on Alexander Macleay, Australian National University, Canberra

Clough, R., Notes on entry for Robert Henderson for *The Oxford Companion to Australian Gardening*, Melbourne, 2002

Gilbert, L., 'Plants, Privileges and Power: Some Glimpses of Elizabeth Bay and Sydney's Botanical Community 1825–1865', M.A., University of Sydney, 1989

Liston, C., 'New South Wales under Governor Brisbane, 1821–1825', Ph. D., University of Sydney, 1980

Norrie, P., 'Study of Original Documents on Viticulture in early NSW and the role of the Macleay family 1788–1883', M.A., University of Sydney, 1993

Richardson, G. D., 'The Archives of the Colonial Secretary's Department of New South Wales, 1788–1856', M.A., University of Sydney, 1951

Underwood, J. and N., Alexander Rose Macleay, December, 1987 (located in *Swainston Papers*)

ORAL INTERVIEWS

Cherry, R., Kulnura, 2000

Clough, R., Sydney, 2000

Downes, J., Brownlow Hill, Camden, 1994, 2011

Horning, D., Macleay Museum, Sydney, 1993

Stewart, I., Bilbster House, Wick, June 2002

Sutherland, I., Wick Heritage Centre, Wick, June 2002

Index